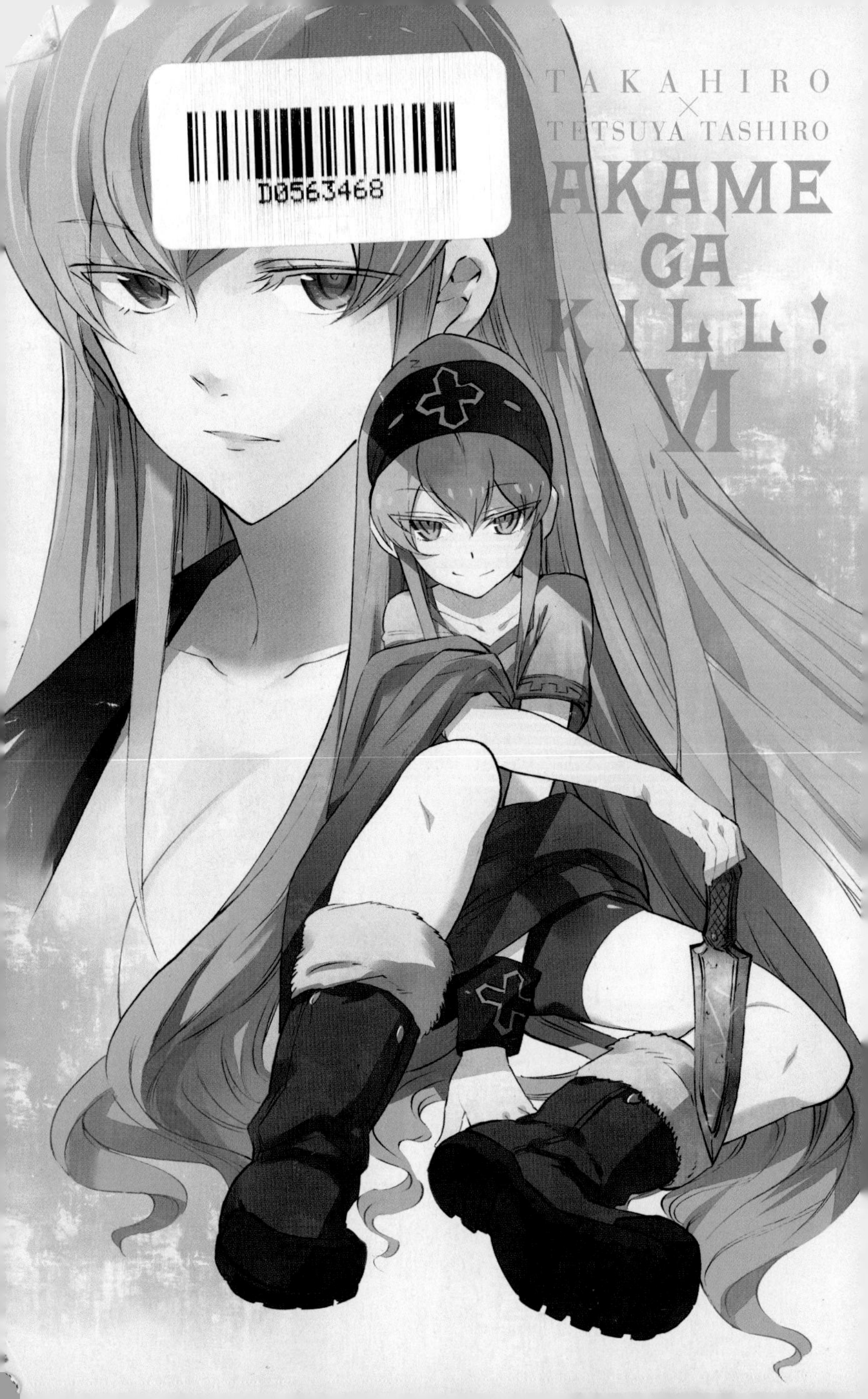
TAKAHIRO
×
TETSUYA TASHIRO
AKAME GA KILL!
VI

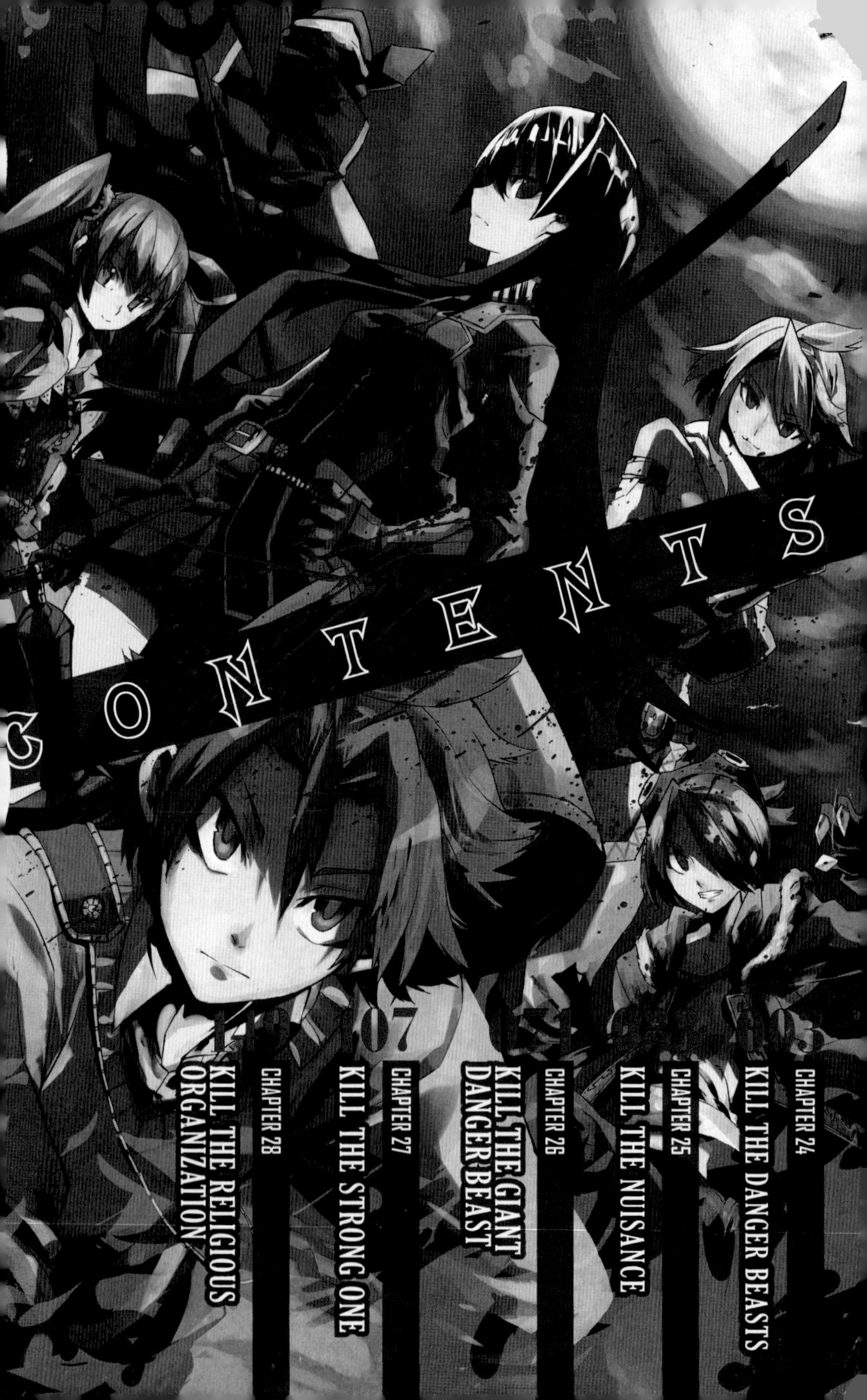
CONTENTS
CHAPTER 24 KILL THE DANGER BEASTS 003
CHAPTER 25 KILL THE NUISANCE 033
CHAPTER 26 KILL THE GIANT DANGER BEAST 051
CHAPTER 27 KILL THE STRONG ONE 107
CHAPTER 28 KILL THE RELIGIOUS ORGANIZATION 149

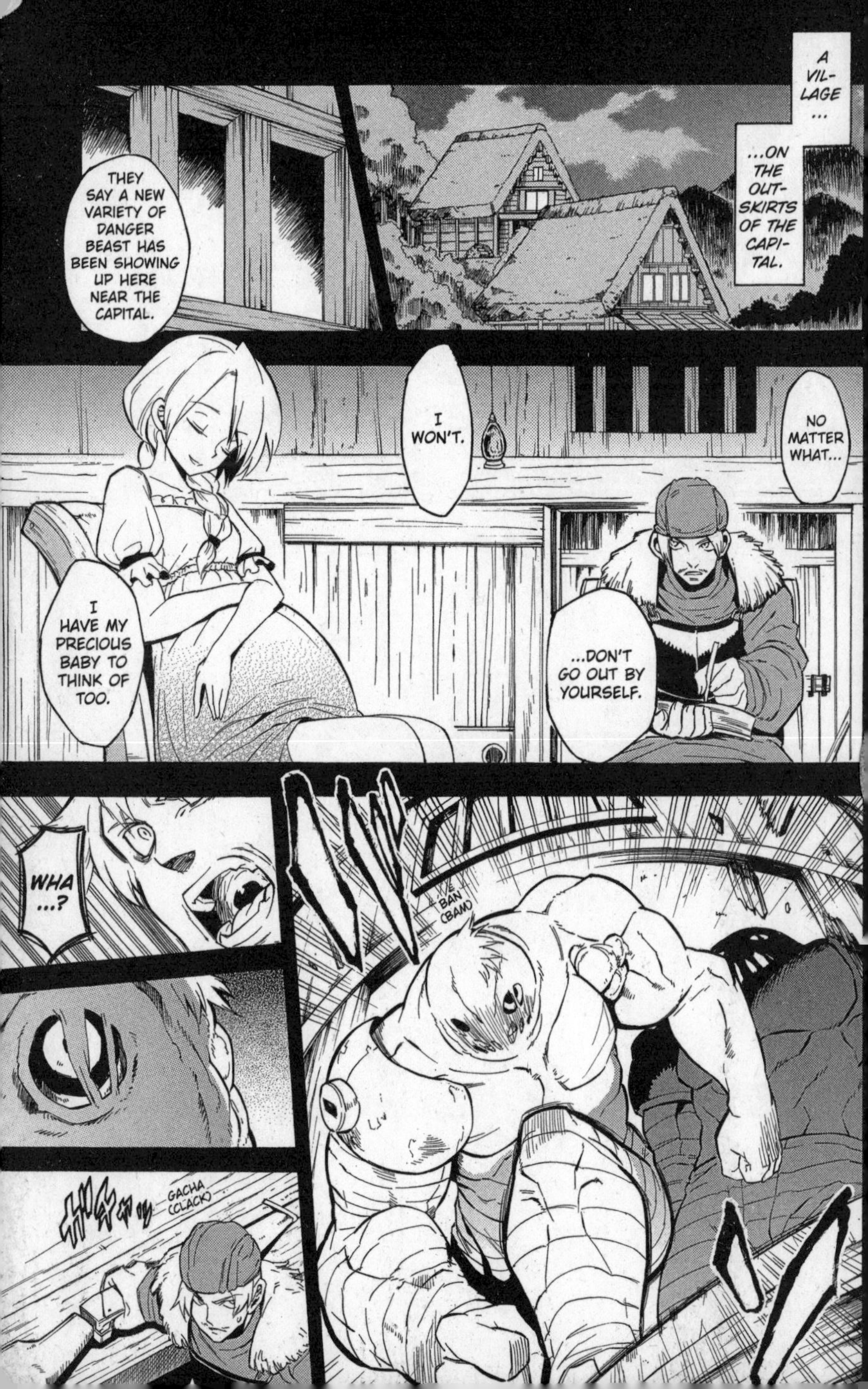

A VIL-LAGE...
...ON THE OUT-SKIRTS OF THE CAPI-TAL.
THEY SAY A NEW VARIETY OF DANGER BEAST HAS BEEN SHOWING UP HERE NEAR THE CAPITAL.
NO MATTER WHAT...
...DON'T GO OUT BY YOURSELF.
I WON'T.
I HAVE MY PRECIOUS BABY TO THINK OF TOO.
BAN (BAM)
WHA...?
GACHA (CLACK)

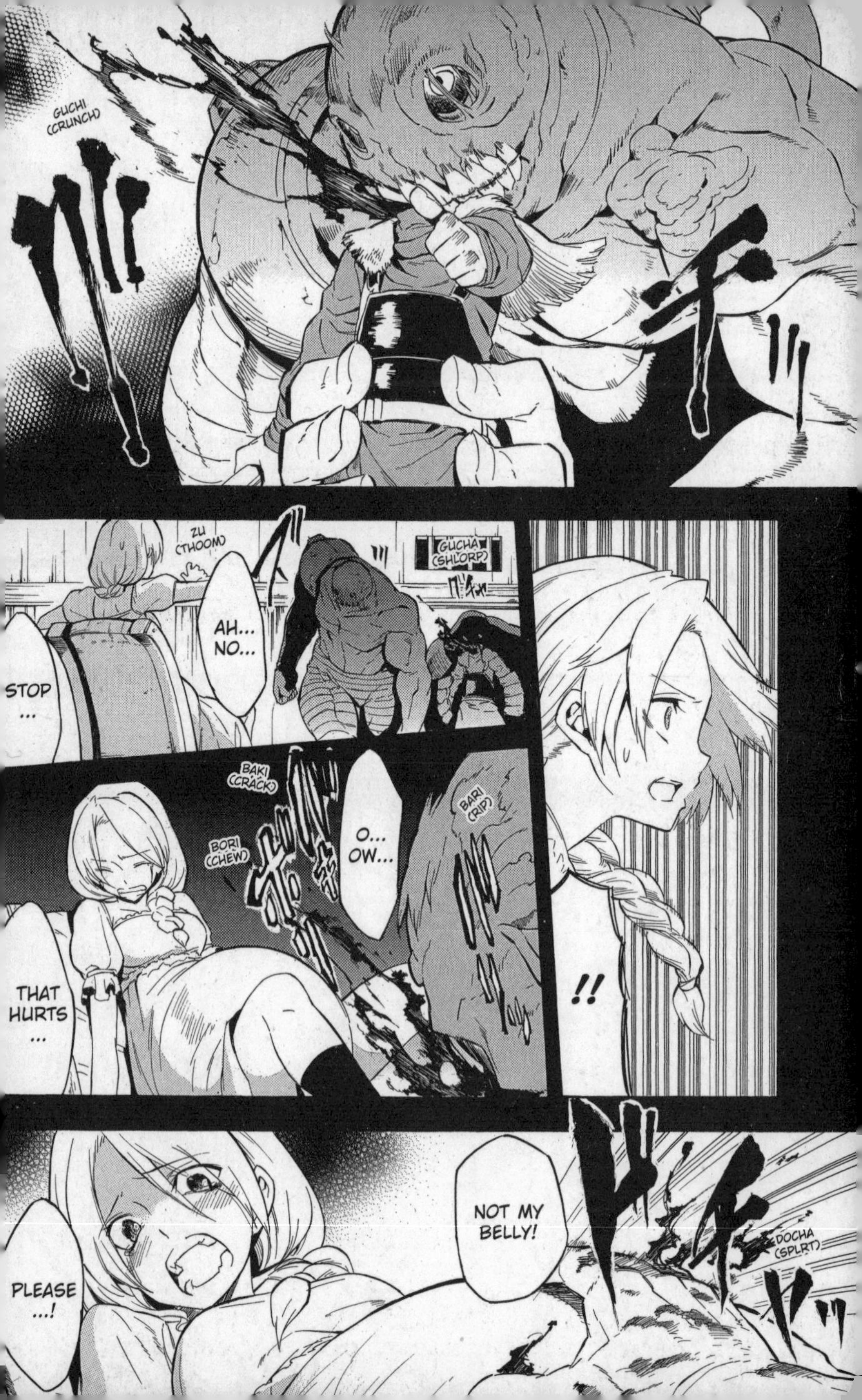

GUCHI (CRUNCH)
ZU (THOOM)
GUCHA (SHLORP)
AH... NO...
STOP ...
!!
BAKI (CRACK)
BORI (CHEW)
BARI (RIP)
O... OW...
THAT HURTS ...
DOCHA (SPLRT)
NOT MY BELLY!
PLEASE ...!

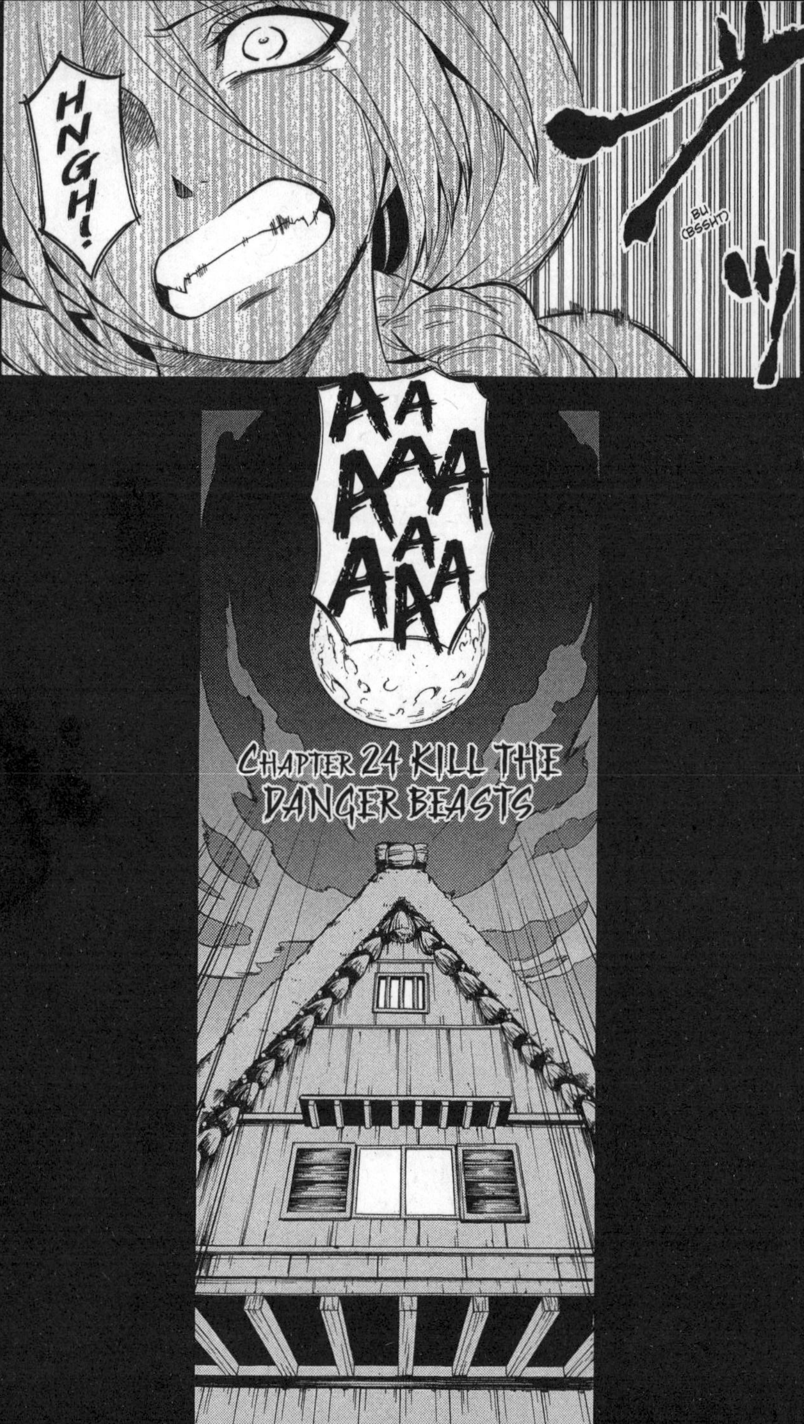
BU (BSSHT)
HNGH!
AAAAAAAAAAA
CHAPTER 24 KILL THE DANGER BEASTS

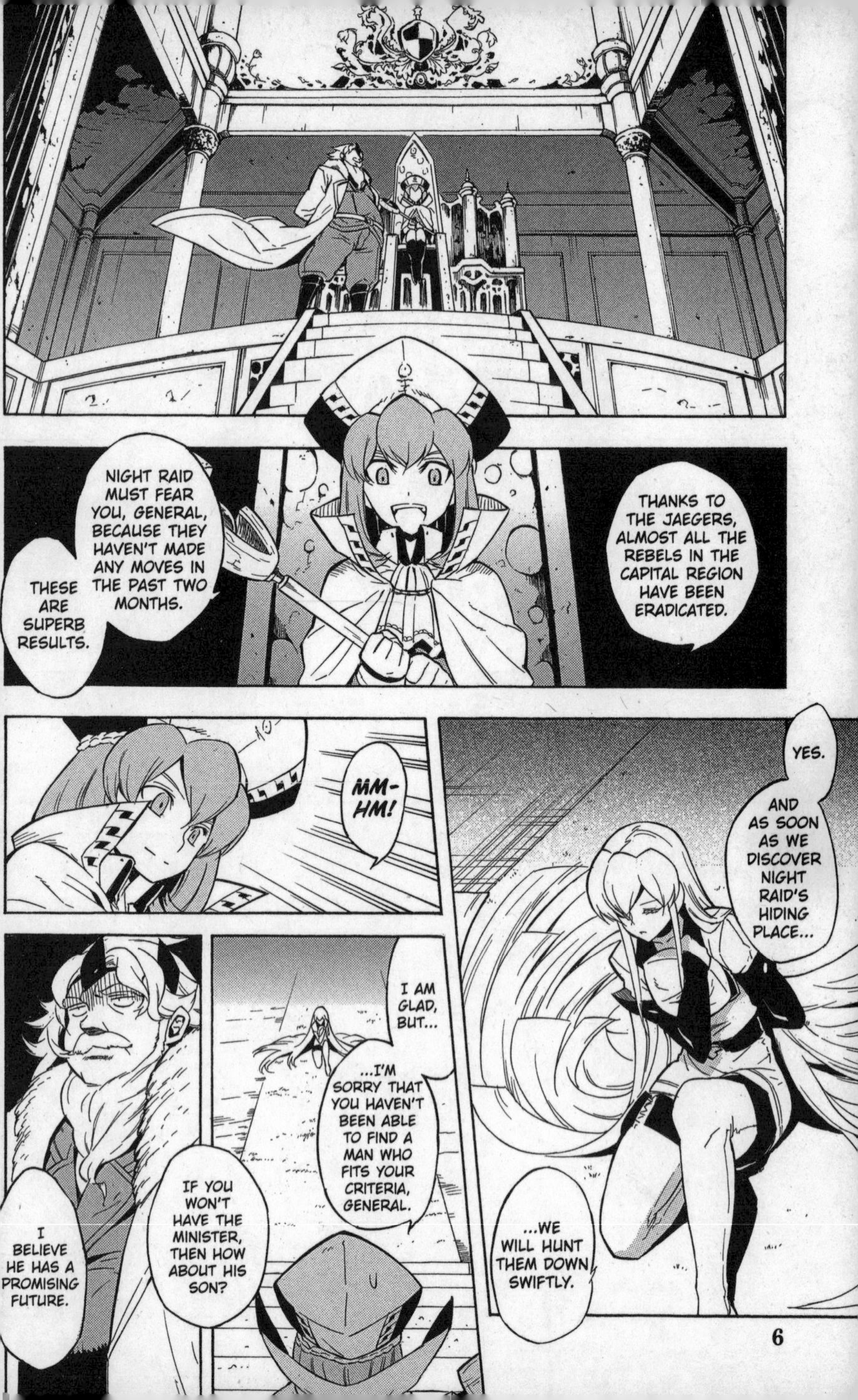
THANKS TO THE JAEGERS, ALMOST ALL THE REBELS IN THE CAPITAL REGION HAVE BEEN ERADICATED.
NIGHT RAID MUST FEAR YOU, GENERAL, BECAUSE THEY HAVEN'T MADE ANY MOVES IN THE PAST TWO MONTHS.
THESE ARE SUPERB RESULTS.
YES.
AND AS SOON AS WE DISCOVER NIGHT RAID'S HIDING PLACE...
...WE WILL HUNT THEM DOWN SWIFTLY.
MM-HM!
I AM GLAD, BUT...
...I'M SORRY THAT YOU HAVEN'T BEEN ABLE TO FIND A MAN WHO FITS YOUR CRITERIA, GENERAL.
IF YOU WON'T HAVE THE MINISTER, THEN HOW ABOUT HIS SON?
I BELIEVE HE HAS A PROMISING FUTURE.

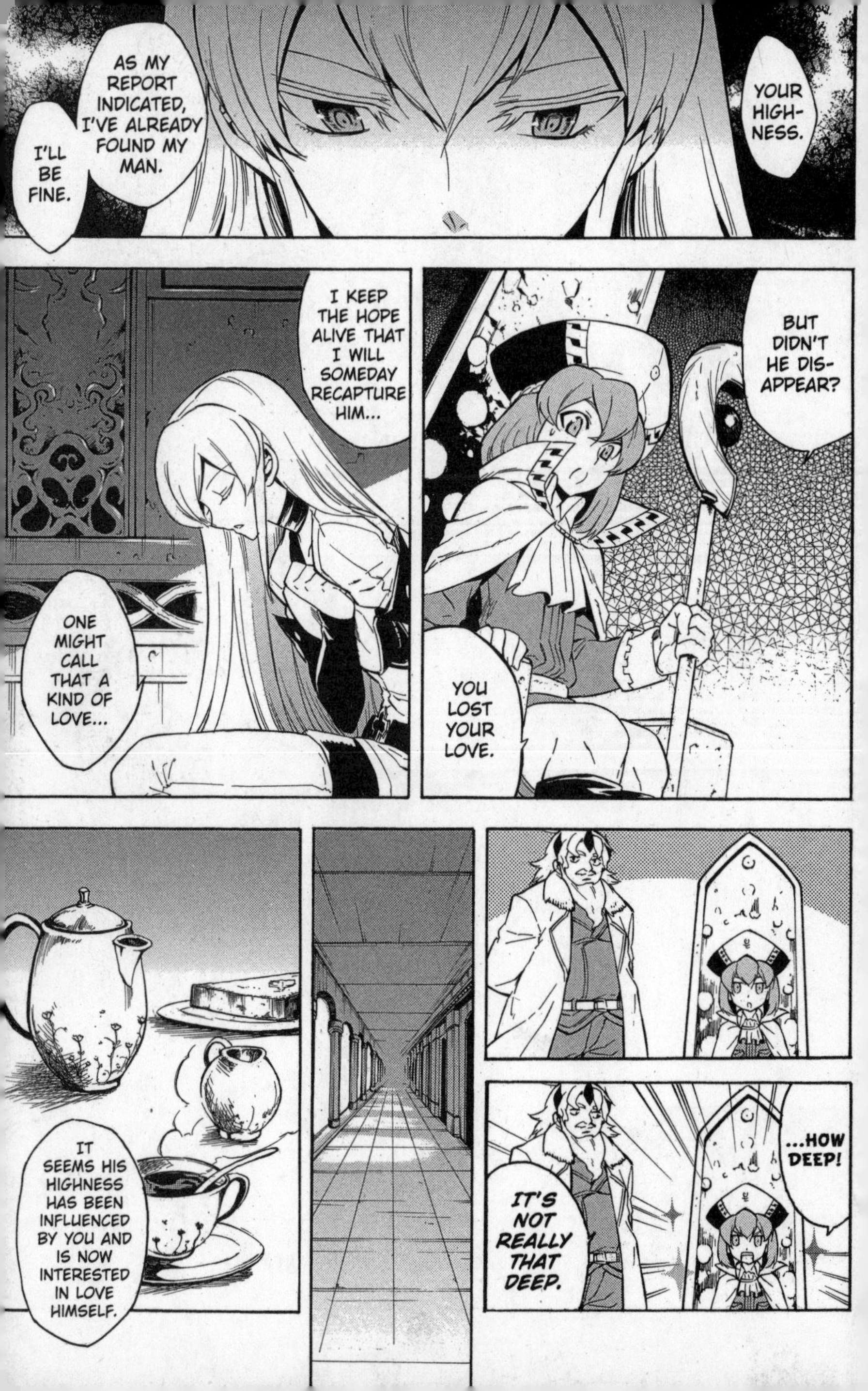
YOUR HIGH-NESS.
AS MY REPORT INDICATED, I'VE ALREADY FOUND MY MAN.
I'LL BE FINE.
BUT DIDN'T HE DIS-APPEAR?
YOU LOST YOUR LOVE.
I KEEP THE HOPE ALIVE THAT I WILL SOMEDAY RECAPTURE HIM...
ONE MIGHT CALL THAT A KIND OF LOVE...
...HOW DEEP!
IT'S NOT REALLY THAT DEEP.
IT SEEMS HIS HIGHNESS HAS BEEN INFLUENCED BY YOU AND IS NOW INTERESTED IN LOVE HIMSELF.

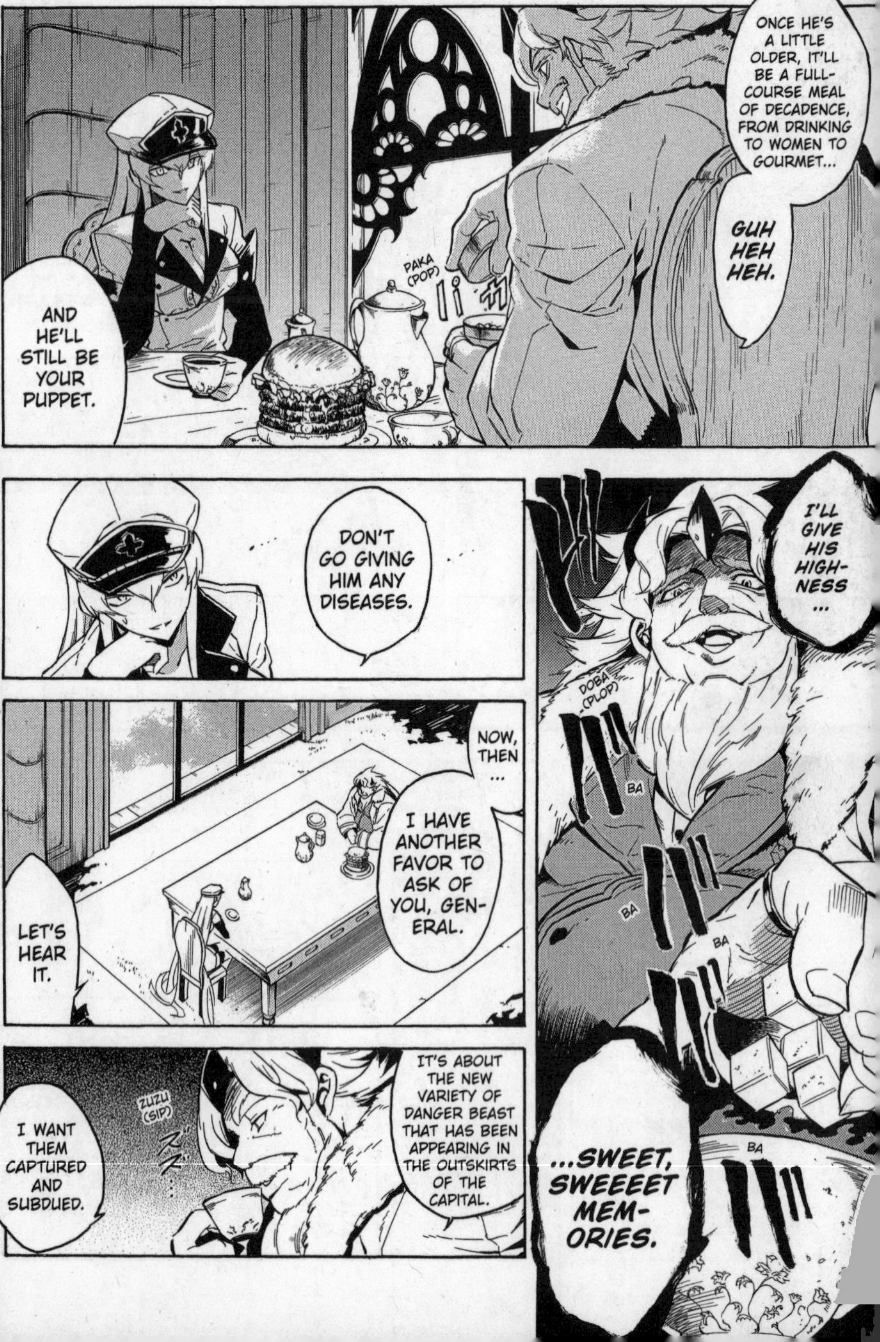
ONCE HE'S A LITTLE OLDER, IT'LL BE A FULL-COURSE MEAL OF DECADENCE, FROM DRINKING TO WOMEN TO GOURMET...
GUH HEH HEH.
PAKA (POP)
AND HE'LL STILL BE YOUR PUPPET.
I'LL GIVE HIS HIGHNESS...
DOBA (PLOP)
BA
BA
BA
BA
...SWEET, SWEEEET MEMORIES.
DON'T GO GIVING HIM ANY DISEASES.
NOW, THEN...
I HAVE ANOTHER FAVOR TO ASK OF YOU, GENERAL.
LET'S HEAR IT.
IT'S ABOUT THE NEW VARIETY OF DANGER BEAST THAT HAS BEEN APPEARING IN THE OUTSKIRTS OF THE CAPITAL.
ZUZU (SIP)
I WANT THEM CAPTURED AND SUBDUED.

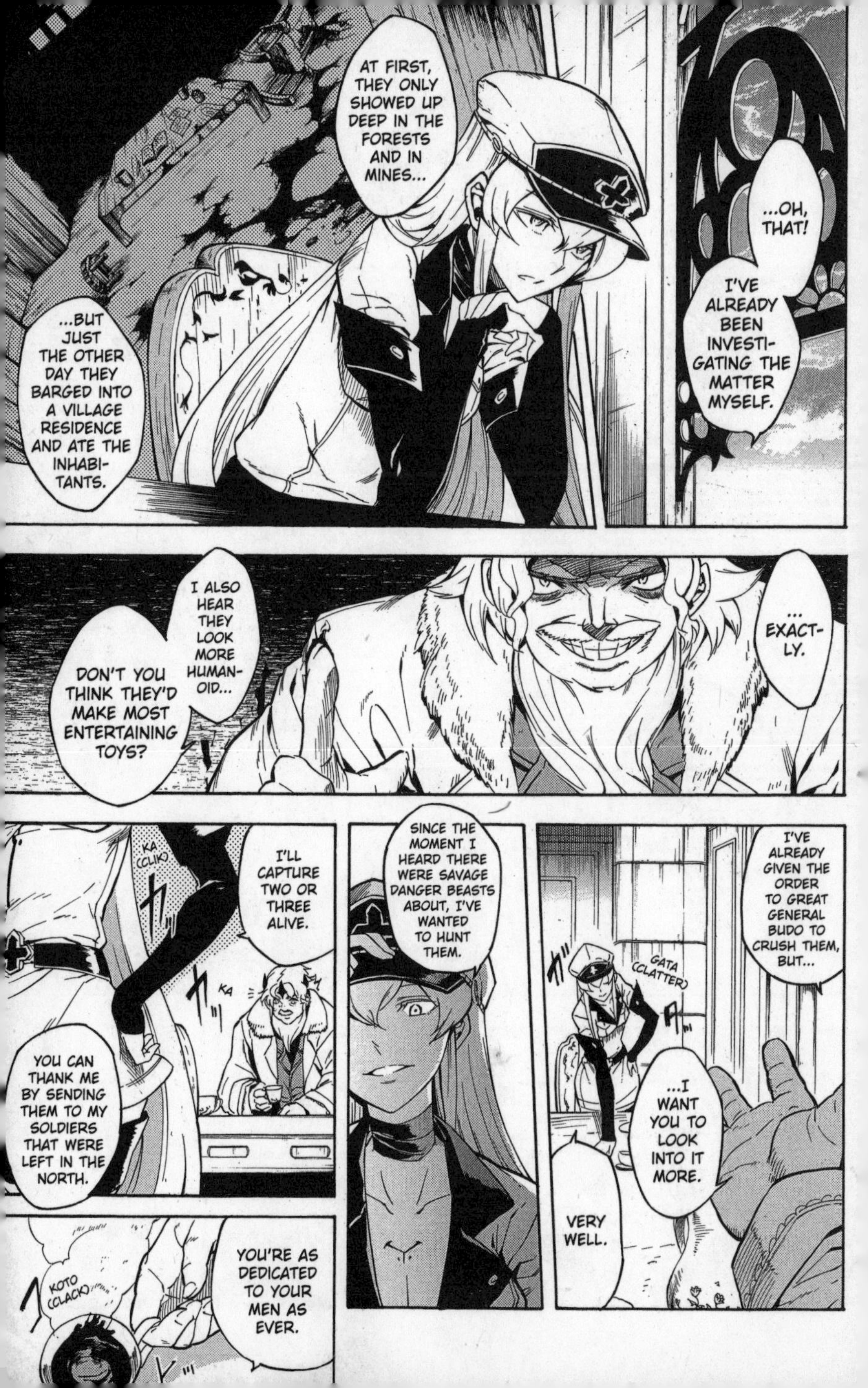
...OH, THAT!
I'VE ALREADY BEEN INVESTIGATING THE MATTER MYSELF.
AT FIRST, THEY ONLY SHOWED UP DEEP IN THE FORESTS AND IN MINES...
...BUT JUST THE OTHER DAY THEY BARGED INTO A VILLAGE RESIDENCE AND ATE THE INHABITANTS.
... EXACTLY.
I ALSO HEAR THEY LOOK MORE HUMANOID...
DON'T YOU THINK THEY'D MAKE MOST ENTERTAINING TOYS?
I'VE ALREADY GIVEN THE ORDER TO GREAT GENERAL BUDO TO CRUSH THEM, BUT...
GATA (CLATTER)
...I WANT YOU TO LOOK INTO IT MORE.
VERY WELL.
SINCE THE MOMENT I HEARD THERE WERE SAVAGE DANGER BEASTS ABOUT, I'VE WANTED TO HUNT THEM.
I'LL CAPTURE TWO OR THREE ALIVE.
KA (CLIK)
KA
YOU CAN THANK ME BY SENDING THEM TO MY SOLDIERS THAT WERE LEFT IN THE NORTH.
KOTO (CLACK)
YOU'RE AS DEDICATED TO YOUR MEN AS EVER.

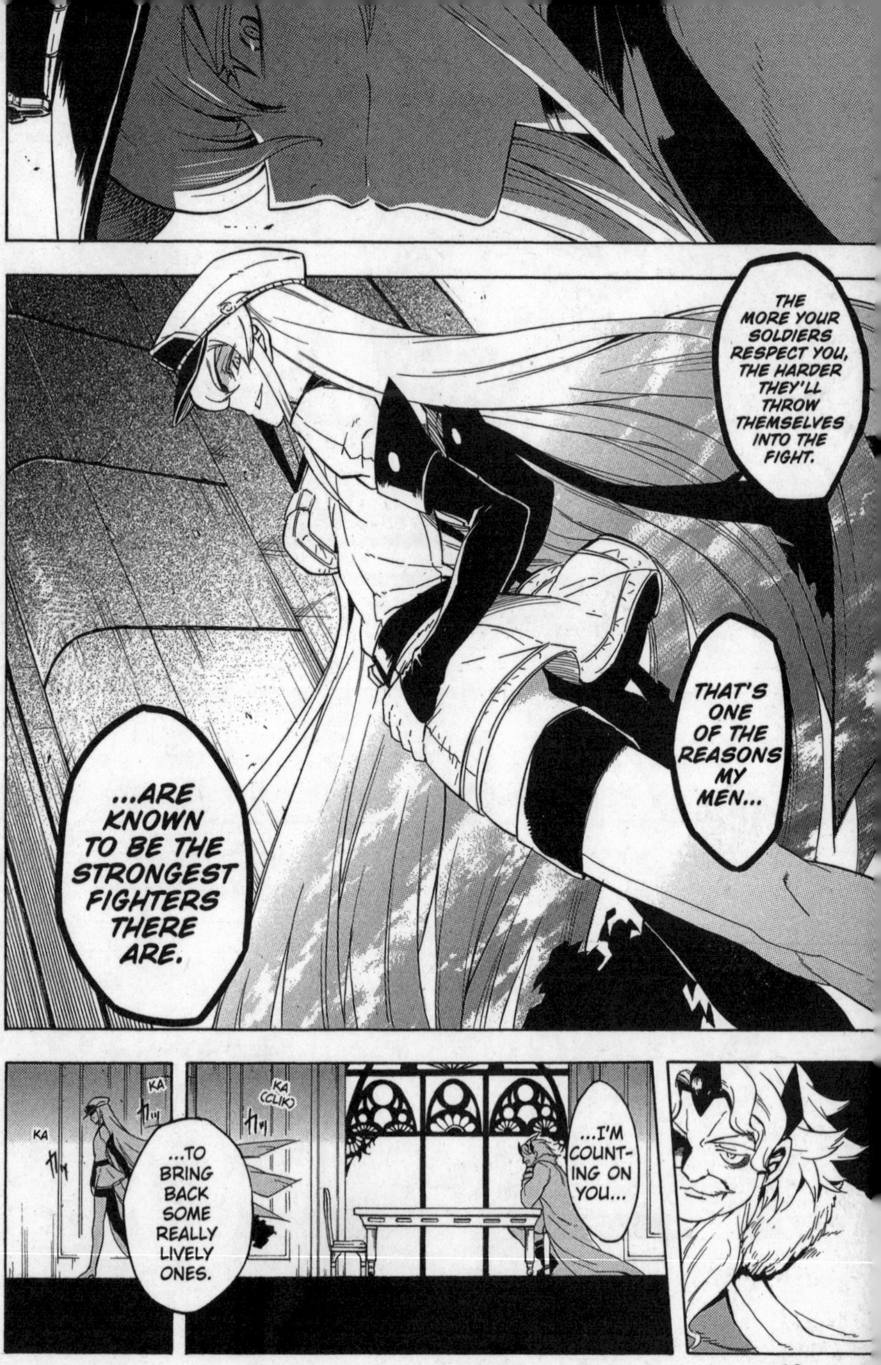
THE MORE YOUR SOLDIERS RESPECT YOU, THE HARDER THEY'LL THROW THEMSELVES INTO THE FIGHT.
THAT'S ONE OF THE REASONS MY MEN...
...ARE KNOWN TO BE THE STRONGEST FIGHTERS THERE ARE.
KA
KA
KA (CLIK)
...TO BRING BACK SOME REALLY LIVELY ONES.
...I'M COUNT-ING ON YOU...

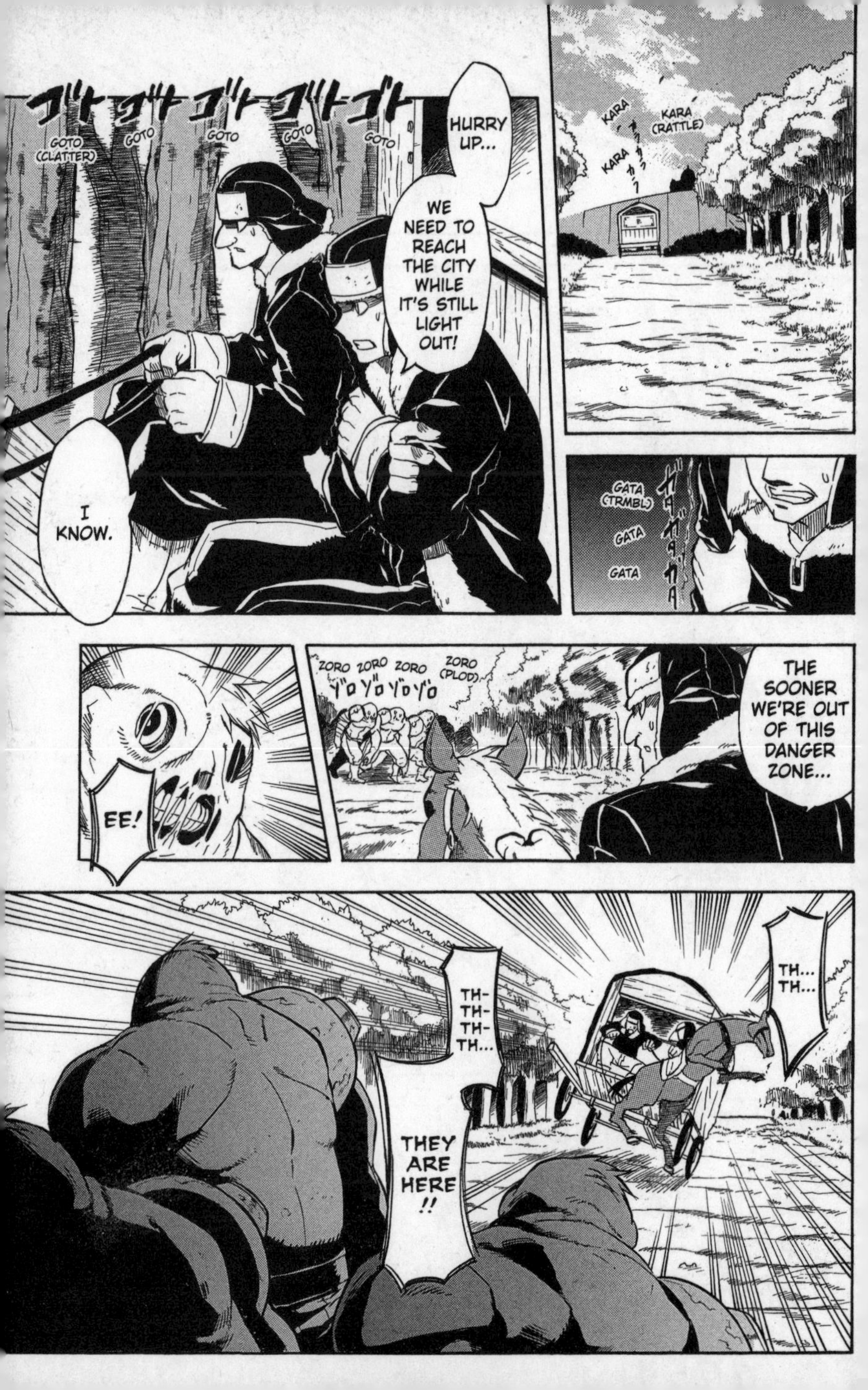
KARA KARA (RATTLE) KARA
GOTO (CLATTER) GOTO GOTO GOTO GOTO
HURRY UP...
WE NEED TO REACH THE CITY WHILE IT'S STILL LIGHT OUT!
I KNOW.
GATA (TRMBL) GATA GATA
THE SOONER WE'RE OUT OF THIS DANGER ZONE...
ZORO ZORO ZORO ZORO (PLOD)
EE!
TH... TH...
TH-TH-TH-TH...
THEY ARE HERE!!

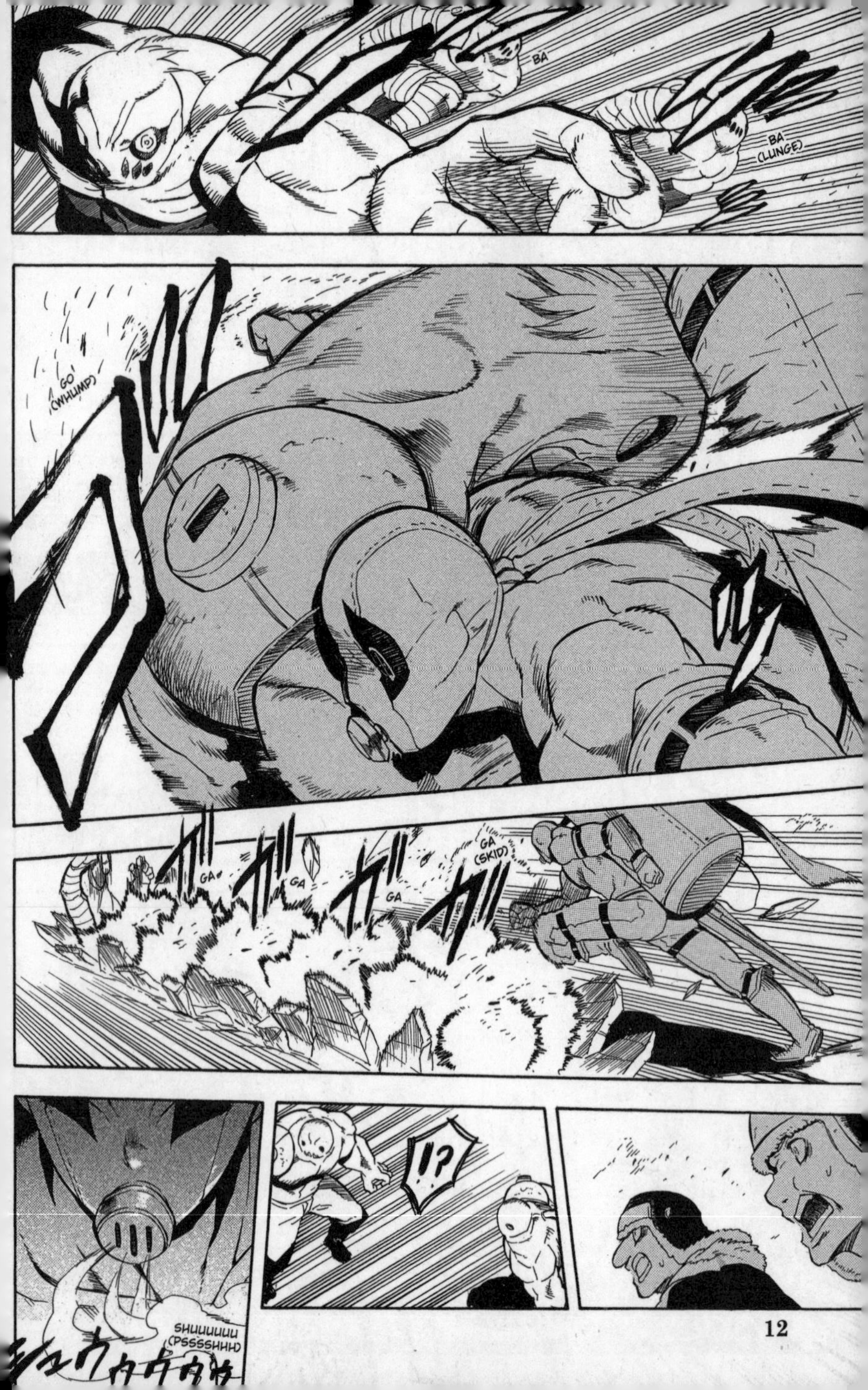
BA
BA
(LUNGE)
GO
(WHUMP)
GA
(SKID)
GA
GA
GA
!?
SHUUUUUUU
(PSSSSHHH)

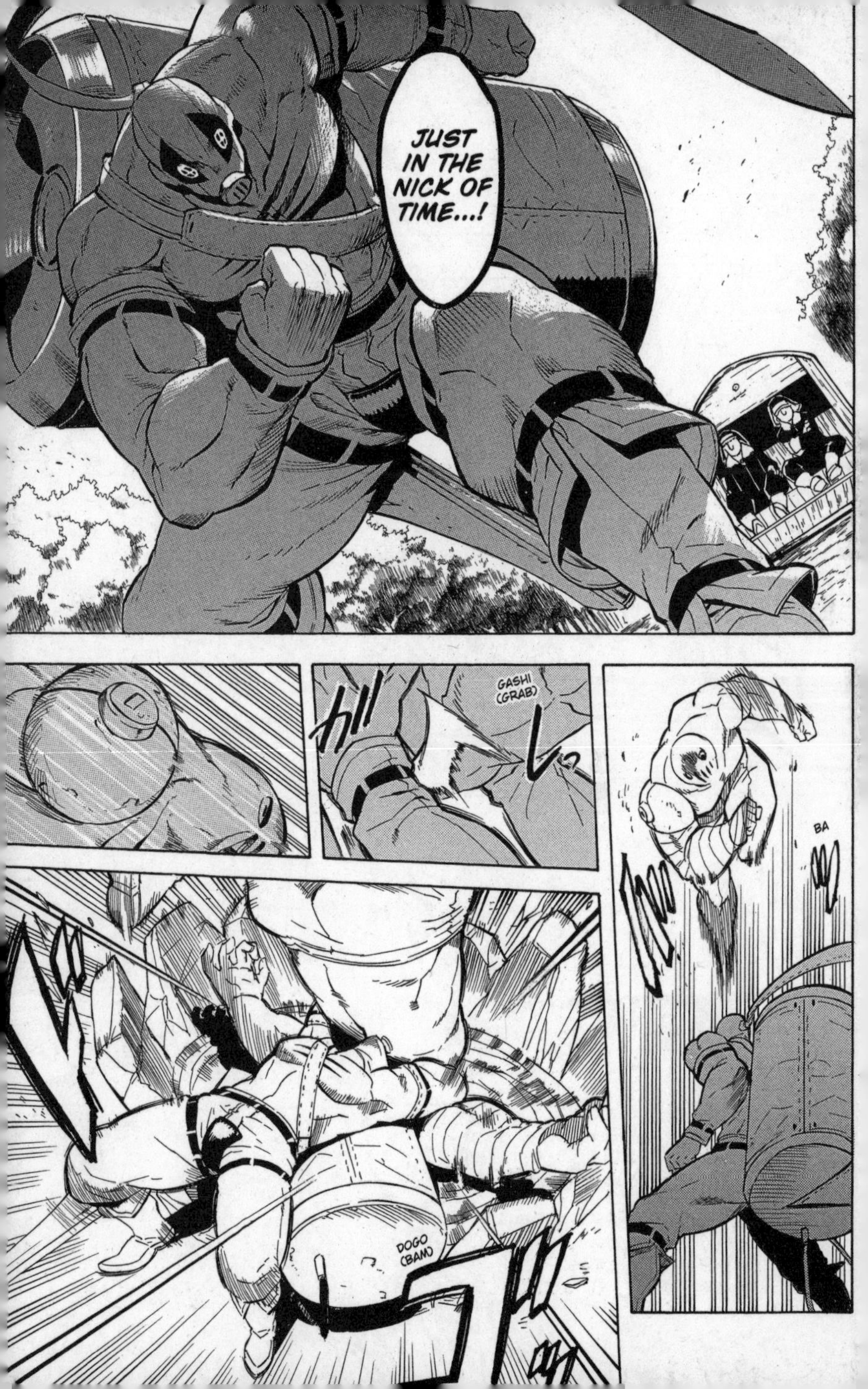
JUST IN THE NICK OF TIME...!
GASHI (GRAB)
BA
DOGO (BAM)

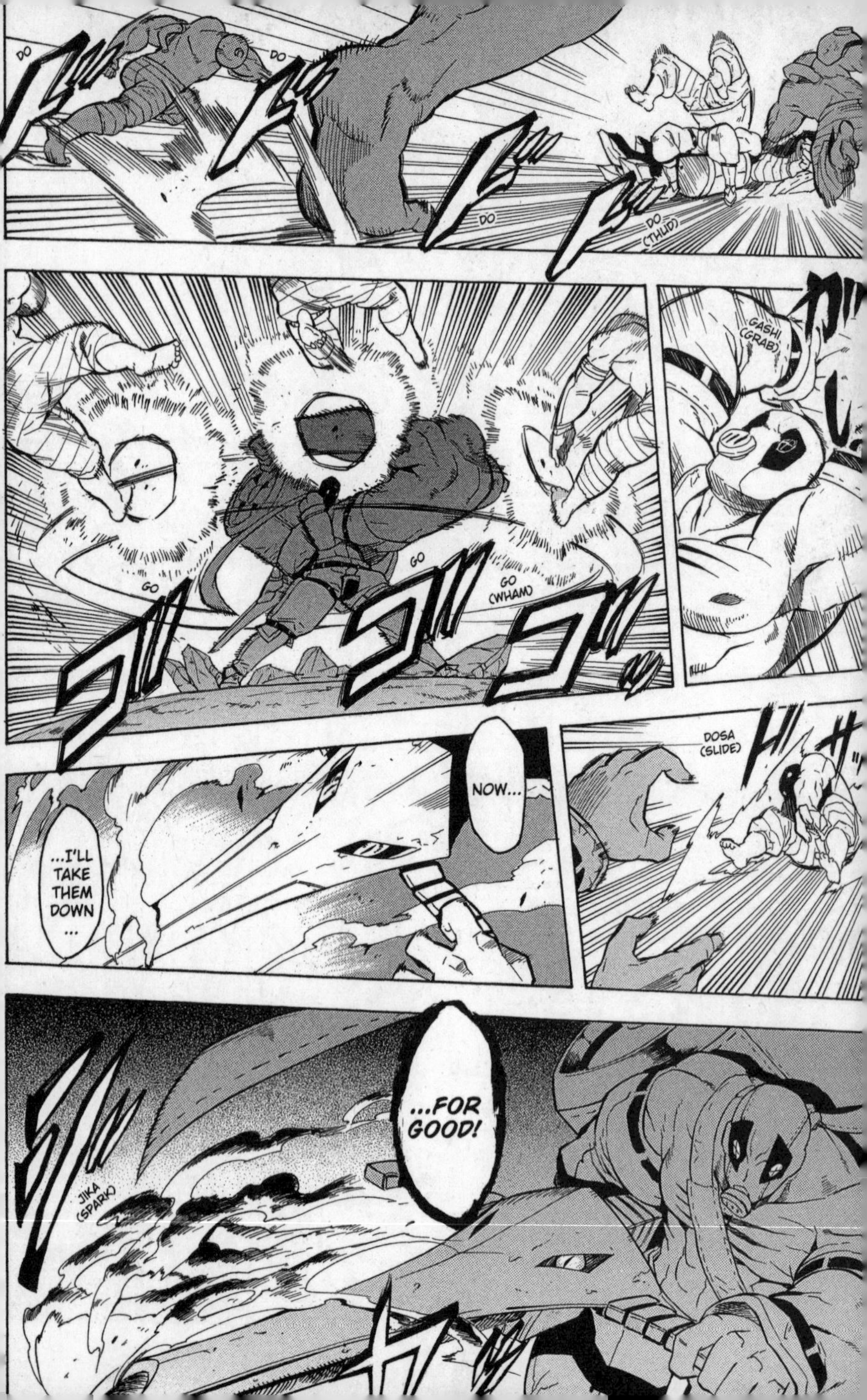
DO
(THUD)
DO
DO
DO
GASHI
(GRAB)
GO
(WHAM)
GO
GO
DOSA
(SLIDE)
NOW...
...I'LL TAKE THEM DOWN ...
...FOR GOOD!
JIKA
(SPARK)

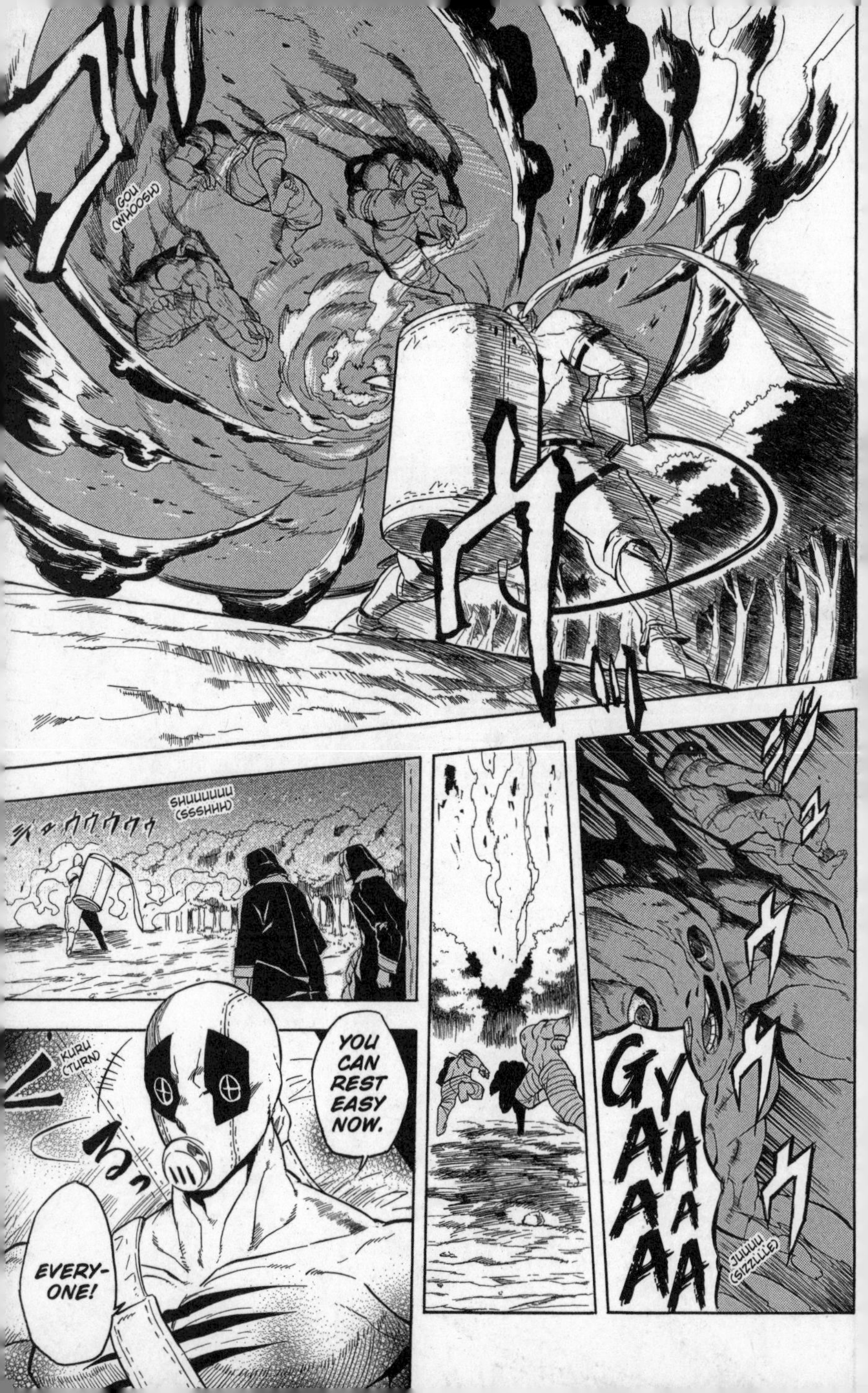
GOU (WHOOSH)
JUUUU (SIZZLLLE)
GYAAAAAAA
SHUUUUUUU (SSSHHH)
シュウウウウウ
YOU CAN REST EASY NOW.
KURU (TURN)
EVERY-ONE!

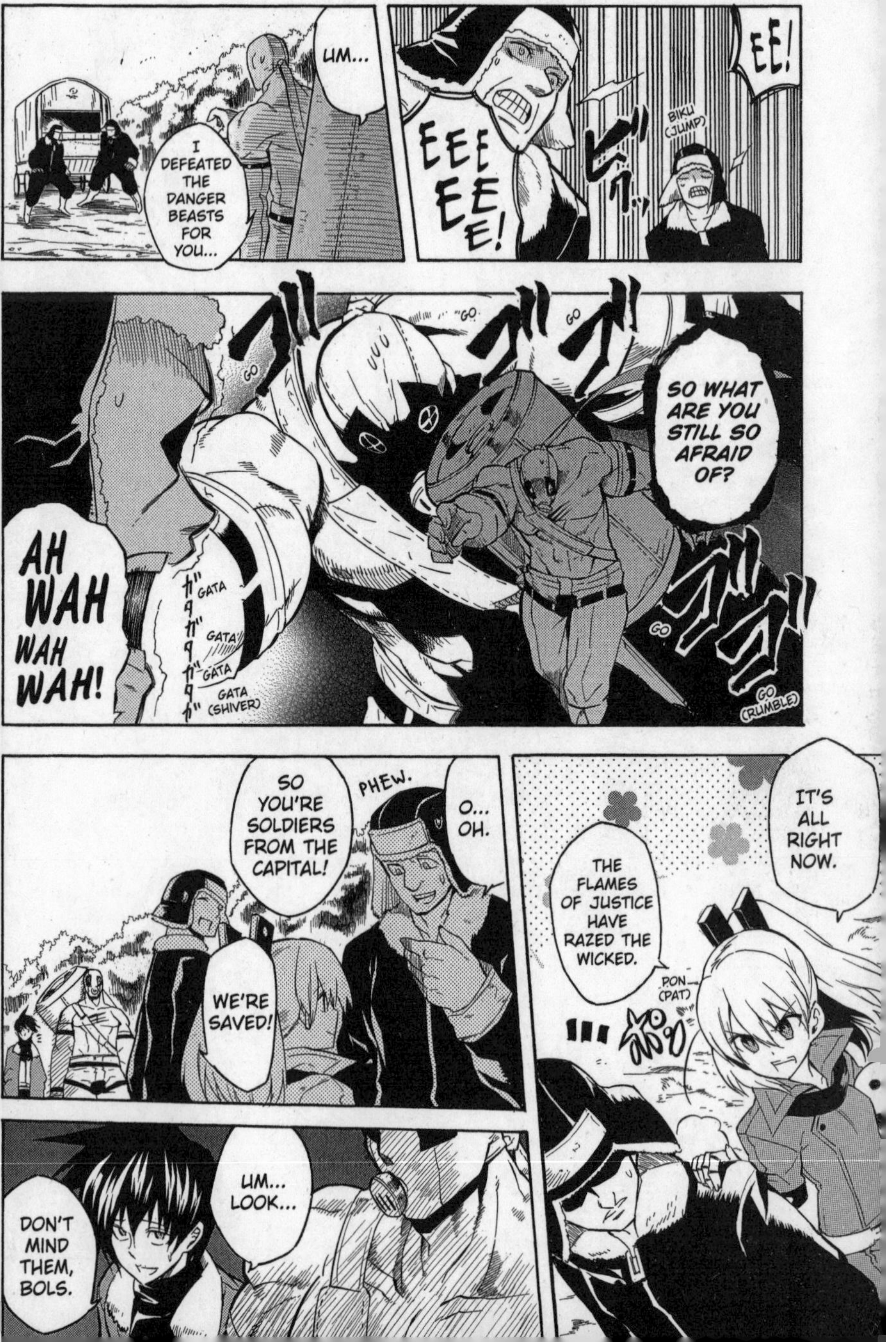
UM...
I DEFEATED THE DANGER BEASTS FOR YOU...
EE!
EEEEEEE!
BIKU (JUMP)
SO WHAT ARE YOU STILL SO AFRAID OF?
GO
GO
GO
GO (RUMBLE)
AH WAH WAH WAH!
GATA
GATA
GATA
GATA (SHIVER)
IT'S ALL RIGHT NOW.
THE FLAMES OF JUSTICE HAVE RAZED THE WICKED.
PON (PAT)
O... OH.
PHEW.
SO YOU'RE SOLDIERS FROM THE CAPITAL!
WE'RE SAVED!
UM... LOOK...
DON'T MIND THEM, BOLS.

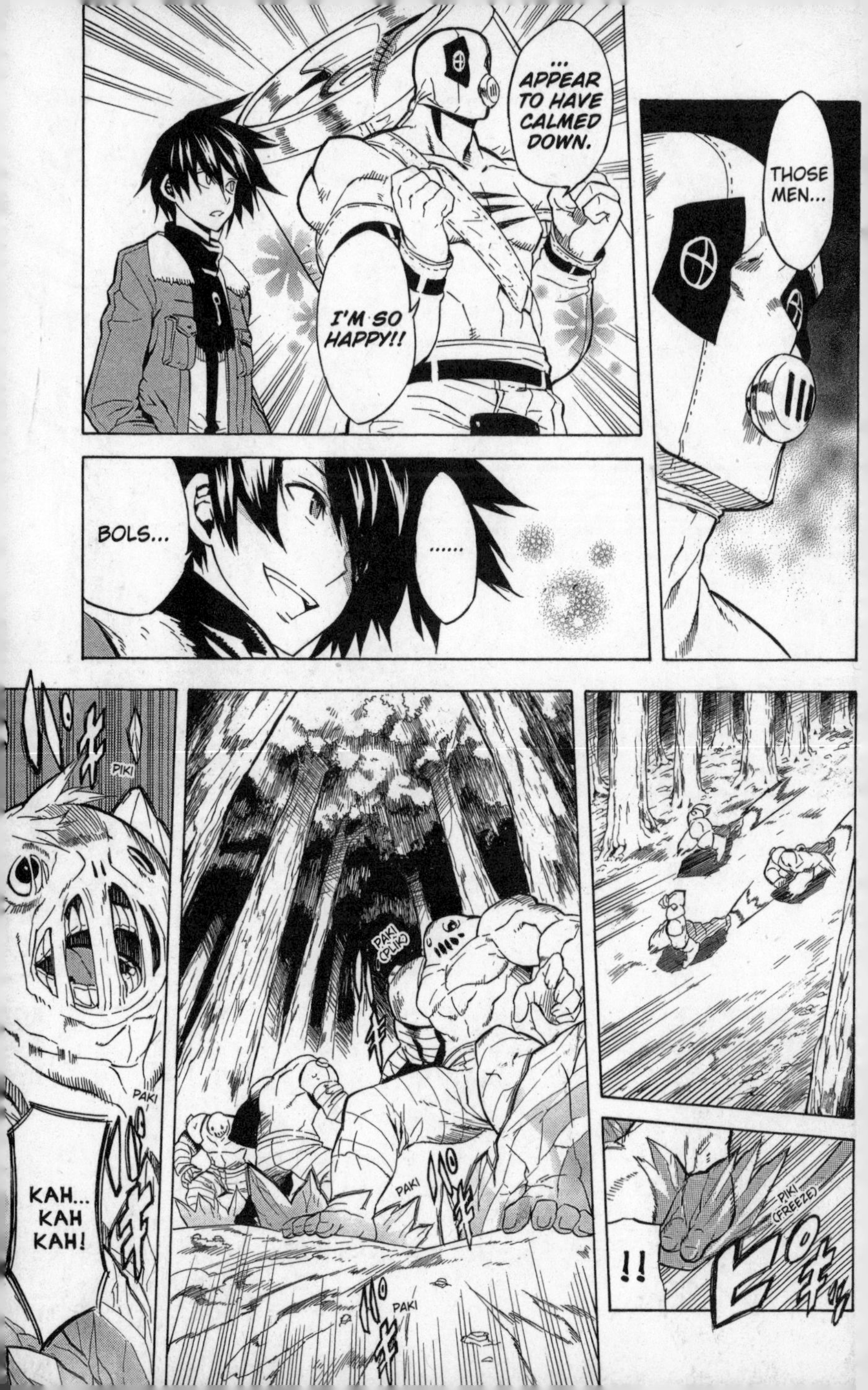
THOSE MEN...
... APPEAR TO HAVE CALMED DOWN.
I'M SO HAPPY!!
......
BOLS...
PIKI (FREEZE)
!!
PAKI (PLIK)
PAKI
PAKI
PIKI
PAKI
KAH... KAH KAH!

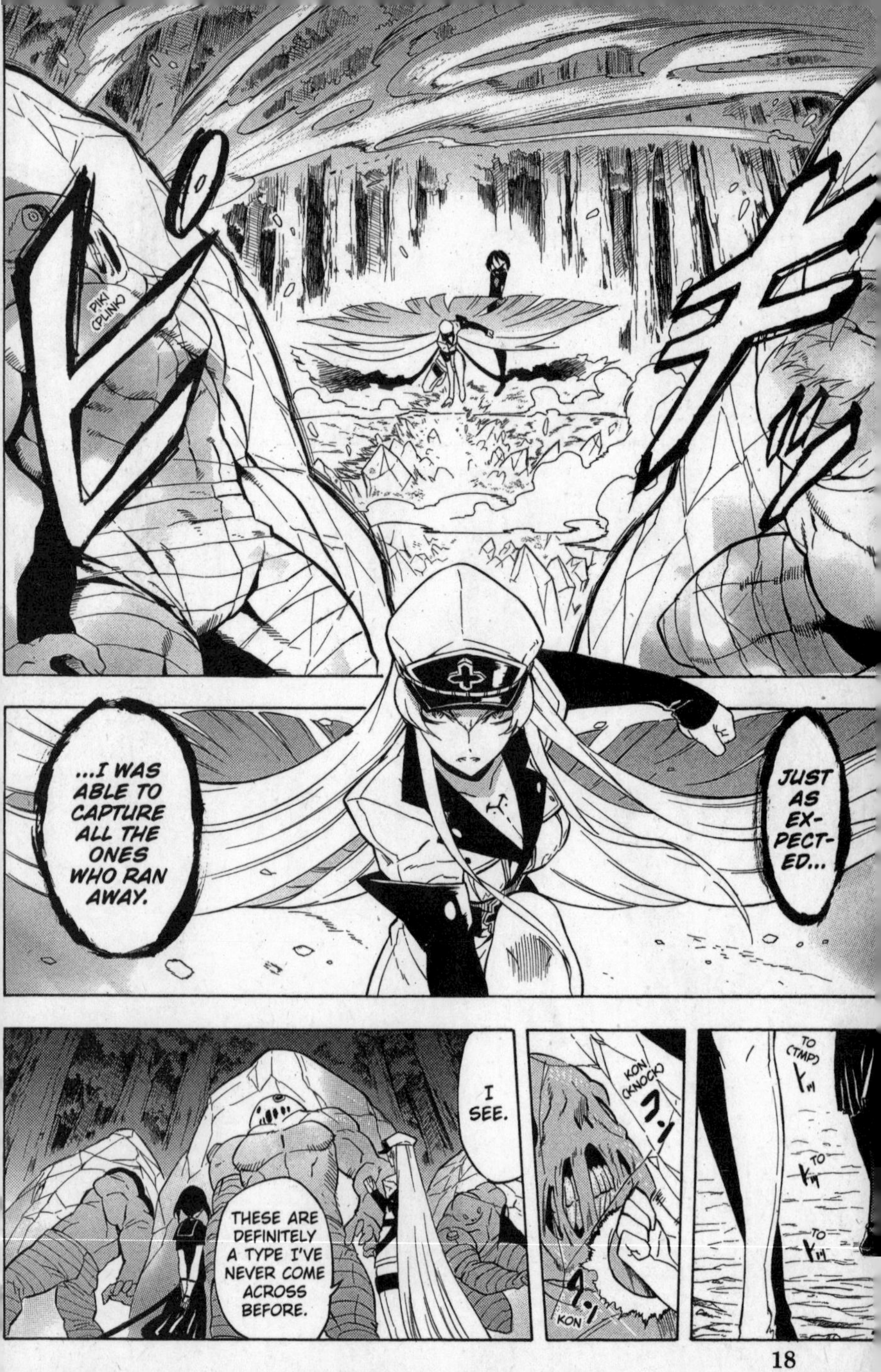
PIKI (PLINK)
JUST AS EXPECTED...
...I WAS ABLE TO CAPTURE ALL THE ONES WHO RAN AWAY.
TO (TMP)
TO
TO
KON (KNOCK)
KON
I SEE.
THESE ARE DEFINITELY A TYPE I'VE NEVER COME ACROSS BEFORE.

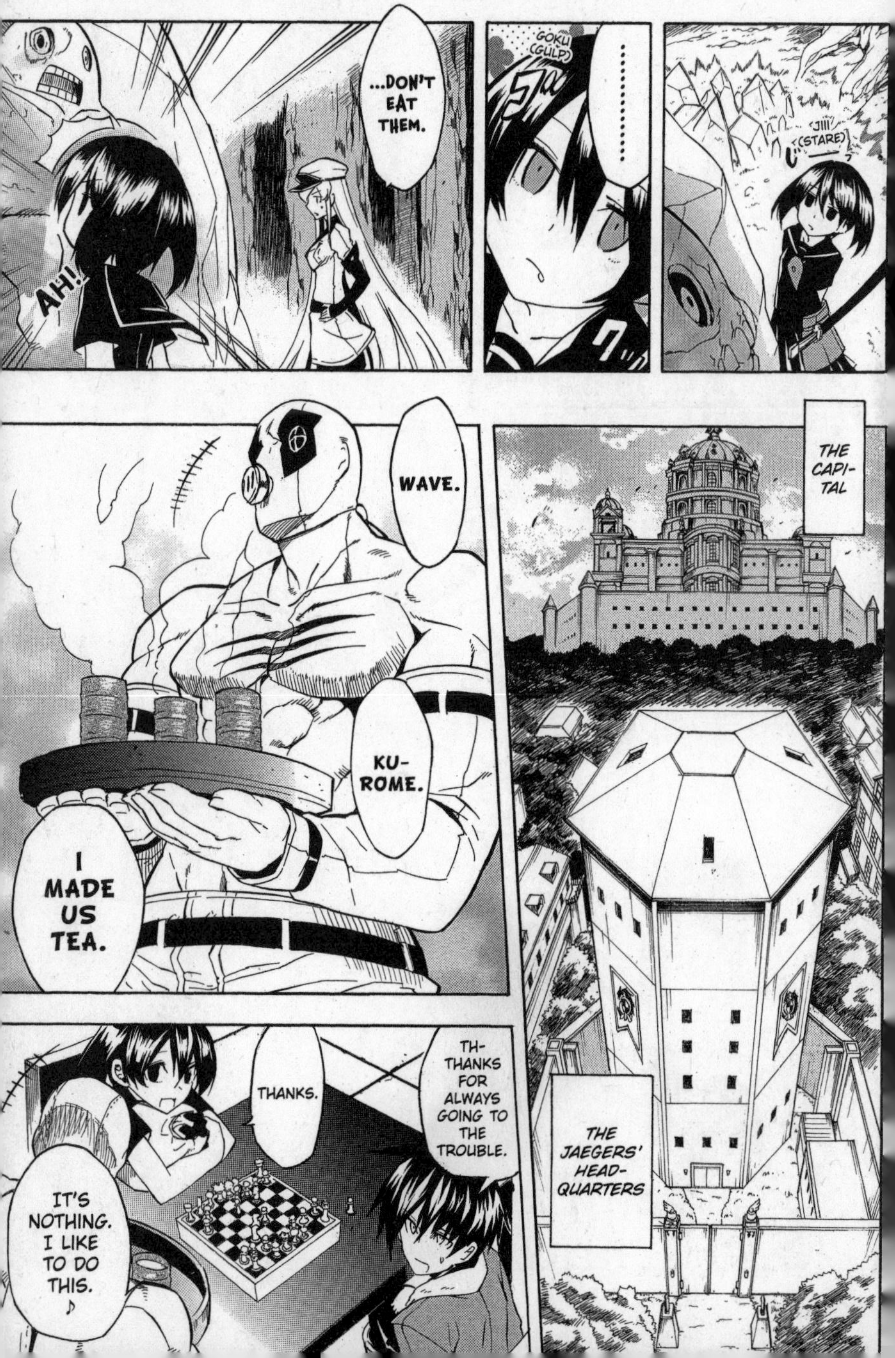
JIII (STARE)
GOKU (GULP)
....
...DON'T EAT THEM.
AH!
THE CAPITAL
THE JAEGERS' HEAD-QUARTERS
WAVE.
KU-ROME.
I MADE US TEA.
TH-THANKS FOR ALWAYS GOING TO THE TROUBLE.
THANKS.
IT'S NOTHING. I LIKE TO DO THIS. ♪

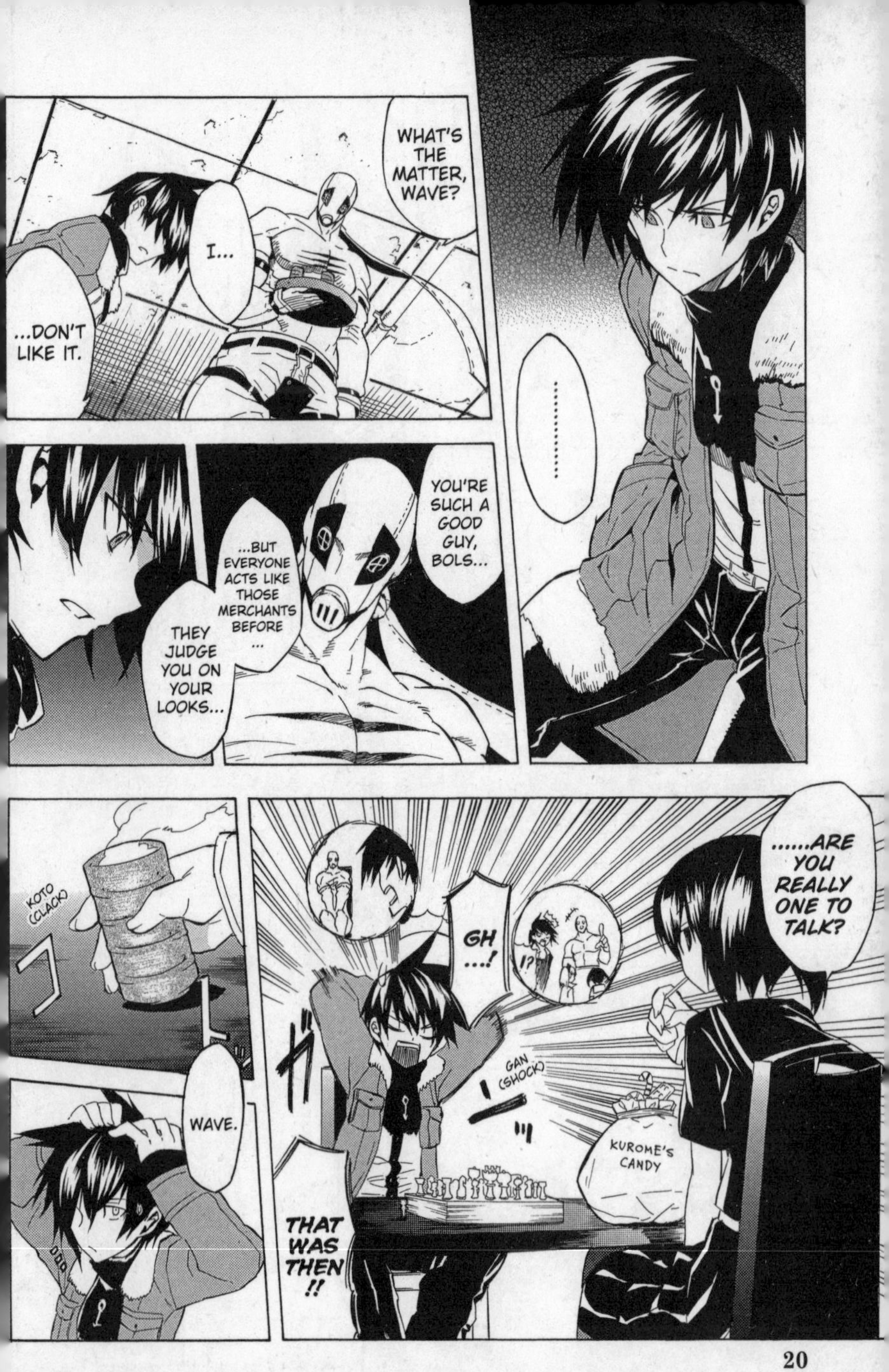
WHAT'S THE MATTER, WAVE?
I...
...DON'T LIKE IT.
......
YOU'RE SUCH A GOOD GUY, BOLS...
...BUT EVERYONE ACTS LIKE THOSE MERCHANTS BEFORE ...
THEY JUDGE YOU ON YOUR LOOKS...
......ARE YOU REALLY ONE TO TALK?
GH ...!
!?
GAN (SHOCK)
KUROME'S CANDY
THAT WAS THEN !!
KOTO (CLACK)
WAVE.

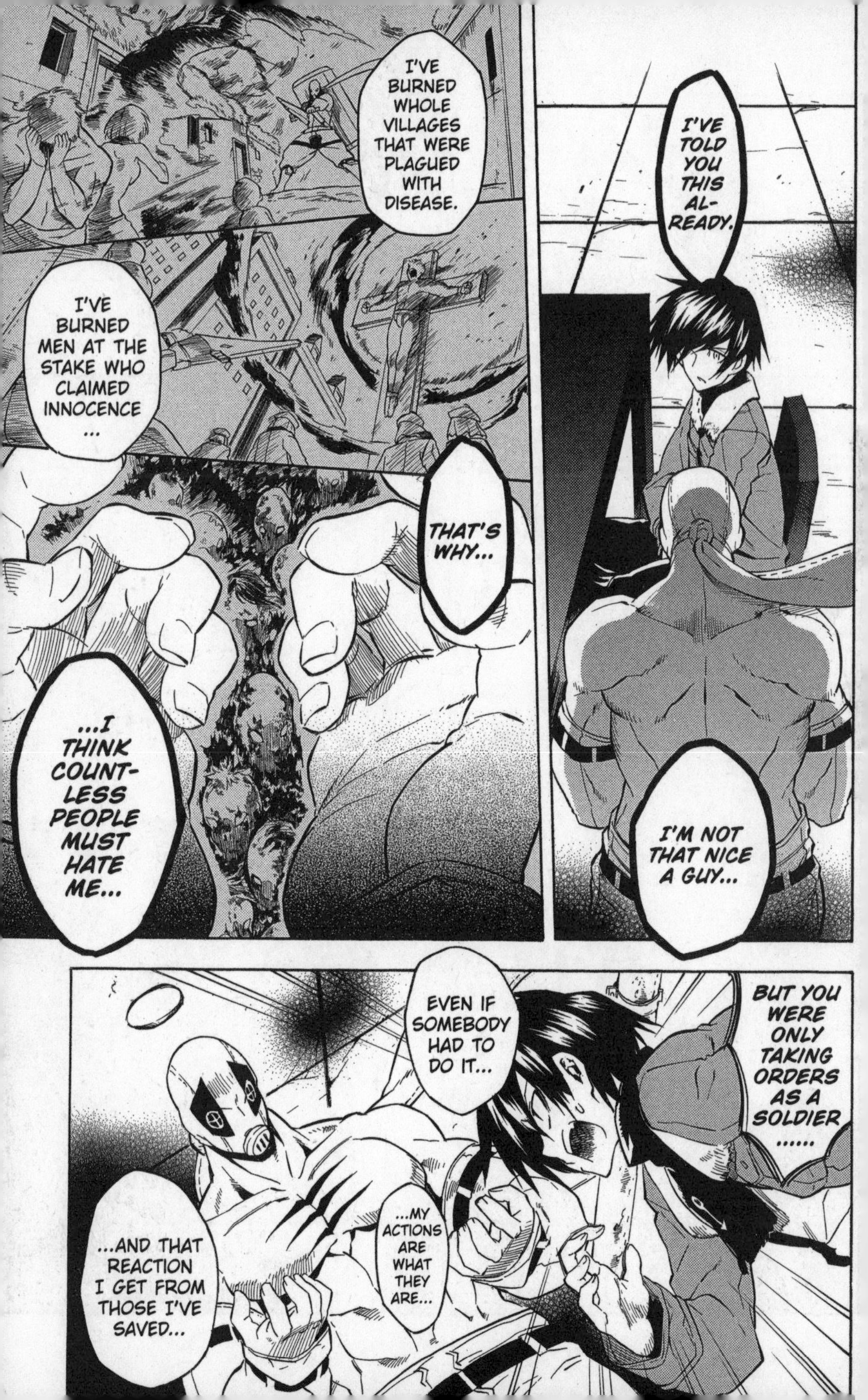
I'VE TOLD YOU THIS AL-READY.
I'VE BURNED WHOLE VILLAGES THAT WERE PLAGUED WITH DISEASE.
I'VE BURNED MEN AT THE STAKE WHO CLAIMED INNOCENCE ...
THAT'S WHY...
...I THINK COUNT-LESS PEOPLE MUST HATE ME...
I'M NOT THAT NICE A GUY...
BUT YOU WERE ONLY TAKING ORDERS AS A SOLDIER ......
EVEN IF SOMEBODY HAD TO DO IT...
...MY ACTIONS ARE WHAT THEY ARE...
...AND THAT REACTION I GET FROM THOSE I'VE SAVED...

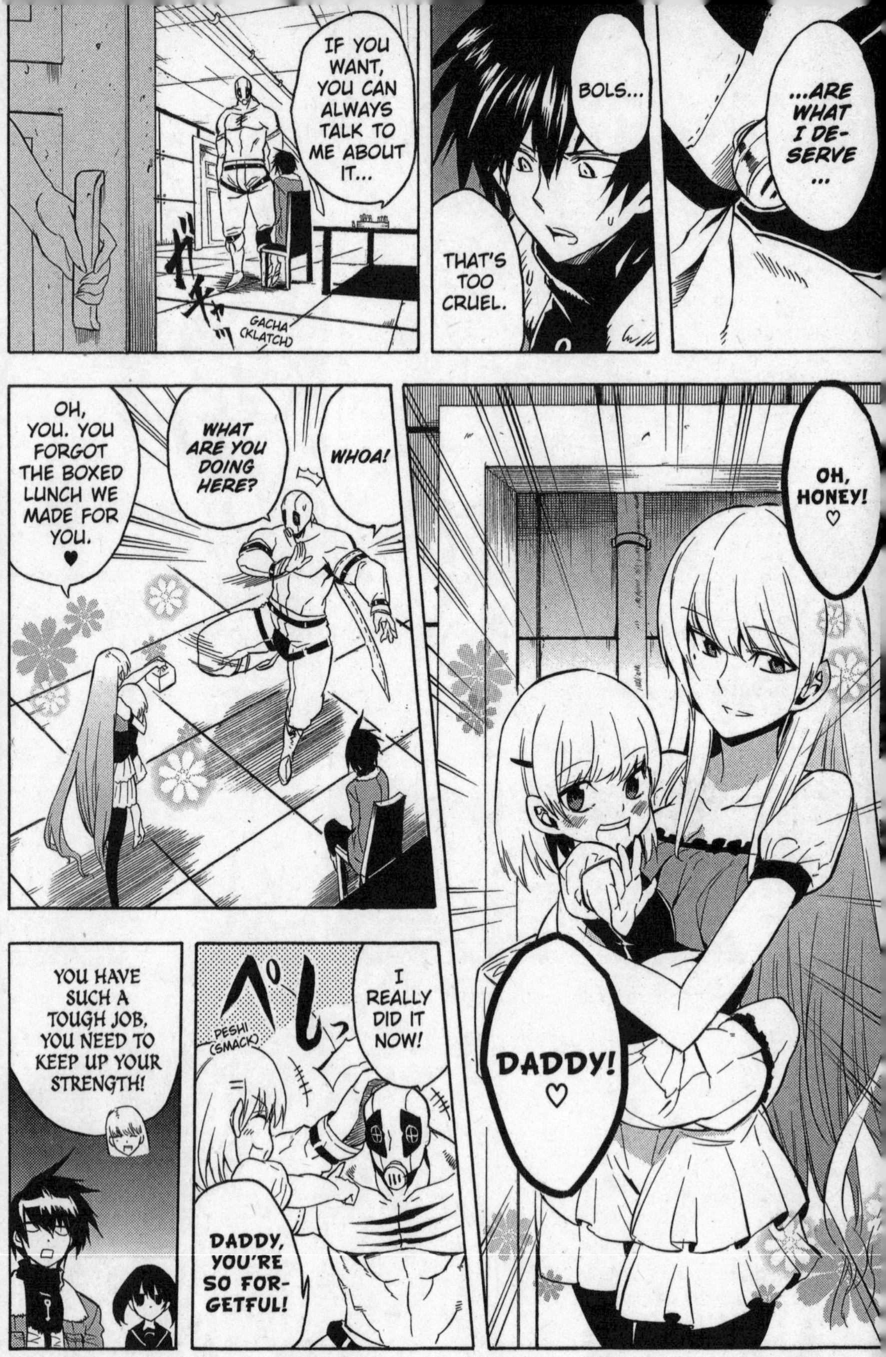
...ARE WHAT I DE-SERVE ...
BOLS...
THAT'S TOO CRUEL.
IF YOU WANT, YOU CAN ALWAYS TALK TO ME ABOUT IT...
GACHA (KLATCH)
OH, HONEY! ♡
DADDY! ♡
WHOA!
WHAT ARE YOU DOING HERE?
OH, YOU. YOU FORGOT THE BOXED LUNCH WE MADE FOR YOU. ♥
I REALLY DID IT NOW!
PESHI (SMACK)
DADDY, YOU'RE SO FOR-GETFUL!
YOU HAVE SUCH A TOUGH JOB, YOU NEED TO KEEP UP YOUR STRENGTH!

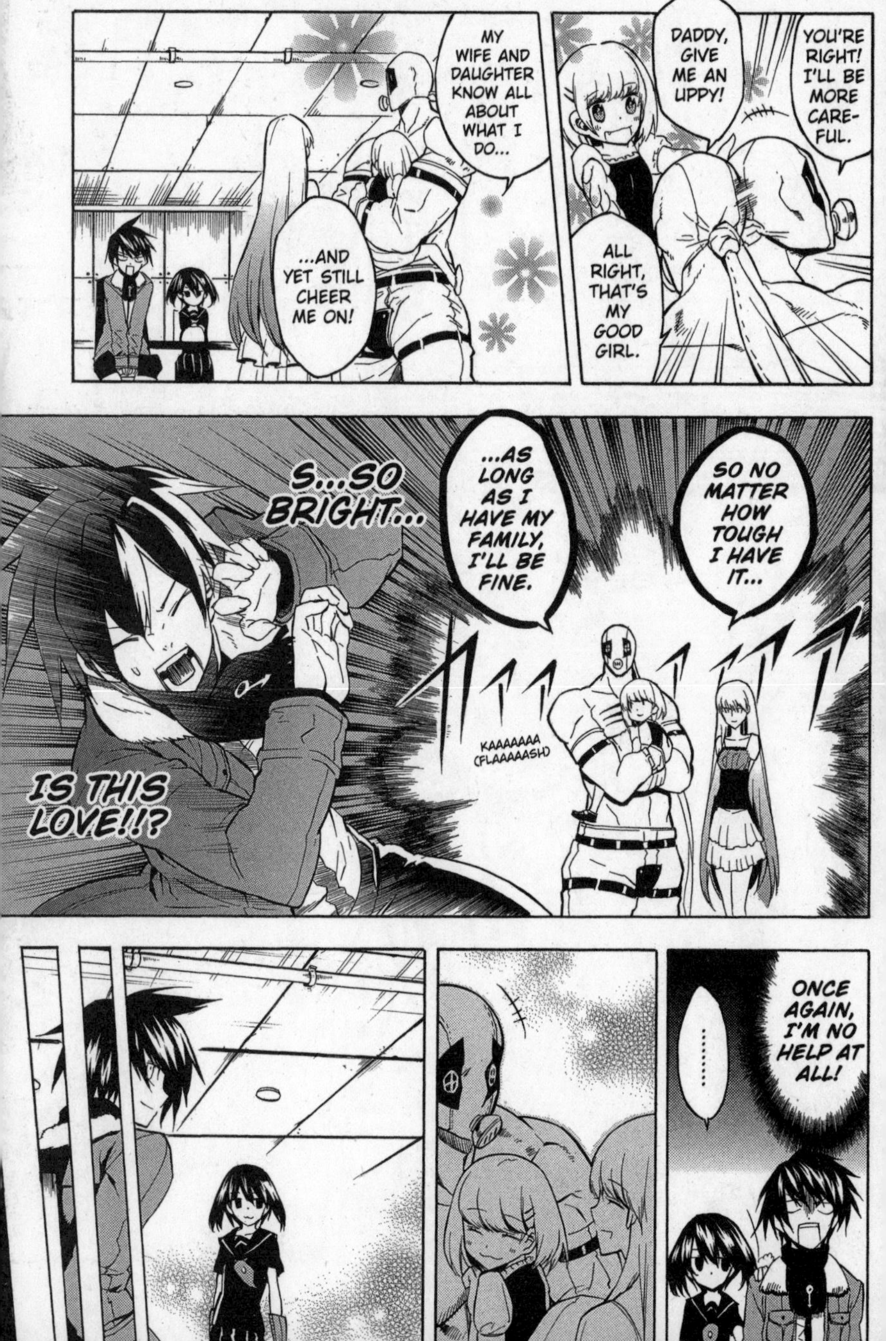

DADDY, GIVE ME AN UPPY!
YOU'RE RIGHT! I'LL BE MORE CARE-FUL.
ALL RIGHT, THAT'S MY GOOD GIRL.
MY WIFE AND DAUGHTER KNOW ALL ABOUT WHAT I DO...
...AND YET STILL CHEER ME ON!
SO NO MATTER HOW TOUGH I HAVE IT...
...AS LONG AS I HAVE MY FAMILY, I'LL BE FINE.
KAAAAAAA (FLAAAAASH)
S...SO BRIGHT...
IS THIS LOVE!!?
ONCE AGAIN, I'M NO HELP AT ALL!
....

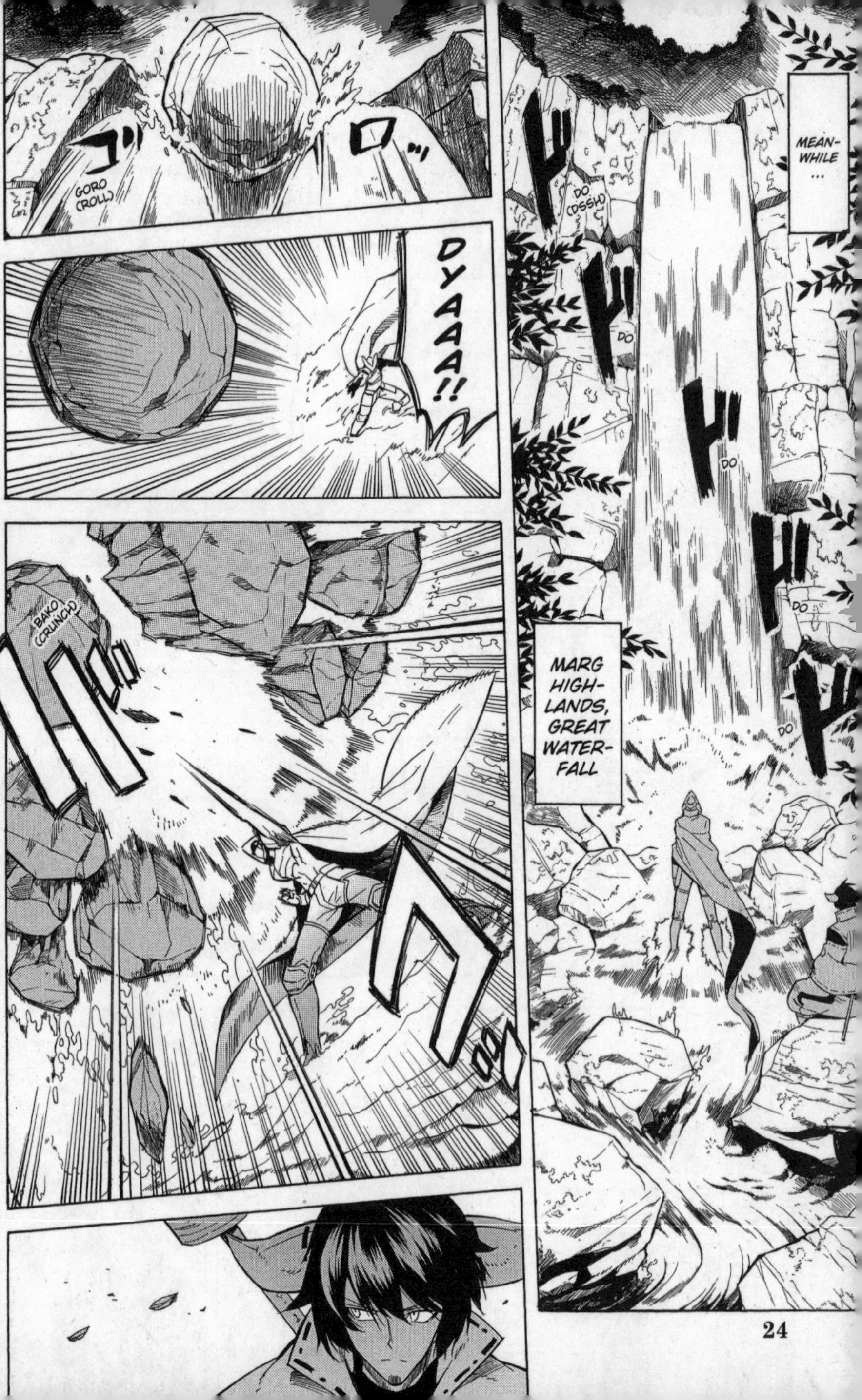
MEAN-WHILE ...
DO (DSSH)
DO
DO
DO
DO
MARG HIGH-LANDS, GREAT WATER-FALL
GORO (ROLL)
DYAAAA!!
BAKO (CRUNCH)

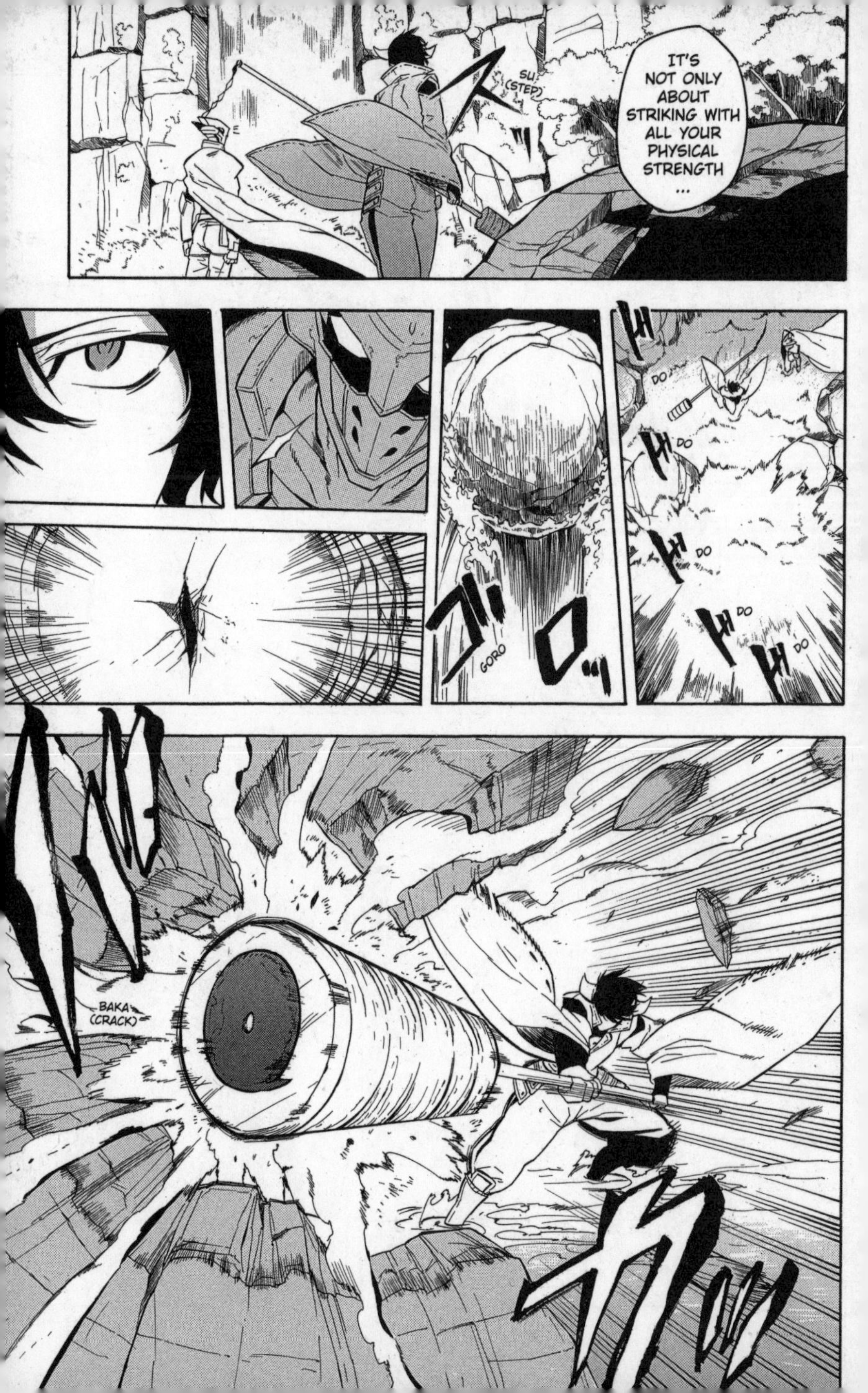

IT'S NOT ONLY ABOUT STRIKING WITH ALL YOUR PHYSICAL STRENGTH ...
SU (STEP)
DO
DO
DO
DO
DO
GORO
BAKA (CRACK)

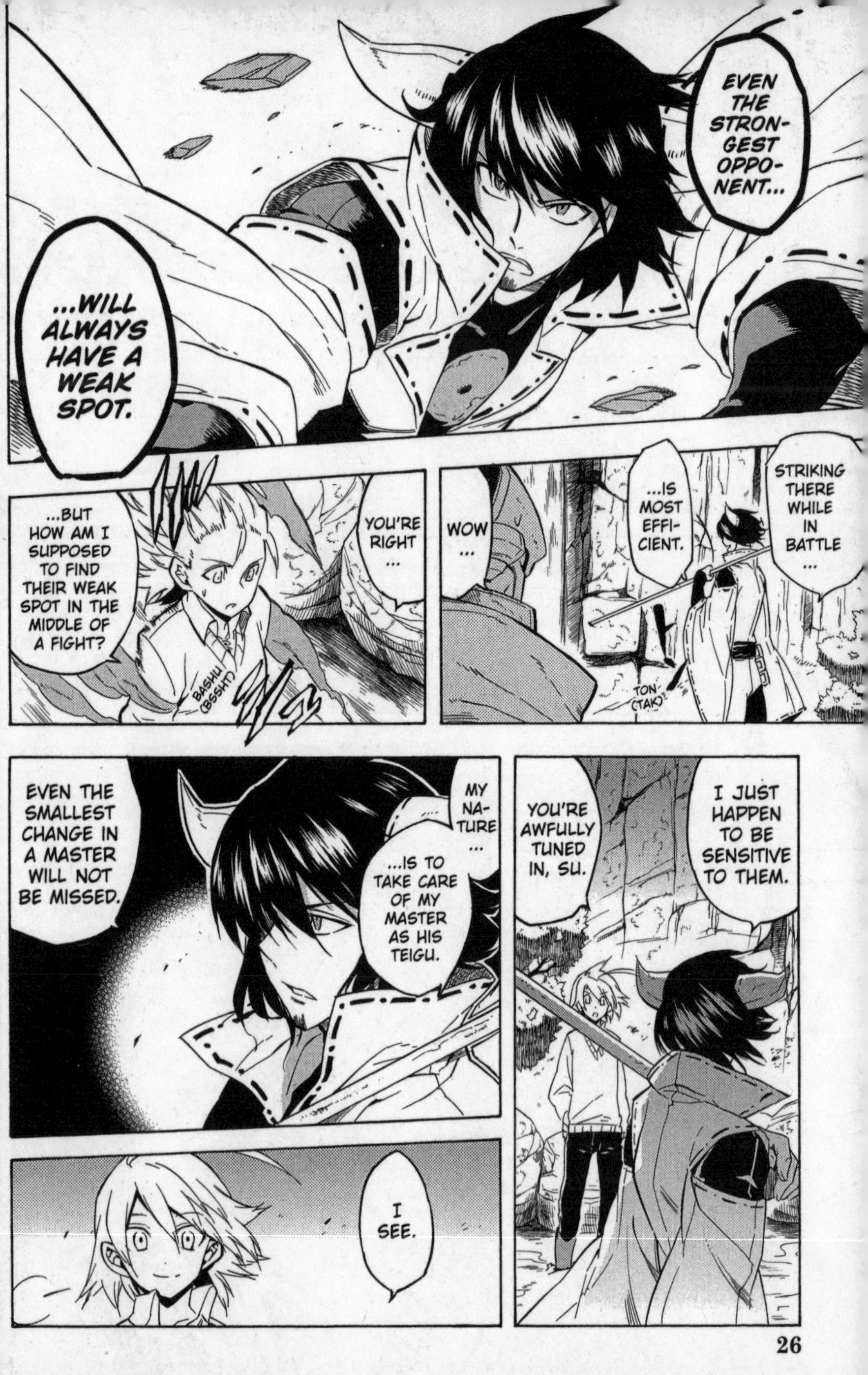
EVEN THE STRONGEST OPPONENT...
...WILL ALWAYS HAVE A WEAK SPOT.
STRIKING THERE WHILE IN BATTLE...
...IS MOST EFFICIENT.
TON (TAK)
WOW...
YOU'RE RIGHT...
...BUT HOW AM I SUPPOSED TO FIND THEIR WEAK SPOT IN THE MIDDLE OF A FIGHT?
BASHU (BSSHT)
I JUST HAPPEN TO BE SENSITIVE TO THEM.
YOU'RE AWFULLY TUNED IN, SU.
MY NATURE...
...IS TO TAKE CARE OF MY MASTER AS HIS TEIGU.
EVEN THE SMALLEST CHANGE IN A MASTER WILL NOT BE MISSED.
I SEE.

THIS IS REALLY REASSURING.
HAVING YOU WITH US PUTS US AT EIGHT PEOPLE, SU.
ZAAAAAA (SSSHHH)
AS LONG AS WE DON'T LOSE ANYONE, I THINK WE'VE GOT A SHOT!
...I'M A TEIGU.
THERE'S NO NEED TO COUNT ME AMONG YOU.
DON'T TALK LIKE THAT!
SU, YOU'RE ALSO A GREAT TEAMMATE!
SU (SWF)
......
TEAM... MATE...

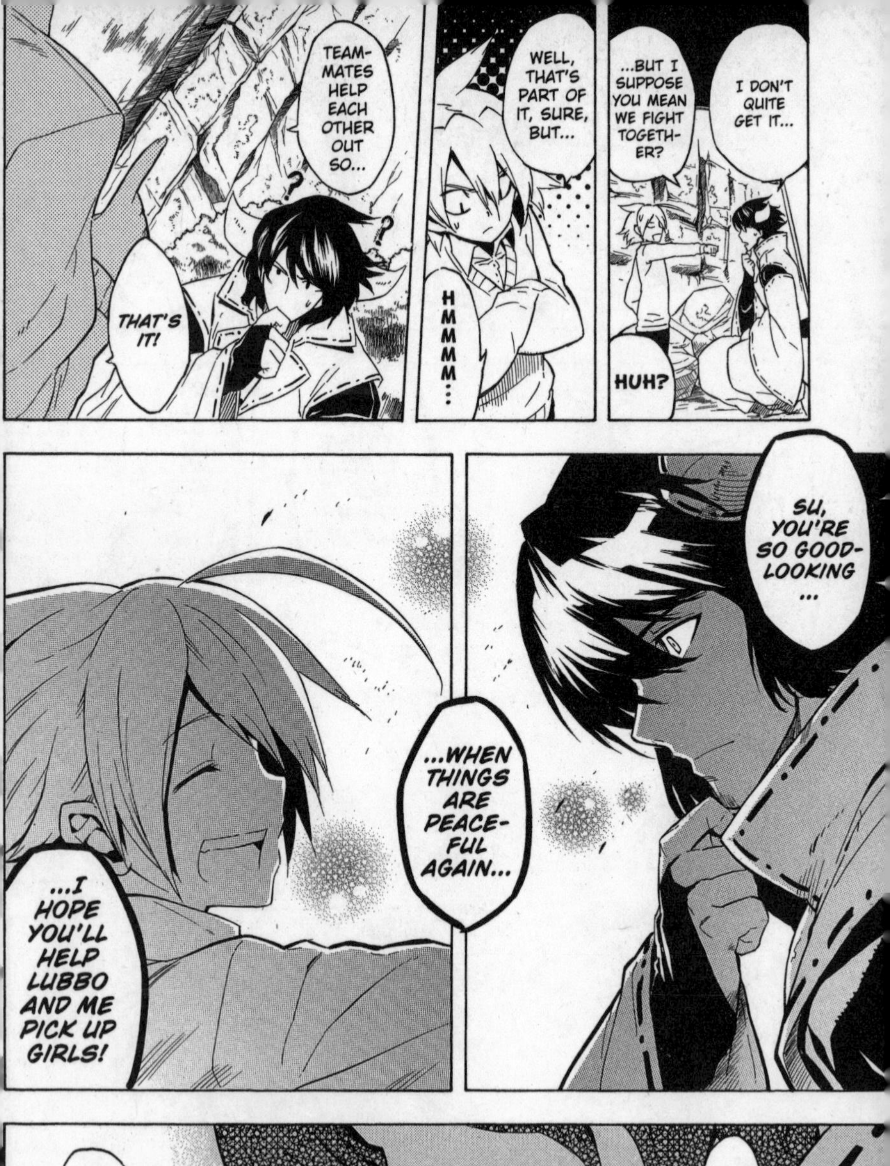
I DON'T QUITE GET IT...
...BUT I SUPPOSE YOU MEAN WE FIGHT TOGETH-ER?
HUH?
WELL, THAT'S PART OF IT, SURE, BUT...
HMMMM...
TEAM-MATES HELP EACH OTHER OUT SO...
THAT'S IT!
SU, YOU'RE SO GOOD-LOOKING...
...WHEN THINGS ARE PEACE-FUL AGAIN...
...I HOPE YOU'LL HELP LUBBO AND ME PICK UP GIRLS!
......
I'M NOT REALLY SURE, BUT...

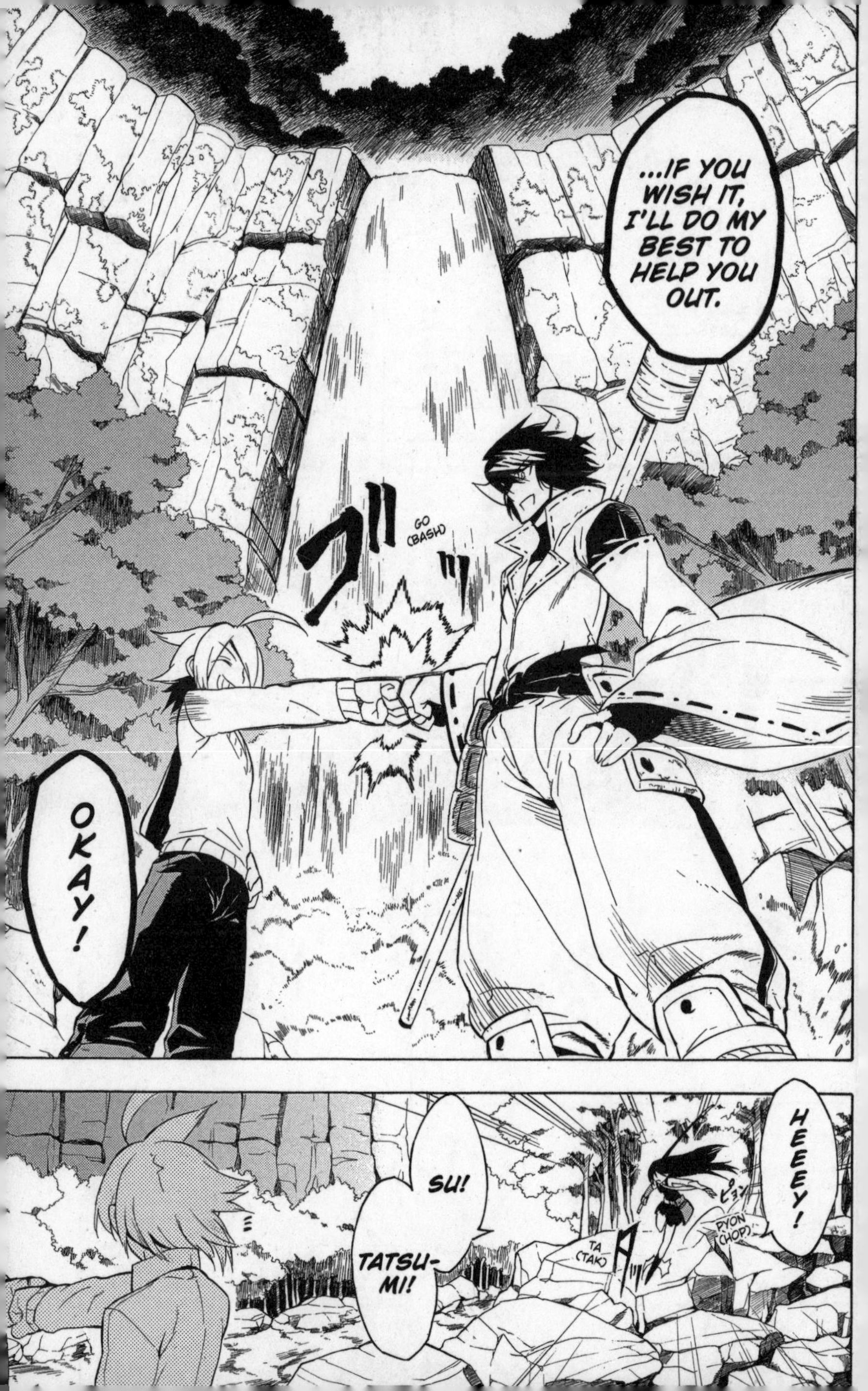
...IF YOU WISH IT, I'LL DO MY BEST TO HELP YOU OUT.
GO (BASH)
OKAY!
HEEEY!
PYON (CHOP)
TA (TAK)
SU!
TATSU-MI!

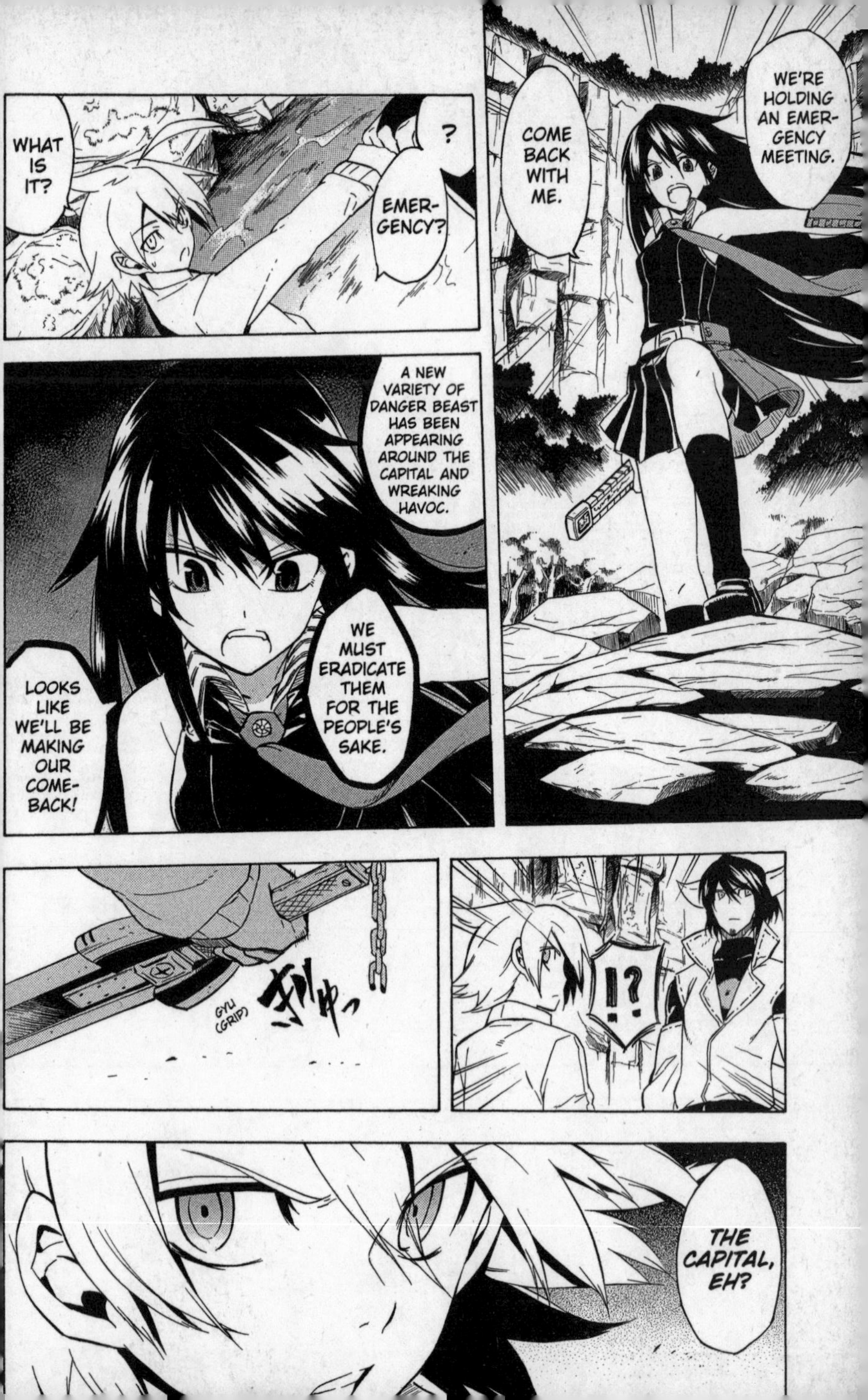
WE'RE HOLDING AN EMER-GENCY MEETING.
COME BACK WITH ME.
?
EMER-GENCY?
WHAT IS IT?
A NEW VARIETY OF DANGER BEAST HAS BEEN APPEARING AROUND THE CAPITAL AND WREAKING HAVOC.
WE MUST ERADICATE THEM FOR THE PEOPLE'S SAKE.
LOOKS LIKE WE'LL BE MAKING OUR COME-BACK!
!?
GYU (GRIP)
THE CAPITAL, EH?

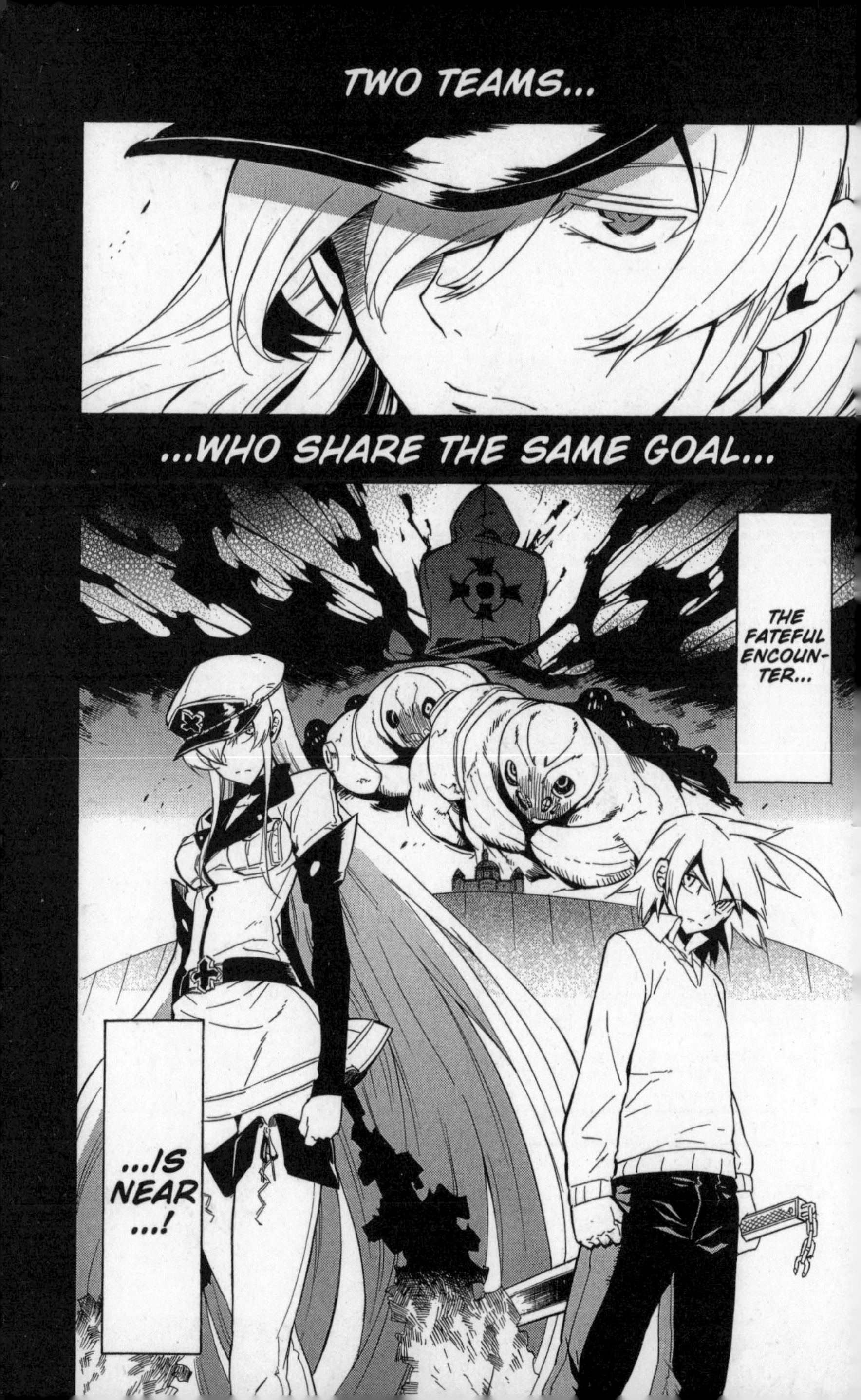
TWO TEAMS...
...WHO SHARE THE SAME GOAL...
THE FATEFUL ENCOUN-TER...
...IS NEAR ...!

Akame ga KILL!
Rough Sketches 1

THE EMBLEMS OF EACH KINGDOM

1'
2'
3'
1
2
3
4
5
6
7
8
9
10

THE EMBLEMS OF EACH KINGDOM

1 · The capital. Located at the heart of the kingdom. The main stage of *Akame ga KILL!*

2 · Matsura Village. Tatsumi's hometown. A mountain village found to the north.

3 · Kakachichi Lake. A natural stronghold. The headquarters for the Revolutionary Army.

4 · Where the battle against the tribe of the north took place under the command of Esdeath.

5 · Where the battle against the tribe of the west took place under the command of Najenda.

6 · Where the battle against the tribe of the south took place. Bulat was affiliated with them.

7 · The sea. Where the Imperial Navy is and where trade takes place. Wave was affiliated with them.

8 · Night Raid's hideout. Was destroyed by Stylish's ambush.

9 · Lake Gyogan.

10 · Headquarters of the new religion.

EMPIRE
The simplified version of the Empire's symbol is: ← THIS
NORTHERN TRIBE 1'
WESTERN TRIBE 2'
SOUTHERN TRIBE 3'

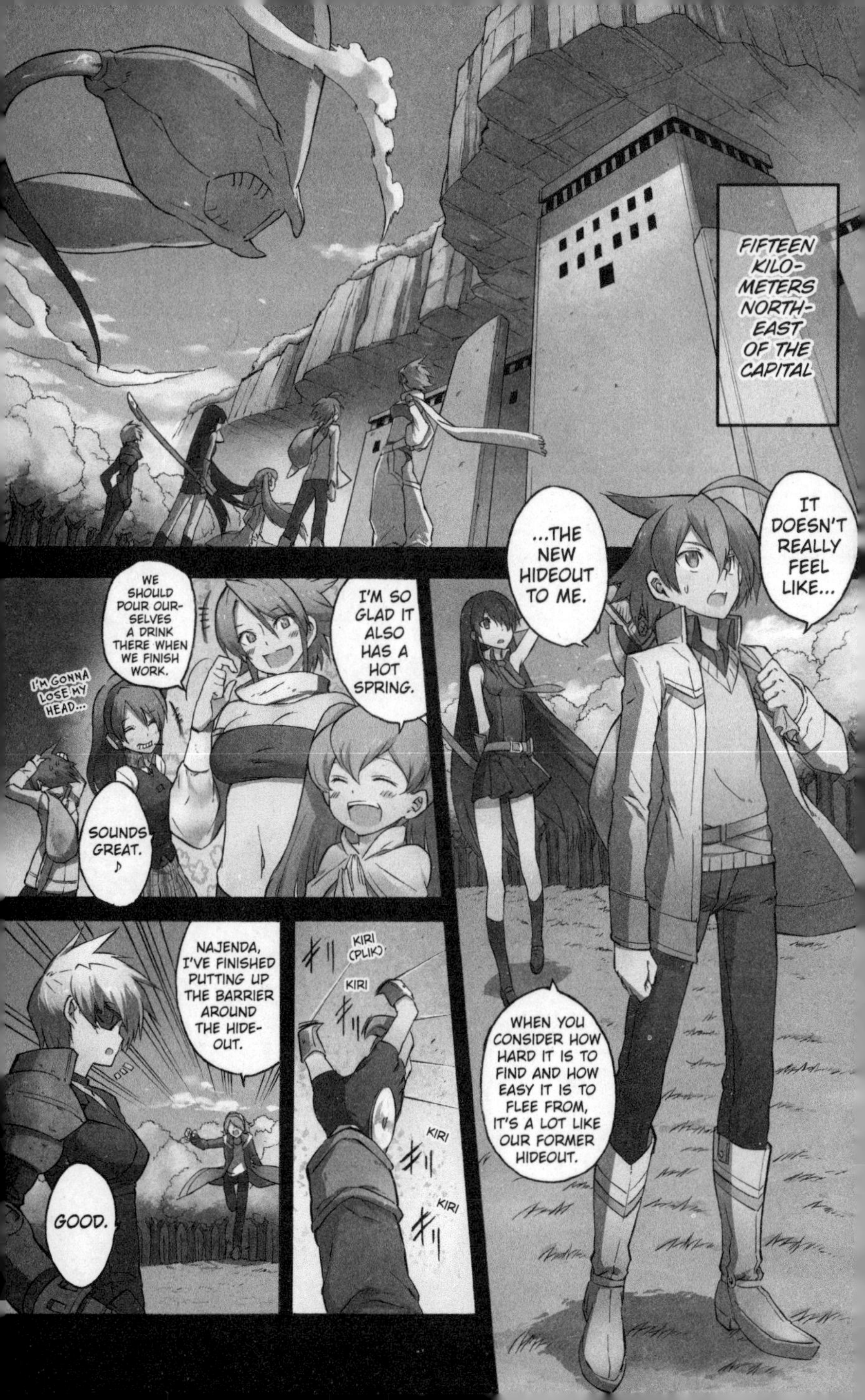
FIFTEEN KILOMETERS NORTHEAST OF THE CAPITAL
IT DOESN'T REALLY FEEL LIKE...
...THE NEW HIDEOUT TO ME.
WHEN YOU CONSIDER HOW HARD IT IS TO FIND AND HOW EASY IT IS TO FLEE FROM, IT'S A LOT LIKE OUR FORMER HIDEOUT.
I'M SO GLAD IT ALSO HAS A HOT SPRING.
WE SHOULD POUR OURSELVES A DRINK THERE WHEN WE FINISH WORK.
I'M GONNA LOSE MY HEAD...
SOUNDS GREAT. ♪
KIRI (PLIK)
KIRI
KIRI
KIRI
NAJENDA, I'VE FINISHED PUTTING UP THE BARRIER AROUND THE HIDEOUT.
GOOD.

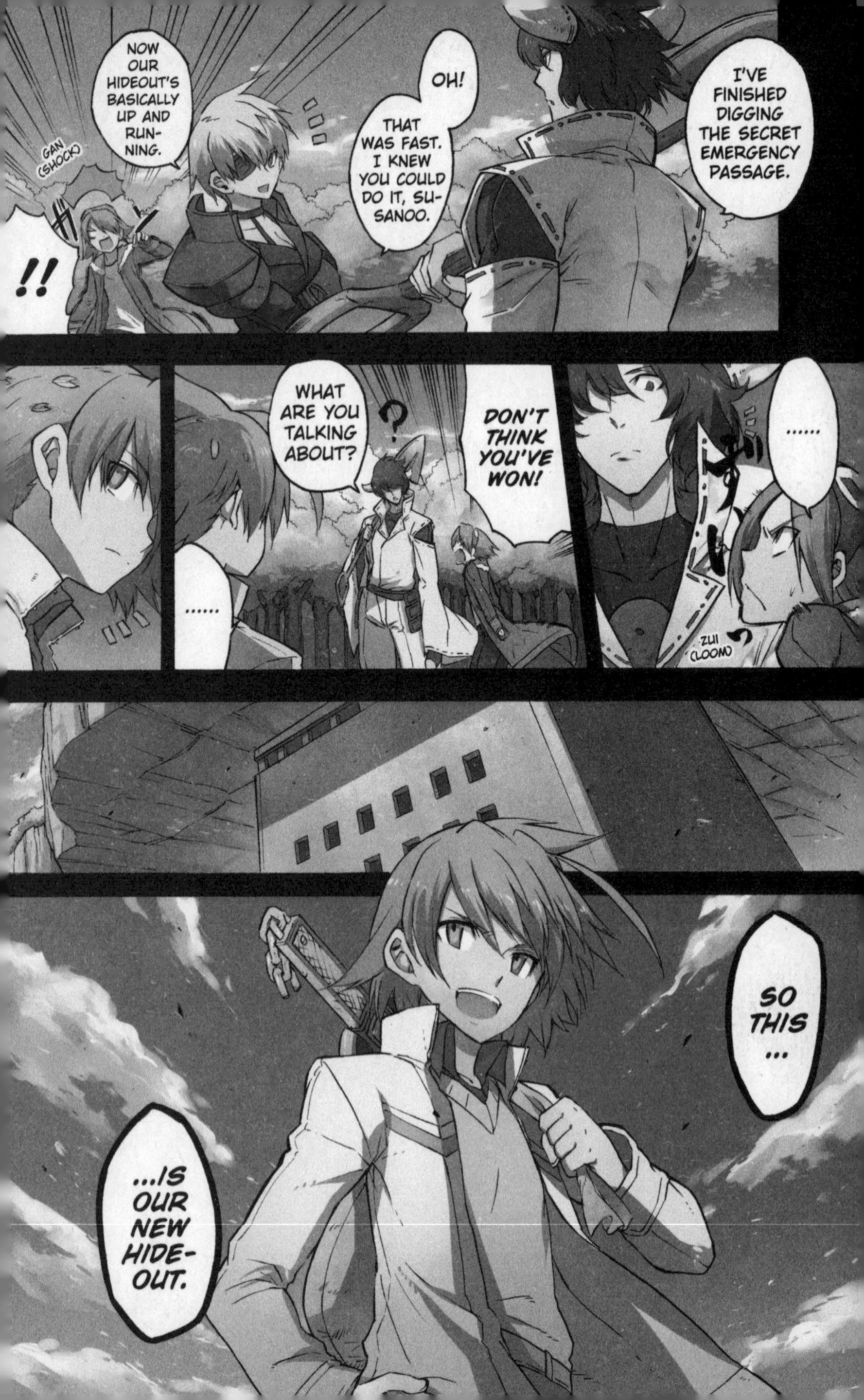

I'VE FINISHED DIGGING THE SECRET EMERGENCY PASSAGE.
OH!
THAT WAS FAST. I KNEW YOU COULD DO IT, SU-SANOO.
NOW OUR HIDEOUT'S BASICALLY UP AND RUN-NING.
GAN (SHOCK)
!!
......
ZUI (LOOM)
DON'T THINK YOU'VE WON!
?
WHAT ARE YOU TALKING ABOUT?
......
SO THIS...
...IS OUR NEW HIDE-OUT.

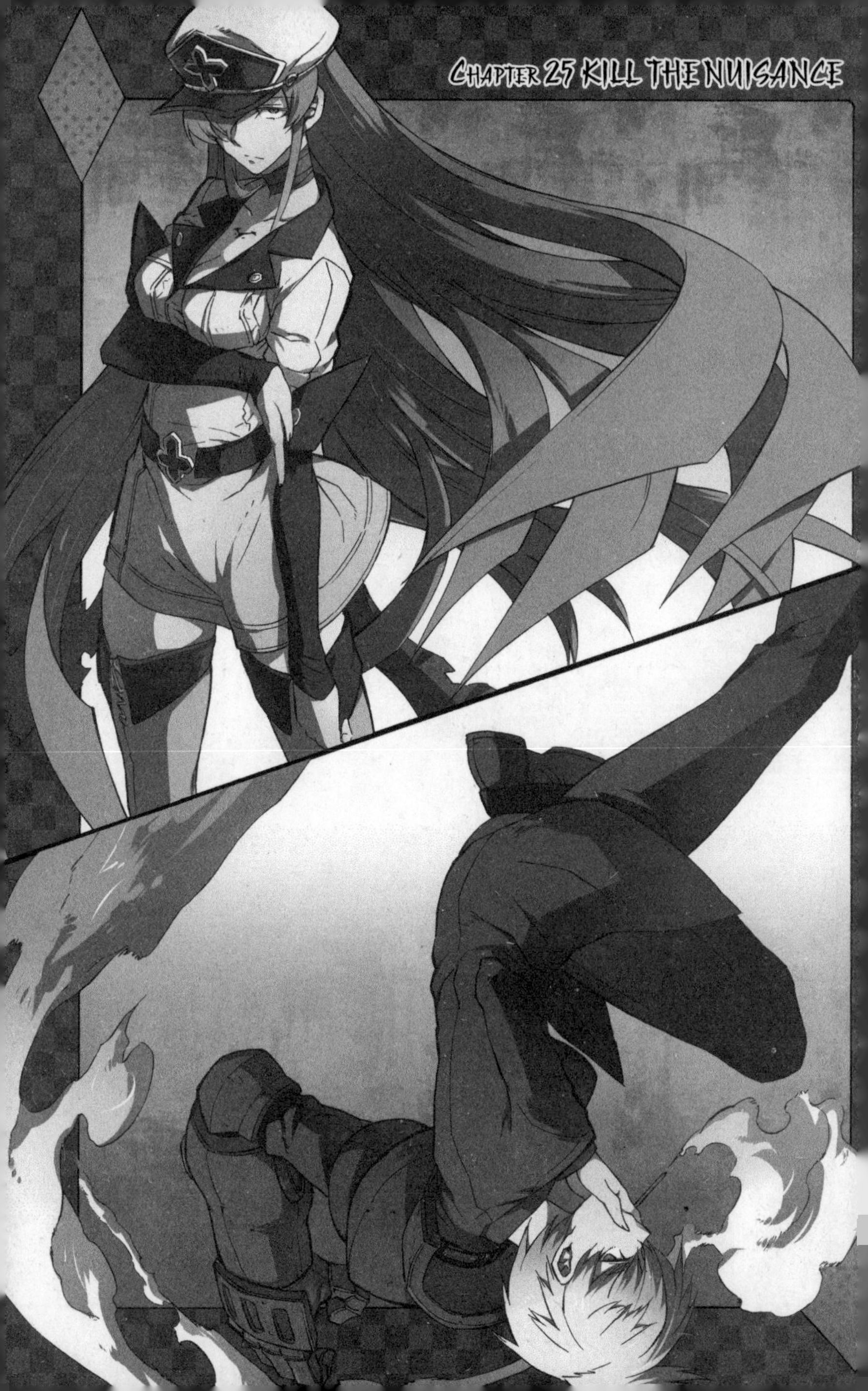
Chapter 25 KILL THE NUISANCE

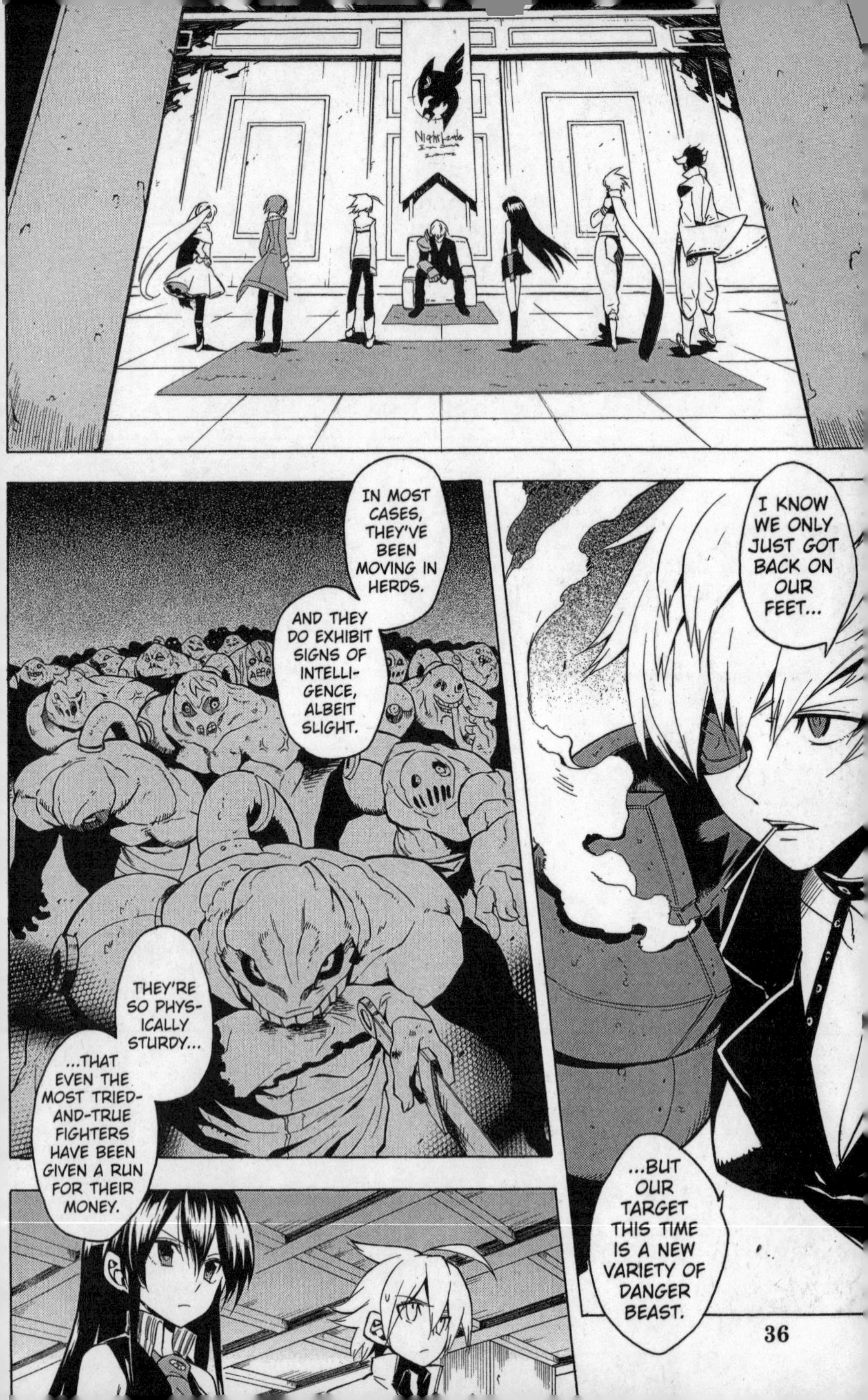
I KNOW WE ONLY JUST GOT BACK ON OUR FEET...
...BUT OUR TARGET THIS TIME IS A NEW VARIETY OF DANGER BEAST.
IN MOST CASES, THEY'VE BEEN MOVING IN HERDS.
AND THEY DO EXHIBIT SIGNS OF INTELLI-GENCE, ALBEIT SLIGHT.
THEY'RE SO PHYS-ICALLY STURDY...
...THAT EVEN THE MOST TRIED-AND-TRUE FIGHTERS HAVE BEEN GIVEN A RUN FOR THEIR MONEY.

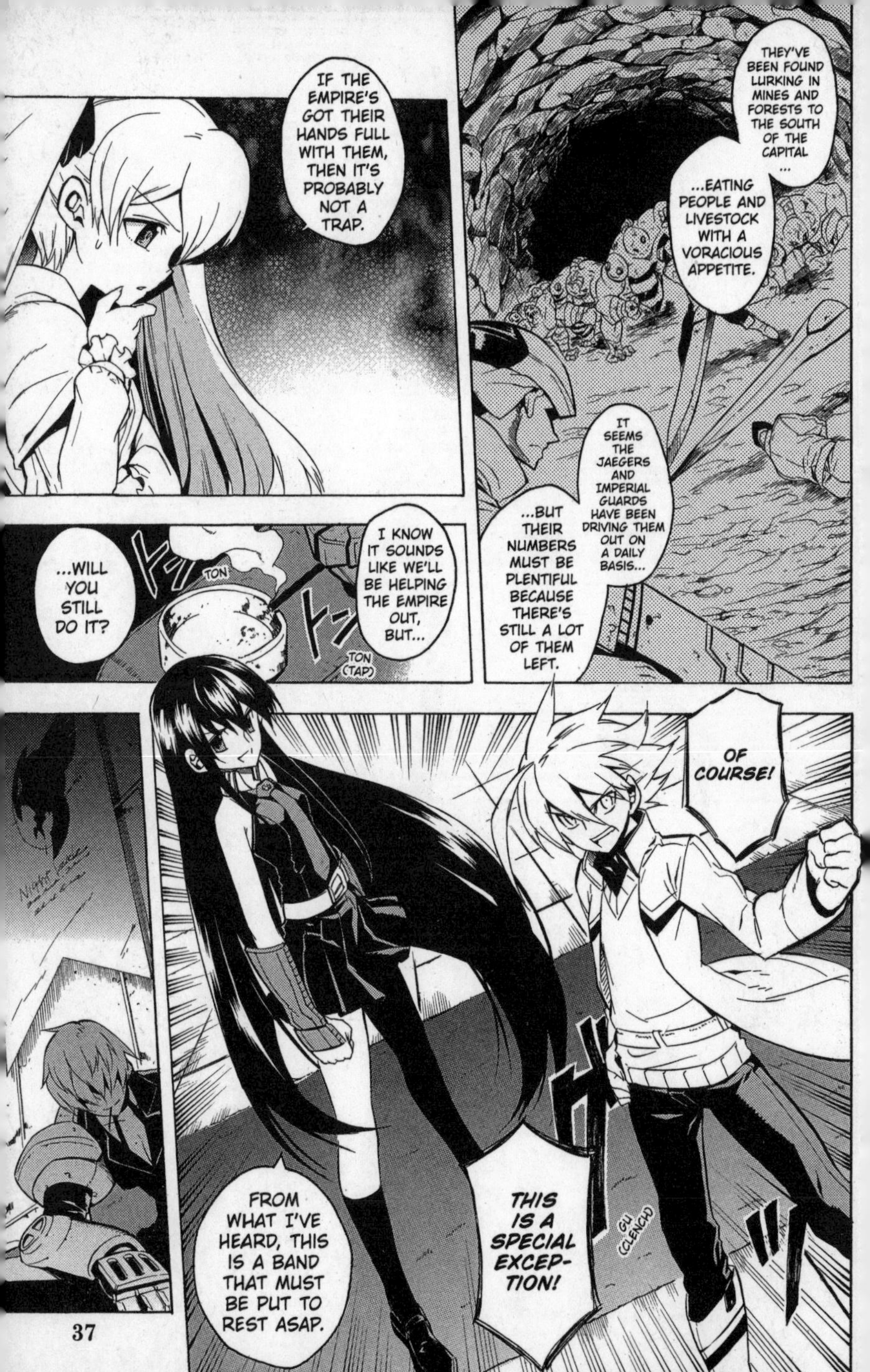
THEY'VE BEEN FOUND LURKING IN MINES AND FORESTS TO THE SOUTH OF THE CAPITAL...
...EATING PEOPLE AND LIVESTOCK WITH A VORACIOUS APPETITE.
IT SEEMS THE JAEGERS AND IMPERIAL GUARDS HAVE BEEN DRIVING THEM OUT ON A DAILY BASIS...
...BUT THEIR NUMBERS MUST BE PLENTIFUL BECAUSE THERE'S STILL A LOT OF THEM LEFT.
IF THE EMPIRE'S GOT THEIR HANDS FULL WITH THEM, THEN IT'S PROBABLY NOT A TRAP.
I KNOW IT SOUNDS LIKE WE'LL BE HELPING THE EMPIRE OUT, BUT...
TON
TON (TAP)
...WILL YOU STILL DO IT?
OF COURSE!
THIS IS A SPECIAL EXCEPTION!
GU (CLENCH)
FROM WHAT I'VE HEARD, THIS IS A BAND THAT MUST BE PUT TO REST ASAP.

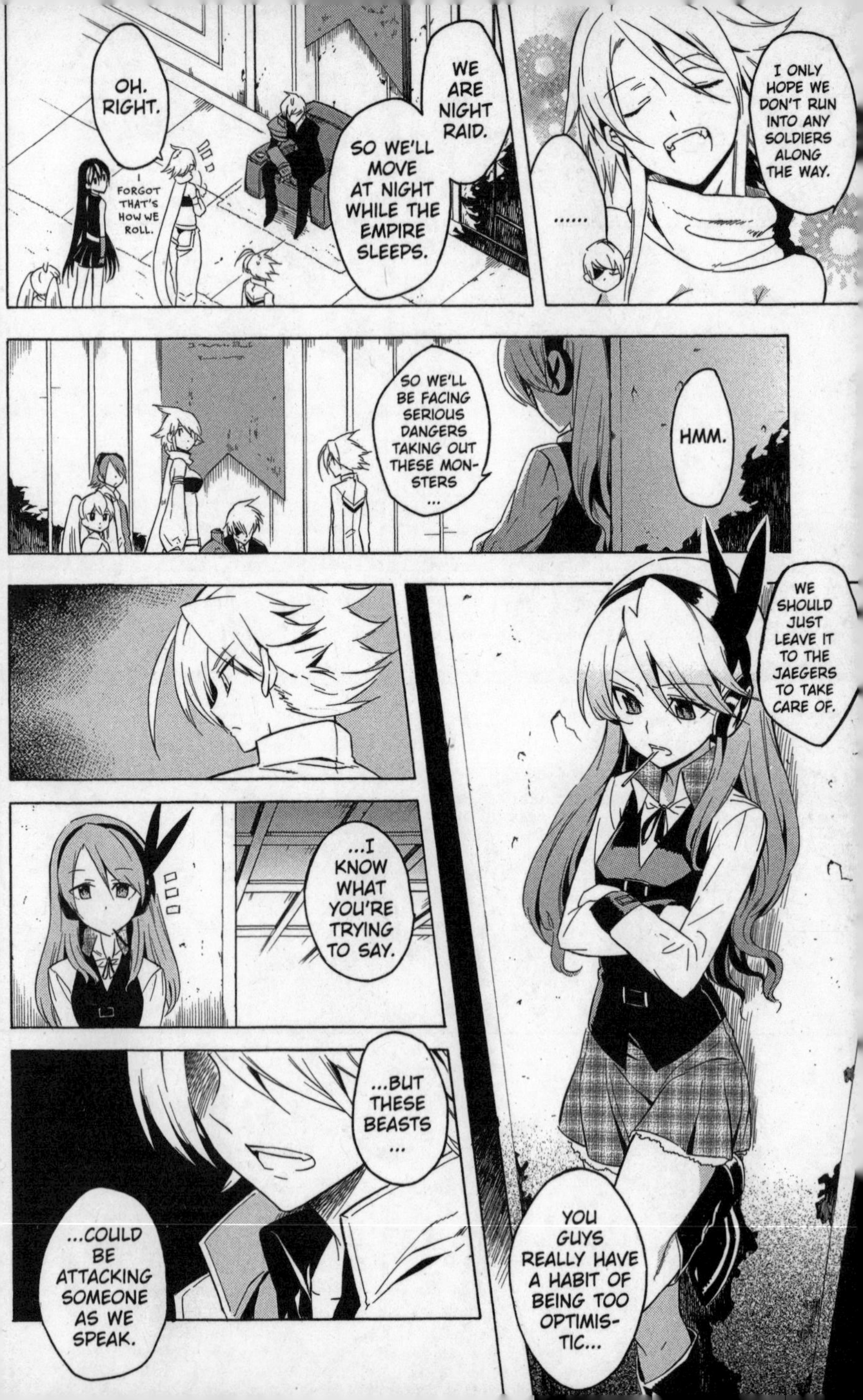
I ONLY HOPE WE DON'T RUN INTO ANY SOLDIERS ALONG THE WAY.
......
WE ARE NIGHT RAID.
SO WE'LL MOVE AT NIGHT WHILE THE EMPIRE SLEEPS.
OH. RIGHT.
I FORGOT THAT'S HOW WE ROLL.
HMM.
SO WE'LL BE FACING SERIOUS DANGERS TAKING OUT THESE MONSTERS ...
WE SHOULD JUST LEAVE IT TO THE JAEGERS TO TAKE CARE OF.
...I KNOW WHAT YOU'RE TRYING TO SAY.
...BUT THESE BEASTS ...
...COULD BE ATTACKING SOMEONE AS WE SPEAK.
YOU GUYS REALLY HAVE A HABIT OF BEING TOO OPTIMISTIC...

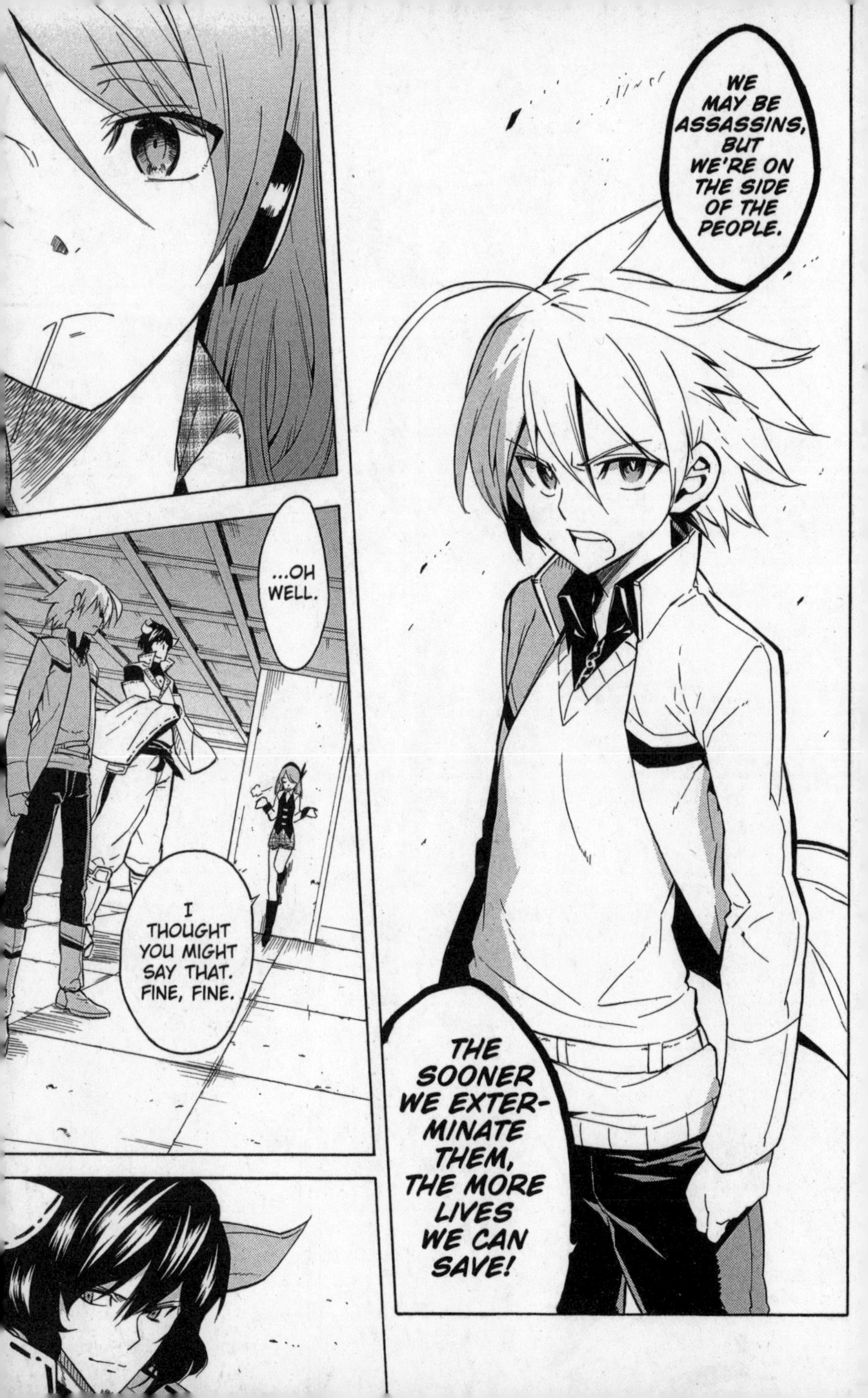
WE MAY BE ASSASSINS, BUT WE'RE ON THE SIDE OF THE PEOPLE.
THE SOONER WE EXTER-MINATE THEM, THE MORE LIVES WE CAN SAVE!
...OH WELL.
I THOUGHT YOU MIGHT SAY THAT. FINE, FINE.

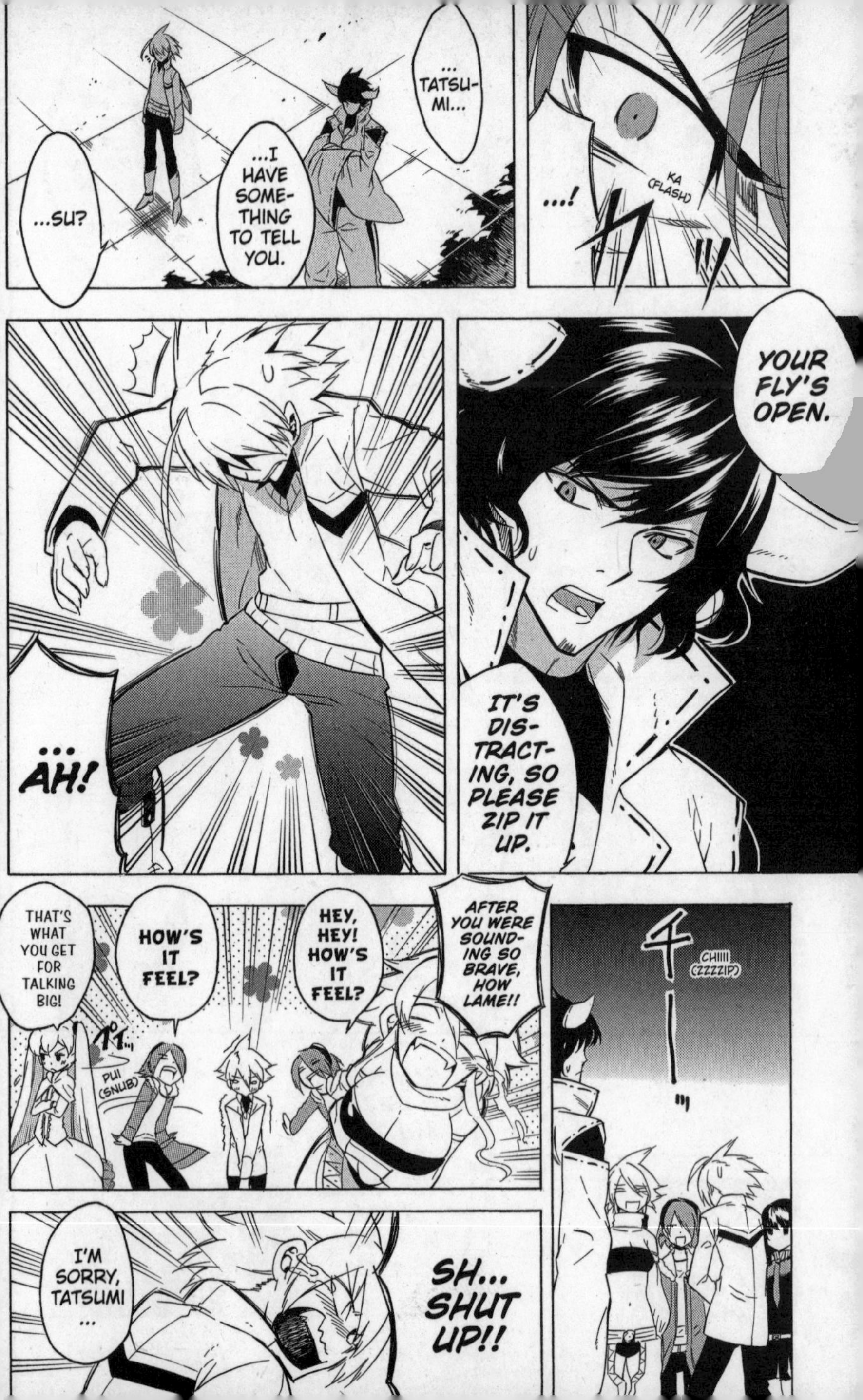

...!
KA (FLASH)
... TATSU-MI...
...I HAVE SOME-THING TO TELL YOU.
...SU?
YOUR FLY'S OPEN.
IT'S DIS-TRACT-ING, SO PLEASE ZIP IT UP.
... ÄH!
CHIIII (ZZZZIP)
AFTER YOU WERE SOUND-ING SO BRAVE, HOW LAME!!
HEY, HEY! HOW'S IT FEEL?
HOW'S IT FEEL?
THAT'S WHAT YOU GET FOR TALKING BIG!
PUI (SNUB)
SH... SHUT UP!!
I'M SORRY, TATSUMI ...

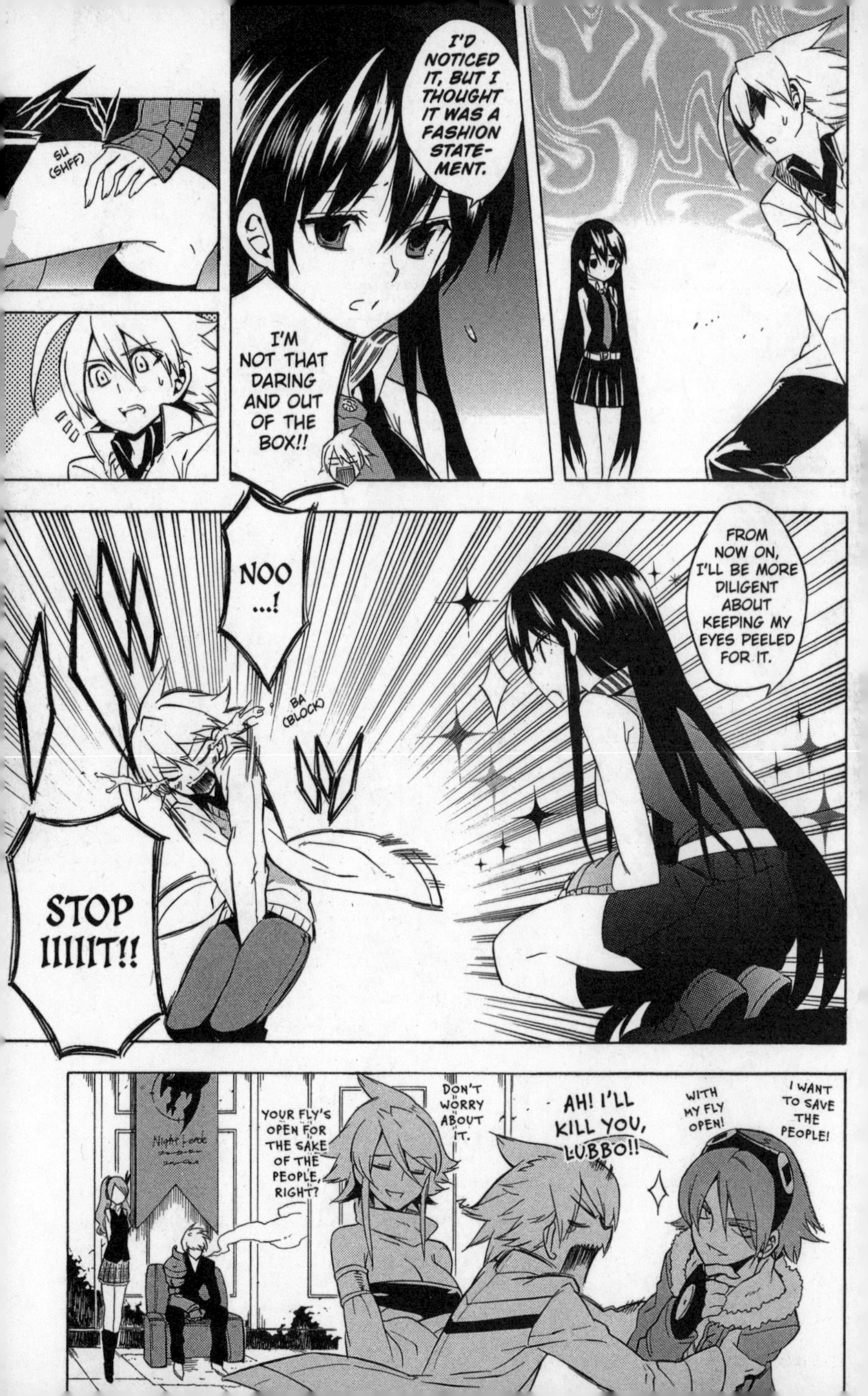
...
I'D NOTICED IT, BUT I THOUGHT IT WAS A FASHION STATEMENT.
I'M NOT THAT DARING AND OUT OF THE BOX!!
SU (SHFF)
FROM NOW ON, I'LL BE MORE DILIGENT ABOUT KEEPING MY EYES PEELED FOR IT.
NOO ...!
BA (BLOCK)
STOP IIIIIT!!
I WANT TO SAVE THE PEOPLE!
WITH MY FLY OPEN!
AH! I'LL KILL YOU, LUBBO!!
DON'T WORRY ABOUT IT.
YOUR FLY'S OPEN FOR THE SAKE OF THE PEOPLE, RIGHT?

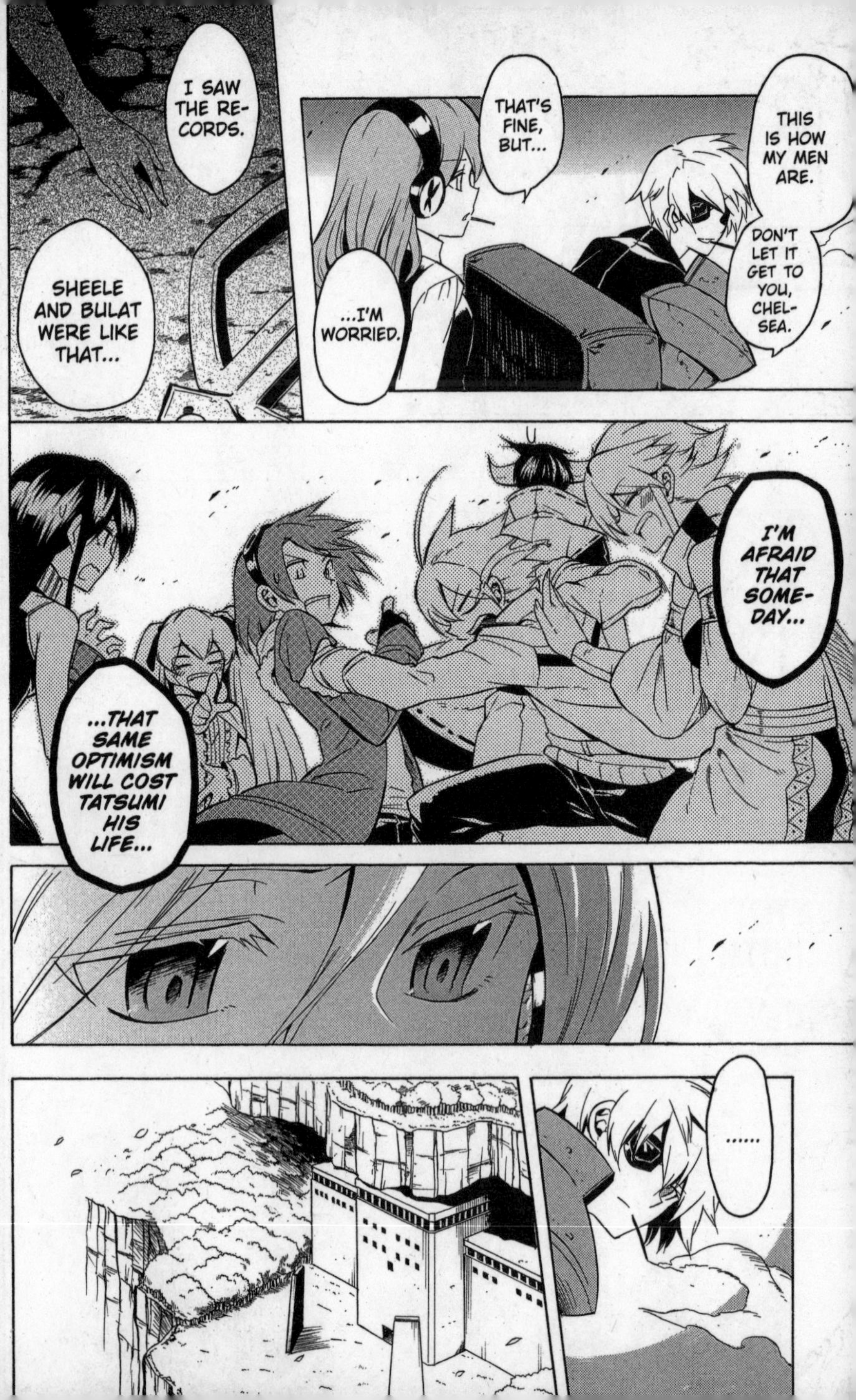
THIS IS HOW MY MEN ARE.
DON'T LET IT GET TO YOU, CHEL-SEA.
THAT'S FINE, BUT...
...I'M WORRIED.
I SAW THE RE-CORDS.
SHEELE AND BULAT WERE LIKE THAT...
I'M AFRAID THAT SOME-DAY...
...THAT SAME OPTIMISM WILL COST TATSUMI HIS LIFE...
......

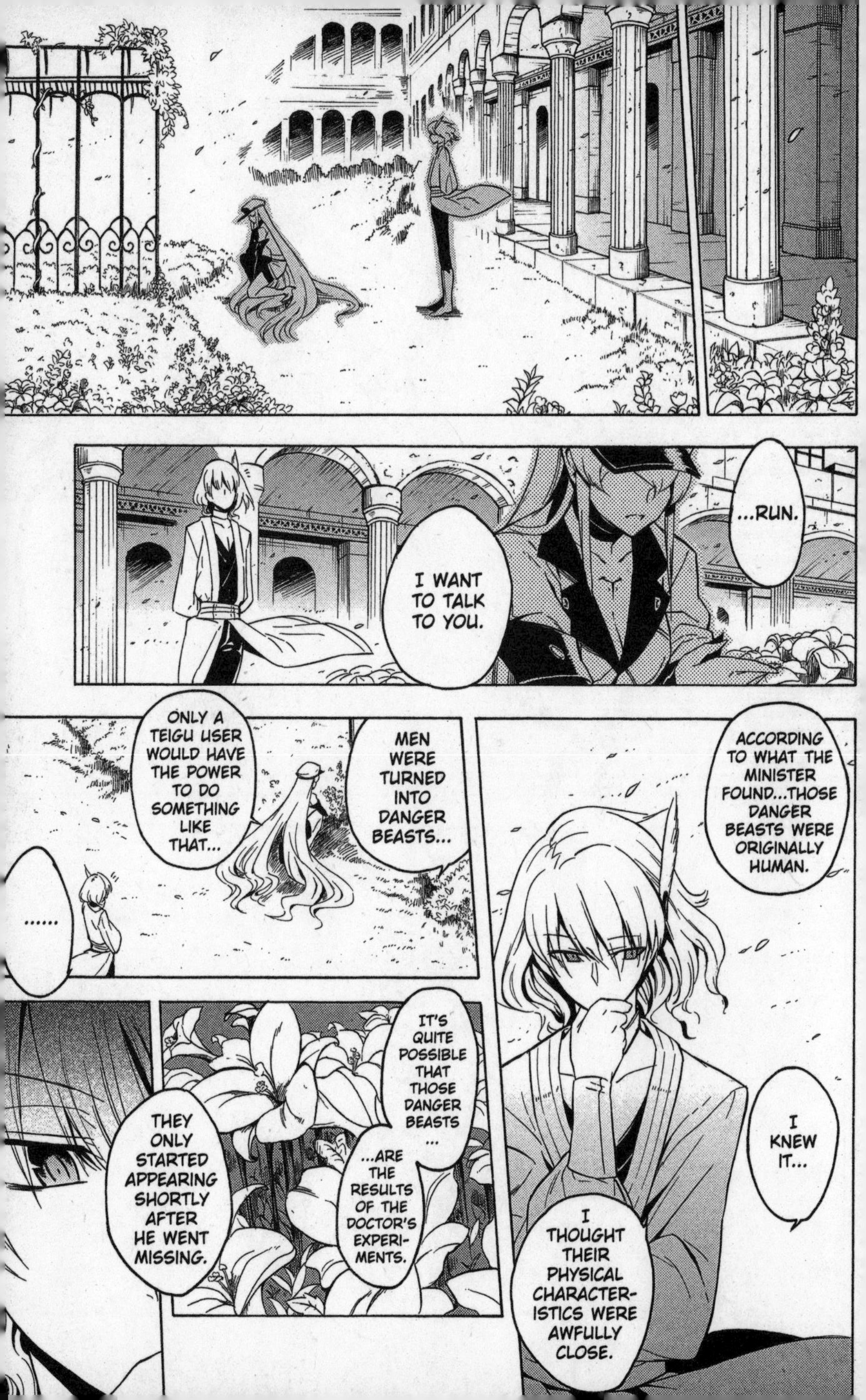
...RUN.
I WANT TO TALK TO YOU.
ACCORDING TO WHAT THE MINISTER FOUND...THOSE DANGER BEASTS WERE ORIGINALLY HUMAN.
MEN WERE TURNED INTO DANGER BEASTS...
ONLY A TEIGU USER WOULD HAVE THE POWER TO DO SOMETHING LIKE THAT...
......
I KNEW IT...
I THOUGHT THEIR PHYSICAL CHARACTERISTICS WERE AWFULLY CLOSE.
IT'S QUITE POSSIBLE THAT THOSE DANGER BEASTS ...
...ARE THE RESULTS OF THE DOCTOR'S EXPERIMENTS.
THEY ONLY STARTED APPEARING SHORTLY AFTER HE WENT MISSING.

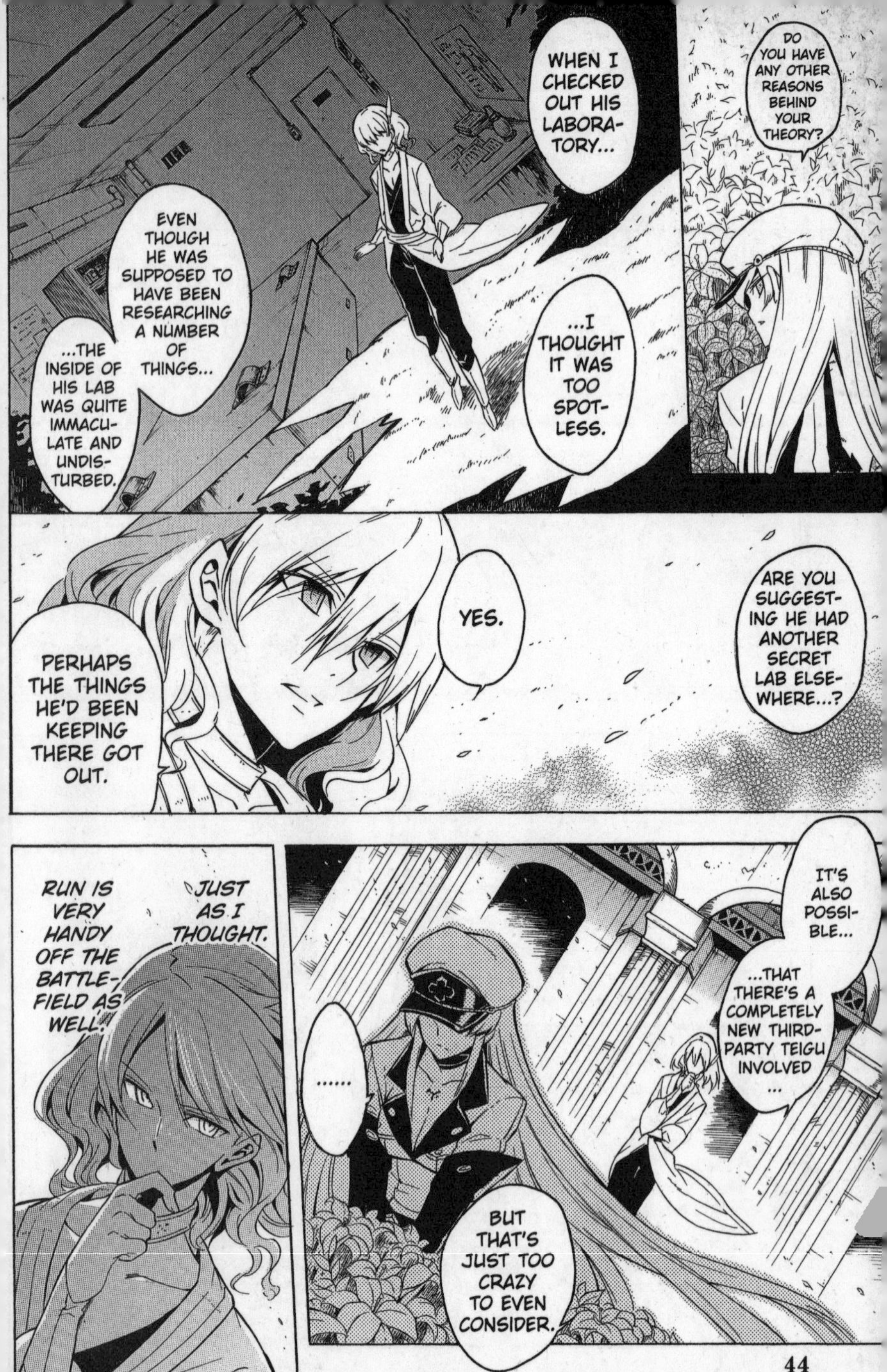
DO YOU HAVE ANY OTHER REASONS BEHIND YOUR THEORY?
WHEN I CHECKED OUT HIS LABORATORY...
...I THOUGHT IT WAS TOO SPOTLESS.
EVEN THOUGH HE WAS SUPPOSED TO HAVE BEEN RESEARCHING A NUMBER OF THINGS...
...THE INSIDE OF HIS LAB WAS QUITE IMMACULATE AND UNDISTURBED.
ARE YOU SUGGESTING HE HAD ANOTHER SECRET LAB ELSEWHERE...?
YES.
PERHAPS THE THINGS HE'D BEEN KEEPING THERE GOT OUT.
IT'S ALSO POSSIBLE...
...THAT THERE'S A COMPLETELY NEW THIRD-PARTY TEIGU INVOLVED...
......
BUT THAT'S JUST TOO CRAZY TO EVEN CONSIDER.
JUST AS I THOUGHT.
RUN IS VERY HANDY OFF THE BATTLEFIELD AS WELL.

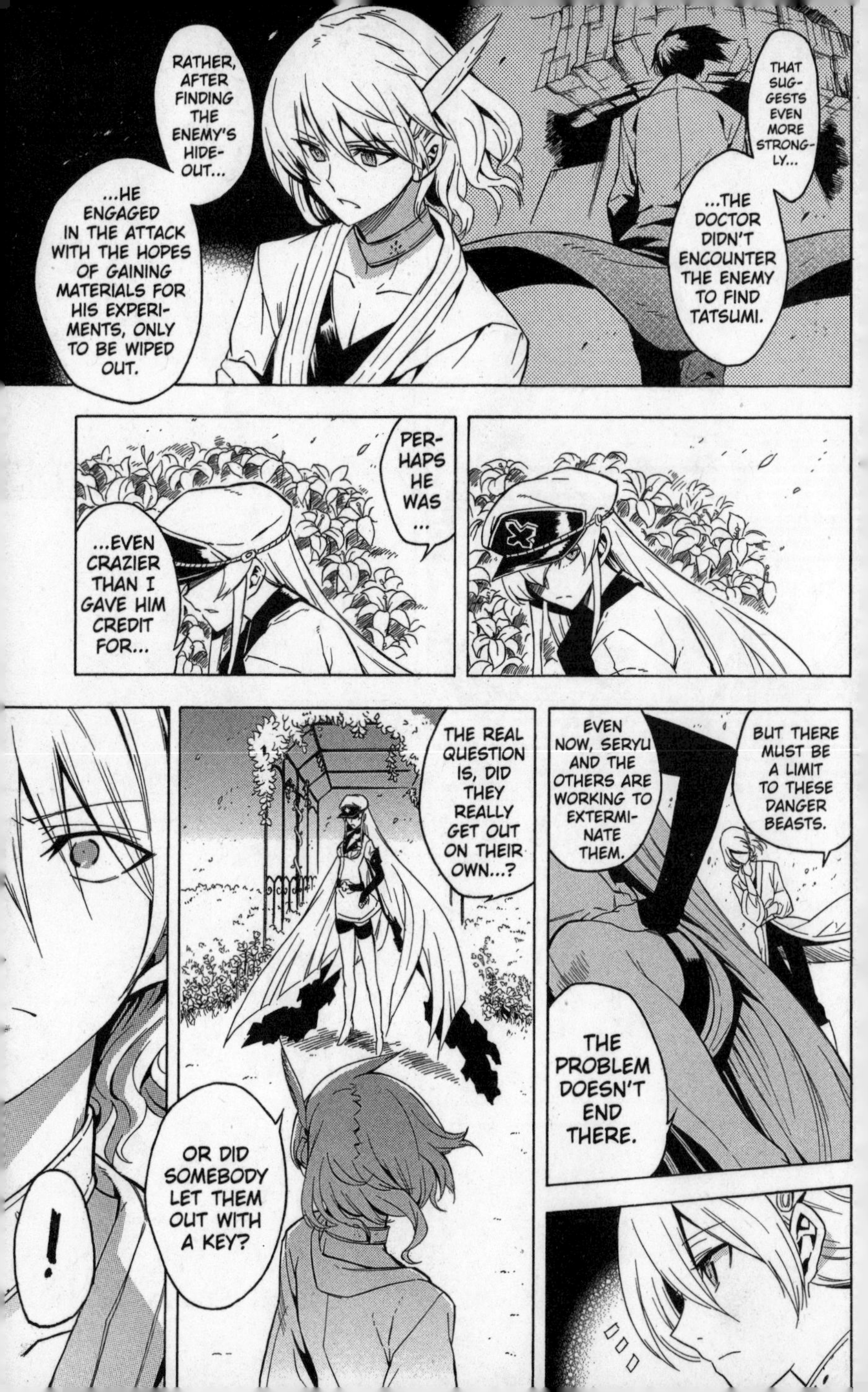
THAT SUGGESTS EVEN MORE STRONGLY...
...THE DOCTOR DIDN'T ENCOUNTER THE ENEMY TO FIND TATSUMI.
RATHER, AFTER FINDING THE ENEMY'S HIDEOUT...
...HE ENGAGED IN THE ATTACK WITH THE HOPES OF GAINING MATERIALS FOR HIS EXPERIMENTS, ONLY TO BE WIPED OUT.
PERHAPS HE WAS...
...EVEN CRAZIER THAN I GAVE HIM CREDIT FOR...
BUT THERE MUST BE A LIMIT TO THESE DANGER BEASTS.
EVEN NOW, SERYU AND THE OTHERS ARE WORKING TO EXTERMINATE THEM.
THE PROBLEM DOESN'T END THERE.
THE REAL QUESTION IS, DID THEY REALLY GET OUT ON THEIR OWN...?
OR DID SOMEBODY LET THEM OUT WITH A KEY?
!

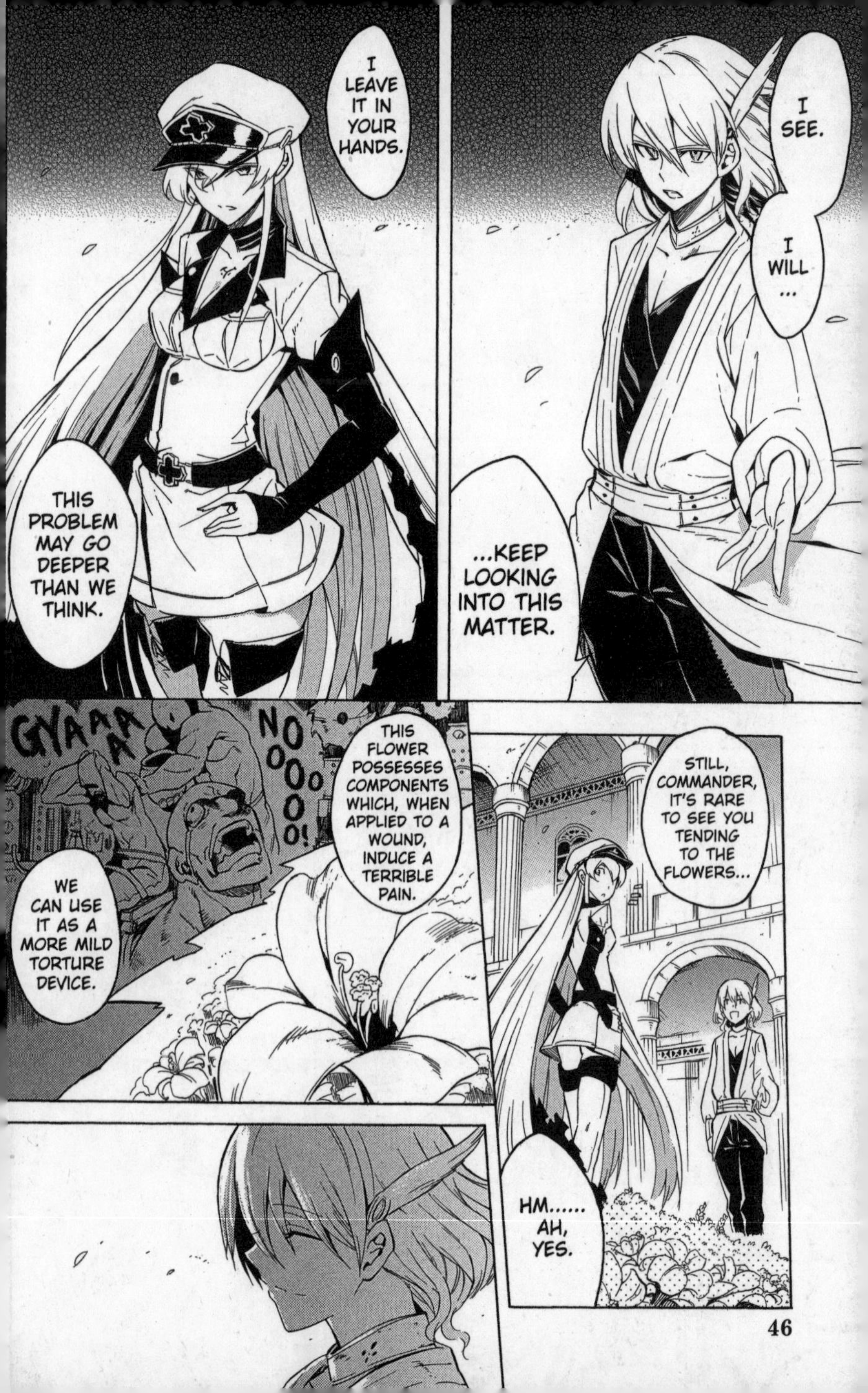
I SEE.
I WILL...
...KEEP LOOKING INTO THIS MATTER.
I LEAVE IT IN YOUR HANDS.
THIS PROBLEM MAY GO DEEPER THAN WE THINK.
STILL, COMMANDER, IT'S RARE TO SEE YOU TENDING TO THE FLOWERS...
HM...... AH, YES.
THIS FLOWER POSSESSES COMPONENTS WHICH, WHEN APPLIED TO A WOUND, INDUCE A TERRIBLE PAIN.
NOOOOOO!
GYAAAA
WE CAN USE IT AS A MORE MILD TORTURE DEVICE.

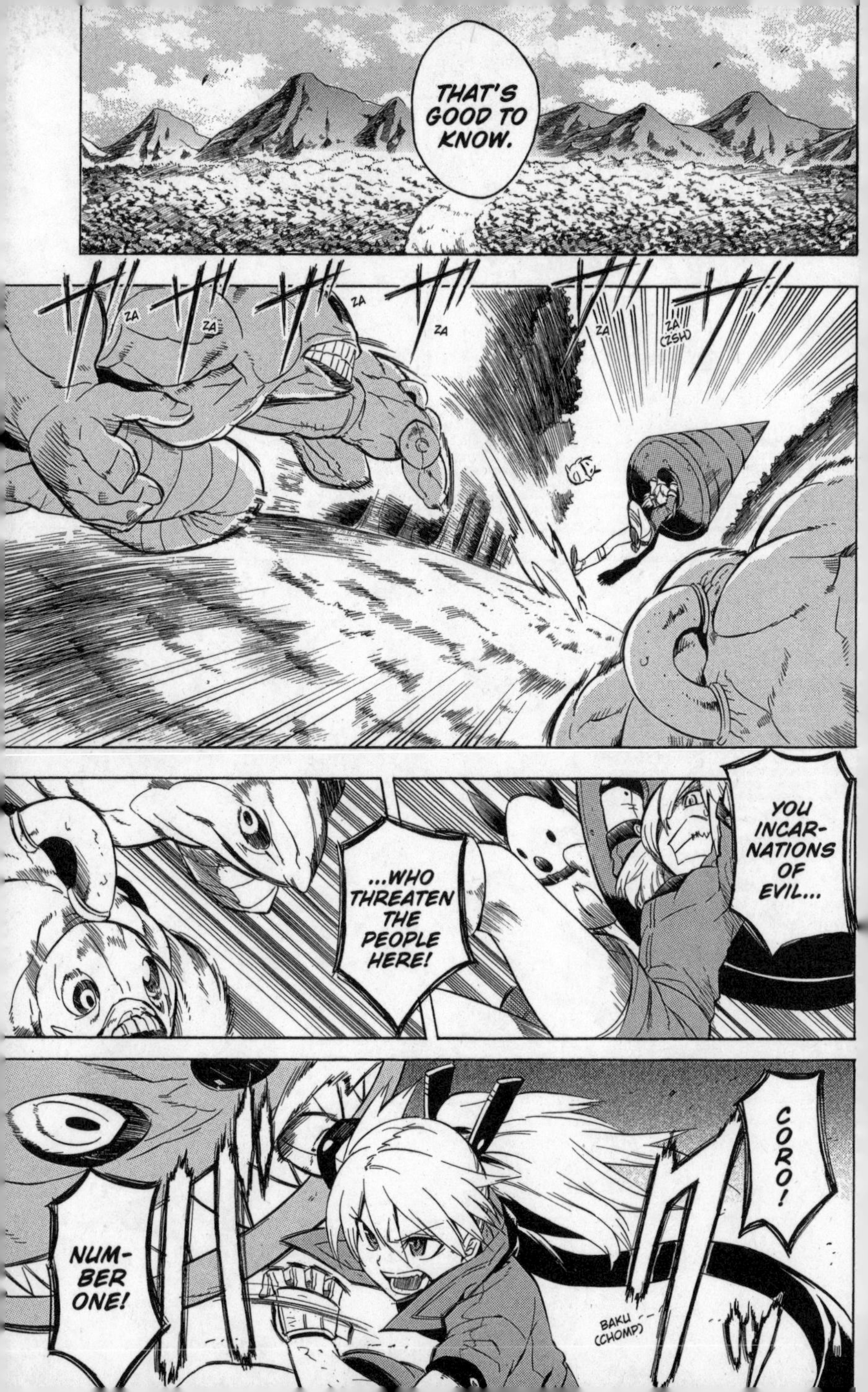
THAT'S GOOD TO KNOW.
ZA
ZA
ZA
ZA
ZA
ZA (ZSH)
YOU INCAR-NATIONS OF EVIL...
...WHO THREATEN THE PEOPLE HERE!
CORO!
NUM-BER ONE!
BAKU (CHOMP)

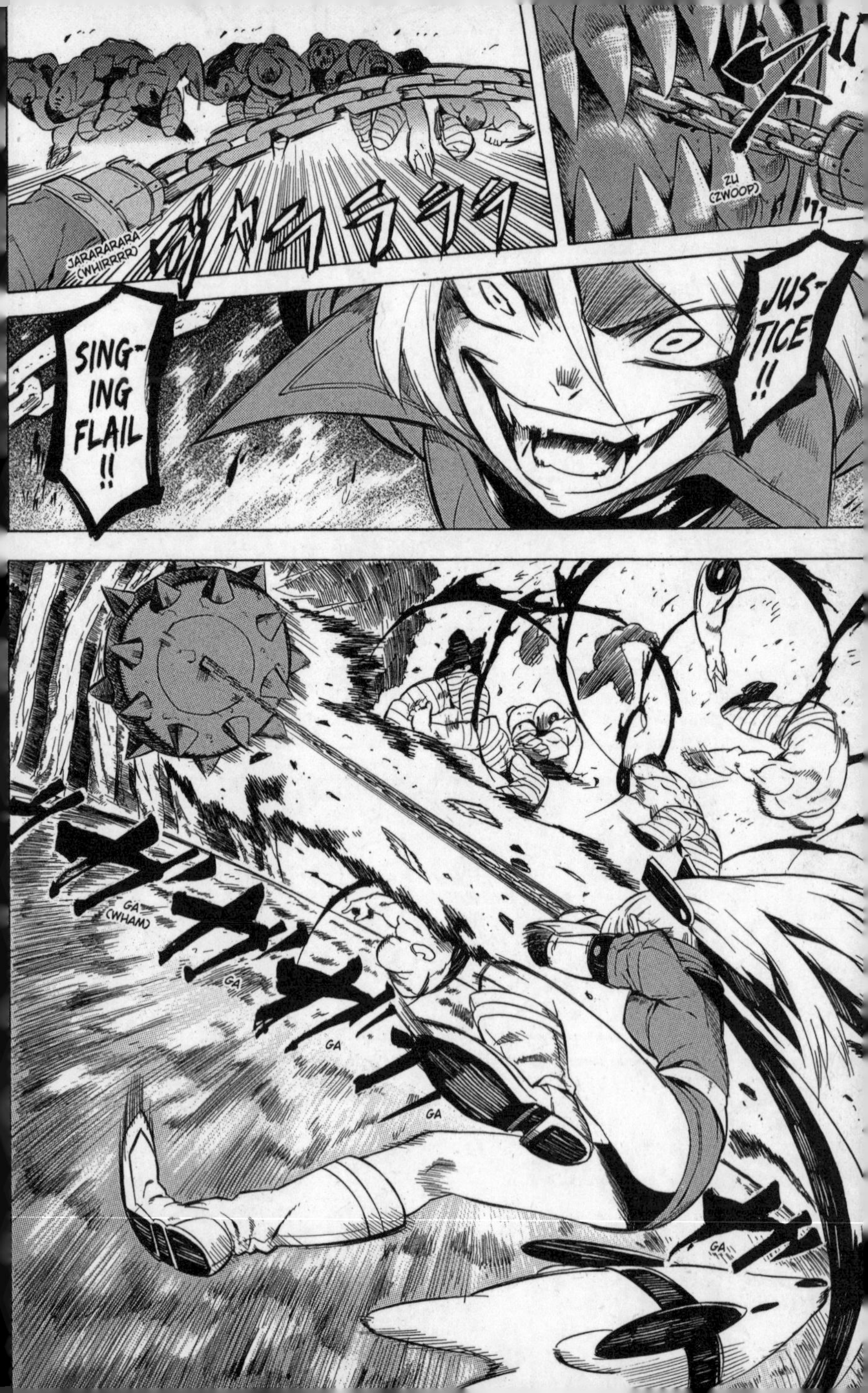
ZU
(ZWOOP)
JARARARARA
(WHIRRRR)
JUS-
TICE
!!
SING-
ING
FLAIL
!!
GA
(WHAM)
GA
GA
GA
GA

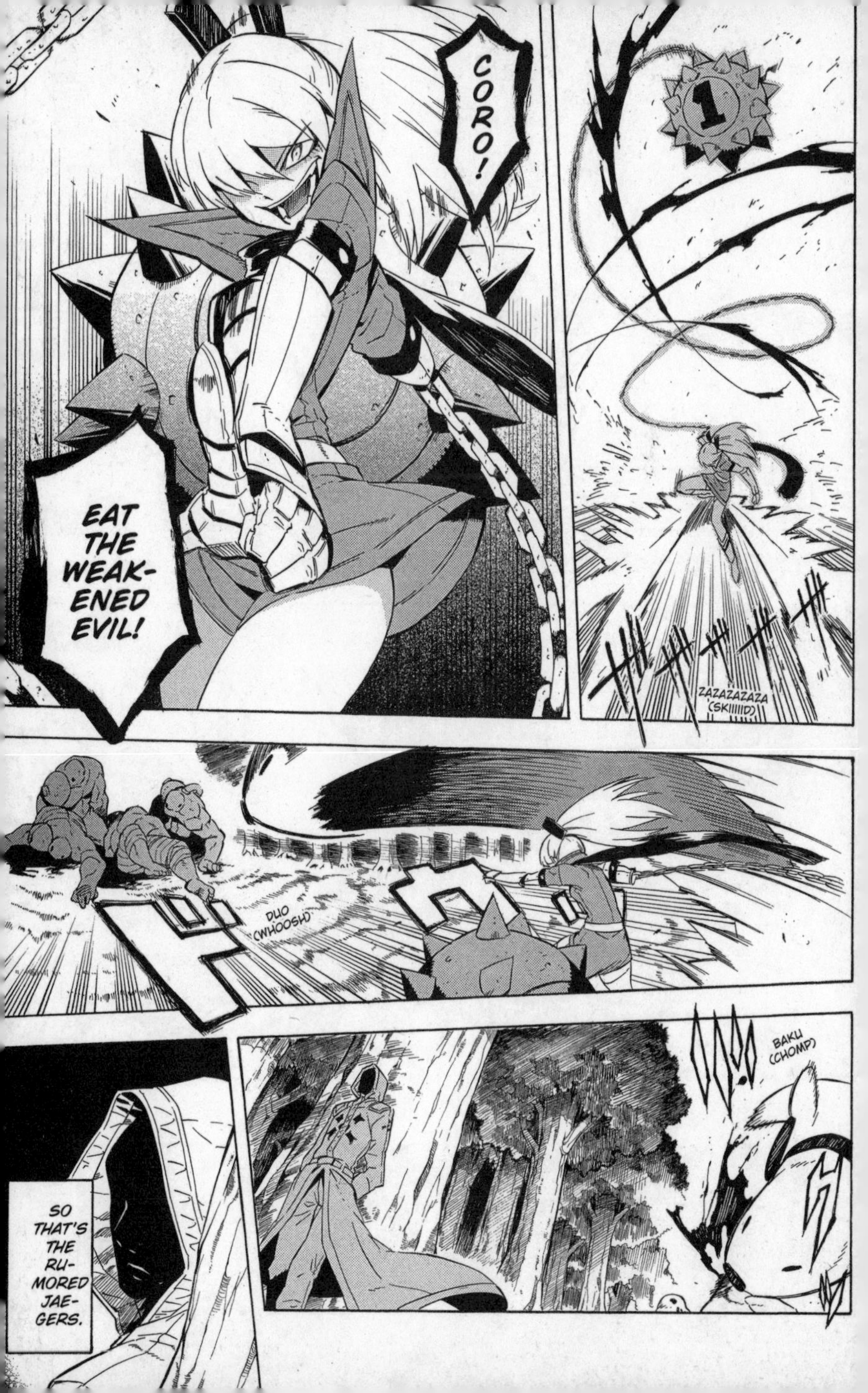
ZAZAZAZAZA (SKIIIIID)
CORO!
EAT THE WEAK-ENED EVIL!
DUO (WHOOSH)
BAKU (CHOMP)
SO THAT'S THE RU-MORED JAE-GERS.

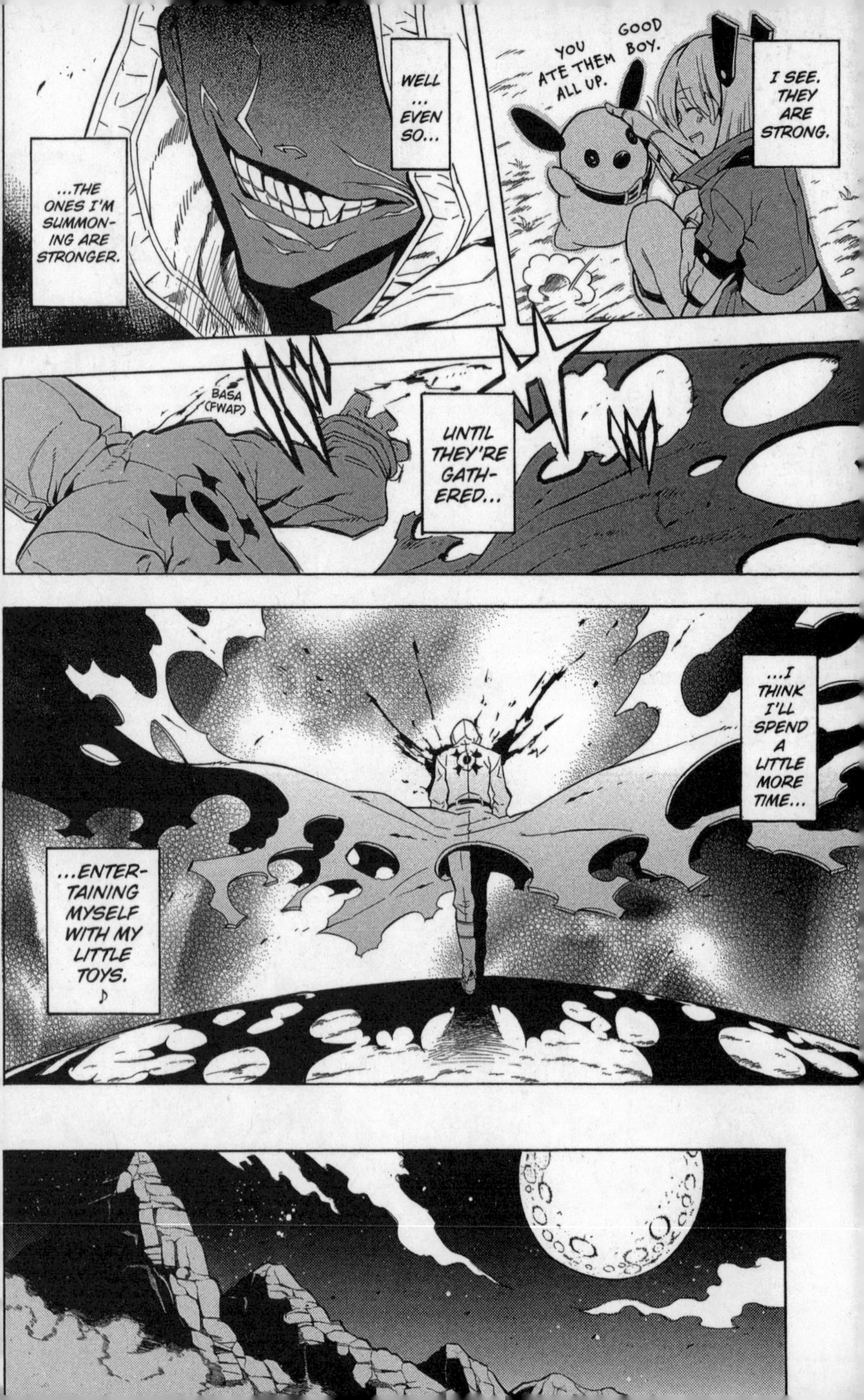
I SEE. THEY ARE STRONG.
GOOD BOY.
YOU ATE THEM ALL UP.
WELL... EVEN SO...
...THE ONES I'M SUMMONING ARE STRONGER.
UNTIL THEY'RE GATHERED...
BASA (FWAP)
...I THINK I'LL SPEND A LITTLE MORE TIME...
...ENTERTAINING MYSELF WITH MY LITTLE TOYS. ♪

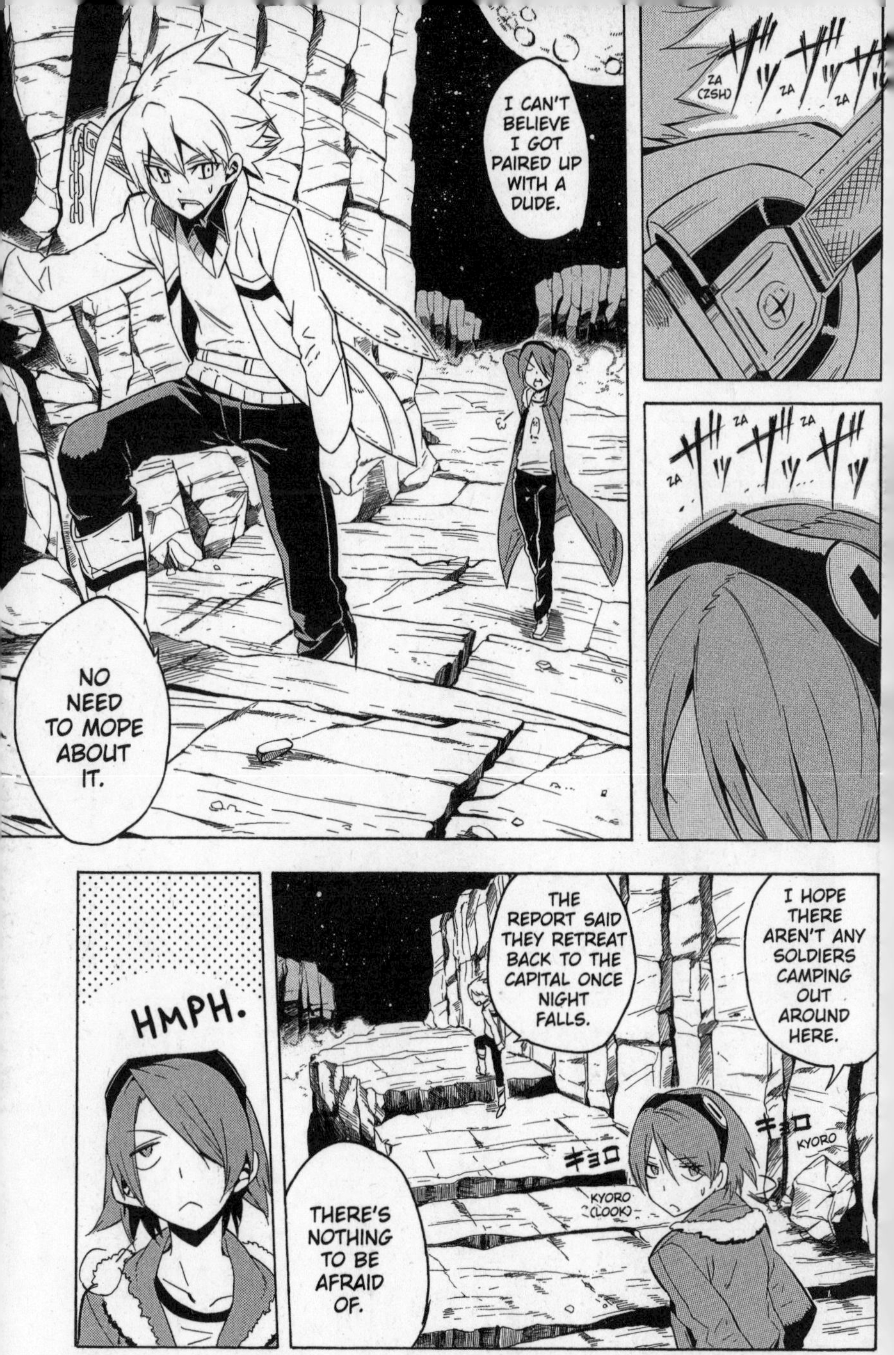
ザッ ザッ ザッ
ZA (ZSH)
ZA
ZA
I CAN'T BELIEVE I GOT PAIRED UP WITH A DUDE.
NO NEED TO MOPE ABOUT IT.
ザッ ザッ ザッ
ZA
ZA
ZA
I HOPE THERE AREN'T ANY SOLDIERS CAMPING OUT AROUND HERE.
THE REPORT SAID THEY RETREAT BACK TO THE CAPITAL ONCE NIGHT FALLS.
キョロ
KYORO
キョロ
KYORO (LOOK)
THERE'S NOTHING TO BE AFRAID OF.
HMPH.

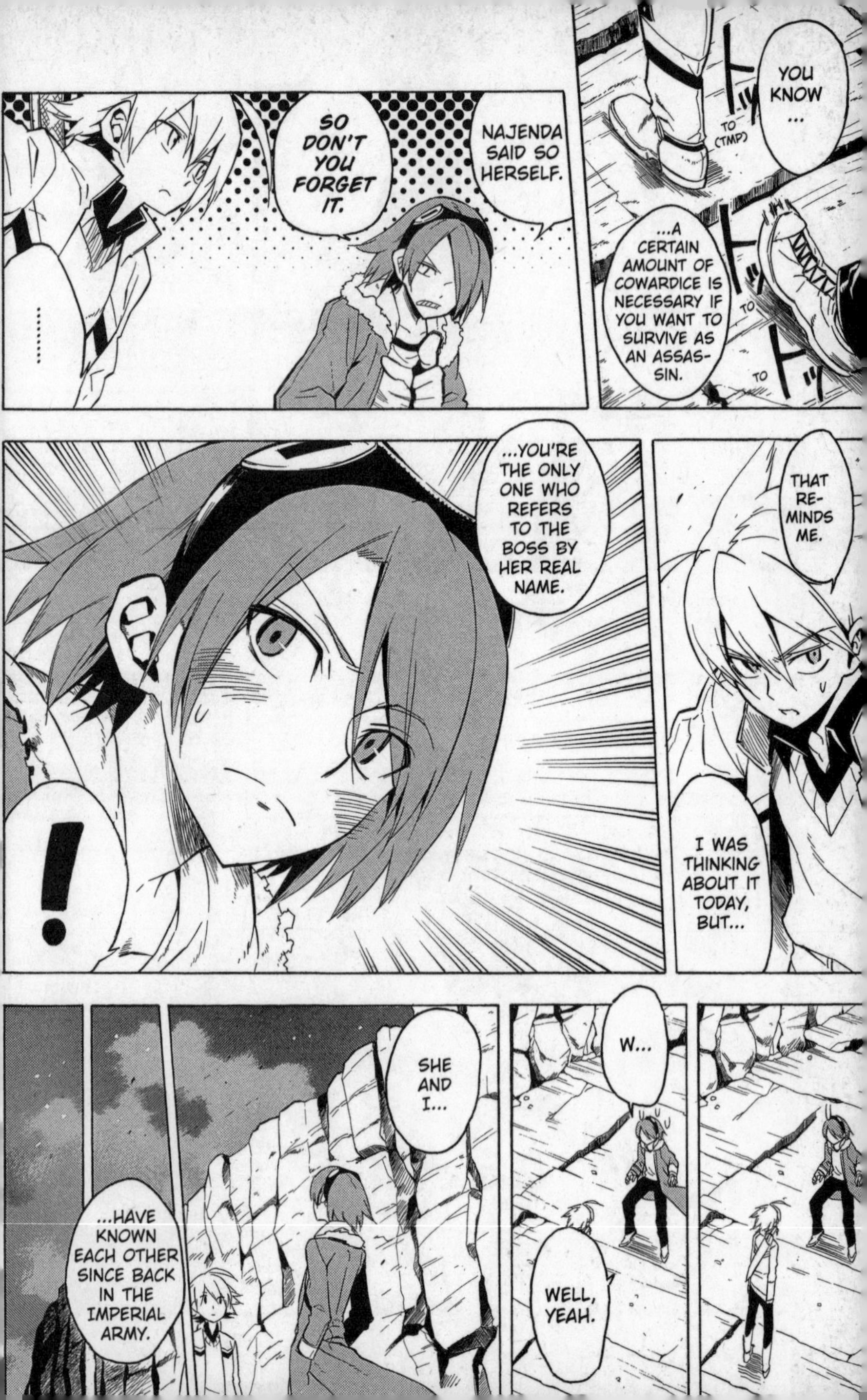
YOU KNOW ...
TO
TO (TMP)
...A CERTAIN AMOUNT OF COWARDICE IS NECESSARY IF YOU WANT TO SURVIVE AS AN ASSAS-SIN.
TO
TO
NAJENDA SAID SO HERSELF.
SO DON'T YOU FORGET IT.
......
THAT RE-MINDS ME.
I WAS THINKING ABOUT IT TODAY, BUT...
...YOU'RE THE ONLY ONE WHO REFERS TO THE BOSS BY HER REAL NAME.
!
W...
WELL, YEAH.
SHE AND I...
...HAVE KNOWN EACH OTHER SINCE BACK IN THE IMPERIAL ARMY.

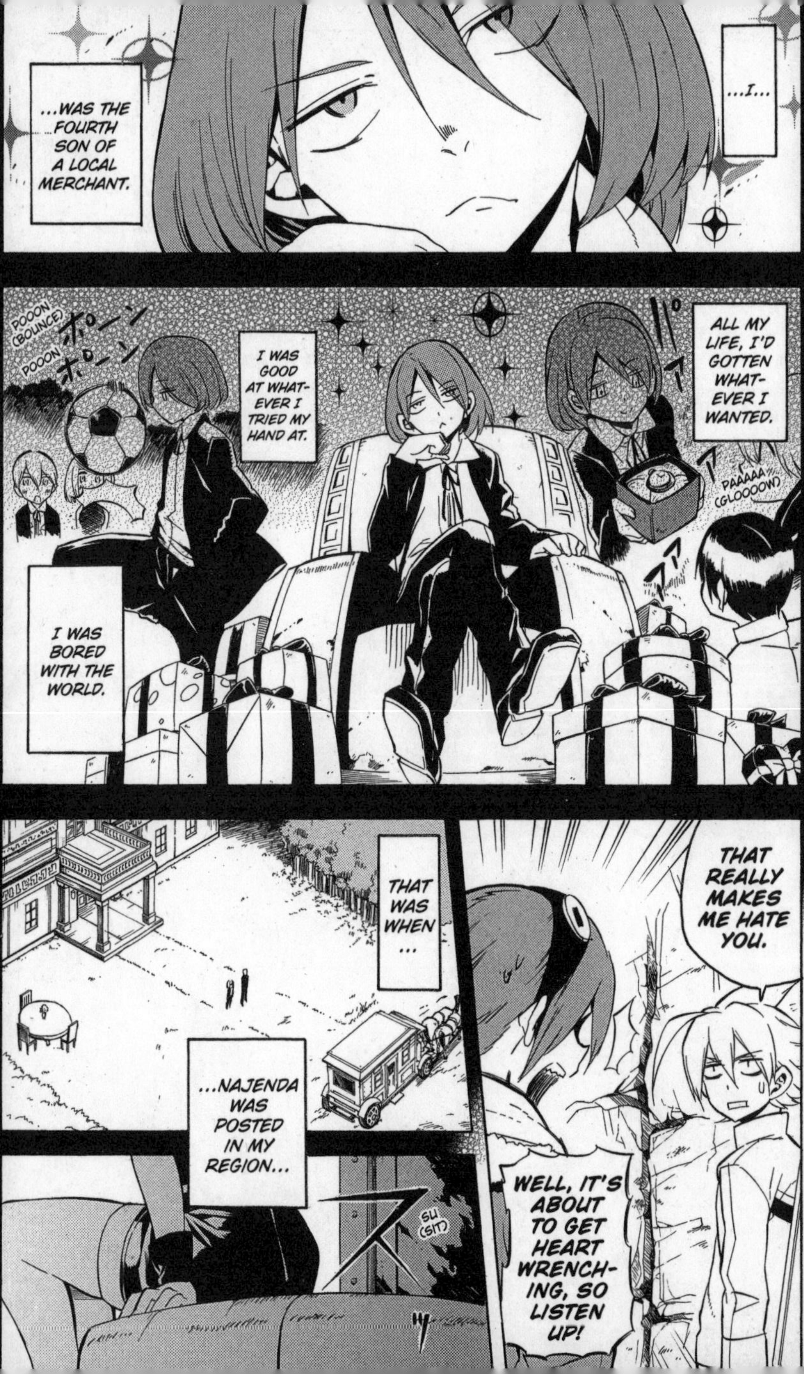
...I...
...WAS THE FOURTH SON OF A LOCAL MERCHANT.
ALL MY LIFE, I'D GOTTEN WHATEVER I WANTED.
PAAAAA (GLOOOOW)
I WAS GOOD AT WHATEVER I TRIED MY HAND AT.
POOOON (BOUNCE)
POOOON
I WAS BORED WITH THE WORLD.
THAT REALLY MAKES ME HATE YOU.
WELL, IT'S ABOUT TO GET HEART WRENCHING, SO LISTEN UP!
THAT WAS WHEN...
...NAJENDA WAS POSTED IN MY REGION...
SU (SIT)

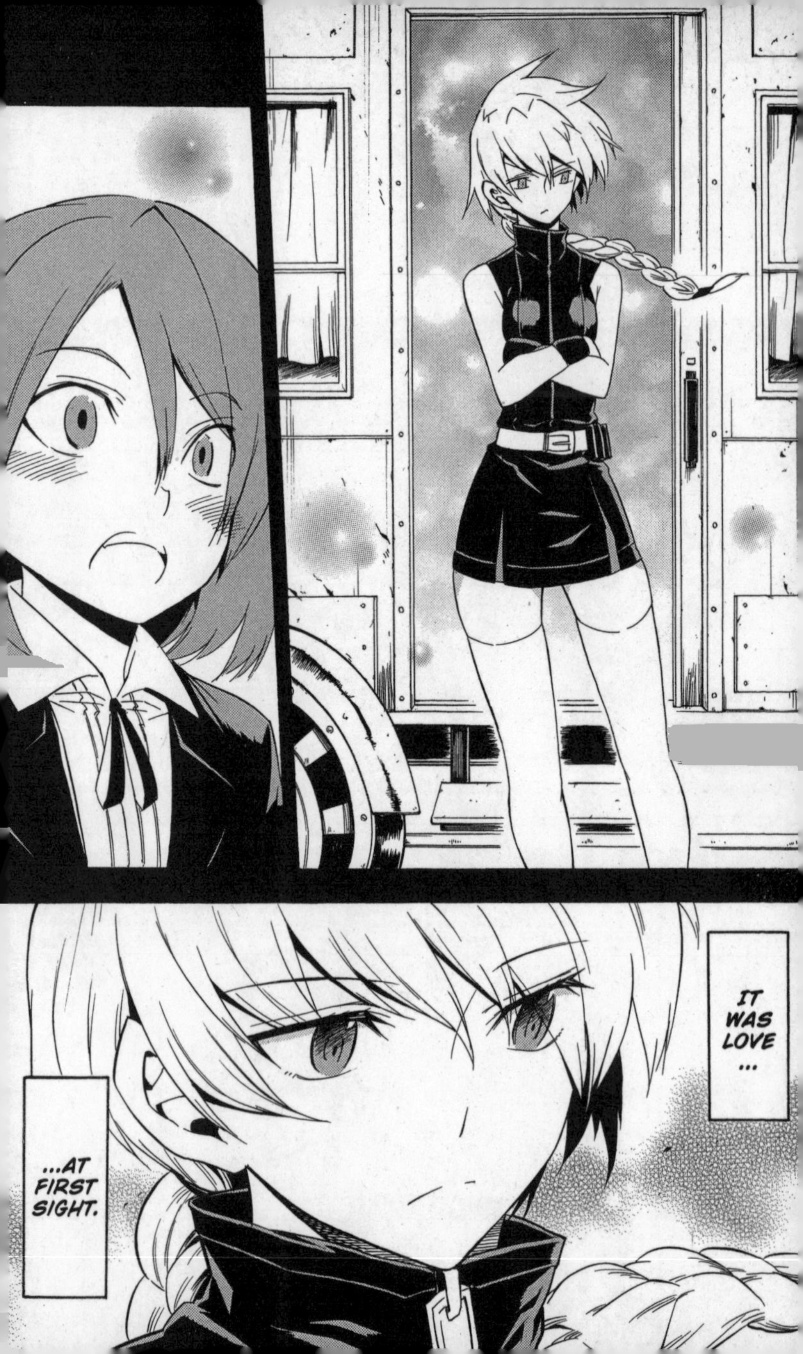
IT WAS LOVE ...
...AT FIRST SIGHT.

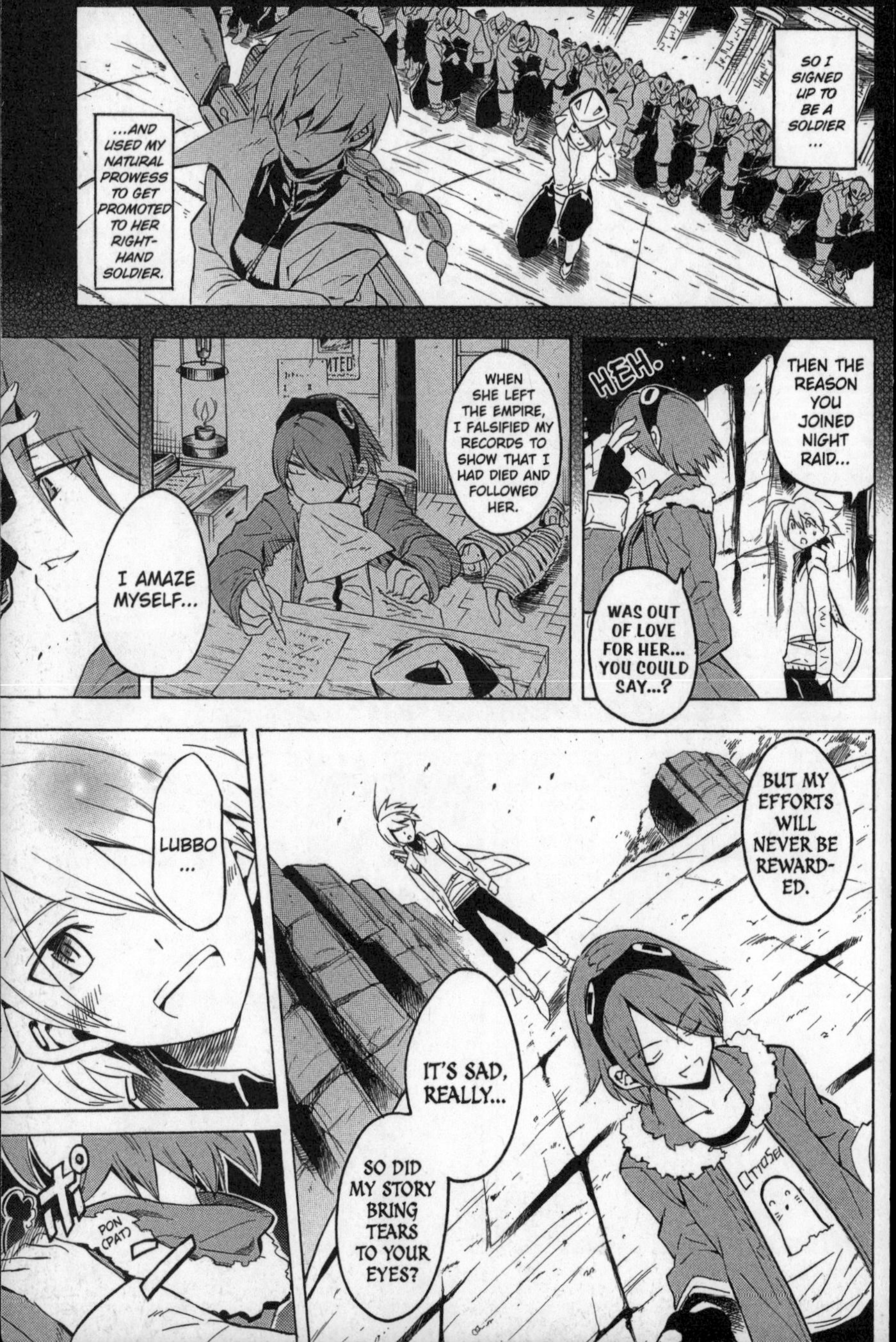
SO I SIGNED UP TO BE A SOLDIER ...
...AND USED MY NATURAL PROWESS TO GET PROMOTED TO HER RIGHT-HAND SOLDIER.
HEH.
THEN THE REASON YOU JOINED NIGHT RAID...
WAS OUT OF LOVE FOR HER... YOU COULD SAY...?
WHEN SHE LEFT THE EMPIRE, I FALSIFIED MY RECORDS TO SHOW THAT I HAD DIED AND FOLLOWED HER.
I AMAZE MYSELF...
BUT MY EFFORTS WILL NEVER BE REWARD-ED.
IT'S SAD, REALLY...
SO DID MY STORY BRING TEARS TO YOUR EYES?
LUBBO ...
PON (PAT)

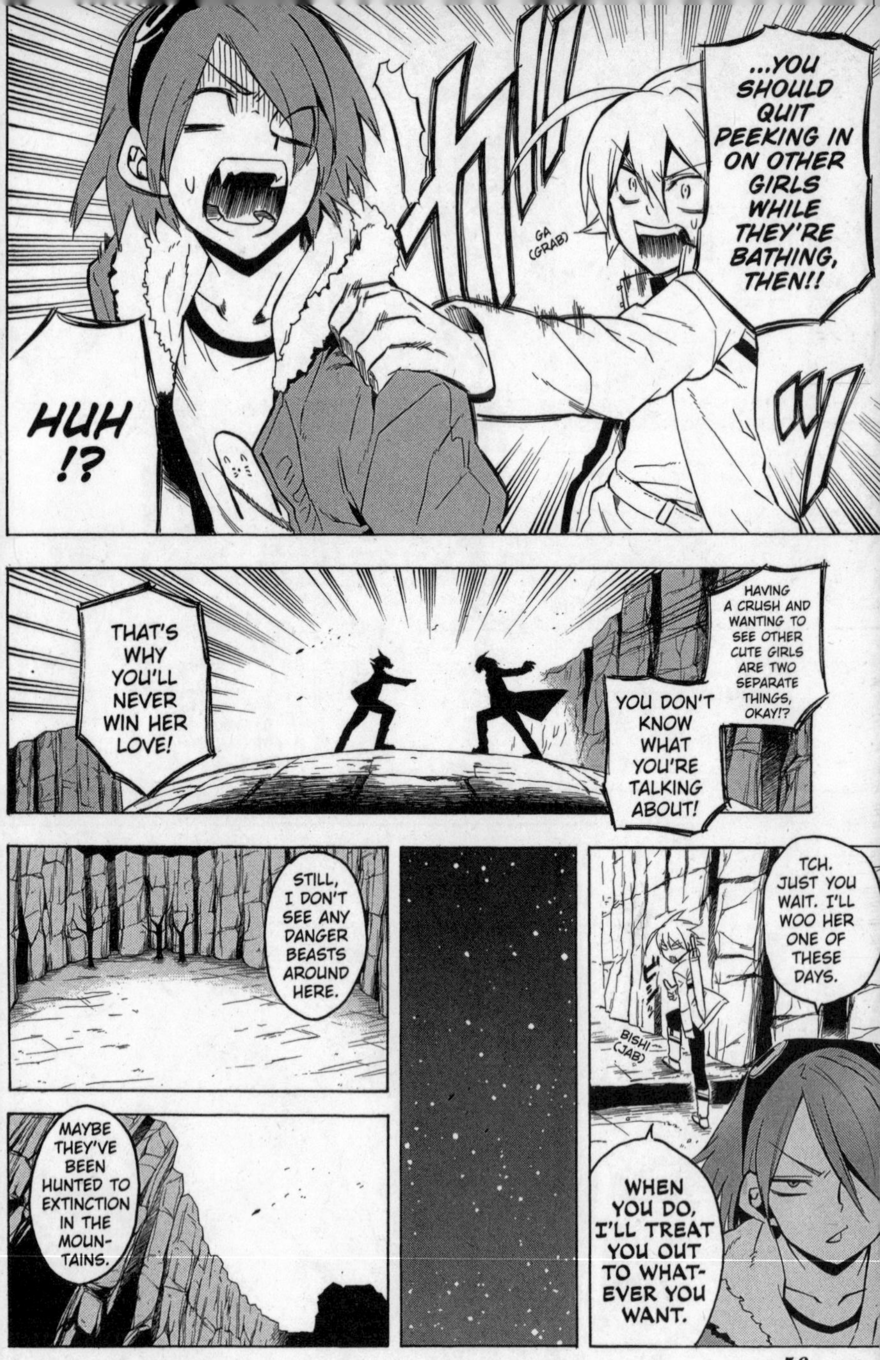
...YOU SHOULD QUIT PEEKING IN ON OTHER GIRLS WHILE THEY'RE BATHING, THEN!!
GA (GRAB)
HUH !?
HAVING A CRUSH AND WANTING TO SEE OTHER CUTE GIRLS ARE TWO SEPARATE THINGS, OKAY!?
YOU DON'T KNOW WHAT YOU'RE TALKING ABOUT!
THAT'S WHY YOU'LL NEVER WIN HER LOVE!
TCH. JUST YOU WAIT. I'LL WOO HER ONE OF THESE DAYS.
BISHI (JAB)
WHEN YOU DO, I'LL TREAT YOU OUT TO WHAT-EVER YOU WANT.
STILL, I DON'T SEE ANY DANGER BEASTS AROUND HERE.
MAYBE THEY'VE BEEN HUNTED TO EXTINCTION IN THE MOUN-TAINS.

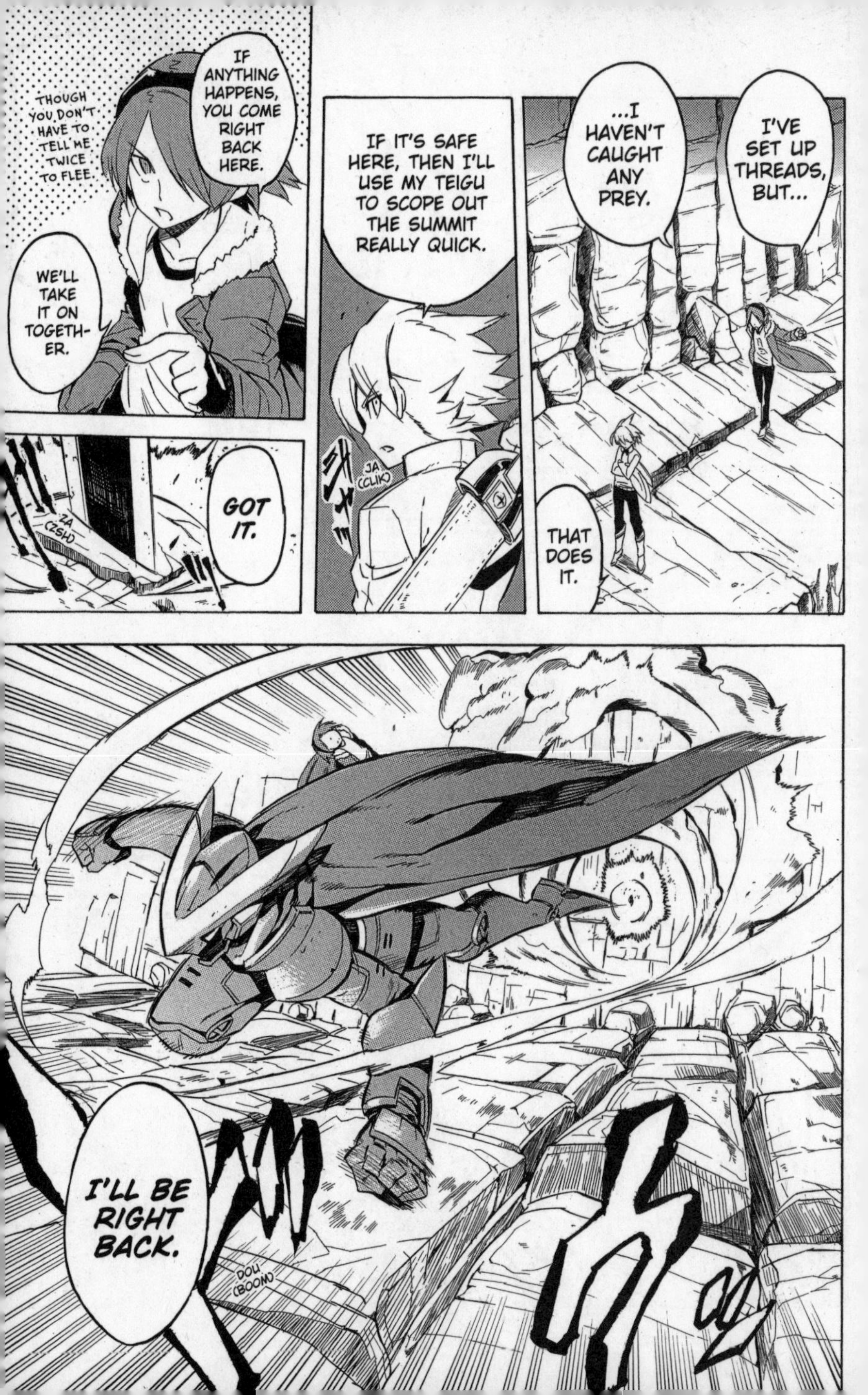
I'VE SET UP THREADS, BUT...
...I HAVEN'T CAUGHT ANY PREY.
THAT DOES IT.
IF IT'S SAFE HERE, THEN I'LL USE MY TEIGU TO SCOPE OUT THE SUMMIT REALLY QUICK.
IF ANYTHING HAPPENS, YOU COME RIGHT BACK HERE.
THOUGH YOU DON'T HAVE TO TELL ME TWICE TO FLEE.
WE'LL TAKE IT ON TOGETH-ER.
JA (CLIK)
GOT IT.
ZA (ZSH)
I'LL BE RIGHT BACK.
DOU (BOOM)

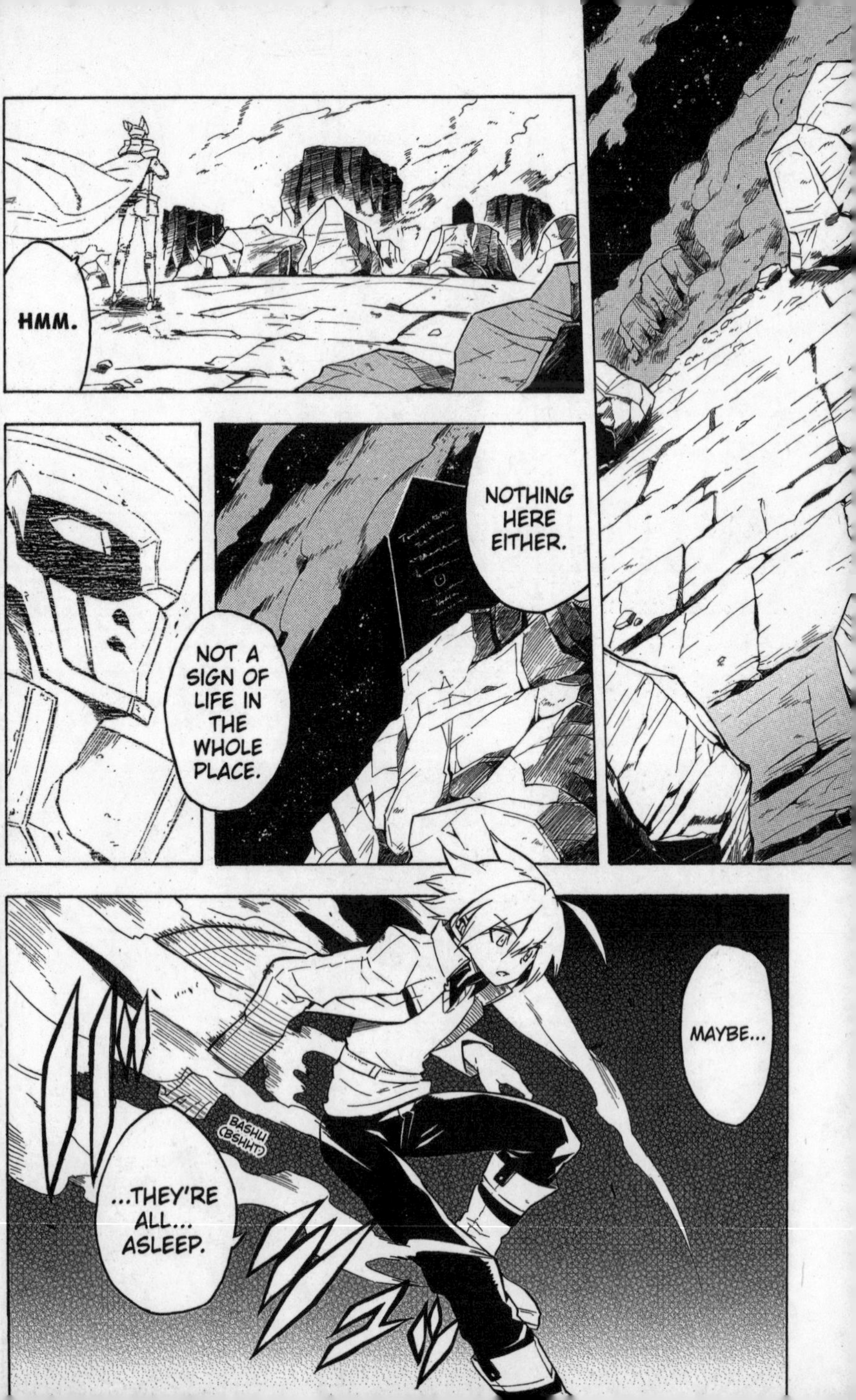
HMM.
NOTHING HERE EITHER.
NOT A SIGN OF LIFE IN THE WHOLE PLACE.
MAYBE...
BASHU (BSHHT)
...THEY'RE ALL... ASLEEP.

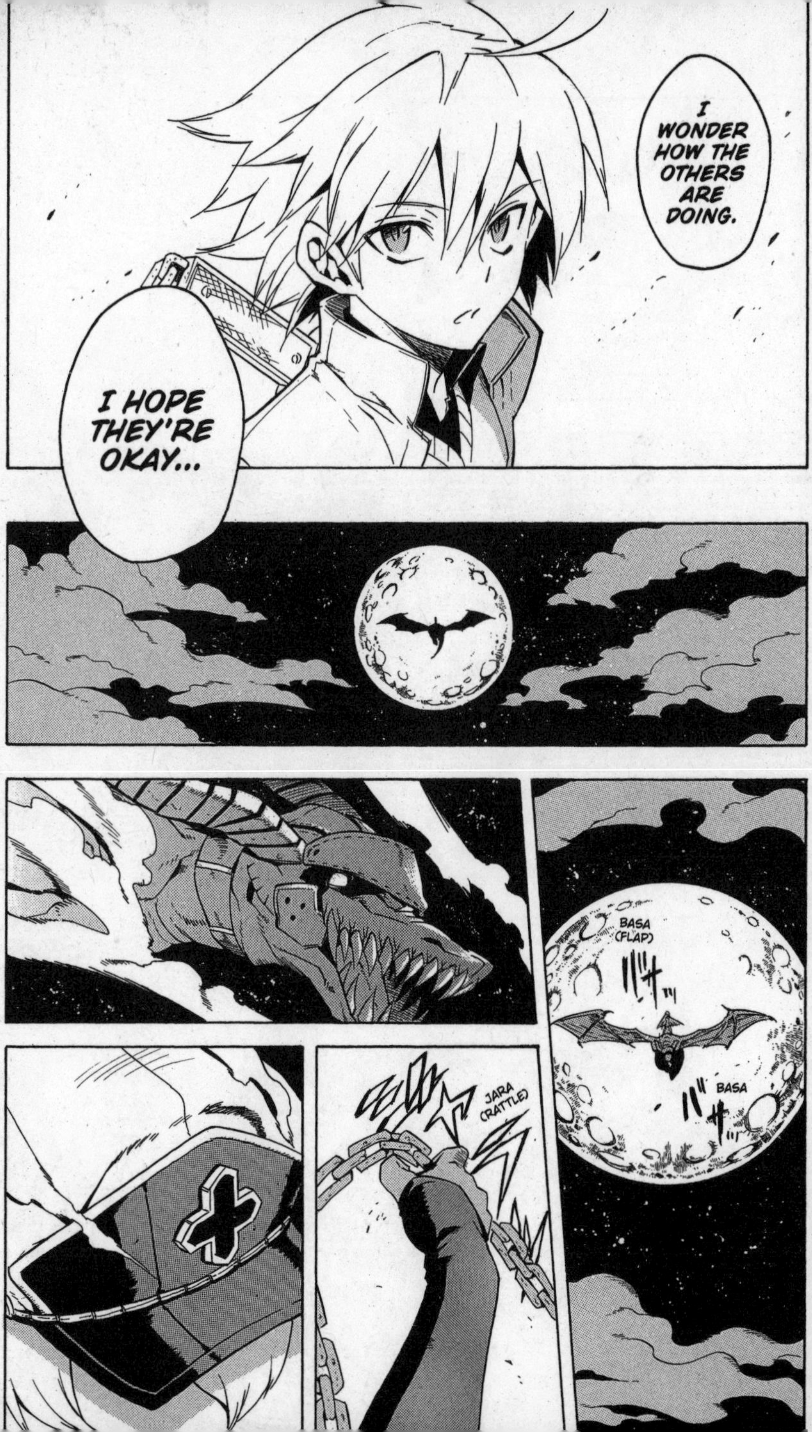
I WONDER HOW THE OTHERS ARE DOING.
I HOPE THEY'RE OKAY...
BASA (FLAP)
BASA
JARA (RATTLE)

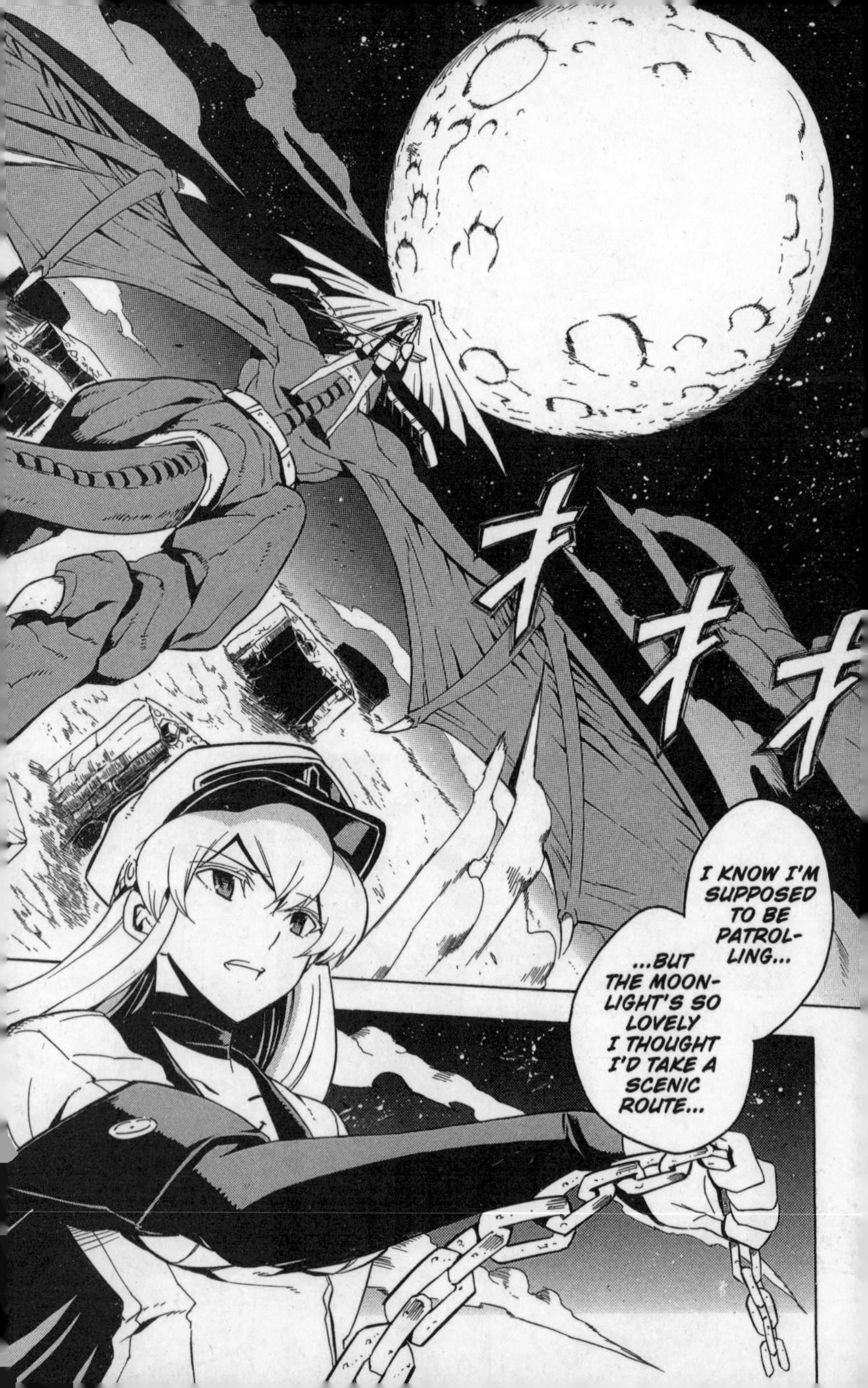

オオオ
I KNOW I'M SUPPOSED TO BE PATROL-LING...
...BUT THE MOON-LIGHT'S SO LOVELY I THOUGHT I'D TAKE A SCENIC ROUTE...

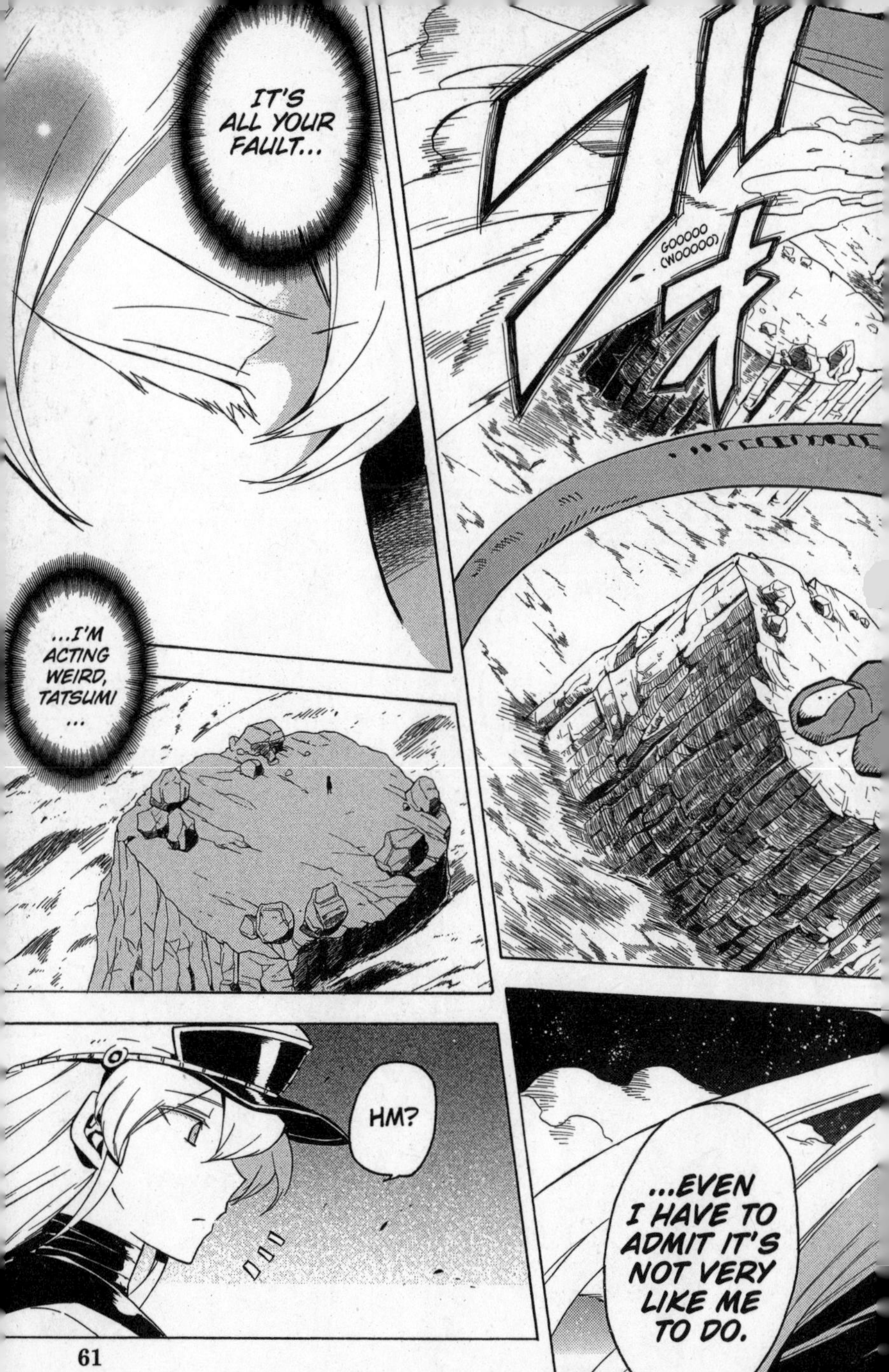

GOOOOO (WOOOOO)
IT'S ALL YOUR FAULT...
...I'M ACTING WEIRD, TATSUMI ...
...EVEN I HAVE TO ADMIT IT'S NOT VERY LIKE ME TO DO.
HM?

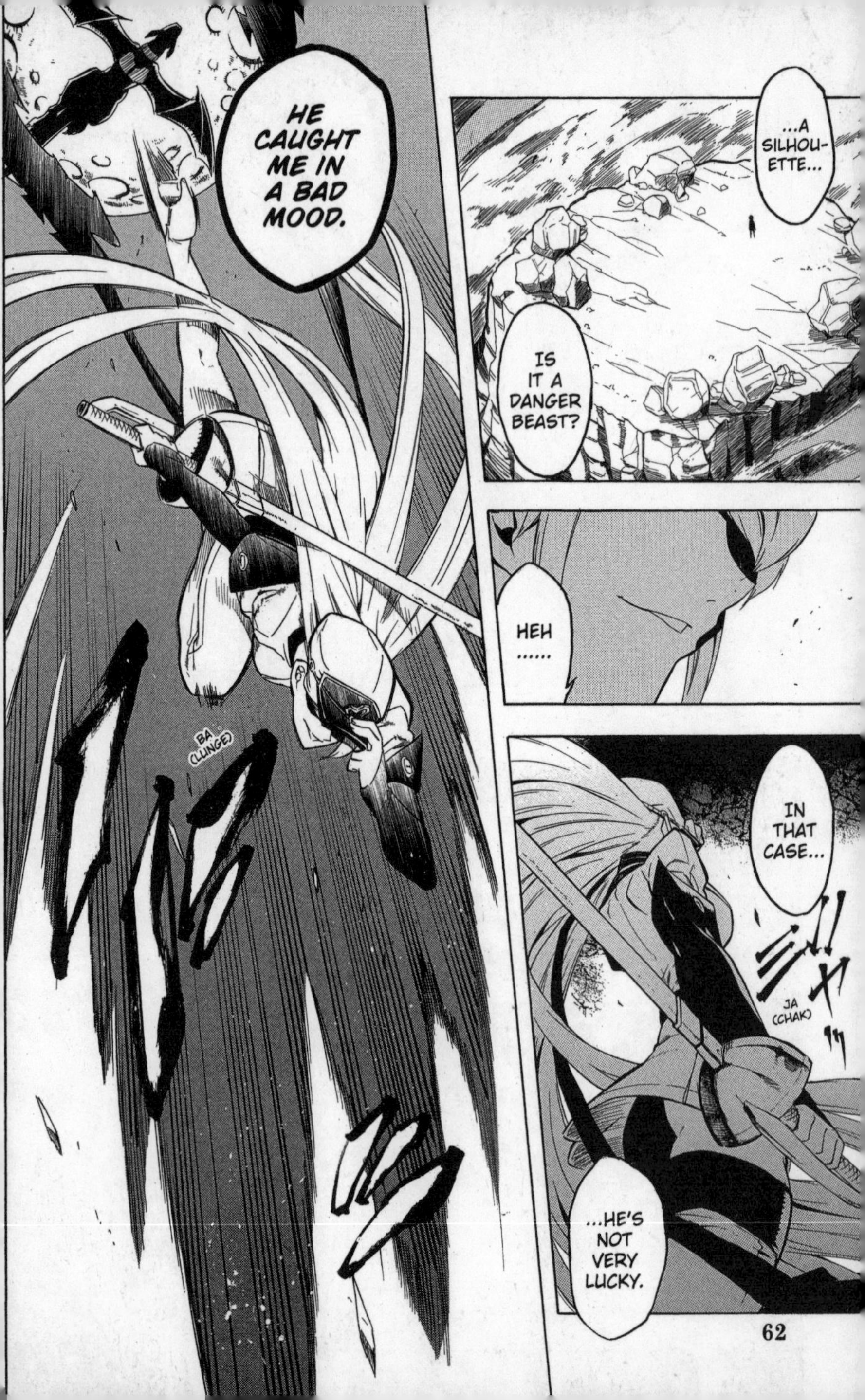
...A SILHOU-ETTE...
IS IT A DANGER BEAST?
HEH ......
IN THAT CASE...
JA (CHAK)
...HE'S NOT VERY LUCKY.
HE CAUGHT ME IN A BAD MOOD.
BA (LUNGE)

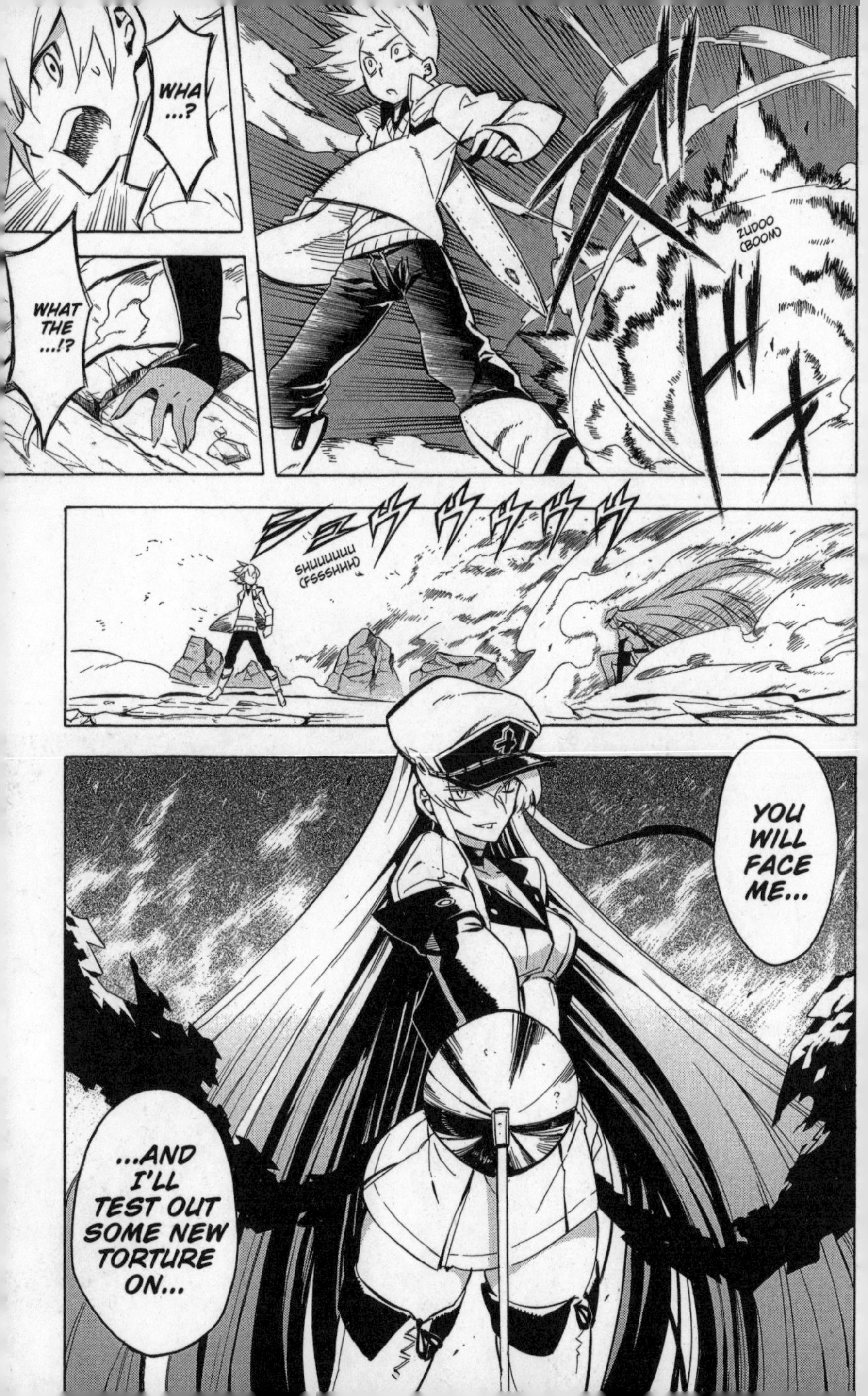
ZUDOO (BOOM)
WHA ...?
WHAT THE ...!?
SHUUUUUUU (FSSSHHH)
YOU WILL FACE ME...
...AND I'LL TEST OUT SOME NEW TORTURE ON...

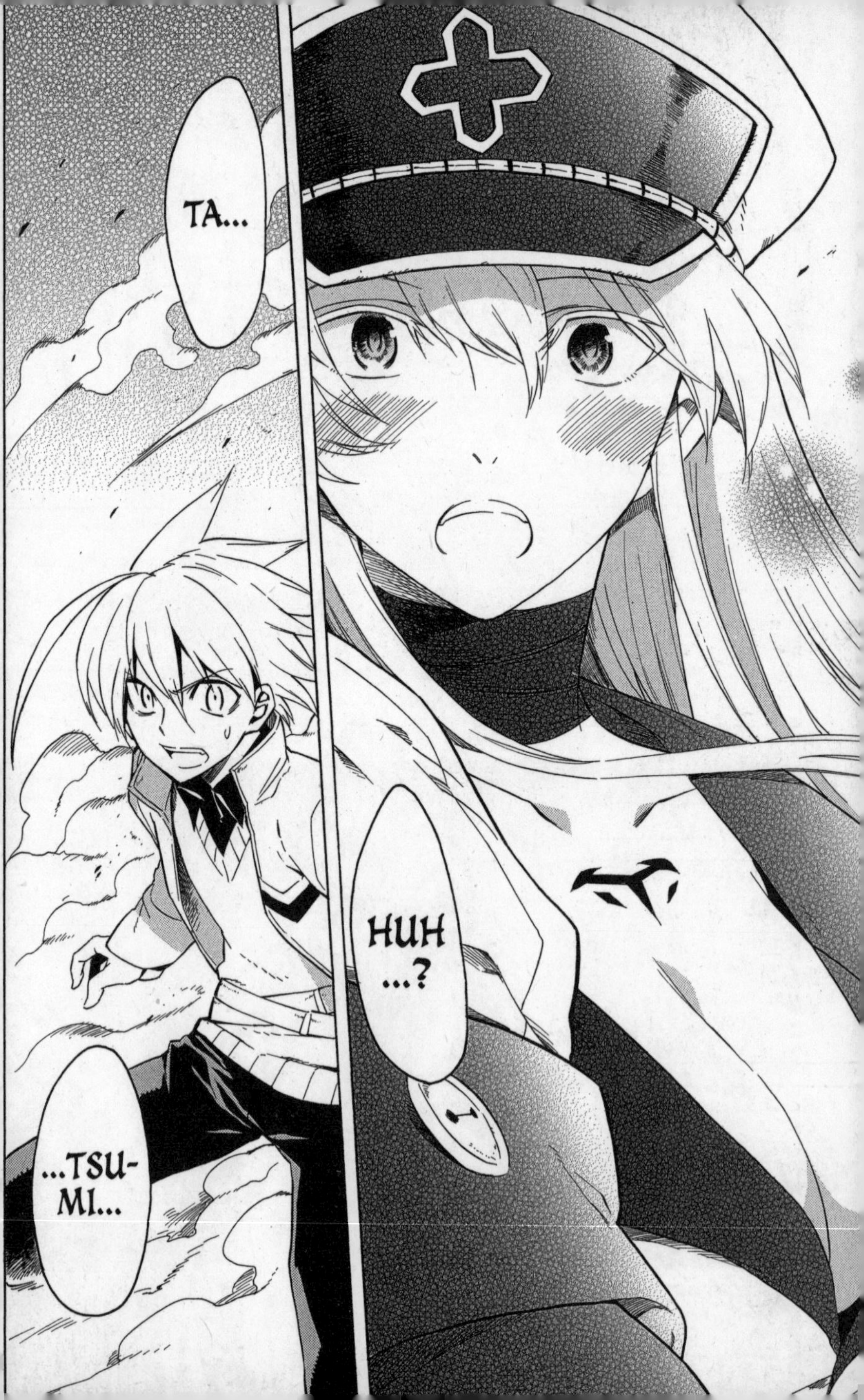
HUH ...?
TA...
...TSU-MI...

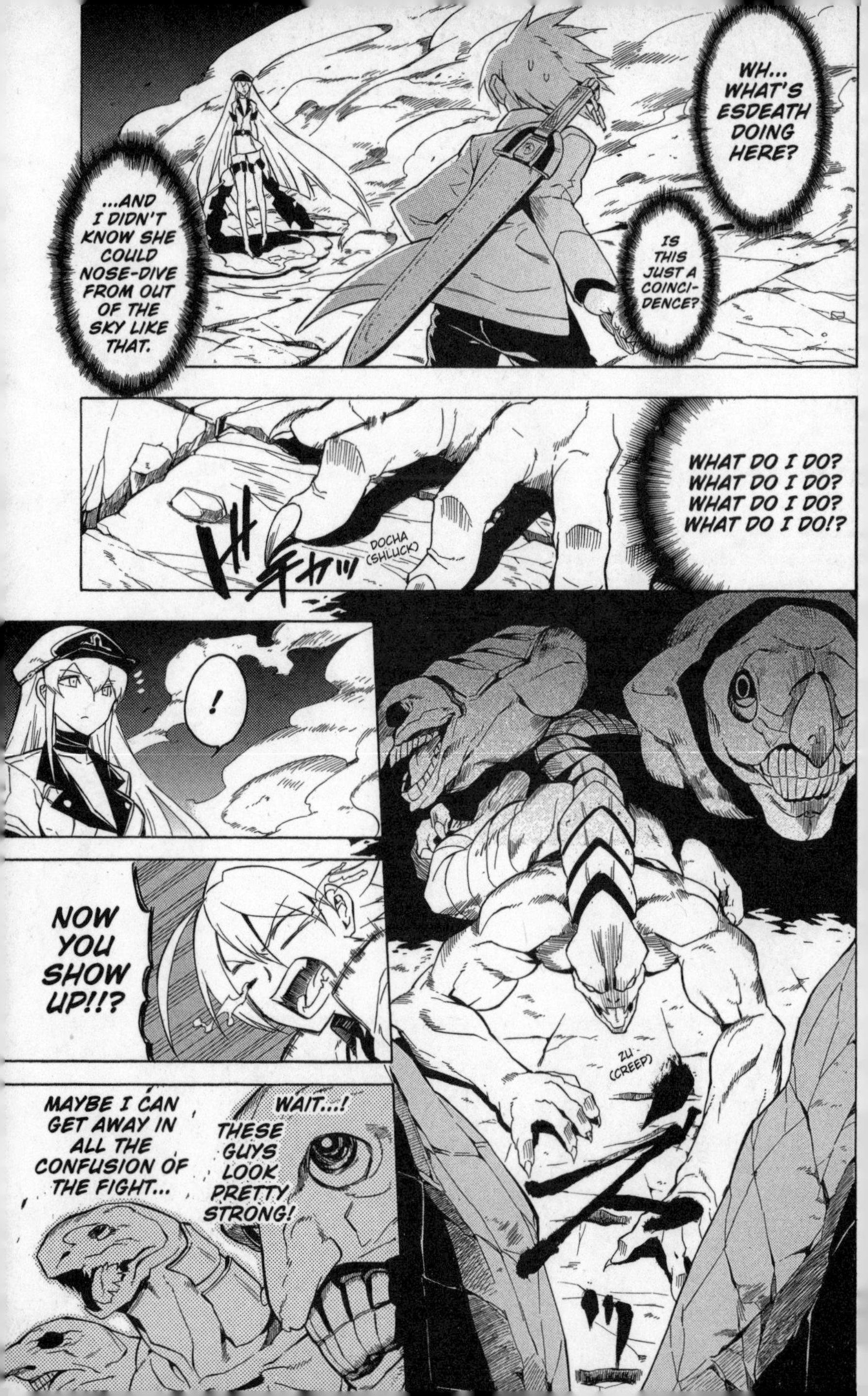
WH... WHAT'S ESDEATH DOING HERE?
IS THIS JUST A COINCI-DENCE?
...AND I DIDN'T KNOW SHE COULD NOSE-DIVE FROM OUT OF THE SKY LIKE THAT.
WHAT DO I DO? WHAT DO I DO? WHAT DO I DO? WHAT DO I DO!?
DOCHA (SHLUCK)
!
ZU (CREEP)
NOW YOU SHOW UP!!?
WAIT...! THESE GUYS LOOK PRETTY STRONG!
MAYBE I CAN GET AWAY IN ALL THE CONFUSION OF THE FIGHT...

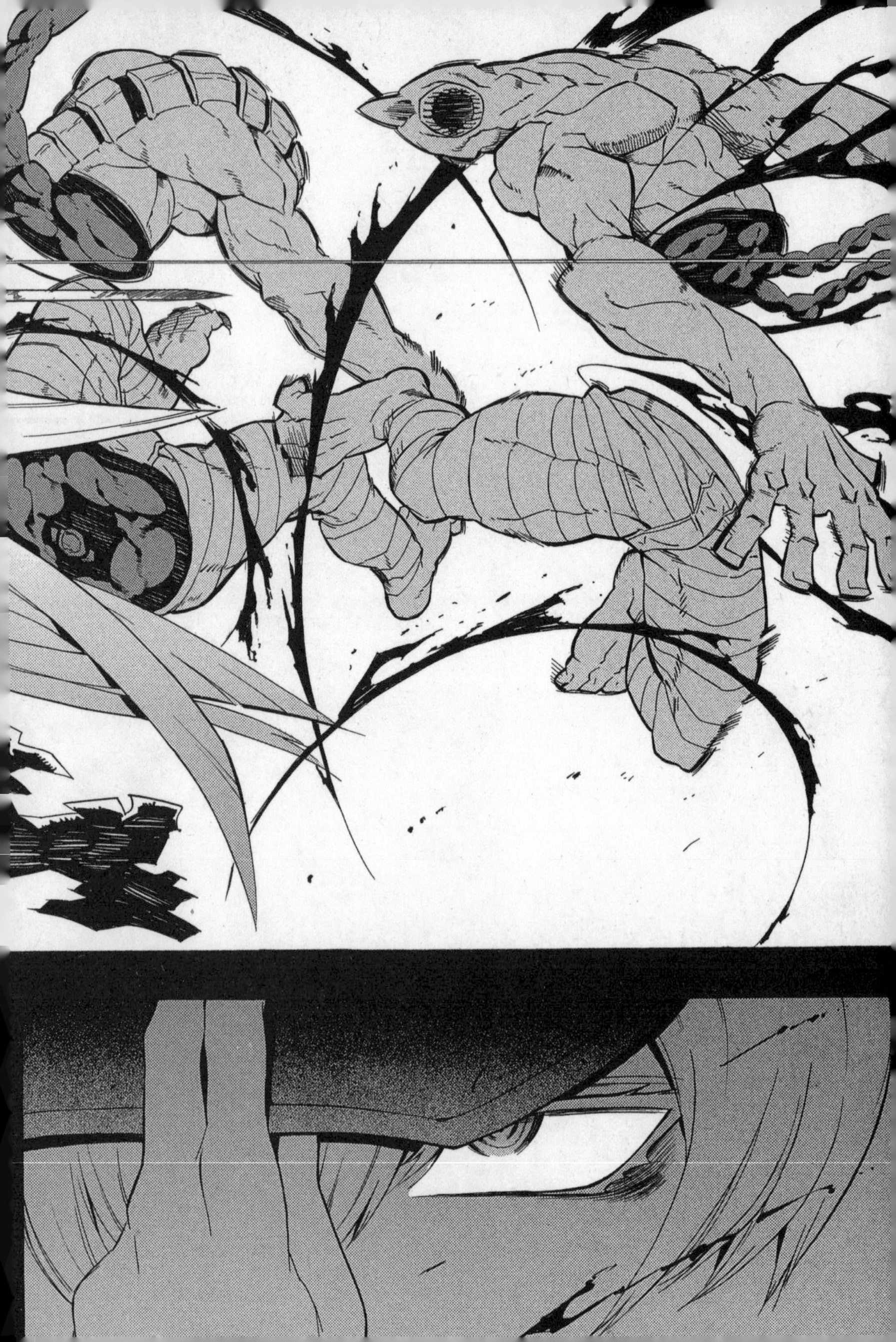

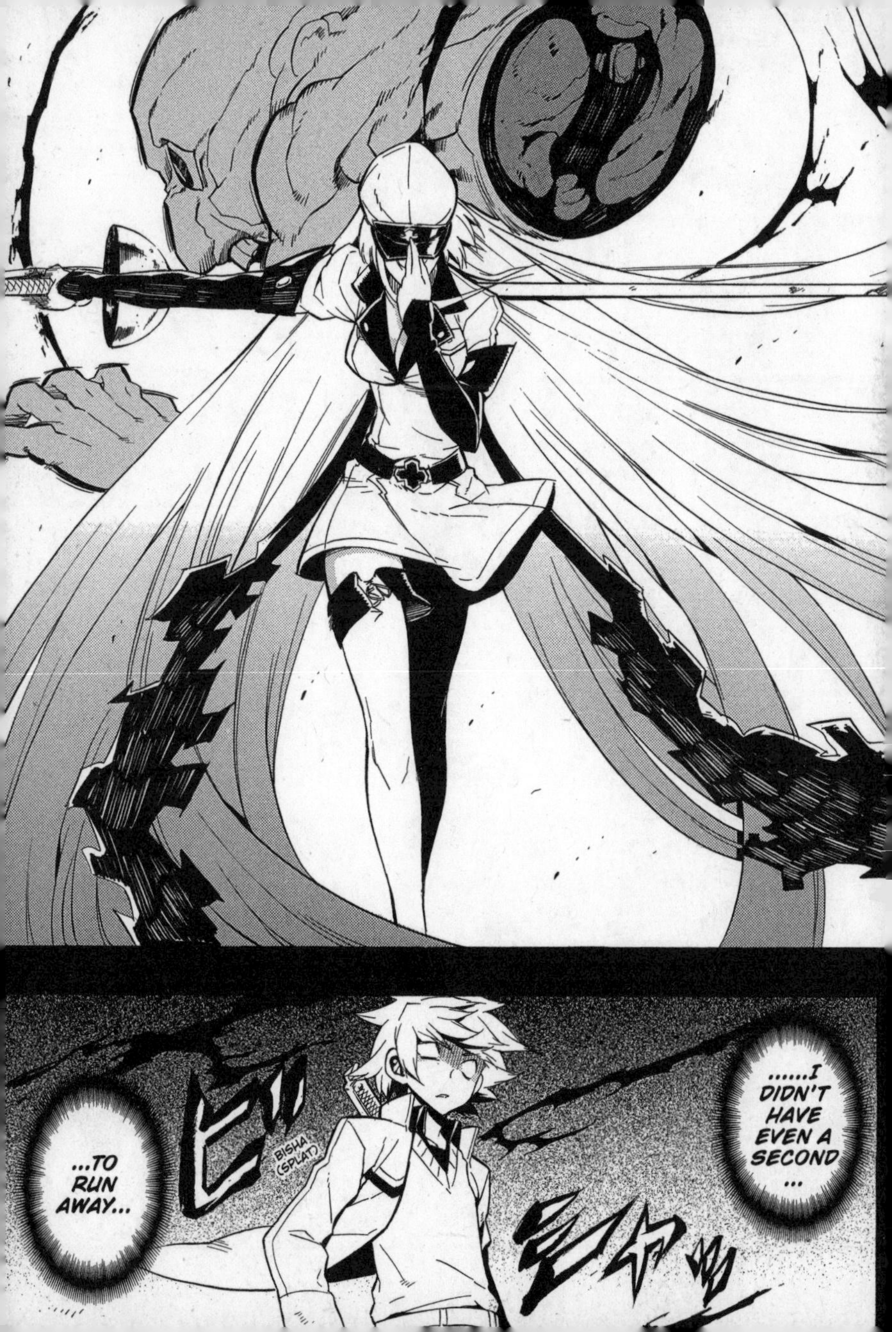
......I DIDN'T HAVE EVEN A SECOND ...
BISHA (SPLAT)
...TO RUN AWAY...

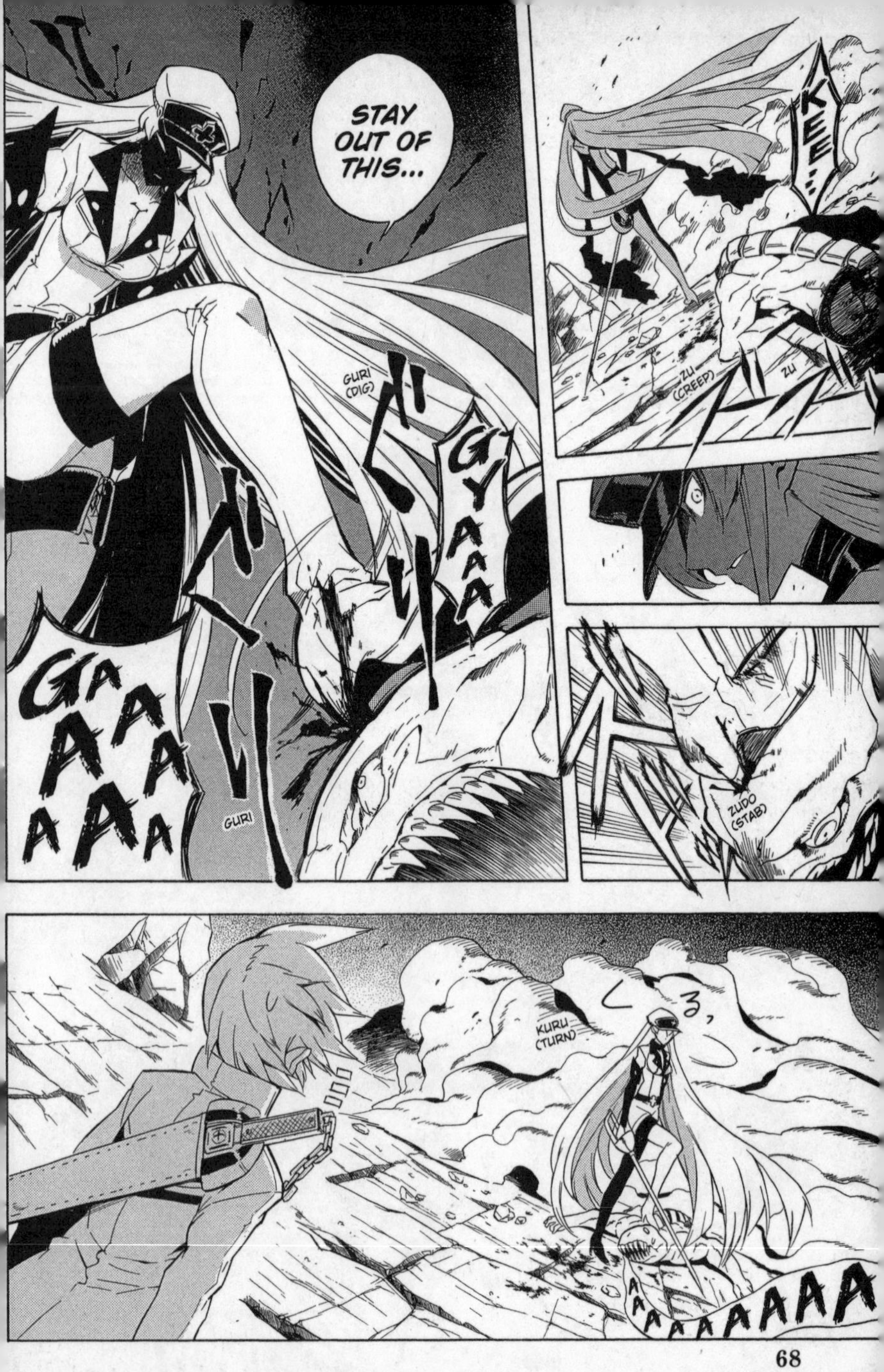
KEE...
ZU (CREEP)
ZU
ZUDO (STAB)
STAY OUT OF THIS...
GURI (DIG)
GYAAA
GAAAAAAAA
GURI
KURU (TURN)
AAAAAAAAAAA

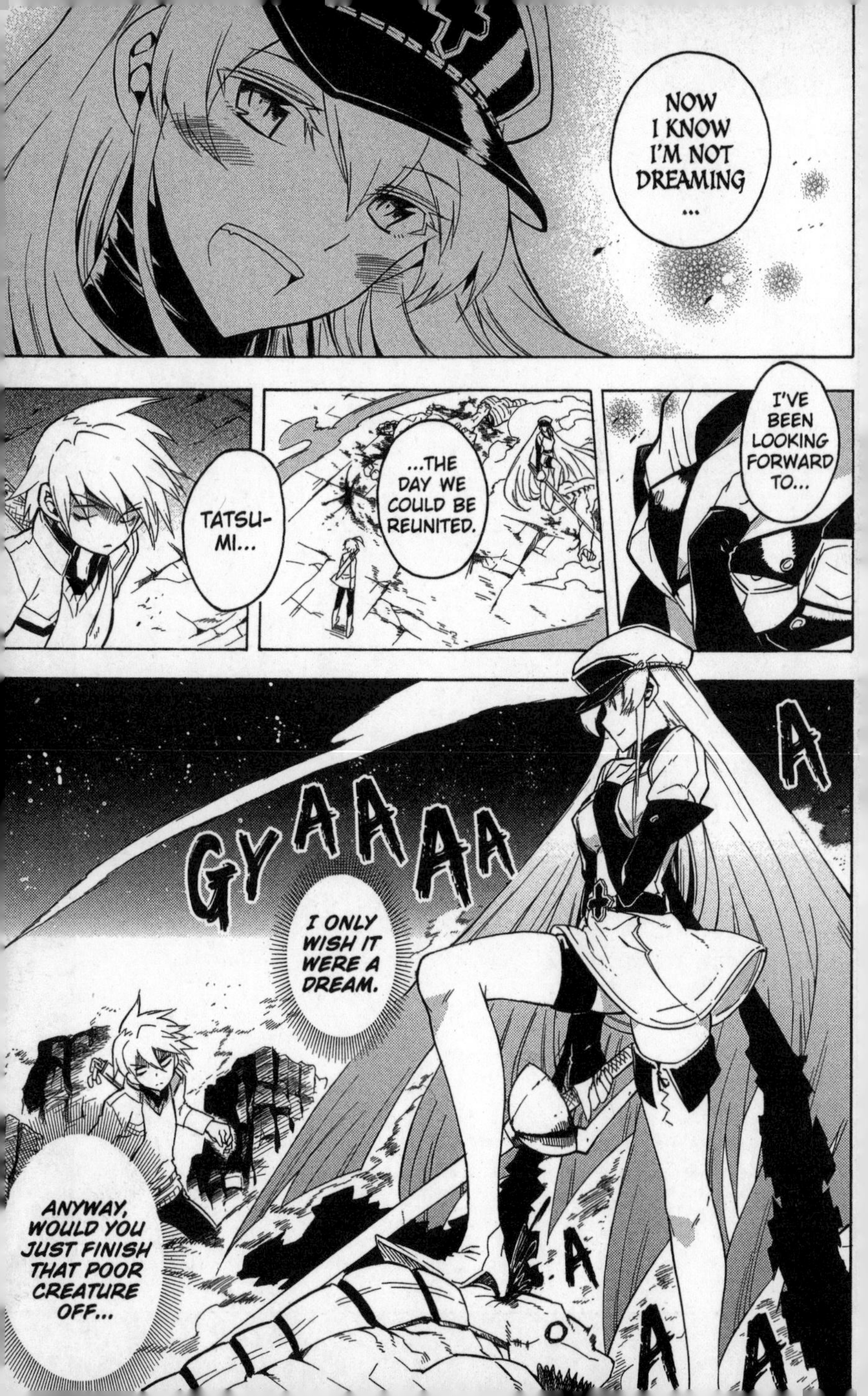
NOW I KNOW I'M NOT DREAMING ...
I'VE BEEN LOOKING FORWARD TO...
...THE DAY WE COULD BE REUNITED.
TATSU-MI...
GYAAAAA
A
I ONLY WISH IT WERE A DREAM.
ANYWAY, WOULD YOU JUST FINISH THAT POOR CREATURE OFF...
A
A
A

Akame ga KILL!
Rough Sketches 2

IMPERIAL SOLDIER GARB

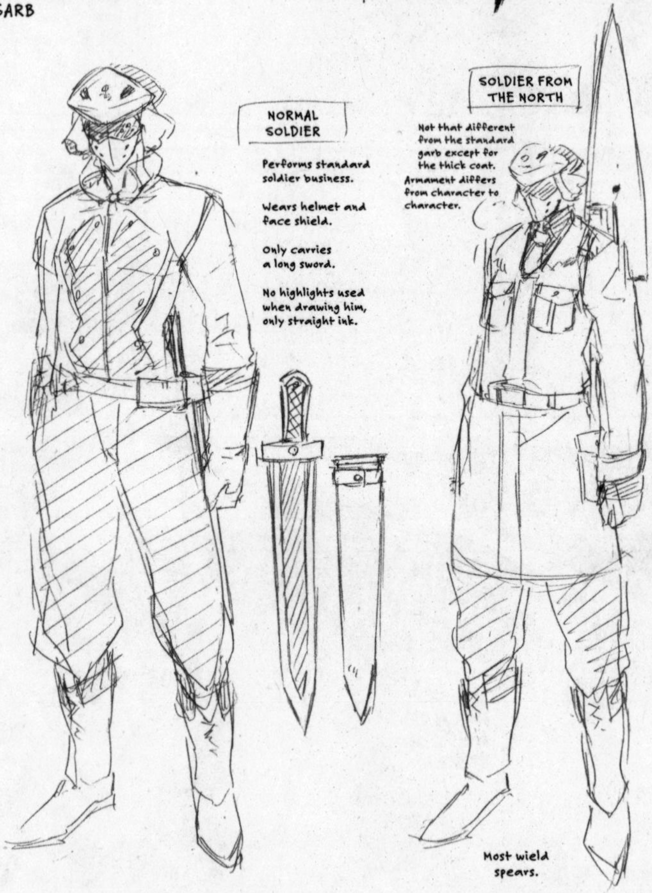
NORMAL SOLDIER
Performs standard soldier business.
Wears helmet and face shield.
Only carries a long sword.
No highlights used when drawing him, only straight ink.
SOLDIER FROM THE NORTH
Not that different from the standard garb except for the thick coat.
Armament differs from character to character.
Most wield spears.

(D) About the face cover and helmet:

Characters who have something important to say in the story will have their face cover and helmet removed so that we can see their facial expressions.

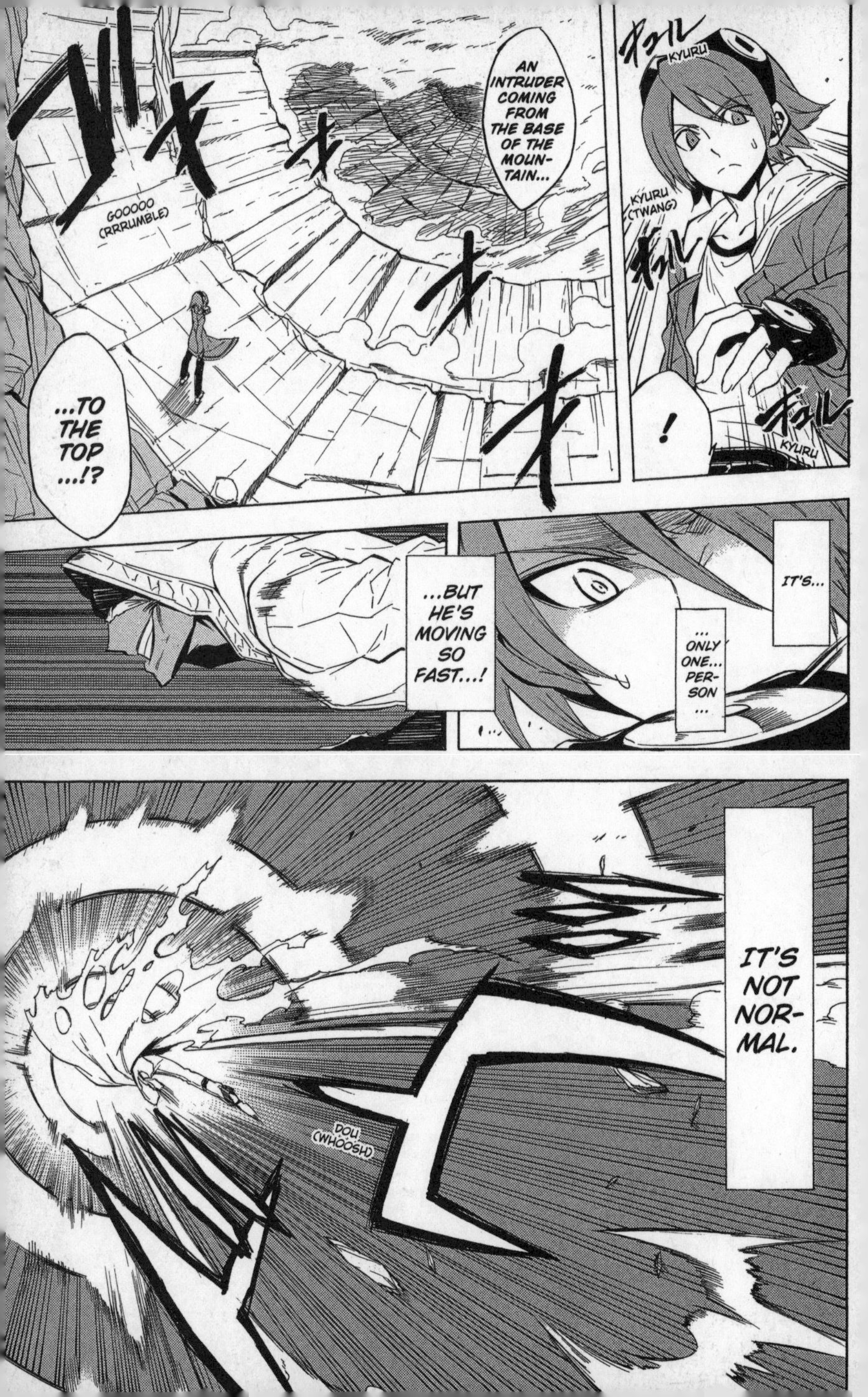
KYURU
KYURU (TWANG)
KYURU
!
AN INTRUDER COMING FROM THE BASE OF THE MOUN-TAIN...
GOOOOO (RRRUMBLE)
...TO THE TOP ...!?
IT'S...
... ONLY ONE... PER-SON ...
...BUT HE'S MOVING SO FAST...!
IT'S NOT NOR-MAL.
DOU (WHOOSH)

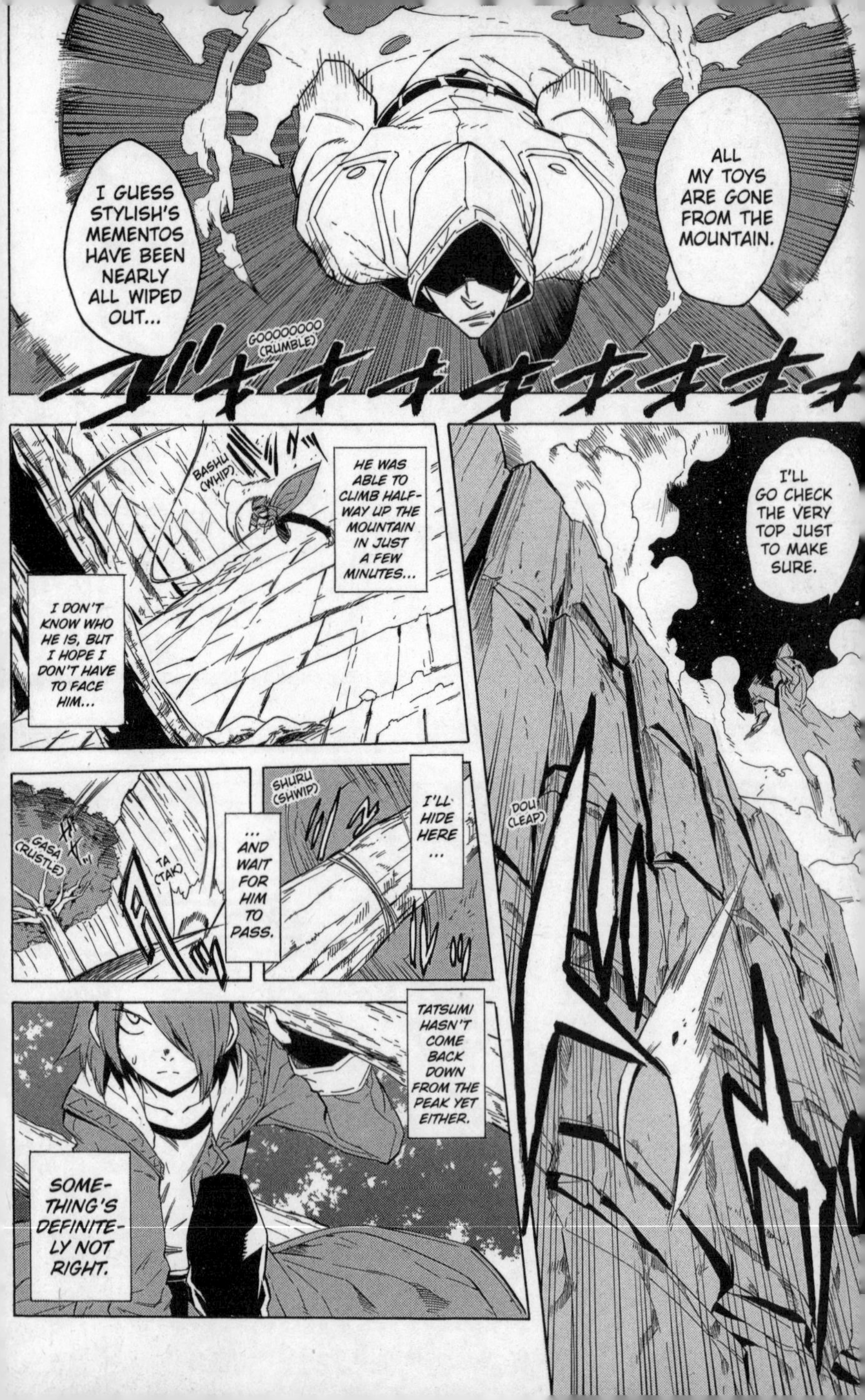

ALL MY TOYS ARE GONE FROM THE MOUNTAIN.
I GUESS STYLISH'S MEMENTOS HAVE BEEN NEARLY ALL WIPED OUT...
GOOOOOOOO (RUMBLE)
I'LL GO CHECK THE VERY TOP JUST TO MAKE SURE.
HE WAS ABLE TO CLIMB HALF-WAY UP THE MOUNTAIN IN JUST A FEW MINUTES...
BASHU (WHIP)
I DON'T KNOW WHO HE IS, BUT I HOPE I DON'T HAVE TO FACE HIM...
DOU (LEAP)
I'LL HIDE HERE...
SHURU (SHWIP)
...AND WAIT FOR HIM TO PASS.
TA (TAK)
GASA (RUSTLE)
TATSUMI HASN'T COME BACK DOWN FROM THE PEAK YET EITHER.
SOME-THING'S DEFINITE-LY NOT RIGHT.

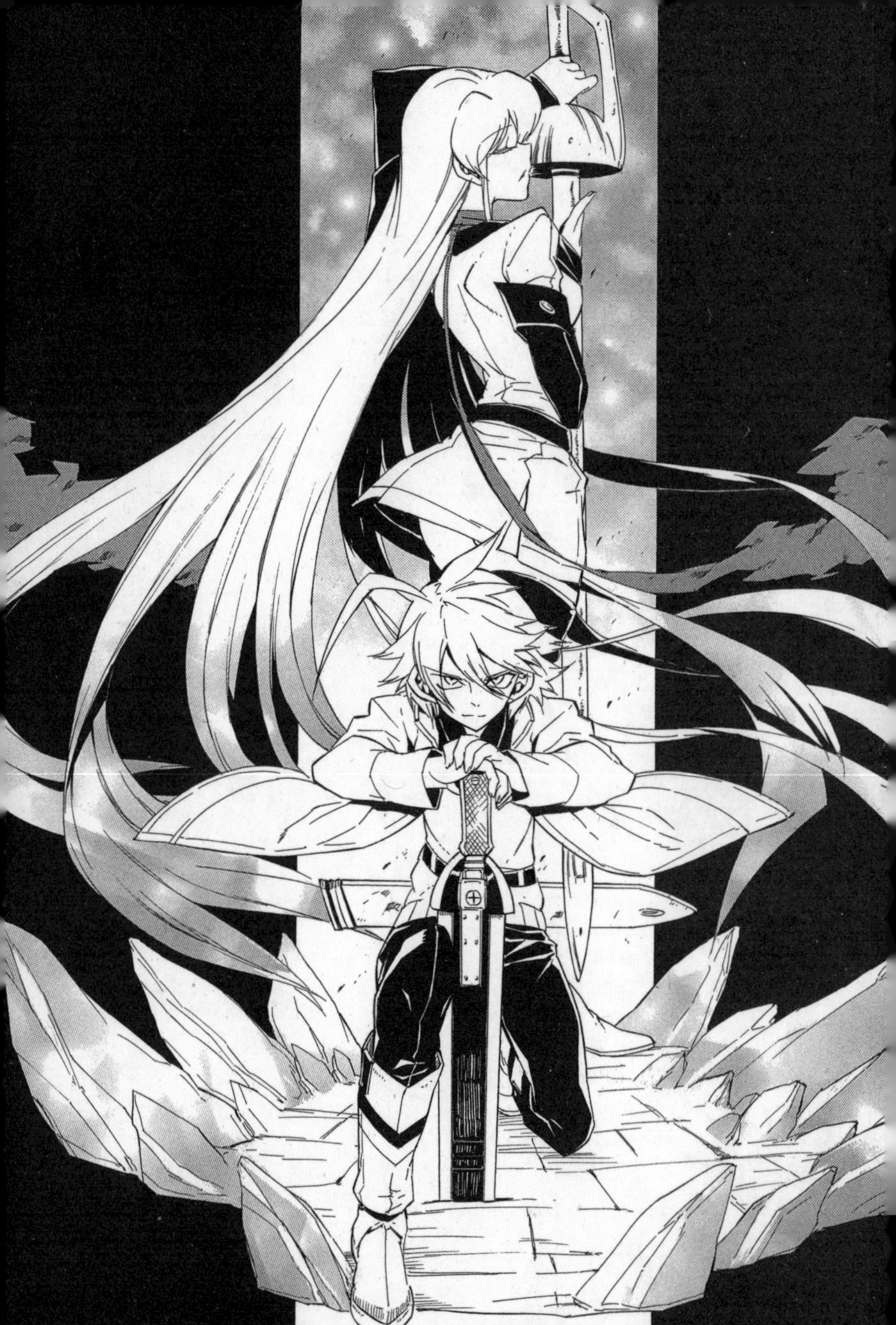

Chapter 26 Kill the Giant Danger Beast

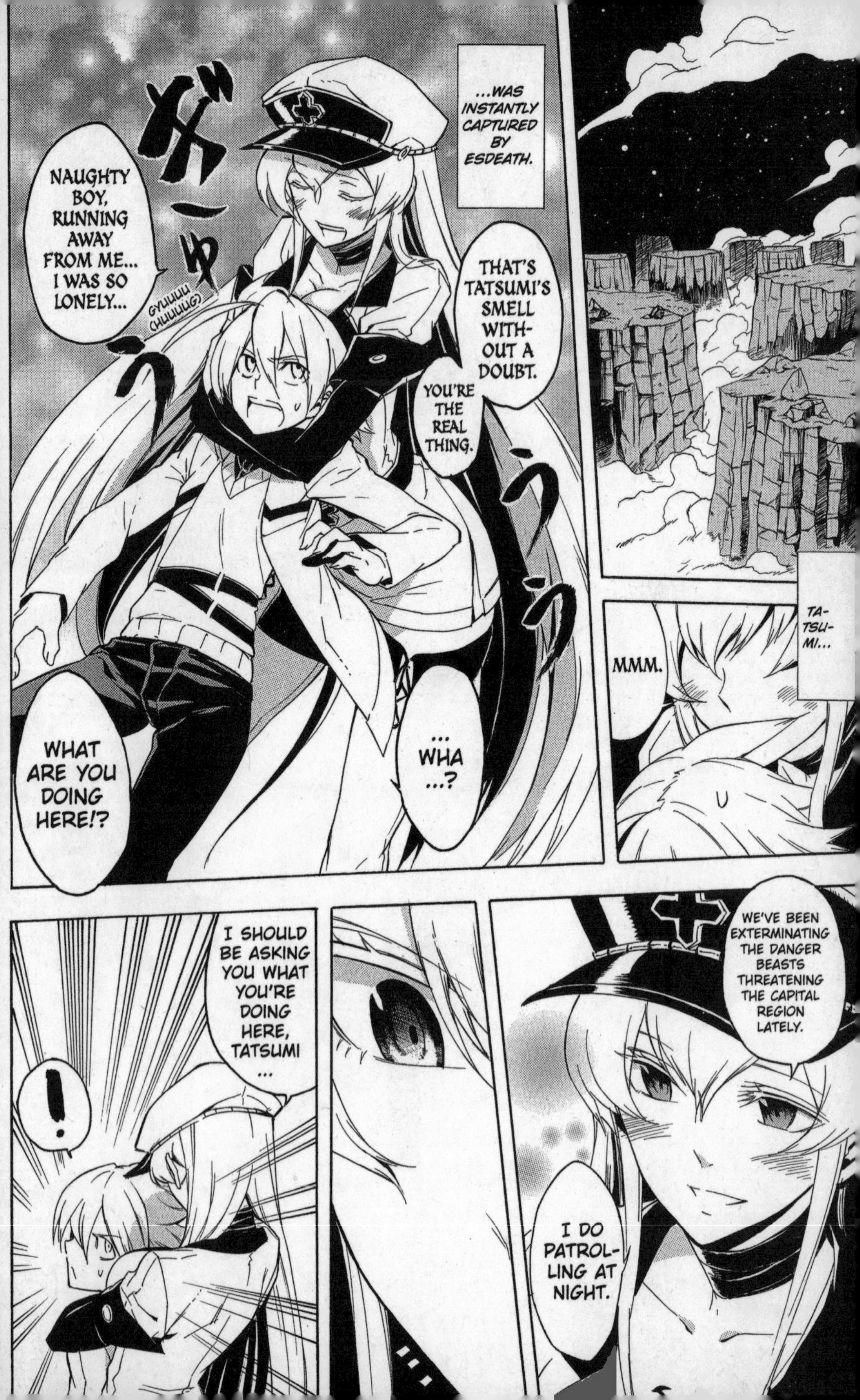
TA-TSU-MI...
MMM.
...WAS INSTANTLY CAPTURED BY ESDEATH.
NAUGHTY BOY, RUNNING AWAY FROM ME... I WAS SO LONELY...
GYUUUU (HUUUUUG)
THAT'S TATSUMI'S SMELL WITH-OUT A DOUBT.
YOU'RE THE REAL THING.
...WHA...?
WHAT ARE YOU DOING HERE!?
WE'VE BEEN EXTERMINATING THE DANGER BEASTS THREATENING THE CAPITAL REGION LATELY.
I DO PATROL-LING AT NIGHT.
I SHOULD BE ASKING YOU WHAT YOU'RE DOING HERE, TATSUMI...
!

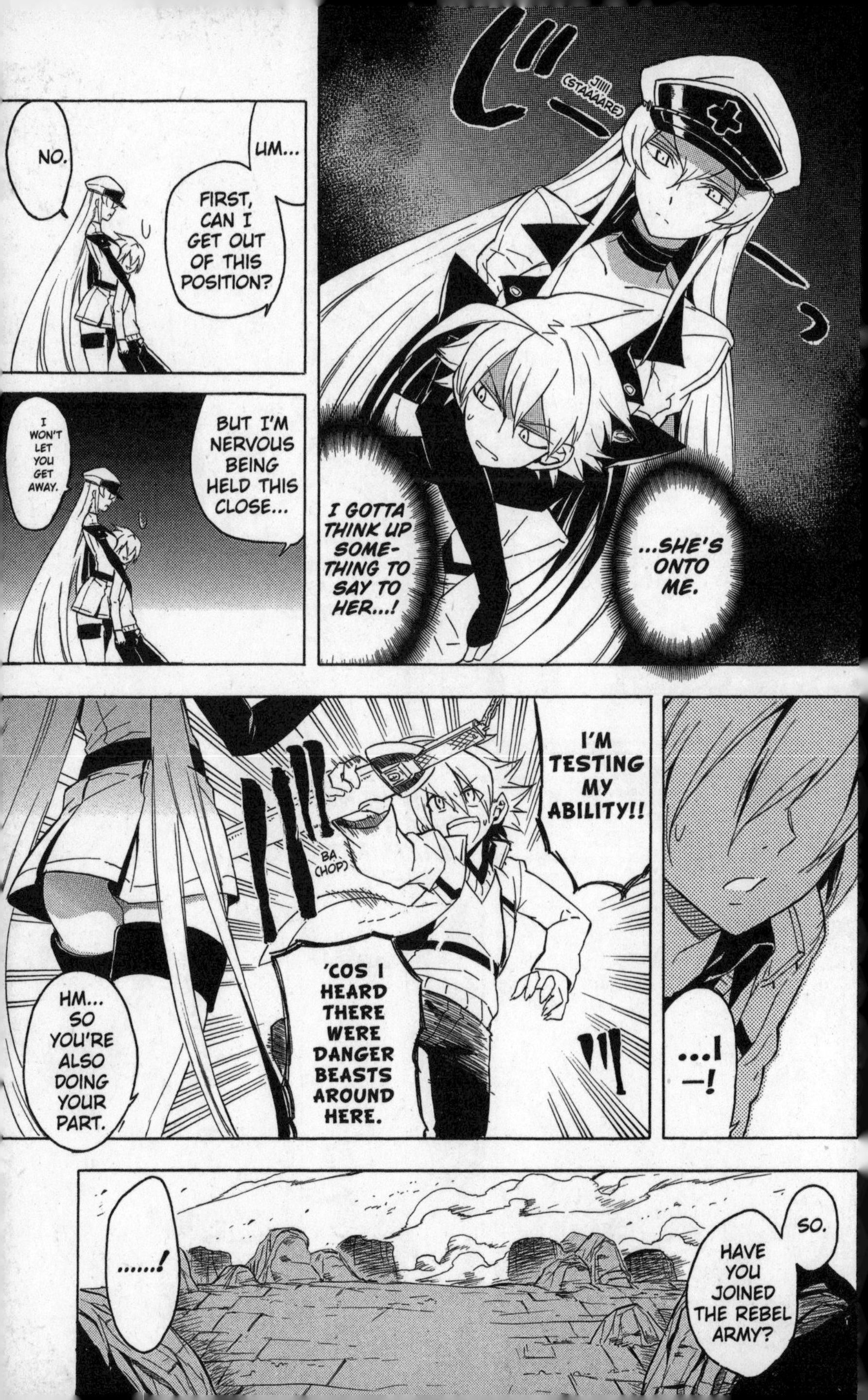

JIIII (STAAAARE)
...SHE'S ONTO ME.
I GOTTA THINK UP SOME-THING TO SAY TO HER...!
UM...
FIRST, CAN I GET OUT OF THIS POSITION?
NO.
BUT I'M NERVOUS BEING HELD THIS CLOSE...
I WON'T LET YOU GET AWAY.
...I —!
I'M TESTING MY ABILITY!!
BA (CHOP)
'COS I HEARD THERE WERE DANGER BEASTS AROUND HERE.
HM... SO YOU'RE ALSO DOING YOUR PART.
SO.
HAVE YOU JOINED THE REBEL ARMY?
......!

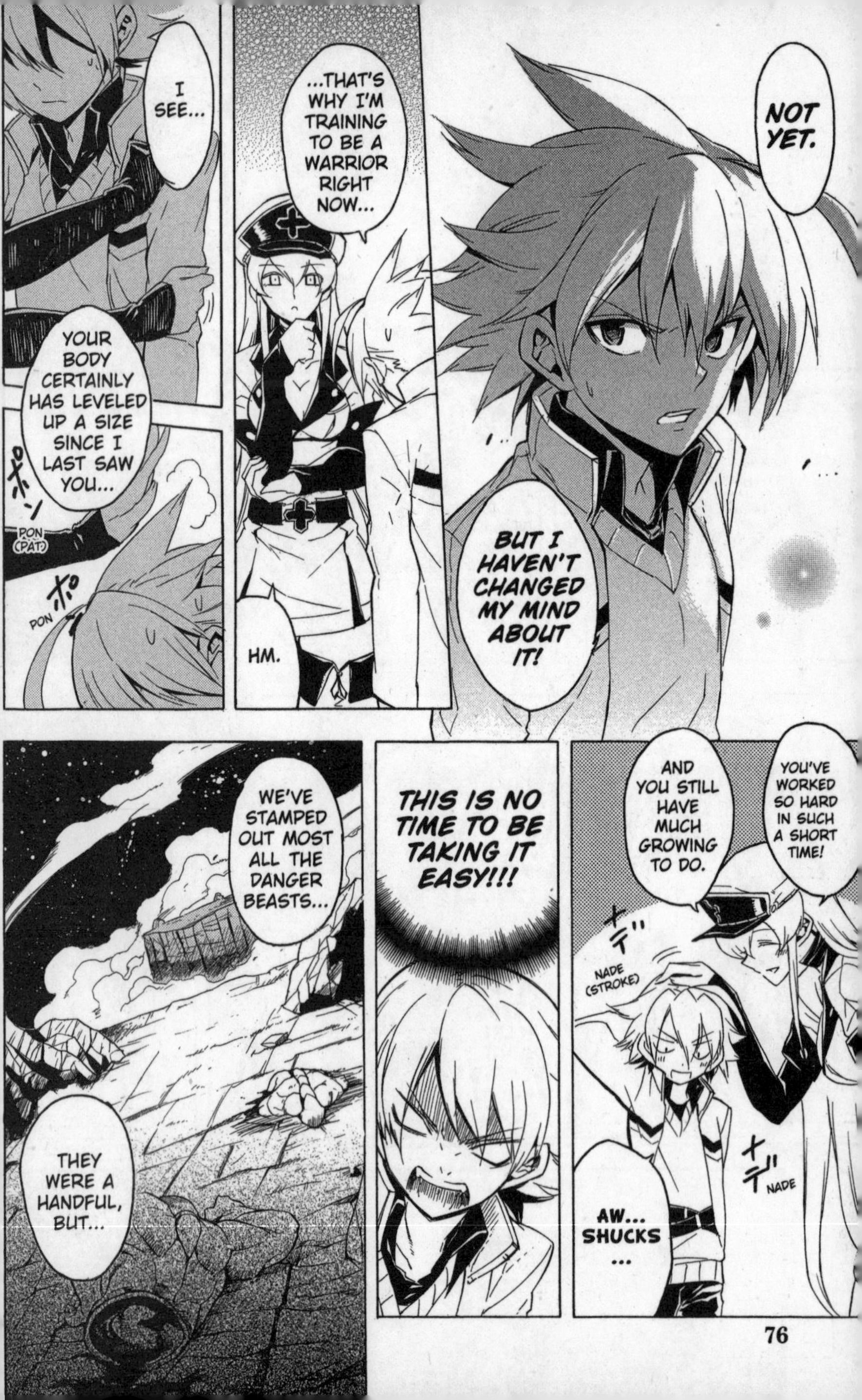
NOT YET.
BUT I HAVEN'T CHANGED MY MIND ABOUT IT!
...THAT'S WHY I'M TRAINING TO BE A WARRIOR RIGHT NOW...
HM.
I SEE...
YOUR BODY CERTAINLY HAS LEVELED UP A SIZE SINCE I LAST SAW YOU...
PON (PAT)
PON
YOU'VE WORKED SO HARD IN SUCH A SHORT TIME!
AND YOU STILL HAVE MUCH GROWING TO DO.
NADE (STROKE)
NADE
AW... SHUCKS ...
THIS IS NO TIME TO BE TAKING IT EASY!!!
WE'VE STAMPED OUT MOST ALL THE DANGER BEASTS...
THEY WERE A HANDFUL, BUT...

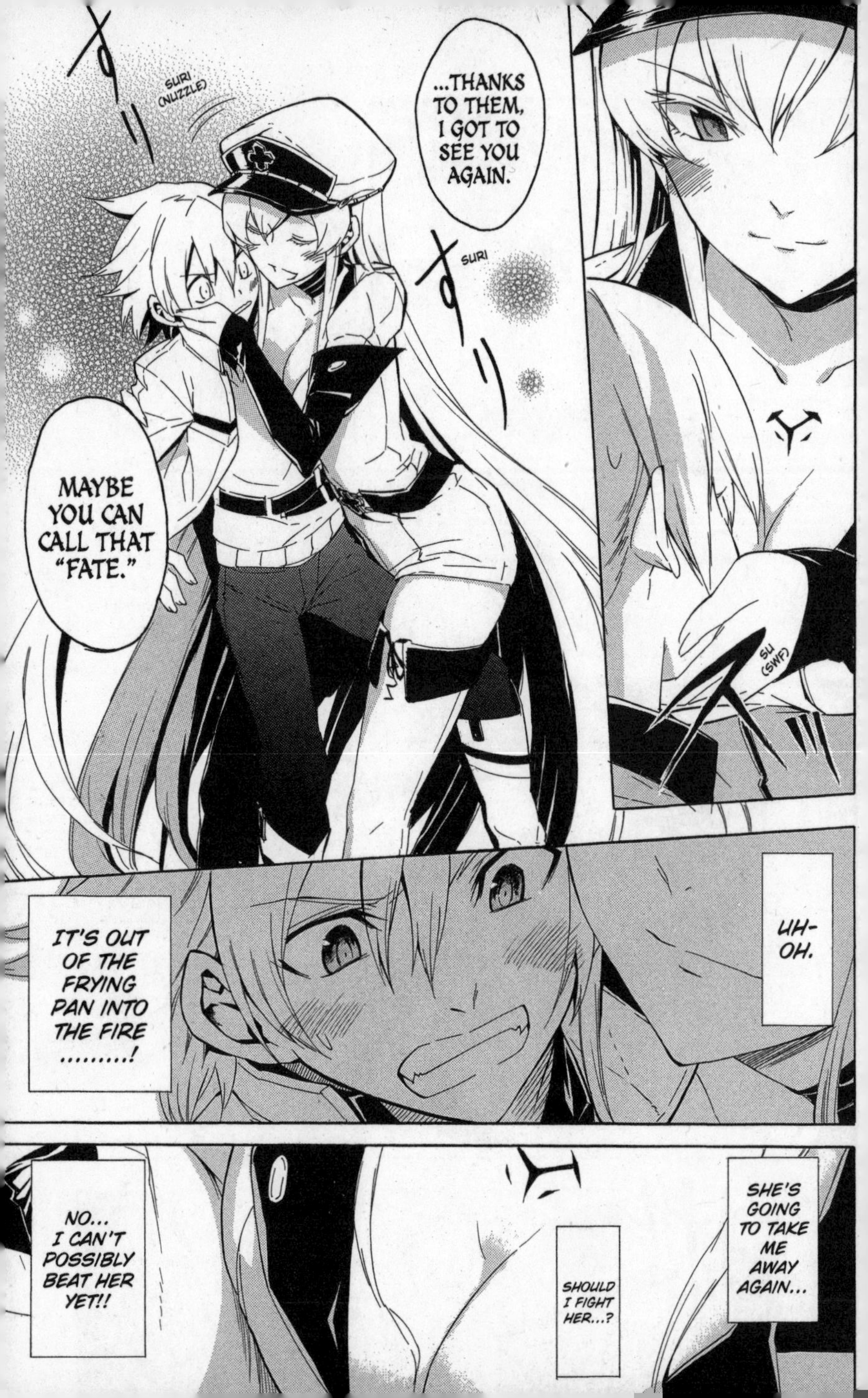

SU (SWF)
...THANKS TO THEM, I GOT TO SEE YOU AGAIN.
SURI (NUZZLE)
SURI
MAYBE YOU CAN CALL THAT "FATE."
UH-OH.
IT'S OUT OF THE FRYING PAN INTO THE FIRE ....!
SHE'S GOING TO TAKE ME AWAY AGAIN...
SHOULD I FIGHT HER...?
NO... I CAN'T POSSIBLY BEAT HER YET!!

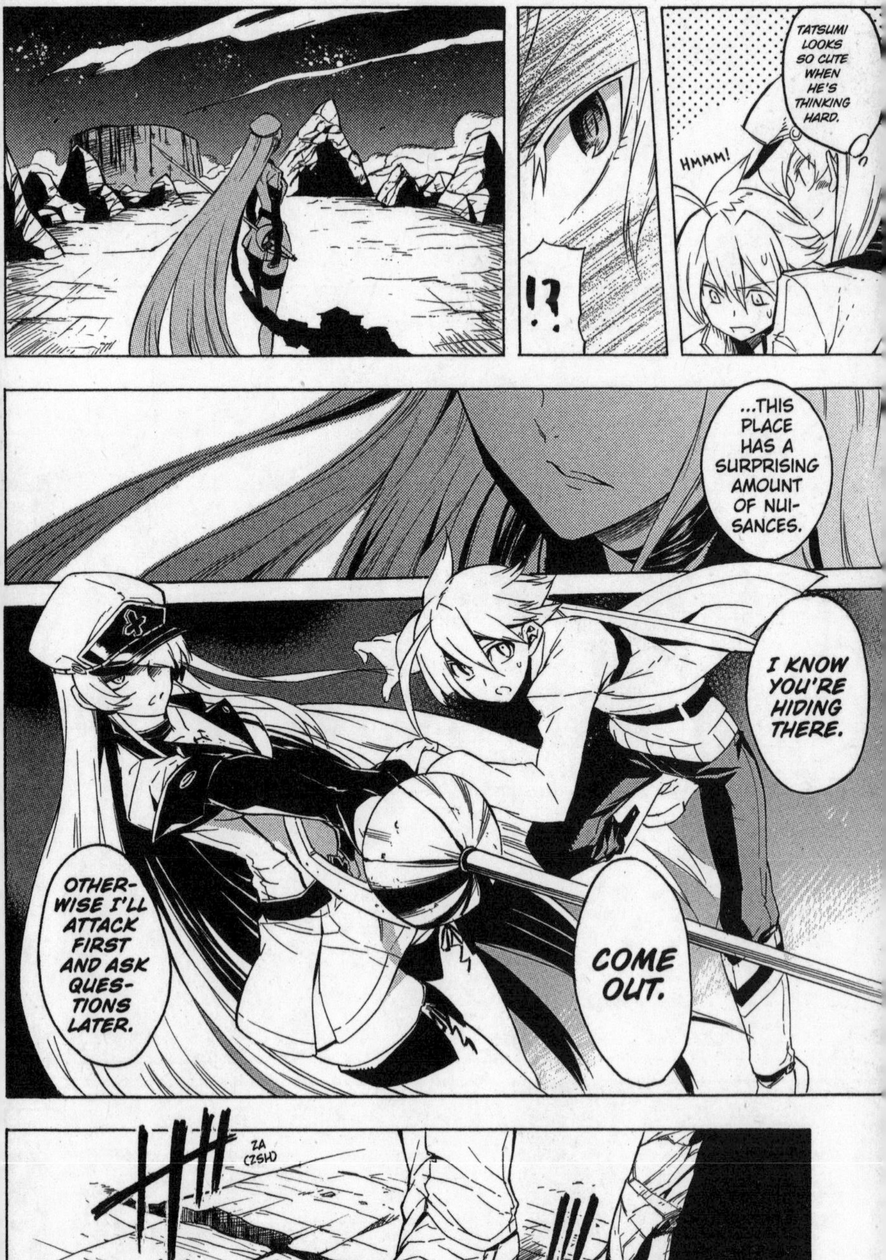
TATSUMI LOOKS SO CUTE WHEN HE'S THINKING HARD.
HMMM!
!?
...THIS PLACE HAS A SURPRISING AMOUNT OF NUI-SANCES.
I KNOW YOU'RE HIDING THERE.
COME OUT.
OTHER-WISE I'LL ATTACK FIRST AND ASK QUES-TIONS LATER.
ZA (ZSH)

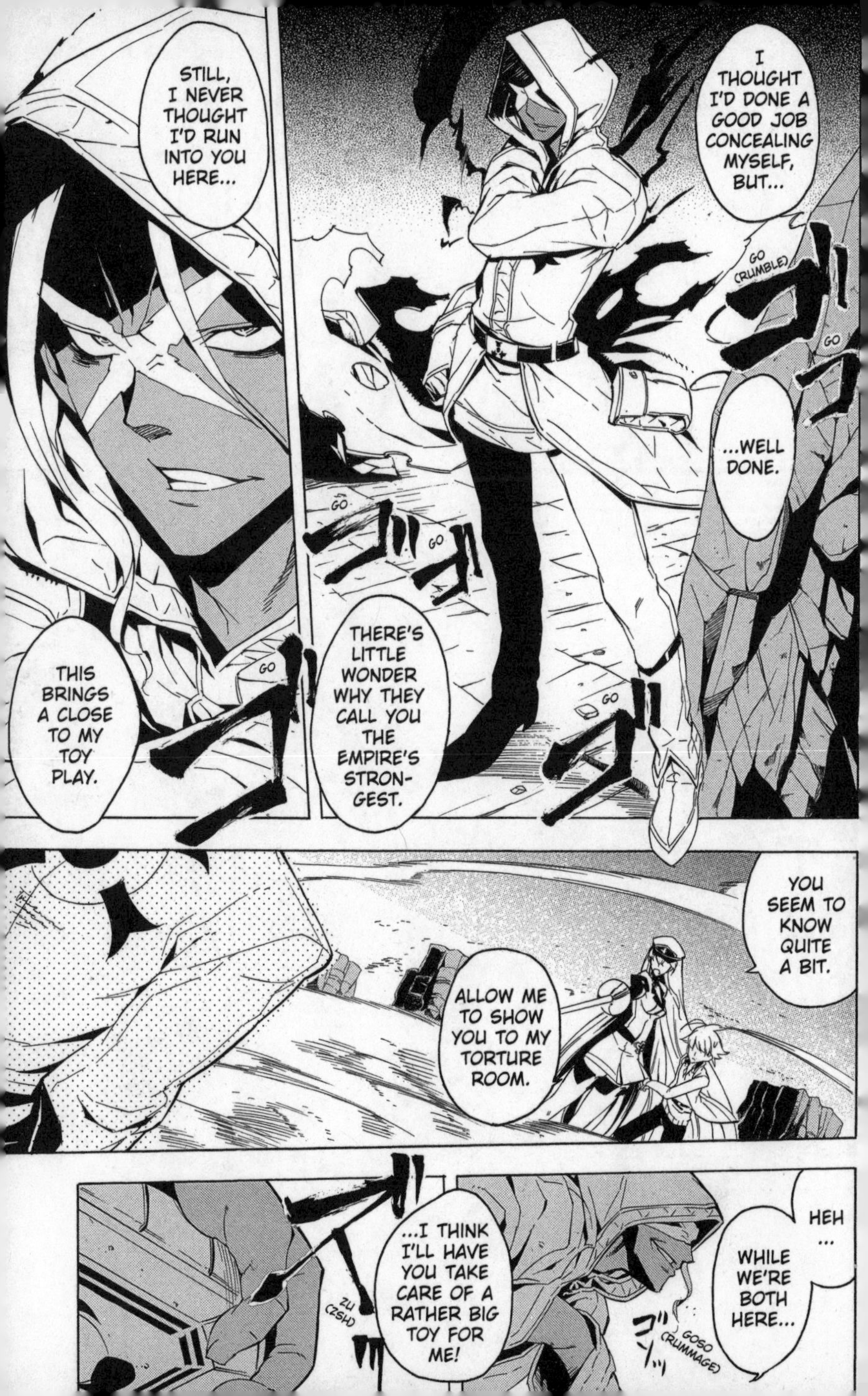
I THOUGHT I'D DONE A GOOD JOB CONCEALING MYSELF, BUT...
GO (RUMBLE)
GO
...WELL DONE.
GO
GO
GO
THERE'S LITTLE WONDER WHY THEY CALL YOU THE EMPIRE'S STRONGEST.
STILL, I NEVER THOUGHT I'D RUN INTO YOU HERE...
GO
THIS BRINGS A CLOSE TO MY TOY PLAY.
YOU SEEM TO KNOW QUITE A BIT.
ALLOW ME TO SHOW YOU TO MY TORTURE ROOM.
HEH ...
WHILE WE'RE BOTH HERE...
GOSO (RUMMAGE)
...I THINK I'LL HAVE YOU TAKE CARE OF A RATHER BIG TOY FOR ME!
ZU (ZSH)

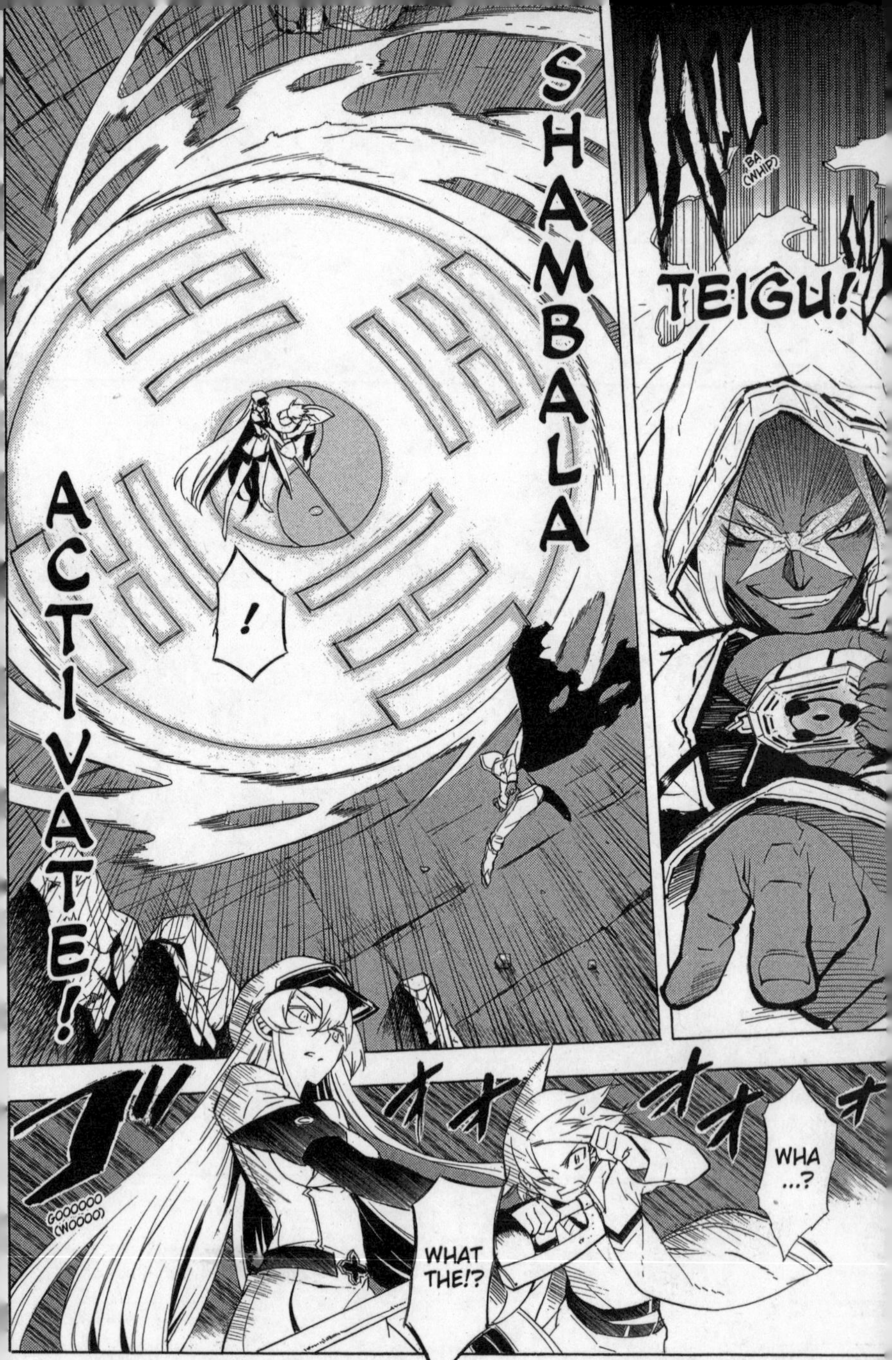
BA (WHIP)
TEIGU!
SHAMBALA
ACTIVATE!
!
GOOOOOO (WOOOO)
WHA ...?
WHAT THE!?

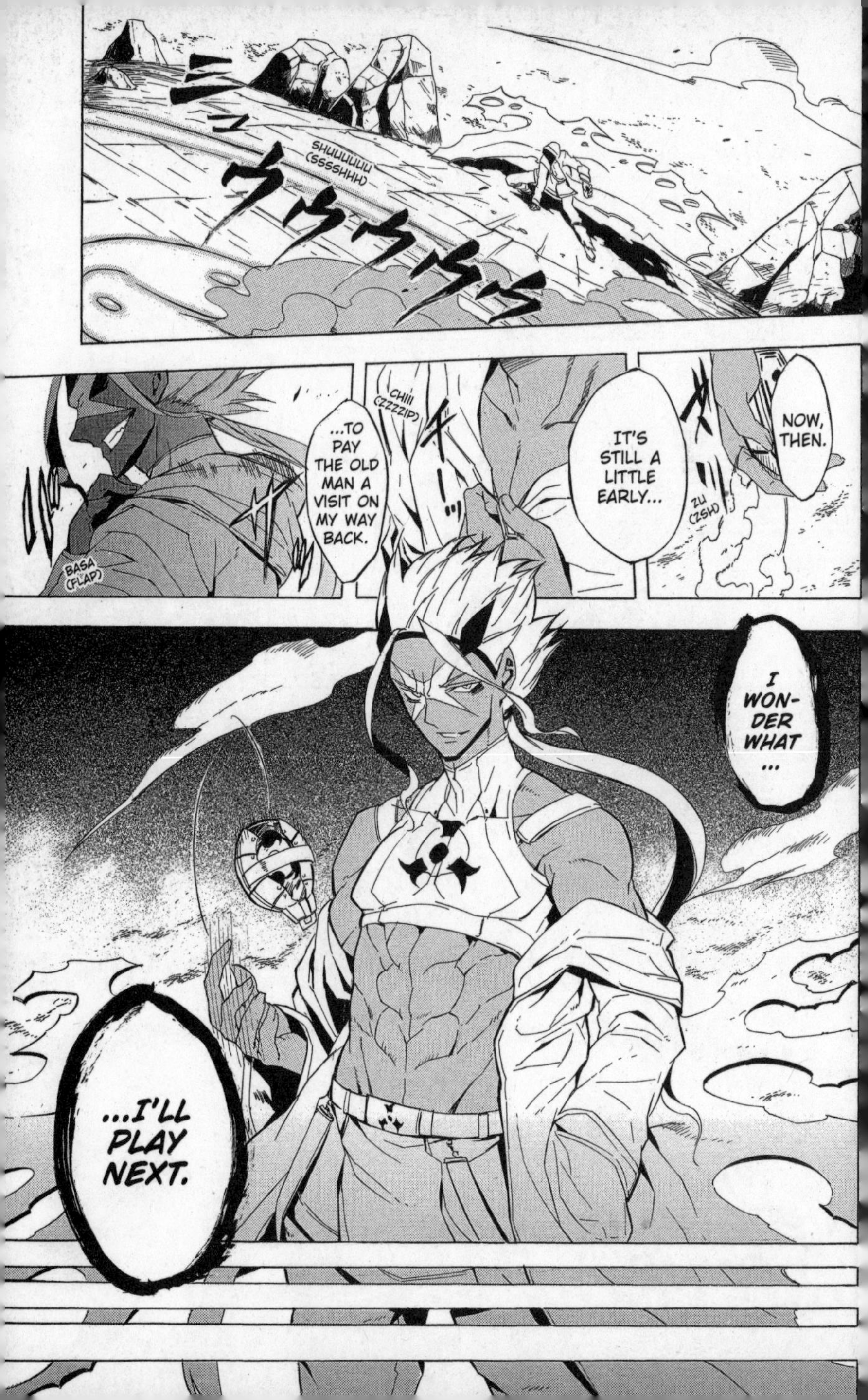
SHUUUUUU (SSSSHHH)
NOW, THEN.
ZU (ZSH)
IT'S STILL A LITTLE EARLY...
CHIII (ZZZZIP)
...TO PAY THE OLD MAN A VISIT ON MY WAY BACK.
BASA (FLAP)
I WON-DER WHAT...
...I'LL PLAY NEXT.

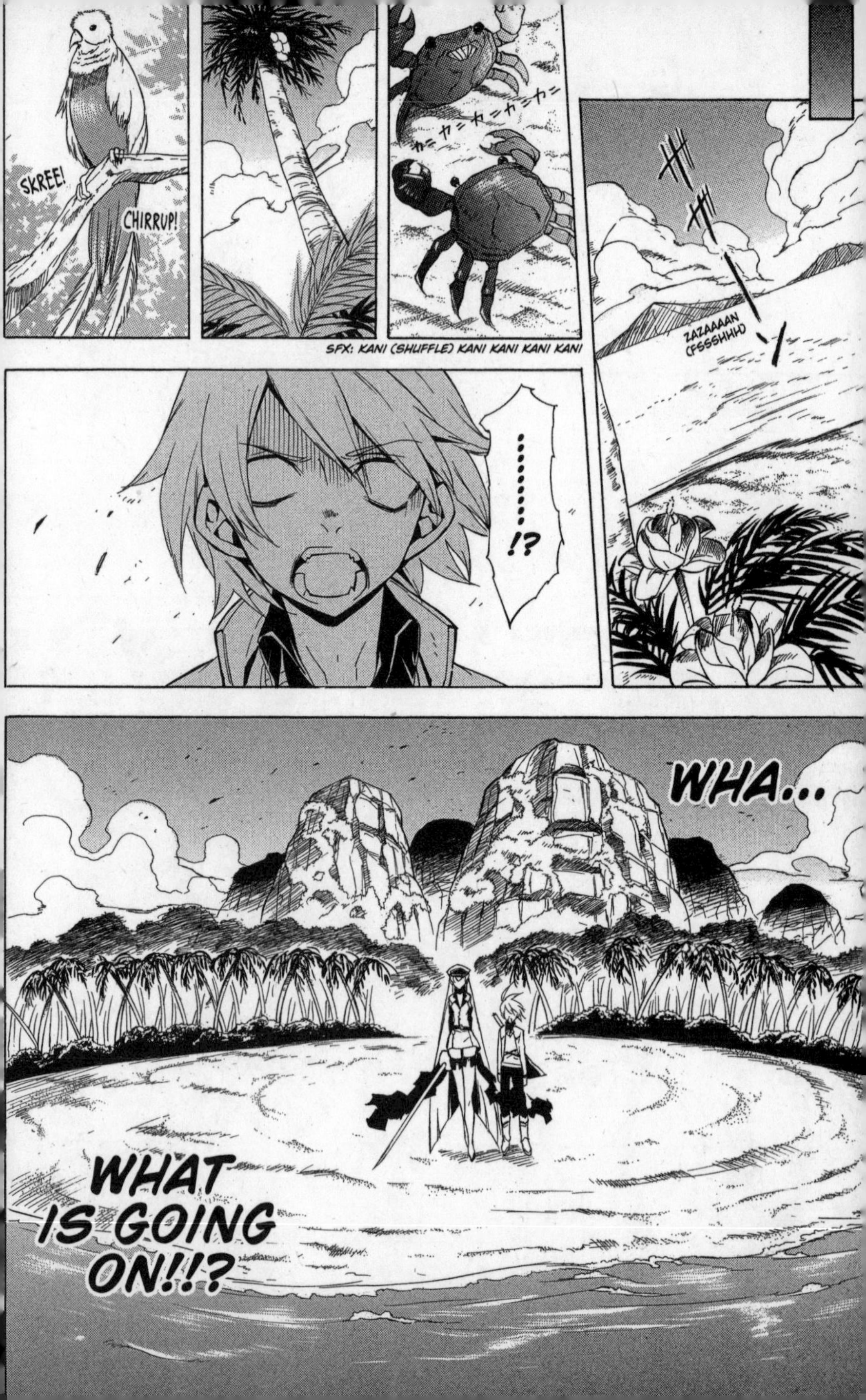

ZAZAAAAN (FSSSHHH)
SFX: KANI (SHUFFLE) KANI KANI KANI KANI
CHIRRUP!
SKREE!
......!?
WHA...
WHAT IS GOING ON!!?

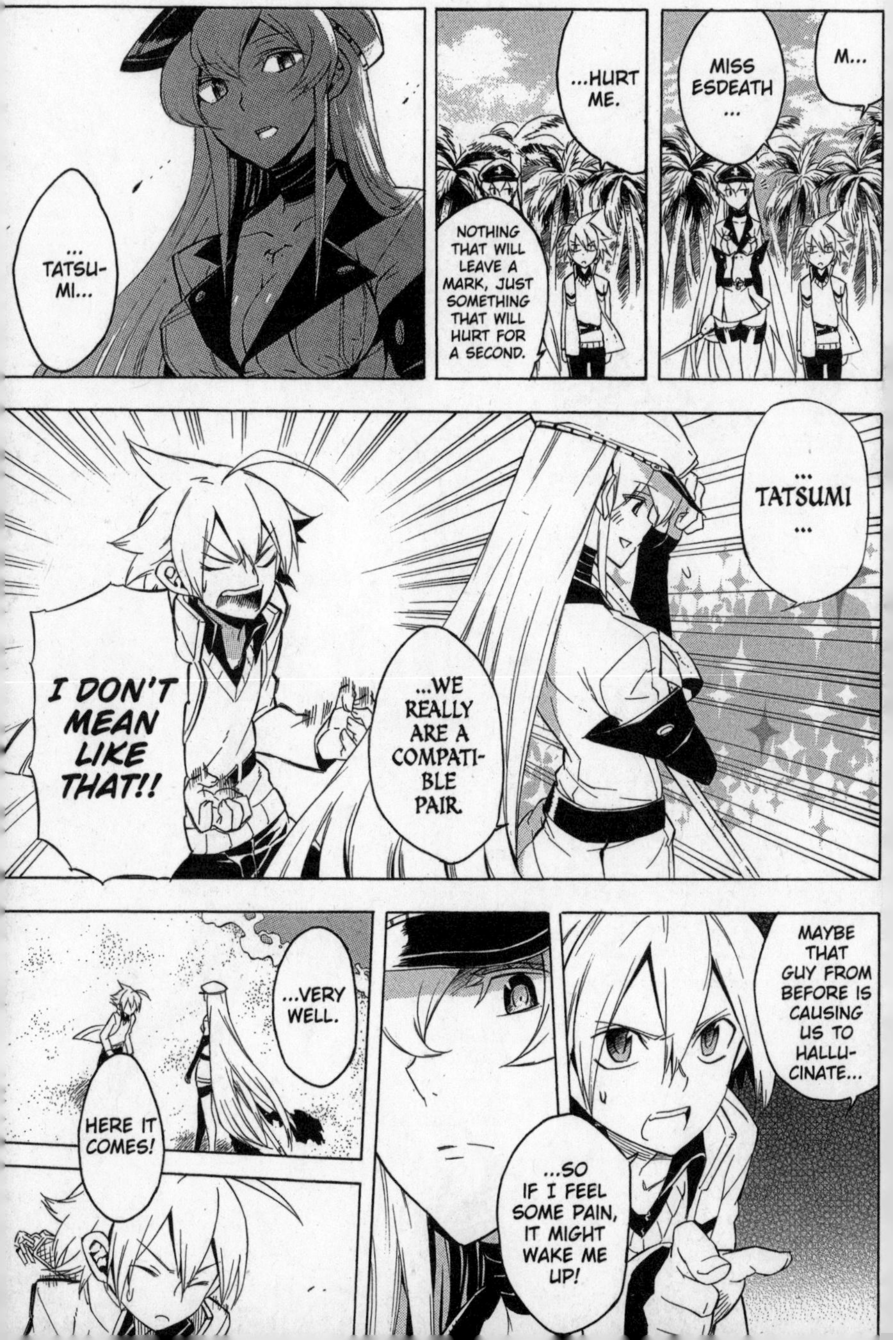
M...
MISS ESDEATH ...
...HURT ME.
NOTHING THAT WILL LEAVE A MARK, JUST SOMETHING THAT WILL HURT FOR A SECOND.
... TATSUMI...
... TATSUMI ...
...WE REALLY ARE A COMPATI-BLE PAIR.
I DON'T MEAN LIKE THAT!!
MAYBE THAT GUY FROM BEFORE IS CAUSING US TO HALLU-CINATE...
...SO IF I FEEL SOME PAIN, IT MIGHT WAKE ME UP!
...VERY WELL.
HERE IT COMES!

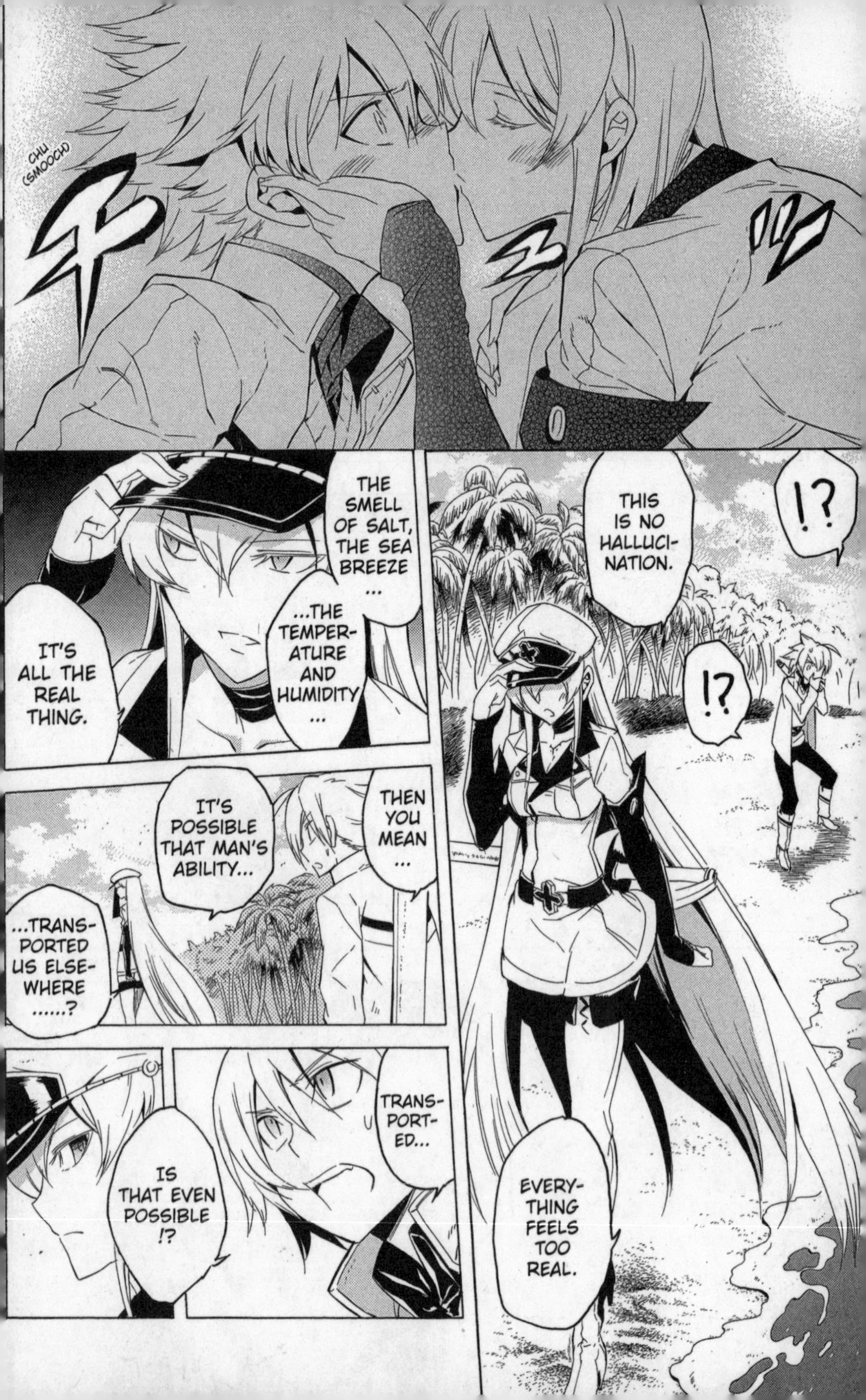
CHU (SMOOCH)
!?
THIS IS NO HALLUCINATION.
!?
THE SMELL OF SALT, THE SEA BREEZE ...
...THE TEMPERATURE AND HUMIDITY ...
IT'S ALL THE REAL THING.
THEN YOU MEAN ...
IT'S POSSIBLE THAT MAN'S ABILITY...
...TRANSPORTED US ELSEWHERE ......?
TRANSPORTED...
IS THAT EVEN POSSIBLE !?
EVERYTHING FEELS TOO REAL.

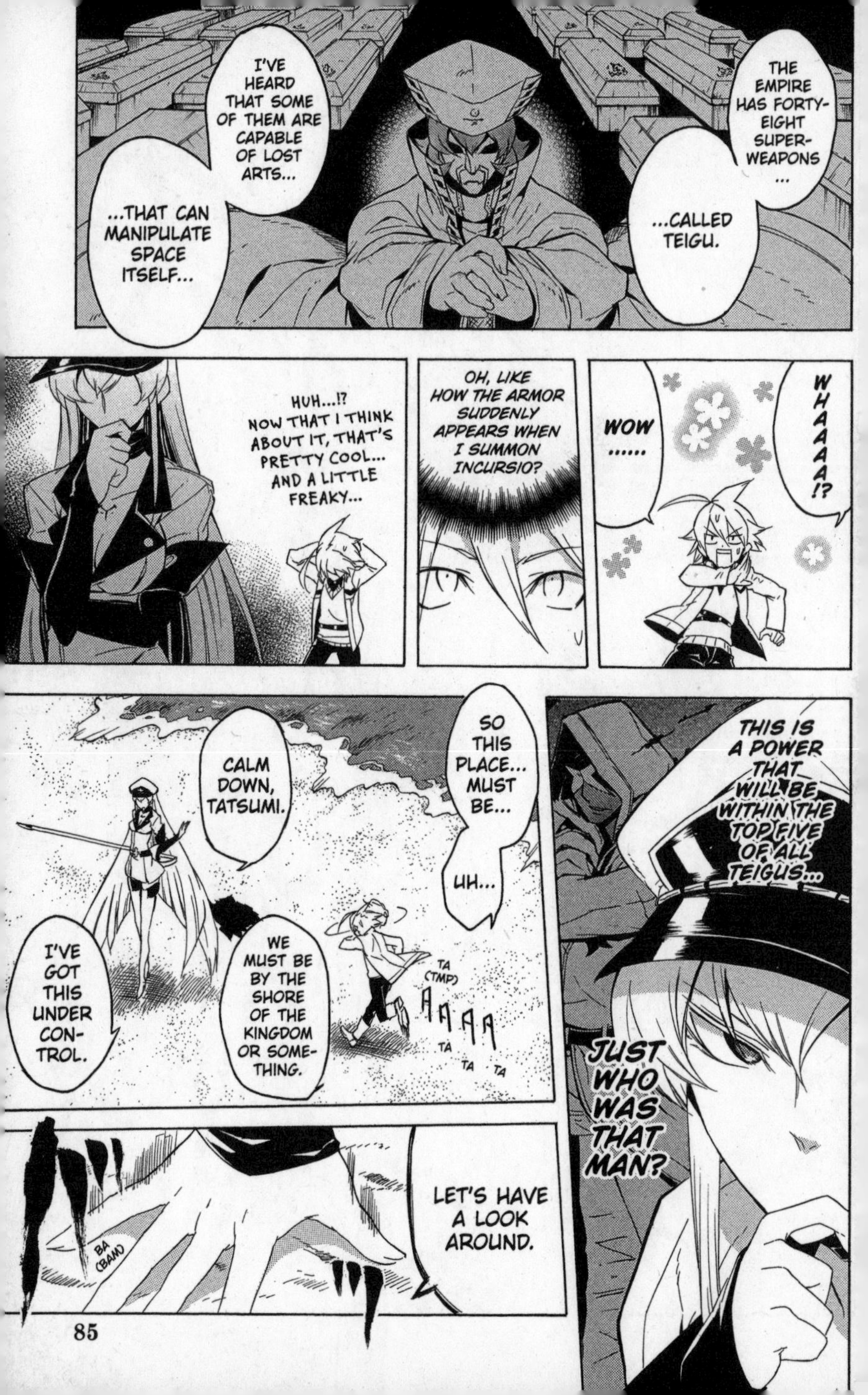
THE EMPIRE HAS FORTY-EIGHT SUPER-WEAPONS...
...CALLED TEIGU.
I'VE HEARD THAT SOME OF THEM ARE CAPABLE OF LOST ARTS...
...THAT CAN MANIPULATE SPACE ITSELF...
WHAAAAA!?
WOW ......
OH, LIKE HOW THE ARMOR SUDDENLY APPEARS WHEN I SUMMON INCURSIO?
HUH...!? NOW THAT I THINK ABOUT IT, THAT'S PRETTY COOL... AND A LITTLE FREAKY...
THIS IS A POWER THAT WILL BE WITHIN THE TOP FIVE OF ALL TEIGUS...
JUST WHO WAS THAT MAN?
SO THIS PLACE... MUST BE...
UH...
CALM DOWN, TATSUMI.
TA (TMP)
TA TA TA
WE MUST BE BY THE SHORE OF THE KINGDOM OR SOMETHING.
I'VE GOT THIS UNDER CONTROL.
LET'S HAVE A LOOK AROUND.
BA (BAM)

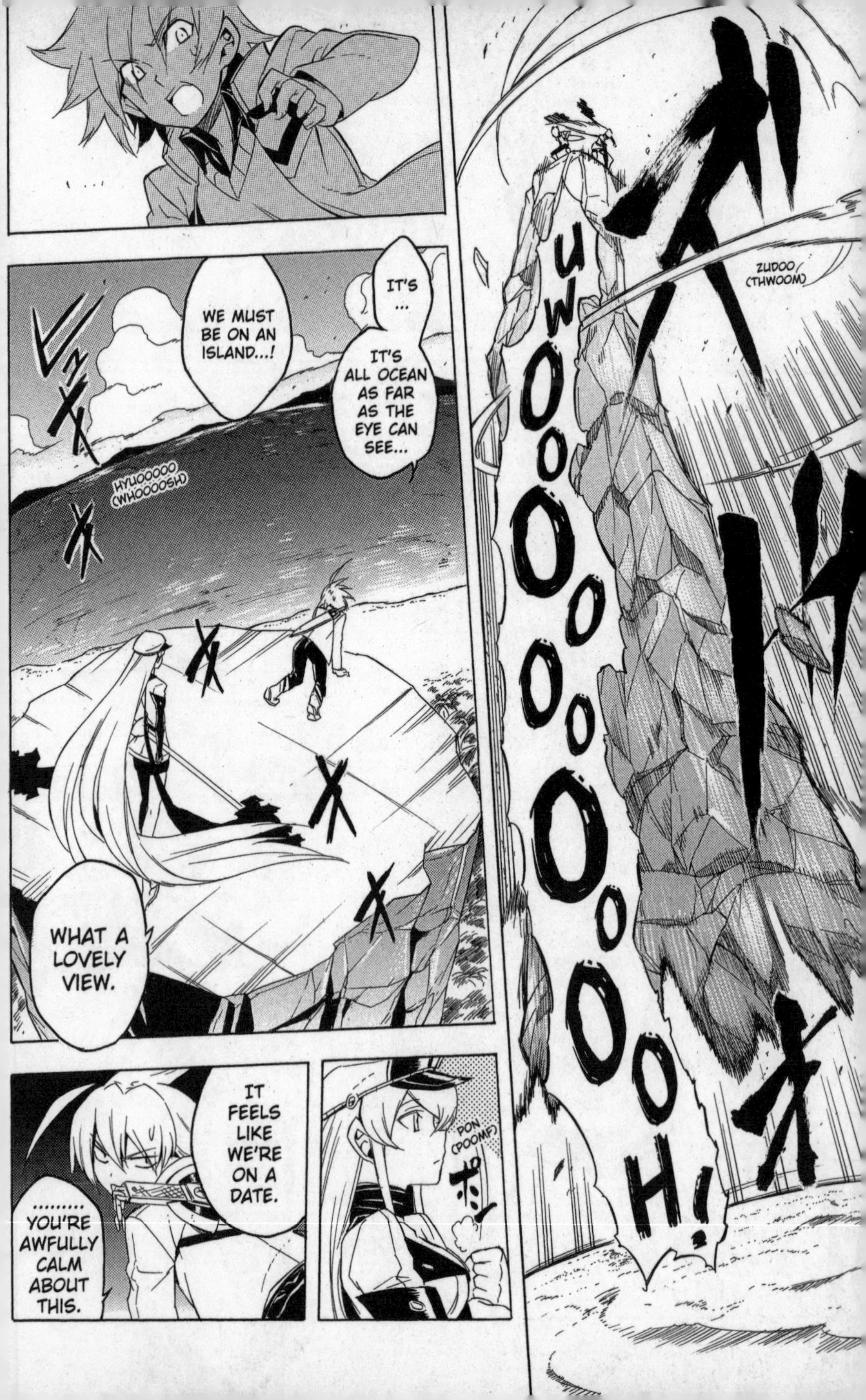

ZUDOO (THWOOM)
UWOOOOOOOOOOOOOH!
...
IT'S ...
IT'S ALL OCEAN AS FAR AS THE EYE CAN SEE...
WE MUST BE ON AN ISLAND...!
HYUOOOOO (WHOOOOSH)
WHAT A LOVELY VIEW.
PON (POOMF)
IT FEELS LIKE WE'RE ON A DATE.
.... YOU'RE AWFULLY CALM ABOUT THIS.

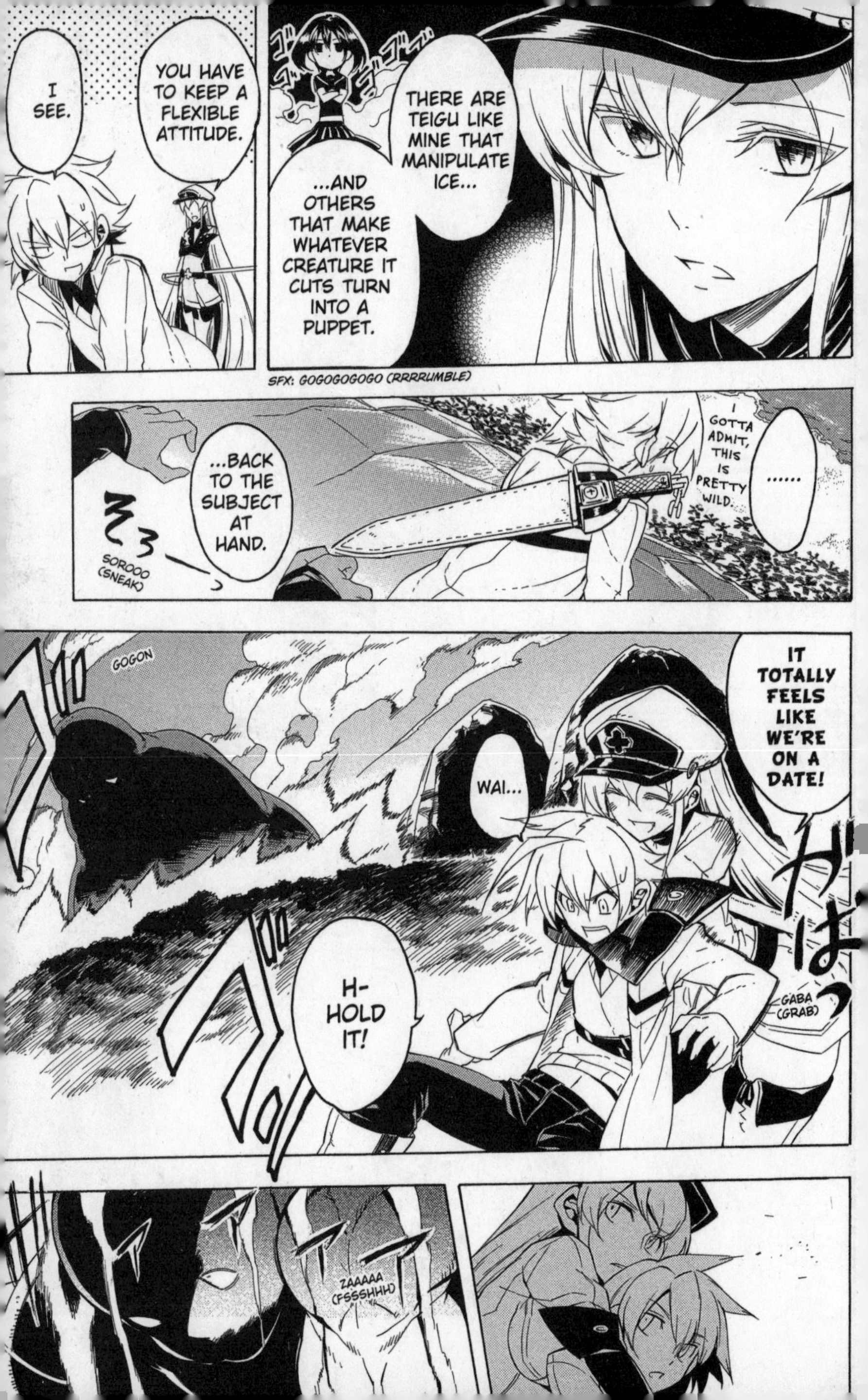
THERE ARE TEIGU LIKE MINE THAT MANIPULATE ICE...
...AND OTHERS THAT MAKE WHATEVER CREATURE IT CUTS TURN INTO A PUPPET.
YOU HAVE TO KEEP A FLEXIBLE ATTITUDE.
I SEE.
SFX: GOGOGOGOGO (RRRRUMBLE)
......
I GOTTA ADMIT, THIS IS PRETTY WILD.
...BACK TO THE SUBJECT AT HAND.
SOROOO (SNEAK)
IT TOTALLY FEELS LIKE WE'RE ON A DATE!
GABA (GRAB)
WAI...
GOGON
H-HOLD IT!
ZAAAAA (FSSSHHH)

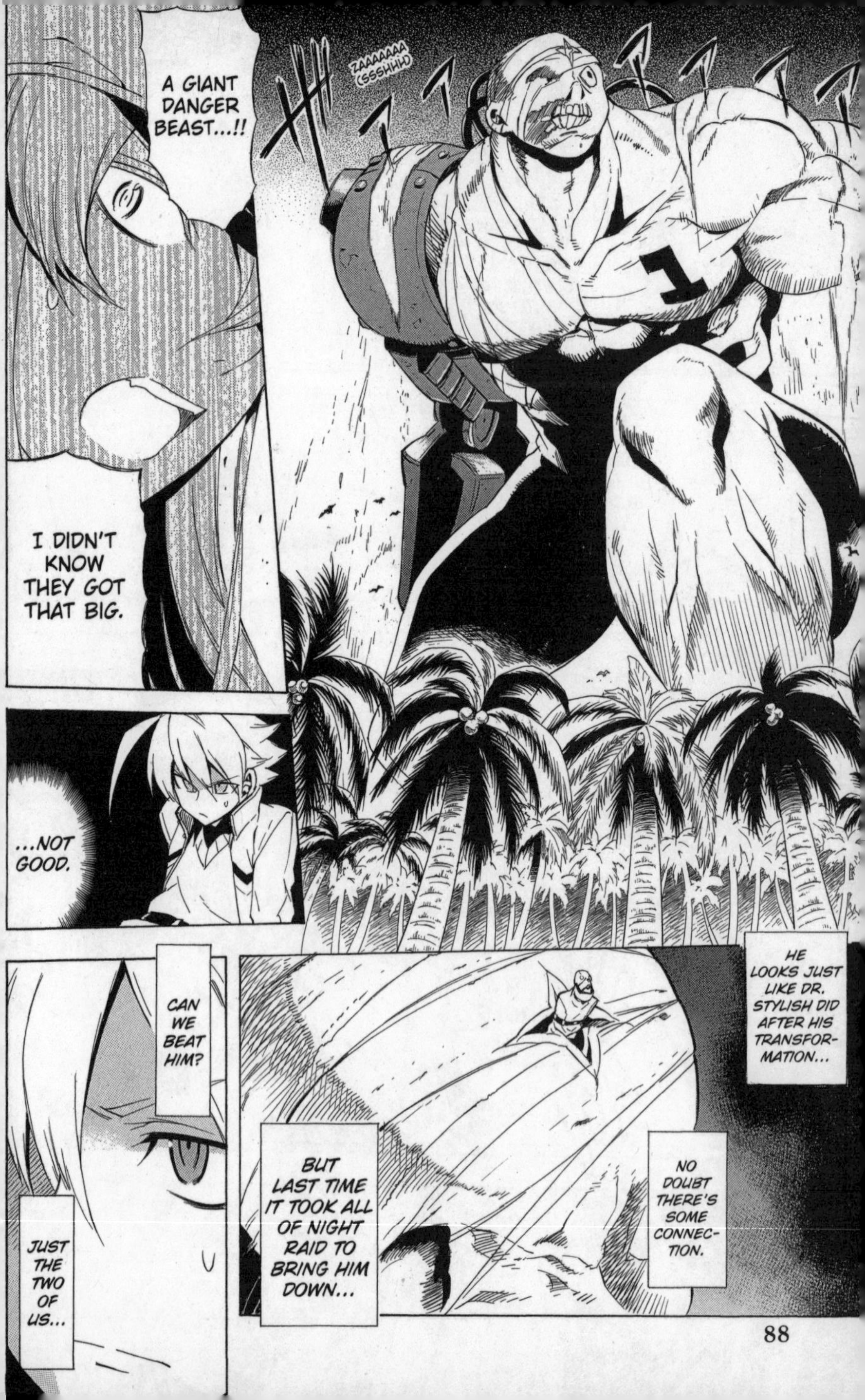
A GIANT DANGER BEAST...!!
ZAAAAAAA (SSSHHH)
I DIDN'T KNOW THEY GOT THAT BIG.
...NOT GOOD.
HE LOOKS JUST LIKE DR. STYLISH DID AFTER HIS TRANSFORMATION...
NO DOUBT THERE'S SOME CONNECTION.
BUT LAST TIME IT TOOK ALL OF NIGHT RAID TO BRING HIM DOWN...
CAN WE BEAT HIM?
JUST THE TWO OF US...

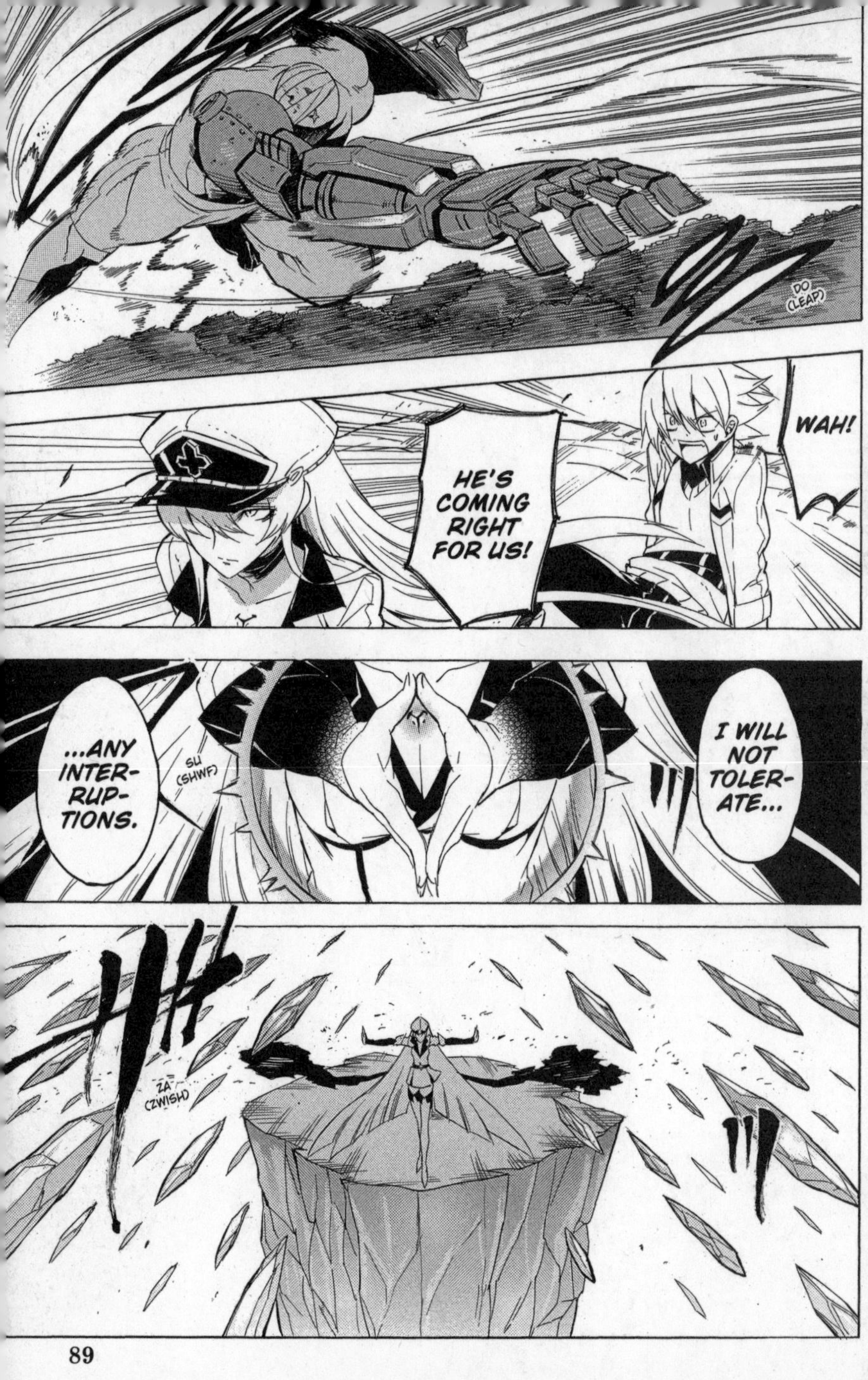
DO
(LEAP)
WAH!
HE'S COMING RIGHT FOR US!
I WILL NOT TOLER-ATE...
SU
(SHWF)
...ANY INTER-RUP-TIONS.
ZA
(ZWISH)

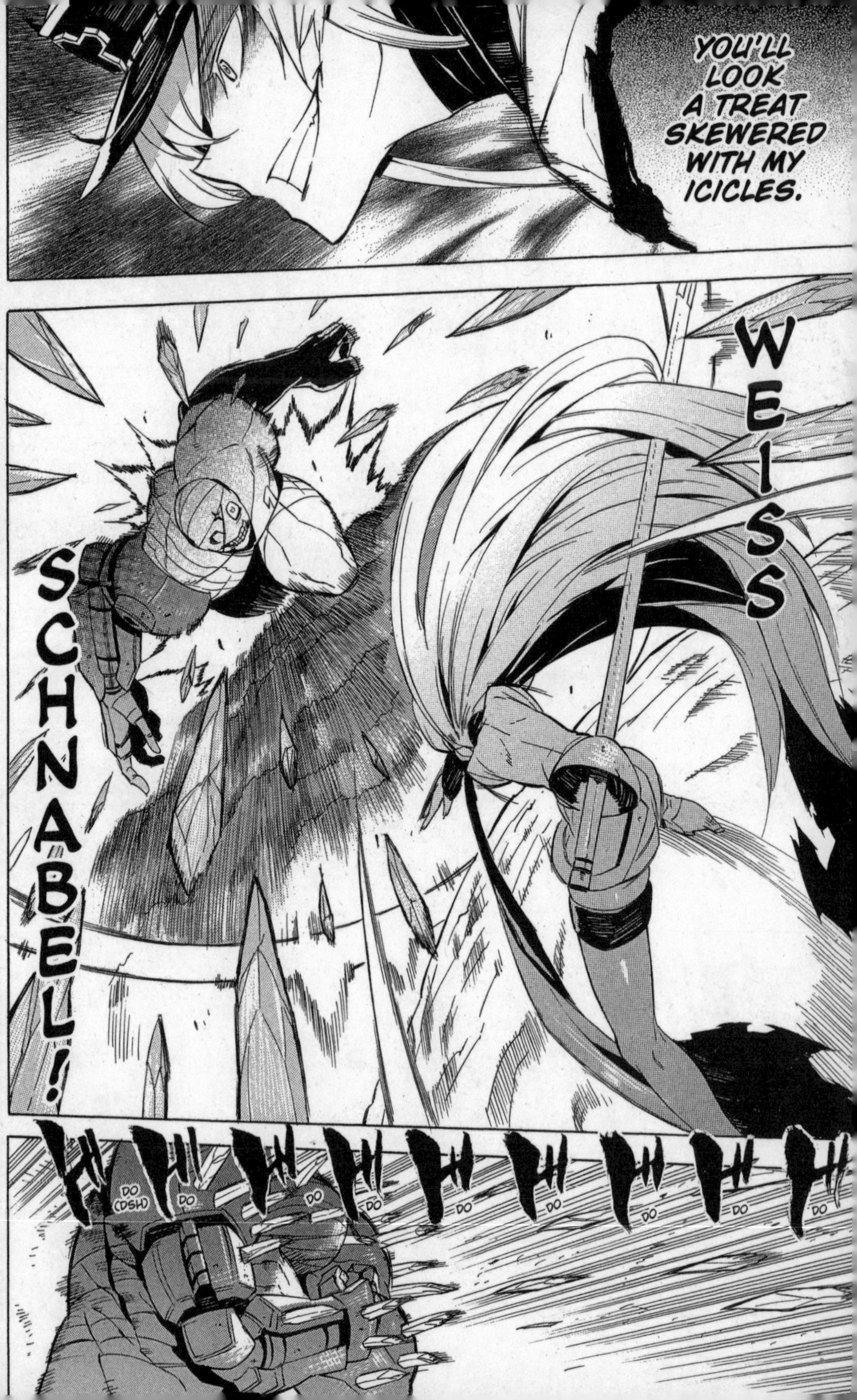
YOU'LL LOOK A TREAT SKEWERED WITH MY ICICLES.
WEISS
SCHNABEL!!
DO (DSH) DO DO DO DO DO DO DO

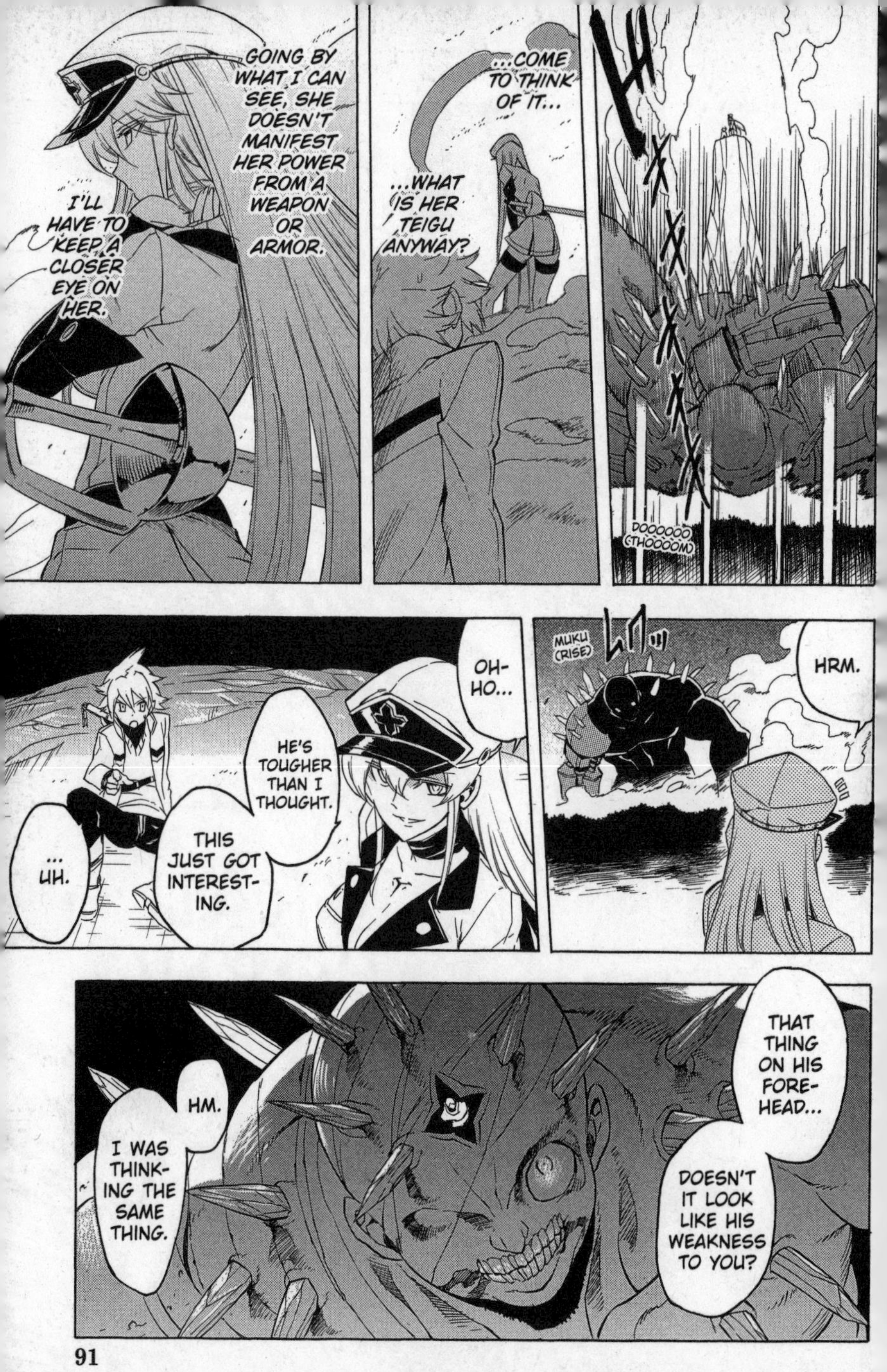
DOOOOOOO (THOOOOM)
...COME TO THINK OF IT...
...WHAT IS HER TEIGU ANYWAY?
GOING BY WHAT I CAN SEE, SHE DOESN'T MANIFEST HER POWER FROM A WEAPON OR ARMOR.
I'LL HAVE TO KEEP A CLOSER EYE ON HER.
MUKU (RISE)
HRM.
OH-HO...
HE'S TOUGHER THAN I THOUGHT.
THIS JUST GOT INTEREST-ING.
... UH.
THAT THING ON HIS FORE-HEAD...
DOESN'T IT LOOK LIKE HIS WEAKNESS TO YOU?
HM.
I WAS THINK-ING THE SAME THING.

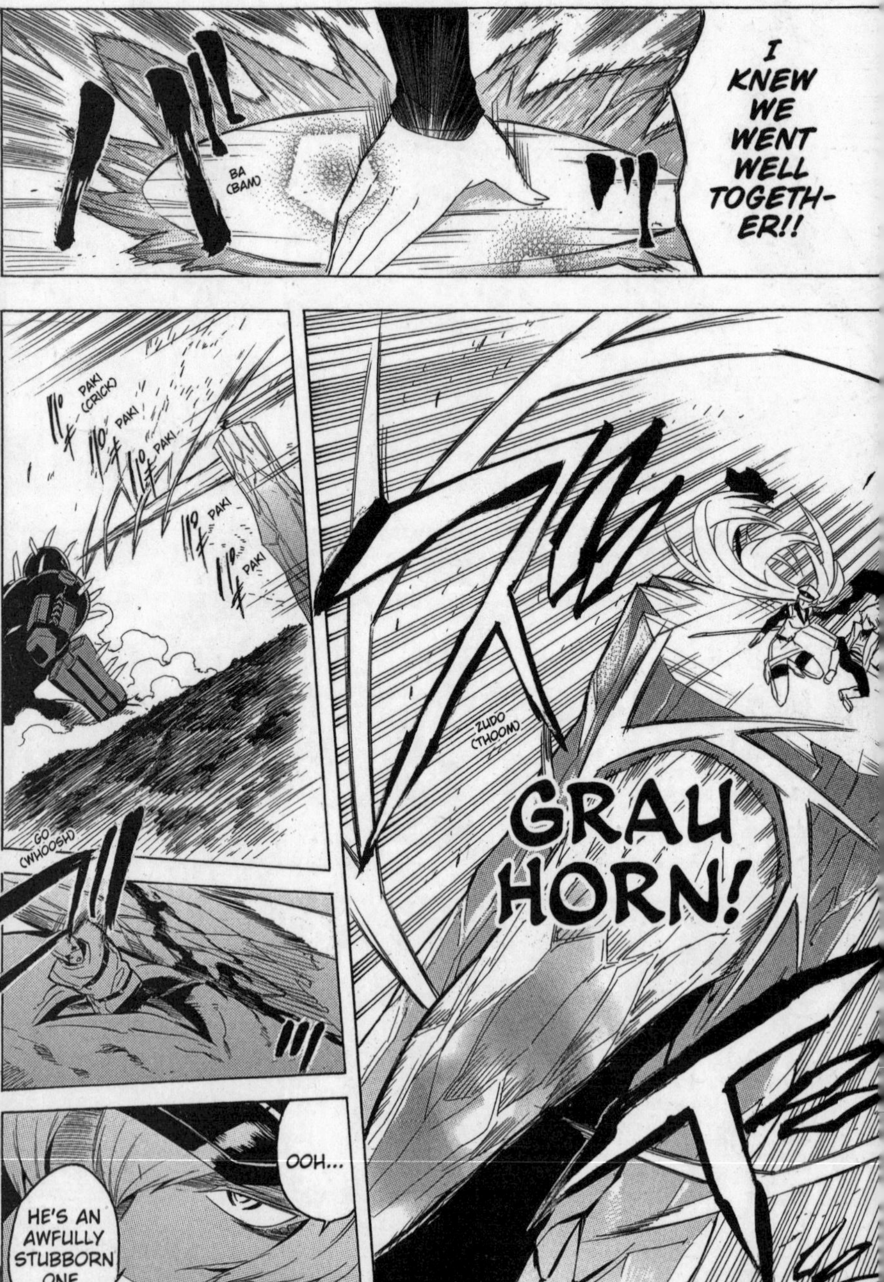

I KNEW WE WENT WELL TOGETHER!!
BA (BAM)
ZUDO (THOOM)
GRAU HORN!
PAKI (CRICK)
PAKI
PAKI
PAKI
PAKI
GO (WHOOSH)
OOH...
HE'S AN AWFULLY STUBBORN ONE.

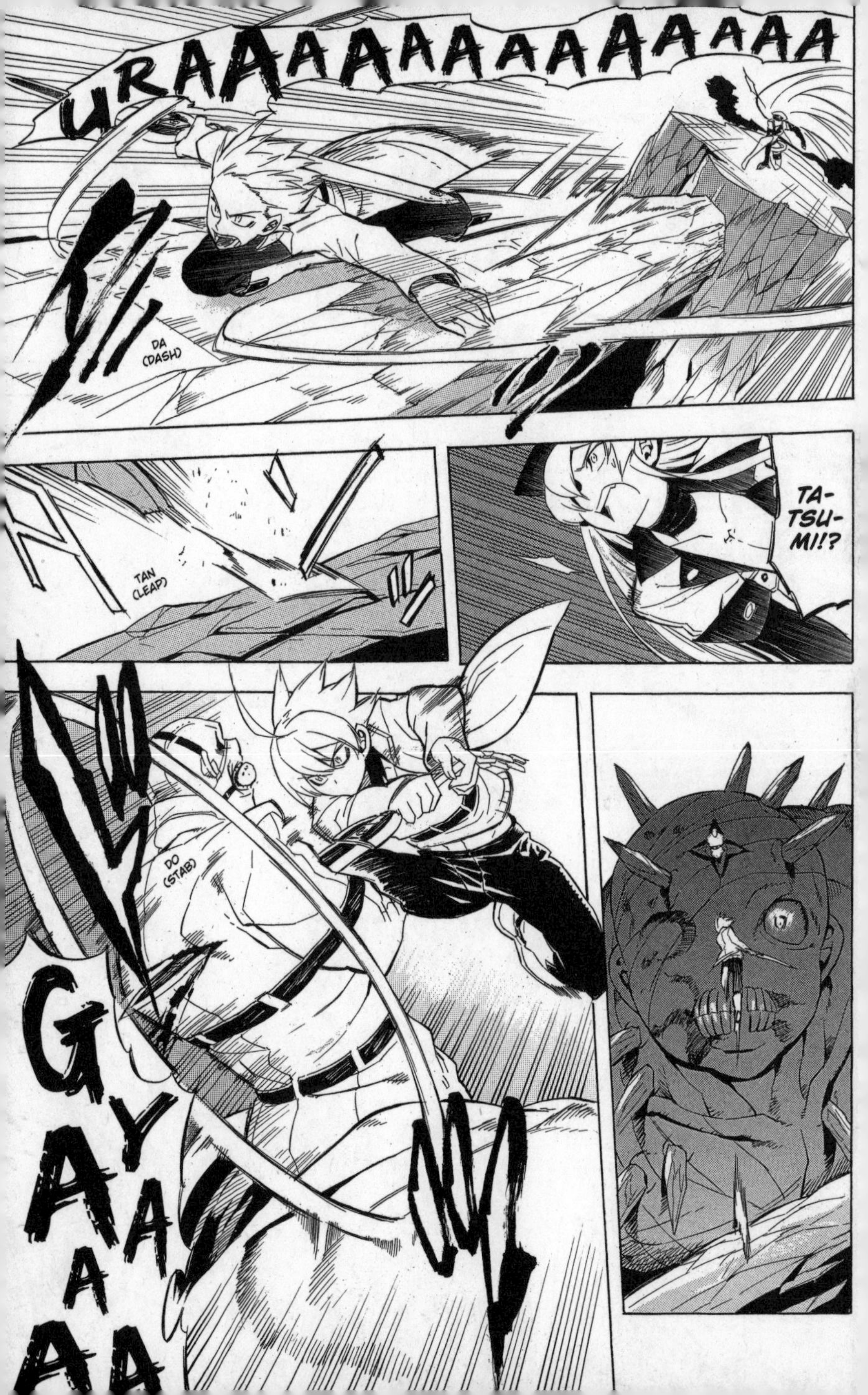
URAAAAAAAAAAAAA
DA (DASH)
TATSUMI!?
TAN (LEAP)
DO (STAB)
GYAAAAA

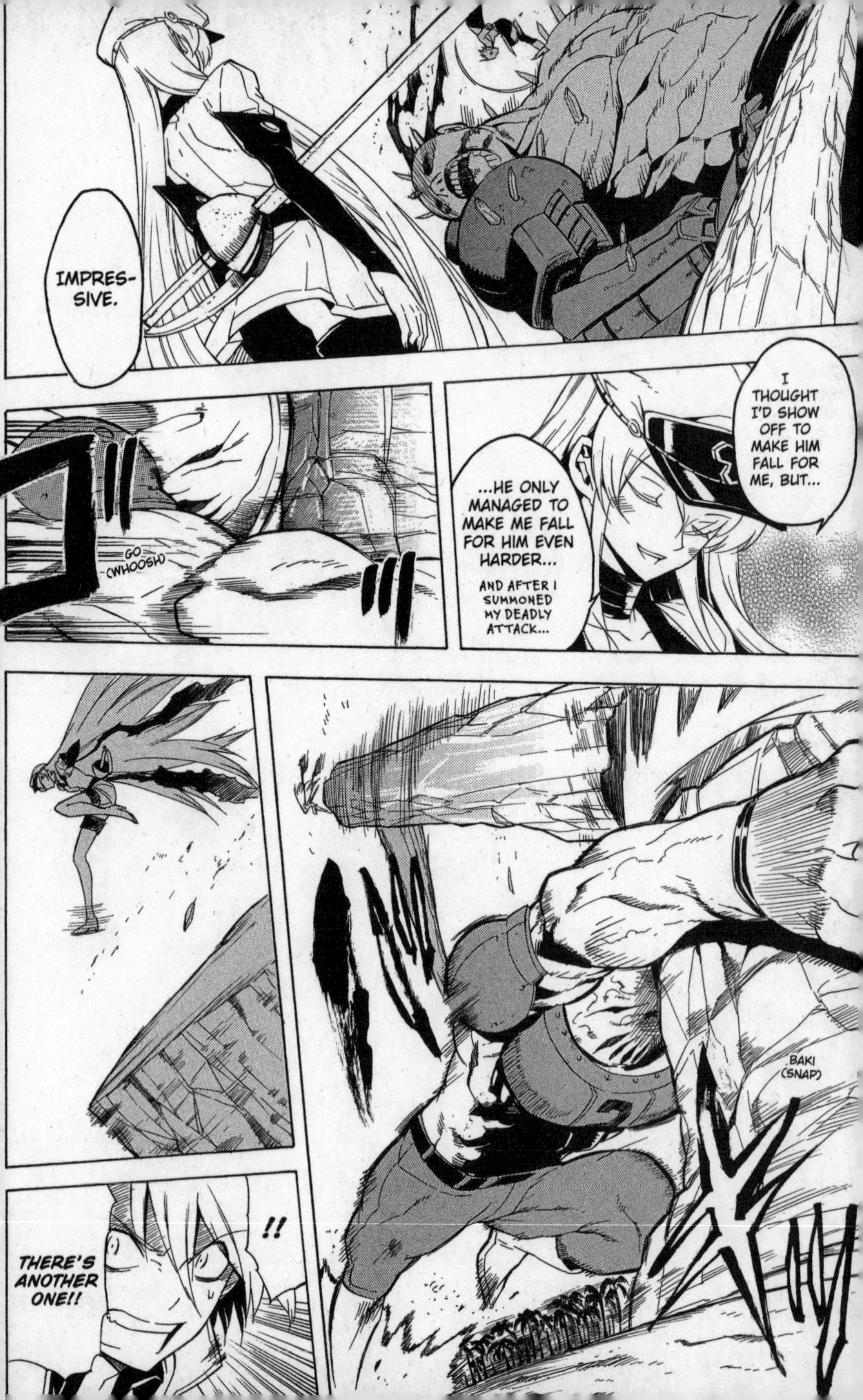
IMPRES-SIVE.
I THOUGHT I'D SHOW OFF TO MAKE HIM FALL FOR ME, BUT...
...HE ONLY MANAGED TO MAKE ME FALL FOR HIM EVEN HARDER...
AND AFTER I SUMMONED MY DEADLY ATTACK...
GO (WHOOSH)
BAKI (SNAP)
!!
THERE'S ANOTHER ONE!!

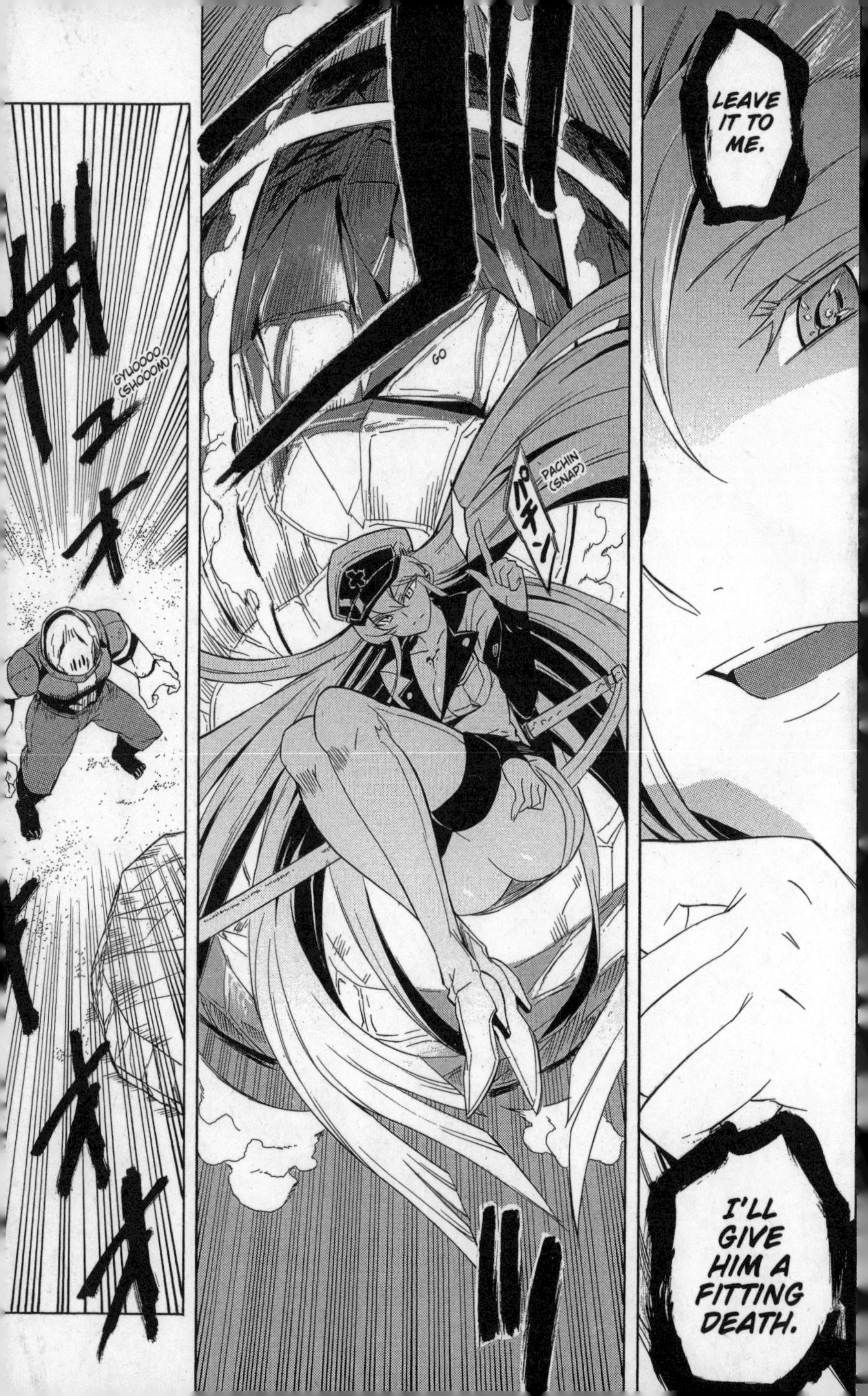
LEAVE IT TO ME.
I'LL GIVE HIM A FITTING DEATH.
PACHIN (SNAP)
GO
GYUOOOO (SHOOOM)

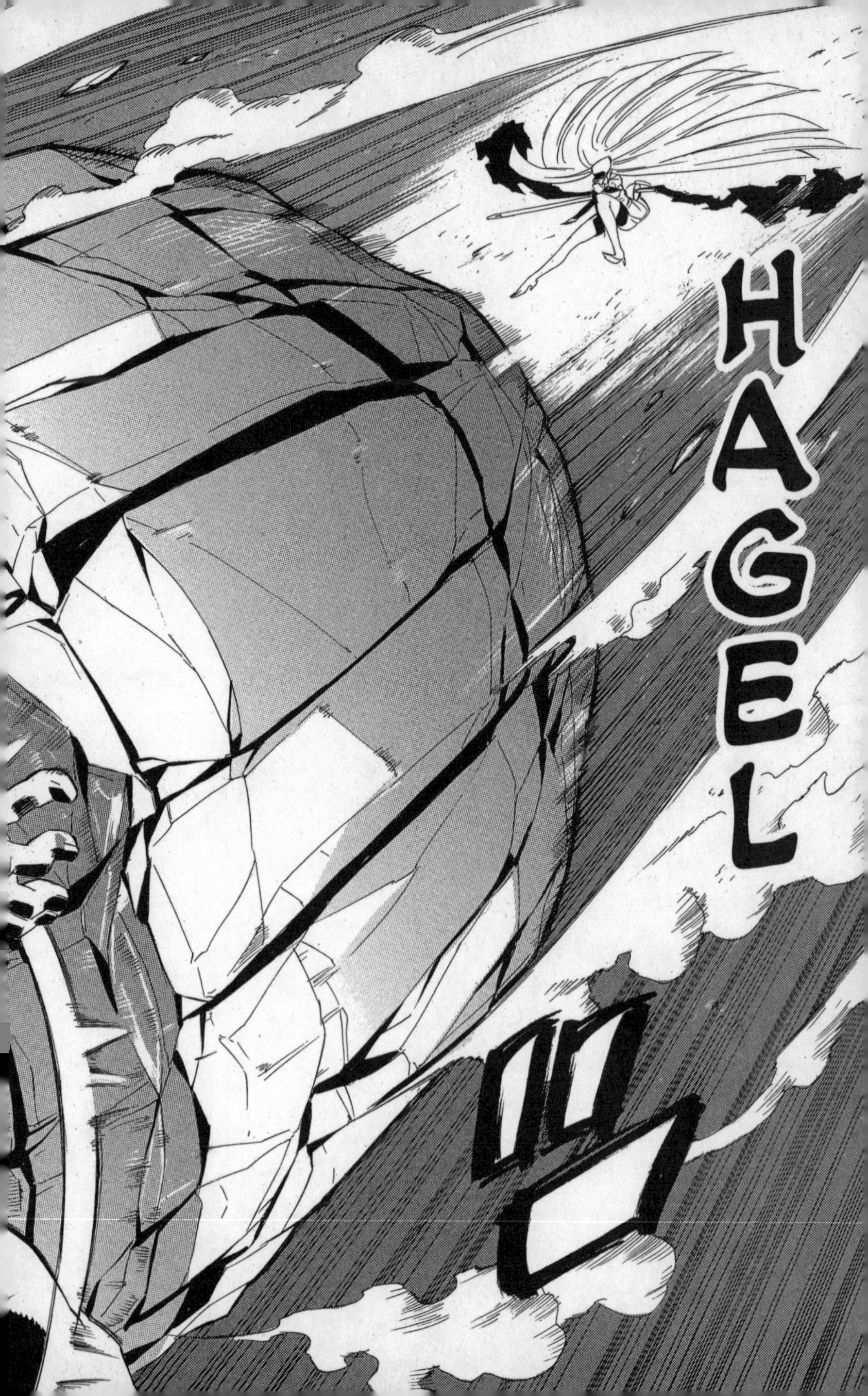
HAGEL

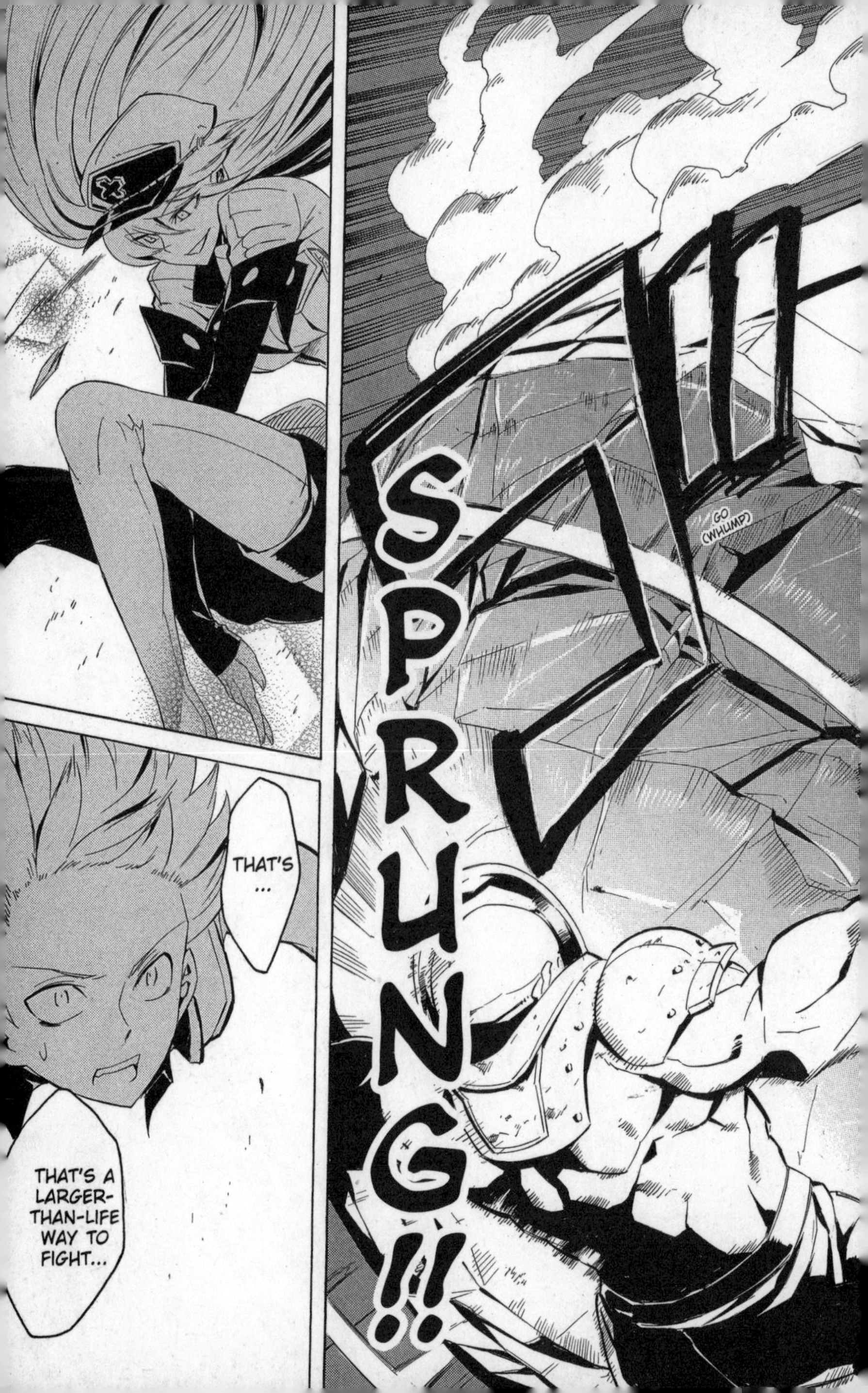
SPRUNG!!
GO (WHUMP)
THAT'S ...
THAT'S A LARGER-THAN-LIFE WAY TO FIGHT...

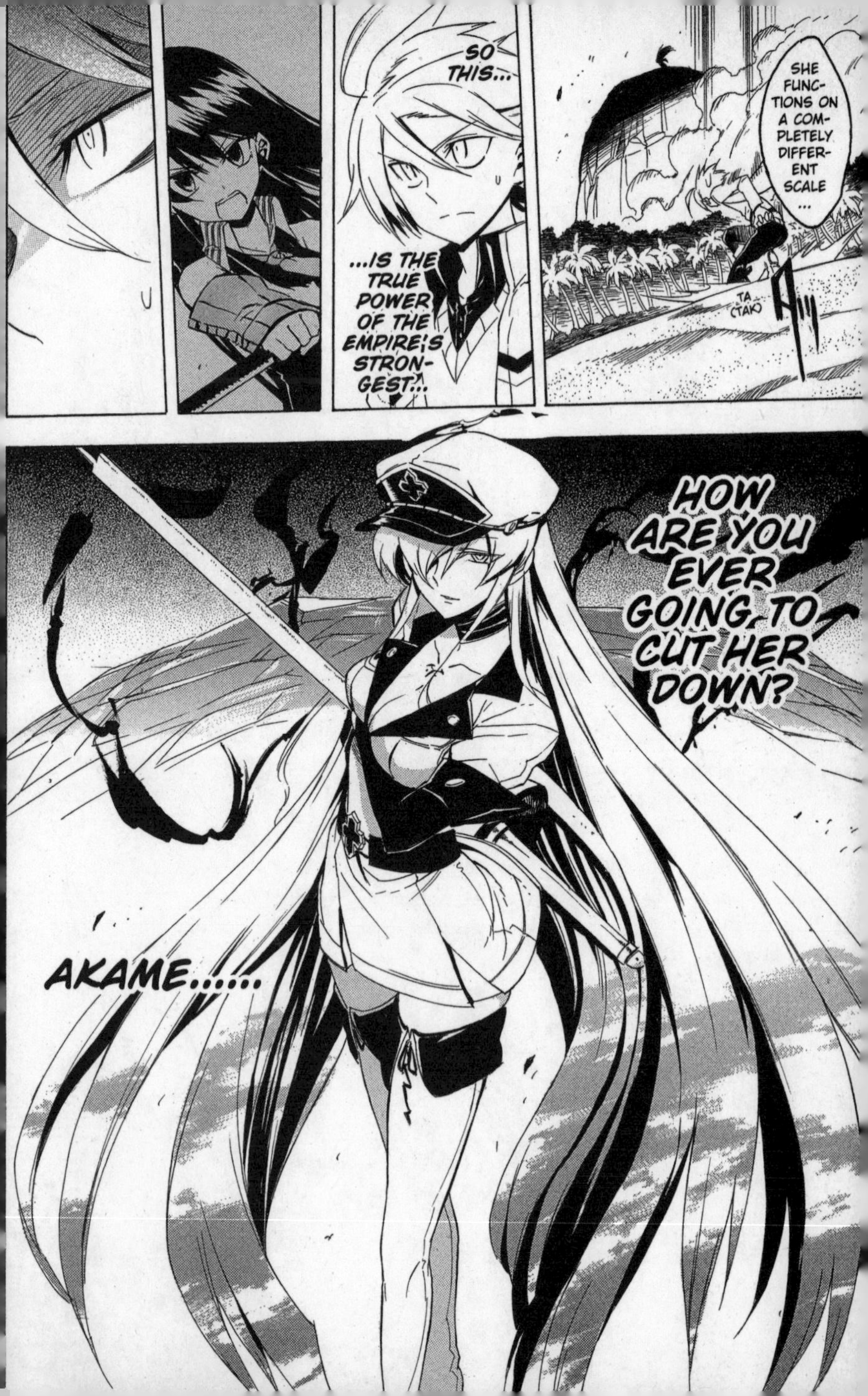
SHE FUNCTIONS ON A COMPLETELY DIFFERENT SCALE...
TA (TAK)
SO THIS...
...IS THE TRUE POWER OF THE EMPIRE'S STRONGEST...
HOW ARE YOU EVER GOING TO CUT HER DOWN?
AKAME......

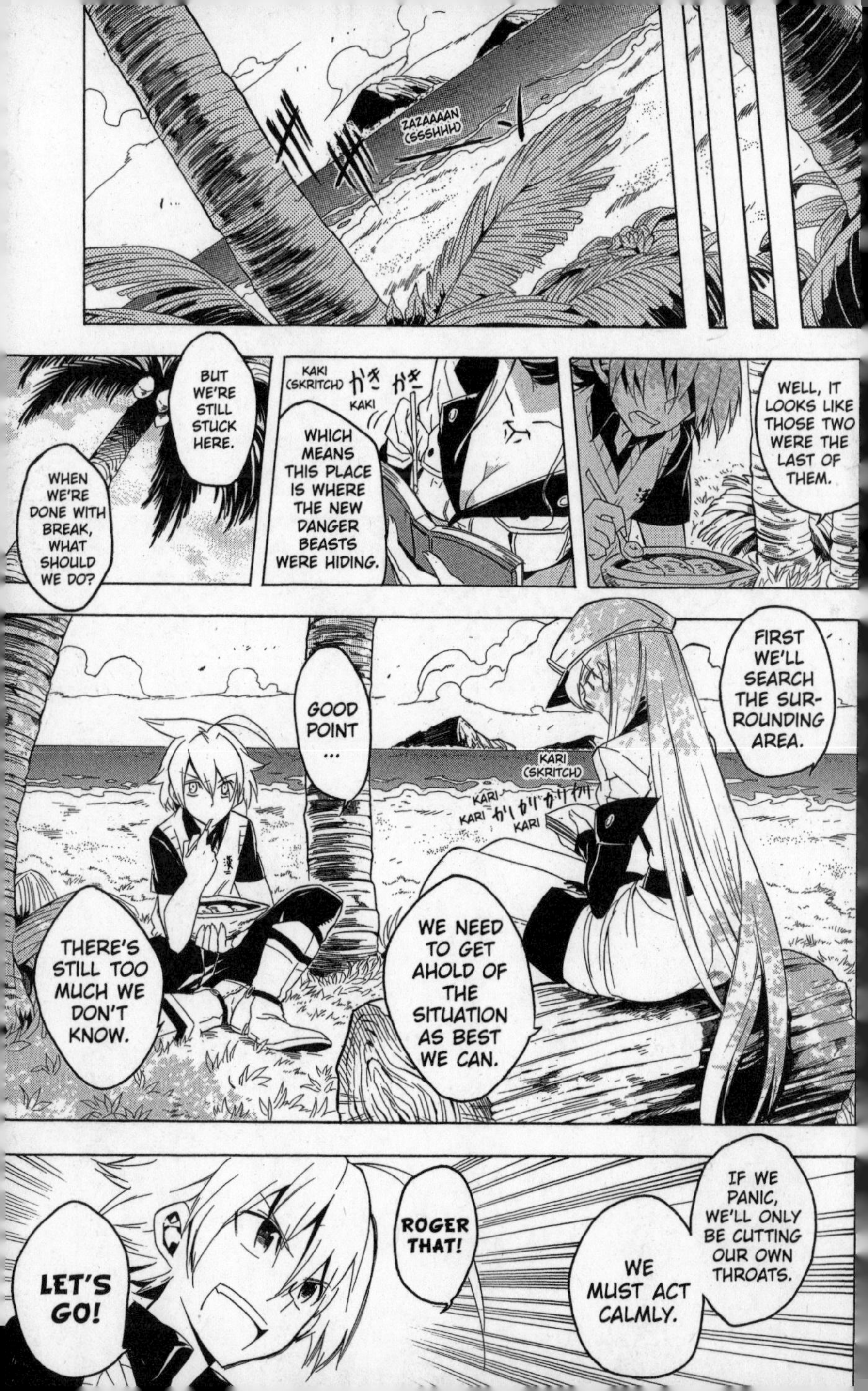
ZAZAAAAN (SSSHHH)
WELL, IT LOOKS LIKE THOSE TWO WERE THE LAST OF THEM.
KAKI (SKRITCH) がき がき KAKI
WHICH MEANS THIS PLACE IS WHERE THE NEW DANGER BEASTS WERE HIDING.
BUT WE'RE STILL STUCK HERE.
WHEN WE'RE DONE WITH BREAK, WHAT SHOULD WE DO?
FIRST WE'LL SEARCH THE SURROUNDING AREA.
KARI (SKRITCH) KARI KARI KARI
GOOD POINT...
WE NEED TO GET AHOLD OF THE SITUATION AS BEST WE CAN.
THERE'S STILL TOO MUCH WE DON'T KNOW.
IF WE PANIC, WE'LL ONLY BE CUTTING OUR OWN THROATS.
WE MUST ACT CALMLY.
ROGER THAT!
LET'S GO!

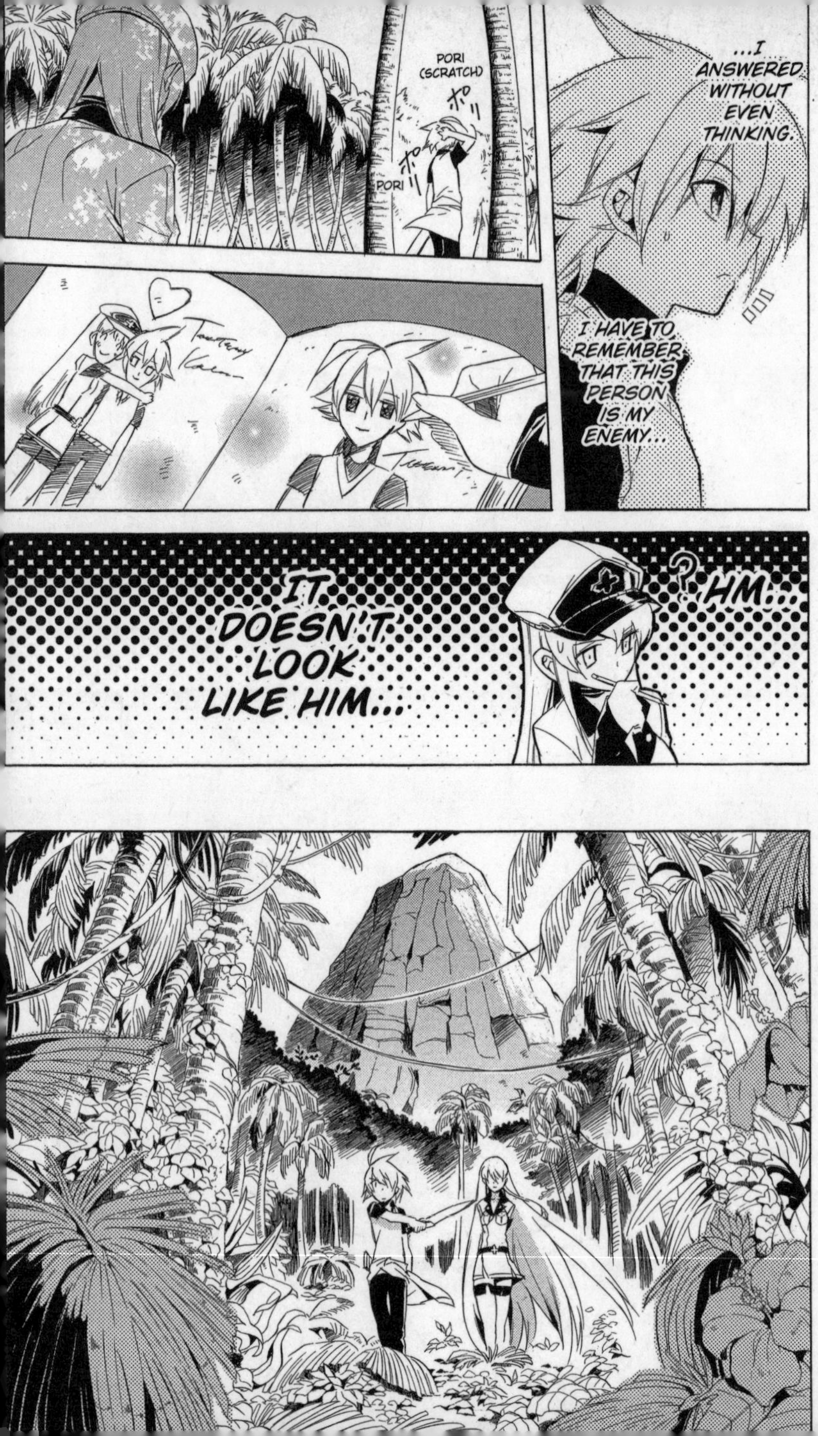
POPI (SCRATCH)
POPI
...I ANSWERED WITHOUT EVEN THINKING.
I HAVE TO REMEMBER THAT THIS PERSON IS MY ENEMY...
IT DOESN'T LOOK LIKE HIM...
HM...?

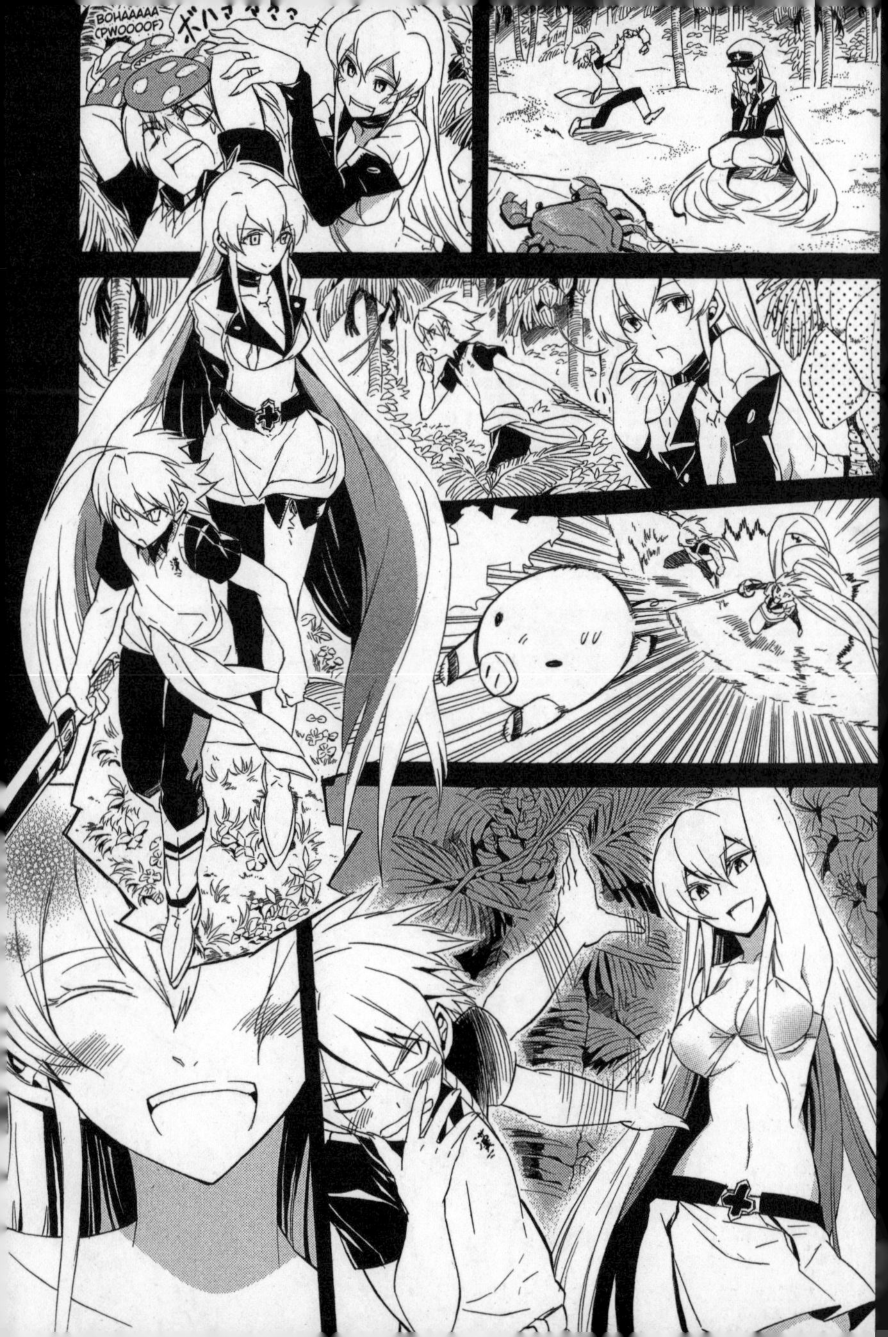
BOHAAAAA (PWOOOOF)
ボハァァァッ

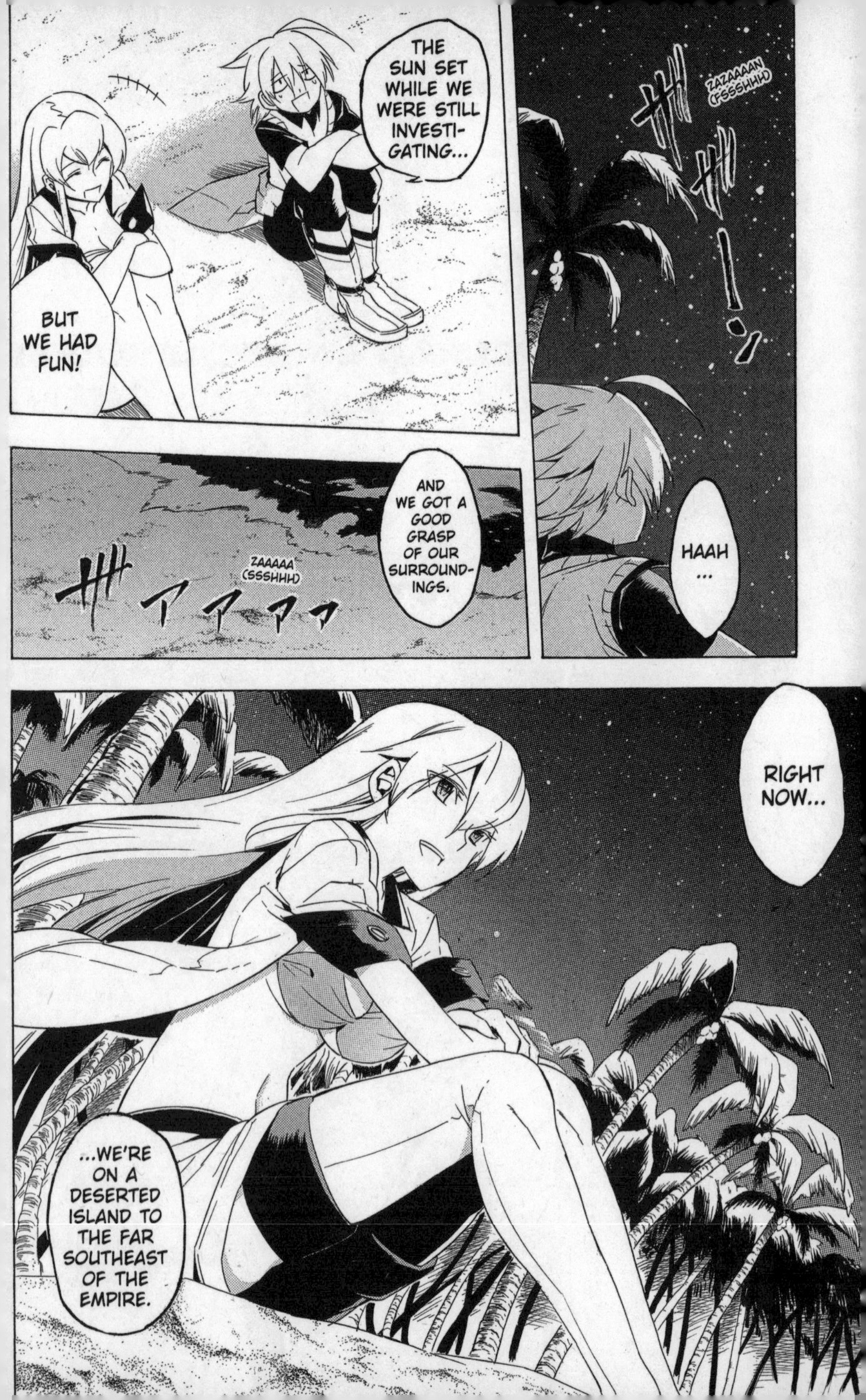
ZAZAAAAN (FSSSHHH)
HAAH...
THE SUN SET WHILE WE WERE STILL INVESTIGATING...
BUT WE HAD FUN!
AND WE GOT A GOOD GRASP OF OUR SURROUNDINGS.
ZAAAAA (SSSHHH)
RIGHT NOW...
...WE'RE ON A DESERTED ISLAND TO THE FAR SOUTHEAST OF THE EMPIRE.

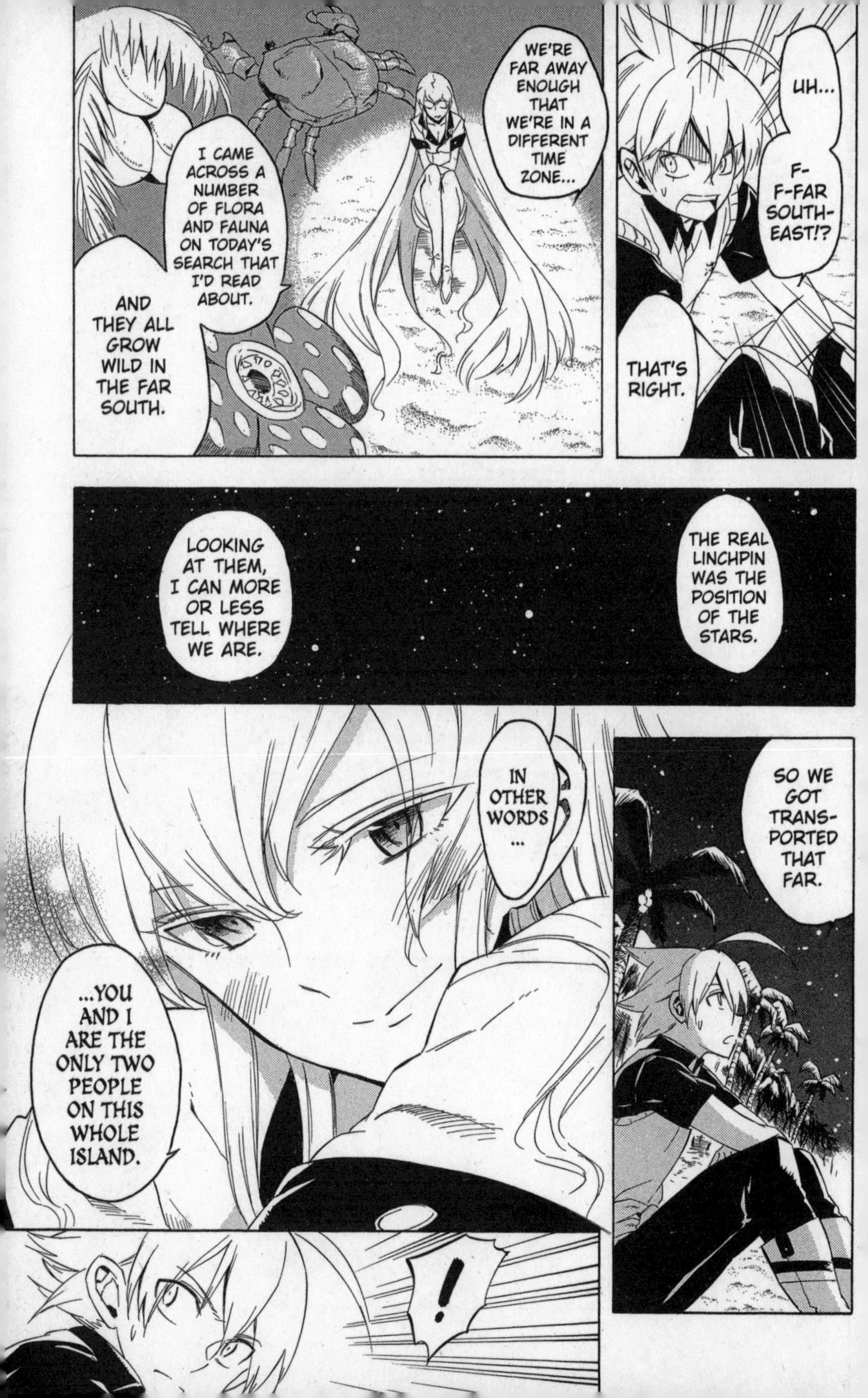
UH...
F- F-FAR SOUTH-EAST!?
THAT'S RIGHT.
WE'RE FAR AWAY ENOUGH THAT WE'RE IN A DIFFERENT TIME ZONE...
I CAME ACROSS A NUMBER OF FLORA AND FAUNA ON TODAY'S SEARCH THAT I'D READ ABOUT.
AND THEY ALL GROW WILD IN THE FAR SOUTH.
THE REAL LINCHPIN WAS THE POSITION OF THE STARS.
LOOKING AT THEM, I CAN MORE OR LESS TELL WHERE WE ARE.
SO WE GOT TRANS-PORTED THAT FAR.
IN OTHER WORDS...
...YOU AND I ARE THE ONLY TWO PEOPLE ON THIS WHOLE ISLAND.
!

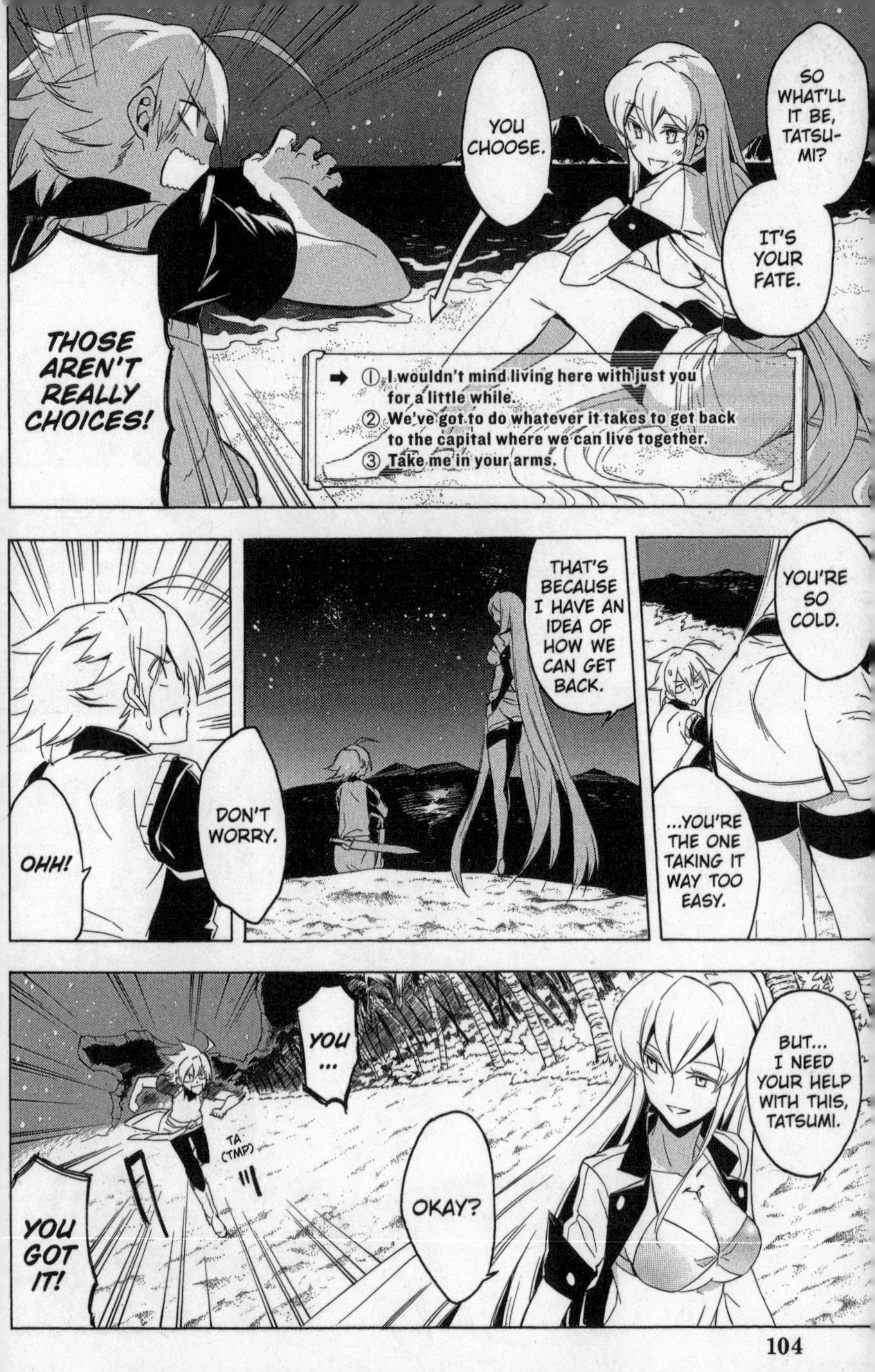
SO WHAT'LL IT BE, TATSUMI?
IT'S YOUR FATE.
YOU CHOOSE.
➡ ① I wouldn't mind living here with just you for a little while.
② We've got to do whatever it takes to get back to the capital where we can live together.
③ Take me in your arms.
THOSE AREN'T REALLY CHOICES!
YOU'RE SO COLD.
...YOU'RE THE ONE TAKING IT WAY TOO EASY.
THAT'S BECAUSE I HAVE AN IDEA OF HOW WE CAN GET BACK.
DON'T WORRY.
OHH!
BUT... I NEED YOUR HELP WITH THIS, TATSUMI.
OKAY?
YOU...
TA (TMP)
YOU GOT IT!

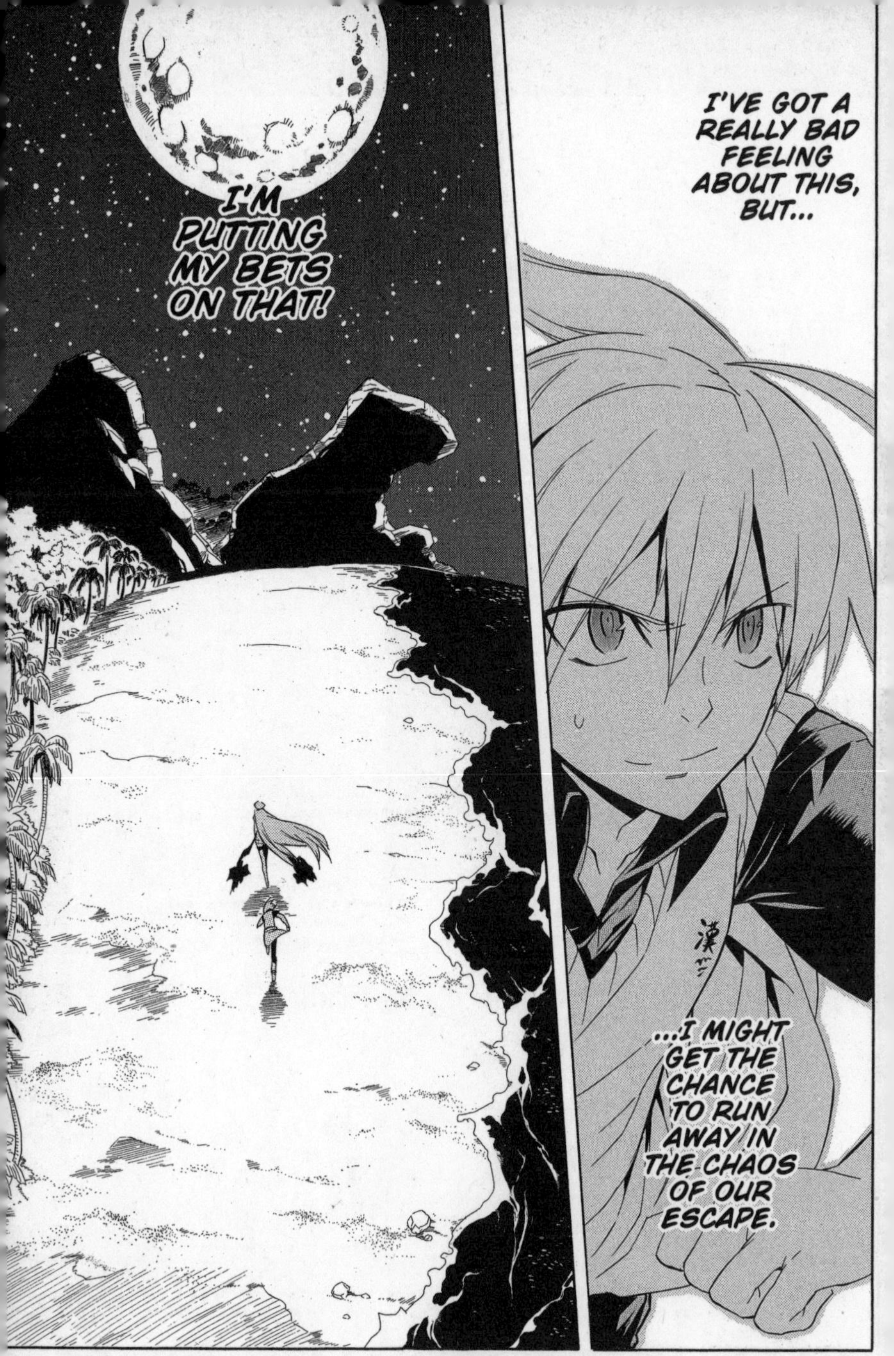
I'VE GOT A REALLY BAD FEELING ABOUT THIS, BUT...
...I MIGHT GET THE CHANCE TO RUN AWAY IN THE CHAOS OF OUR ESCAPE.
I'M PUTTING MY BETS ON THAT!

Akame ga KILL!
Rough Sketches 3

A LOOK AT THE IMPERIAL SOLDIERS' WEAPONS

The weapons used by the Imperial Army's soldiers basically appropriate the same technology used for the teigu. Teigus are based on lost technologies and made up of materials from Danger Beasts that have become extinct, so the soldiers' weapons don't come close in terms of power. Still, the weapons wielded by units like the Jaegers are far more superior and possess strong powers.

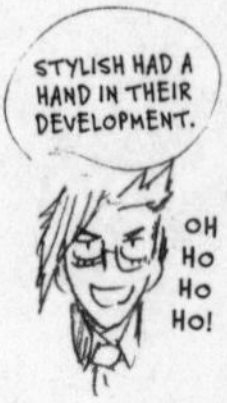

STYLISH HAD A HAND IN THEIR DEVELOPMENT.
OH HO HO HO!

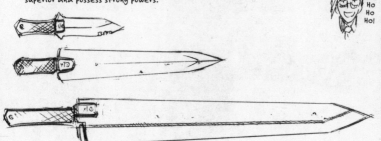

TYPES OF BLADES From top to bottom: dagger, long sword, great sword

These swords possess the ability to mind themselves so no matter how many times they strike, they stay just as sharp. The guards in Chapter 1 were using an outdated style of sword (that made use of Incursio's powers?).

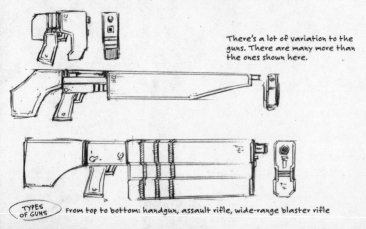

There's a lot of variation to the guns. There are many more than the ones shown here.

TYPES OF GUNS From top to bottom: handgun, assault rifle, wide-range blaster rifle

Only the wide-range blaster rifle doesn't use gunpowder but instead emits spirit energy. Unlike weapons like Pumpkin, they really only pack enough heat to aid in an escape.

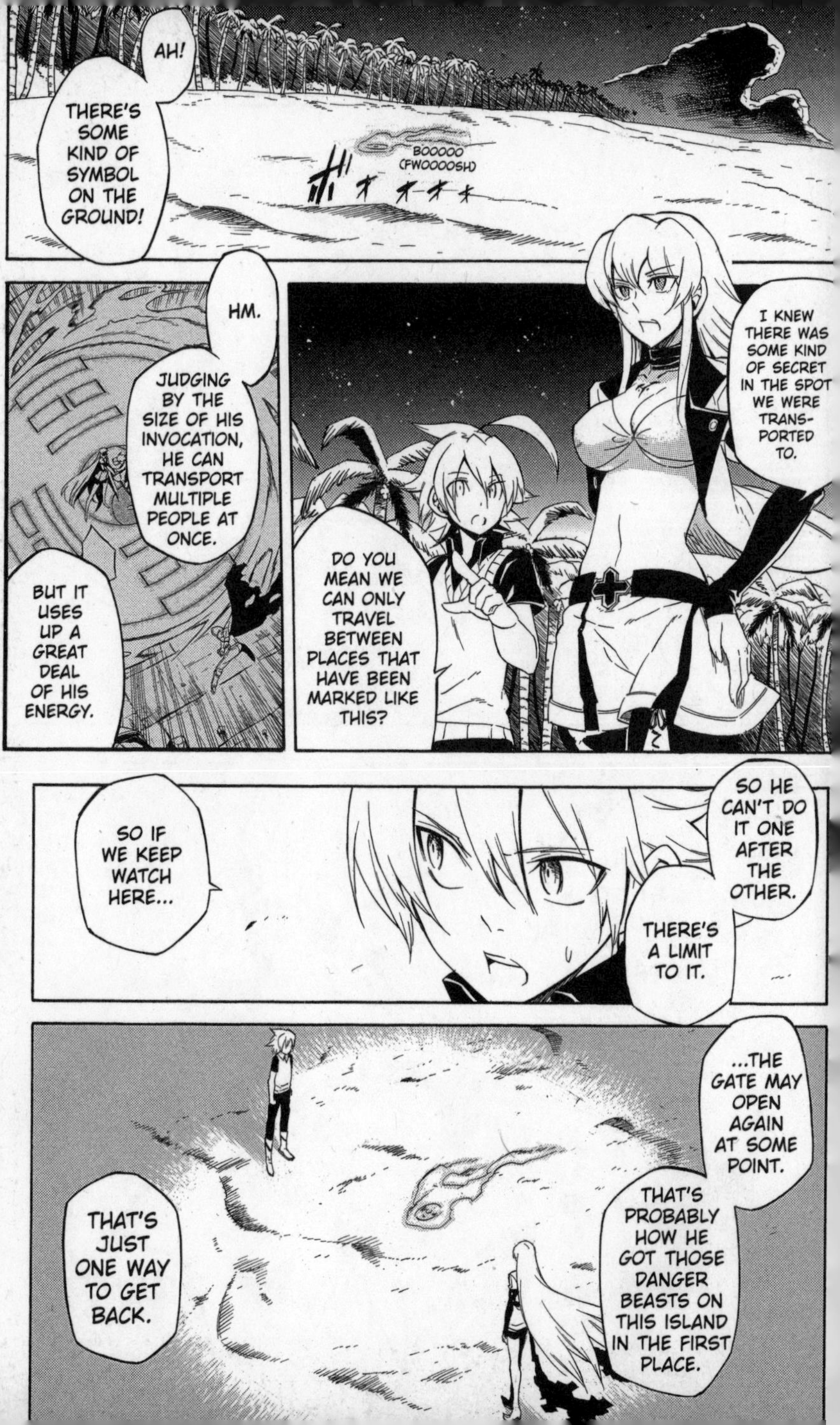
AH!
THERE'S SOME KIND OF SYMBOL ON THE GROUND!
BOOOOO (FWOOOOSH)
I KNEW THERE WAS SOME KIND OF SECRET IN THE SPOT WE WERE TRANS-PORTED TO.
DO YOU MEAN WE CAN ONLY TRAVEL BETWEEN PLACES THAT HAVE BEEN MARKED LIKE THIS?
HM.
JUDGING BY THE SIZE OF HIS INVOCATION, HE CAN TRANSPORT MULTIPLE PEOPLE AT ONCE.
BUT IT USES UP A GREAT DEAL OF HIS ENERGY.
SO HE CAN'T DO IT ONE AFTER THE OTHER.
THERE'S A LIMIT TO IT.
SO IF WE KEEP WATCH HERE...
...THE GATE MAY OPEN AGAIN AT SOME POINT.
THAT'S PROBABLY HOW HE GOT THOSE DANGER BEASTS ON THIS ISLAND IN THE FIRST PLACE.
THAT'S JUST ONE WAY TO GET BACK.

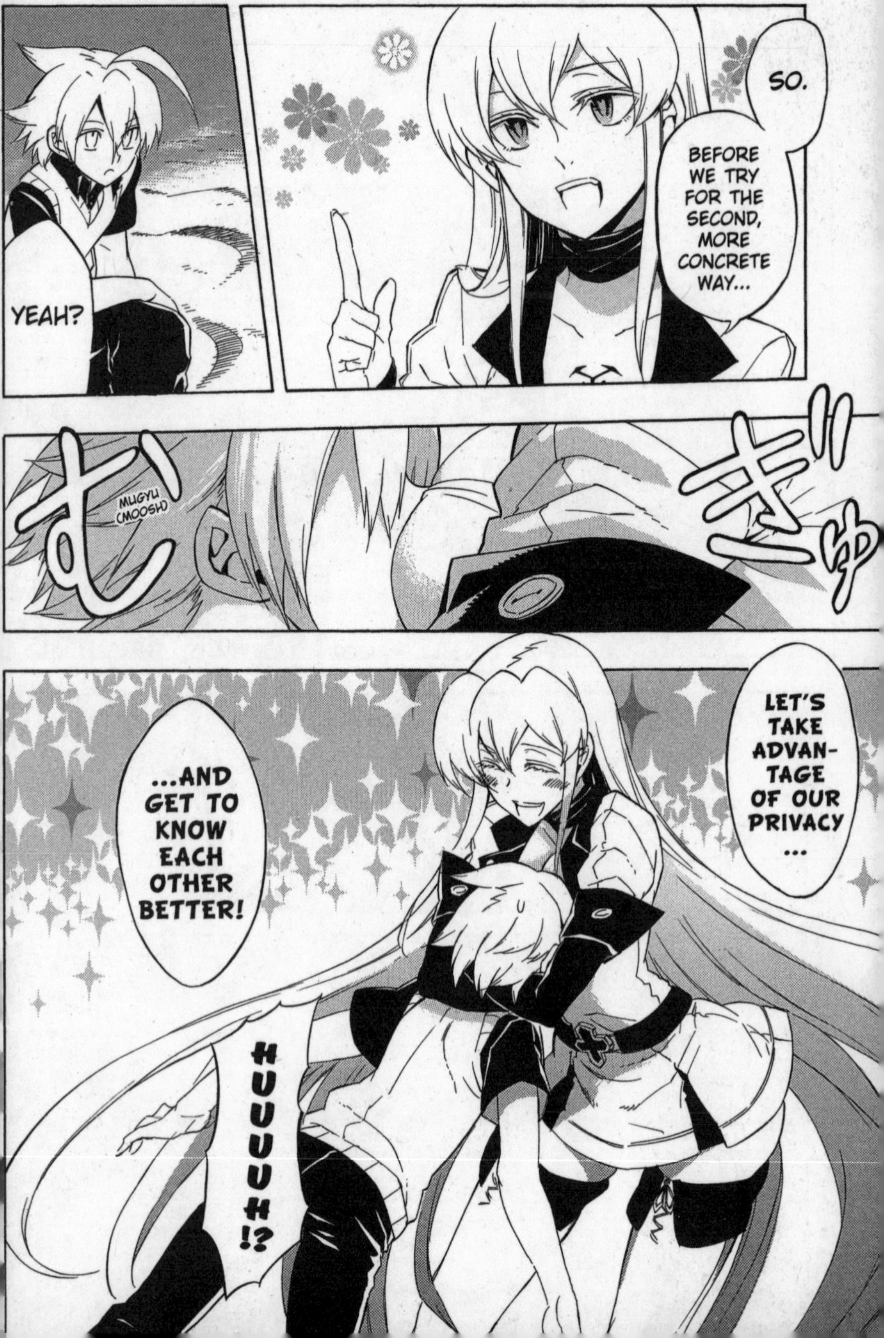
SO.
BEFORE WE TRY FOR THE SECOND, MORE CONCRETE WAY...
YEAH?
ぎゅ
む
MUGYU (MOOSH)
LET'S TAKE ADVAN-TAGE OF OUR PRIVACY...
...AND GET TO KNOW EACH OTHER BETTER!
HUUUUUH!?

CHAPTER 27 KILL THE STRONG ONE

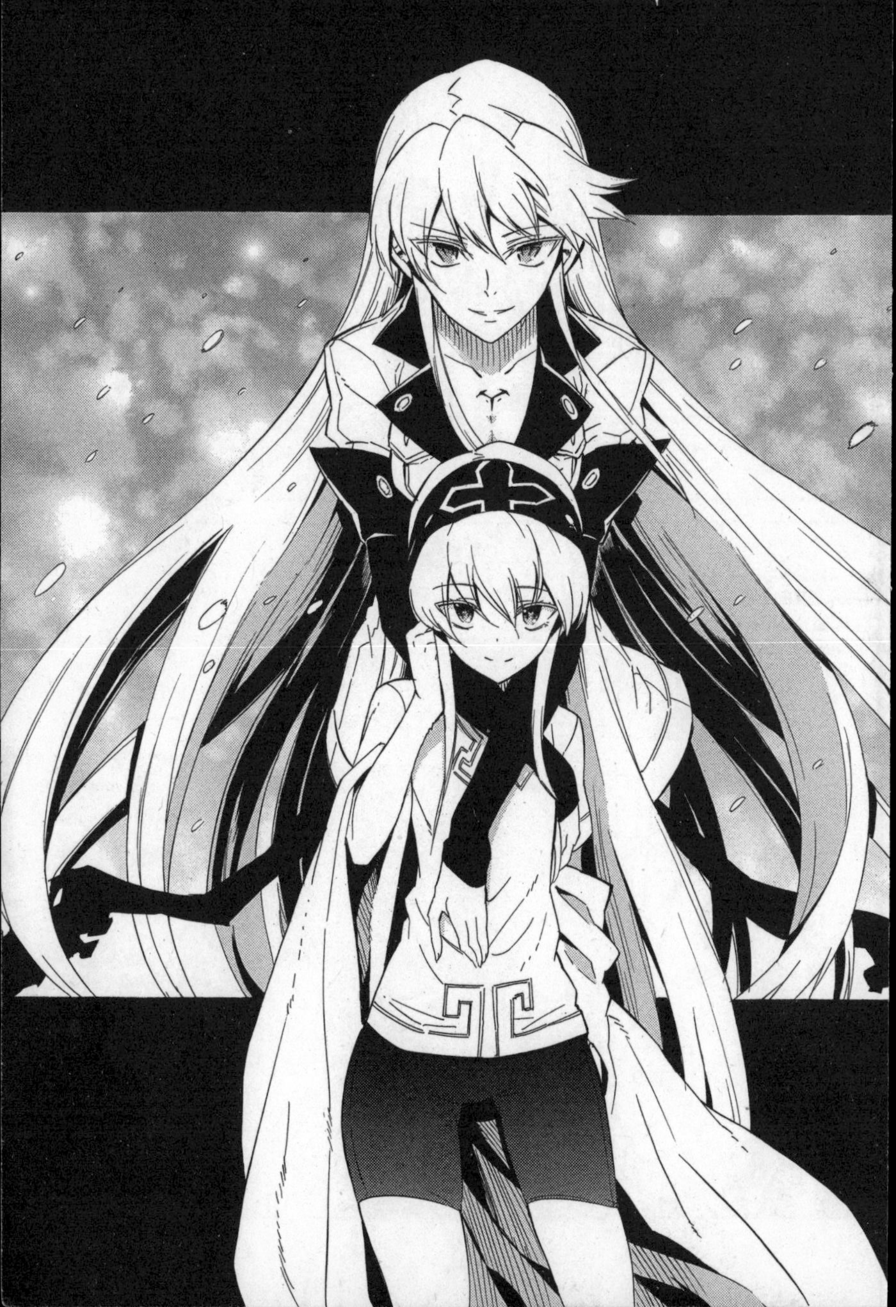

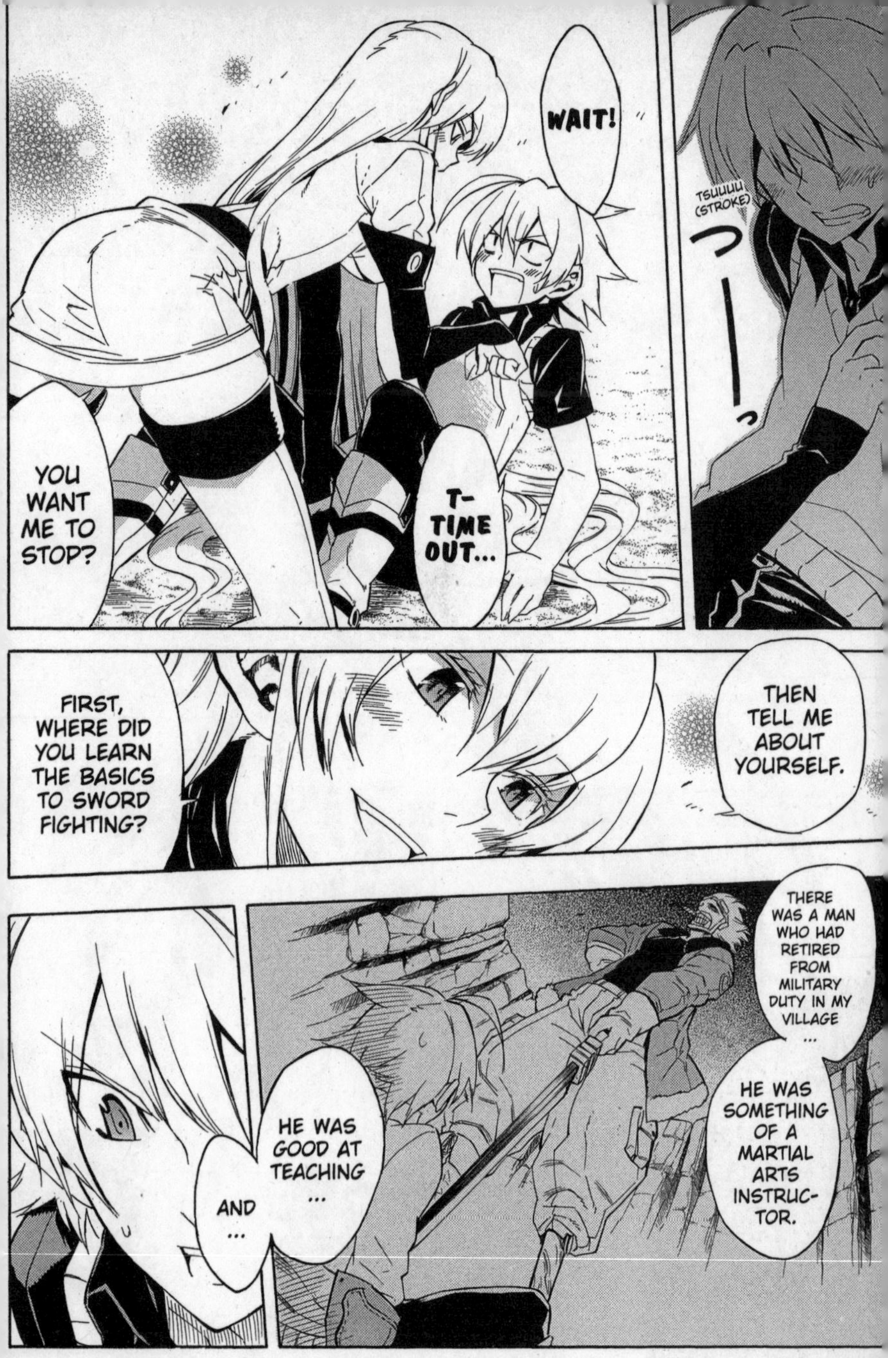
TSUUUU (STROKE)
WAIT!
T-TIME OUT...
YOU WANT ME TO STOP?
THEN TELL ME ABOUT YOURSELF.
FIRST, WHERE DID YOU LEARN THE BASICS TO SWORD FIGHTING?
THERE WAS A MAN WHO HAD RETIRED FROM MILITARY DUTY IN MY VILLAGE ...
HE WAS SOMETHING OF A MARTIAL ARTS INSTRUCTOR.
HE WAS GOOD AT TEACHING ...
AND ...

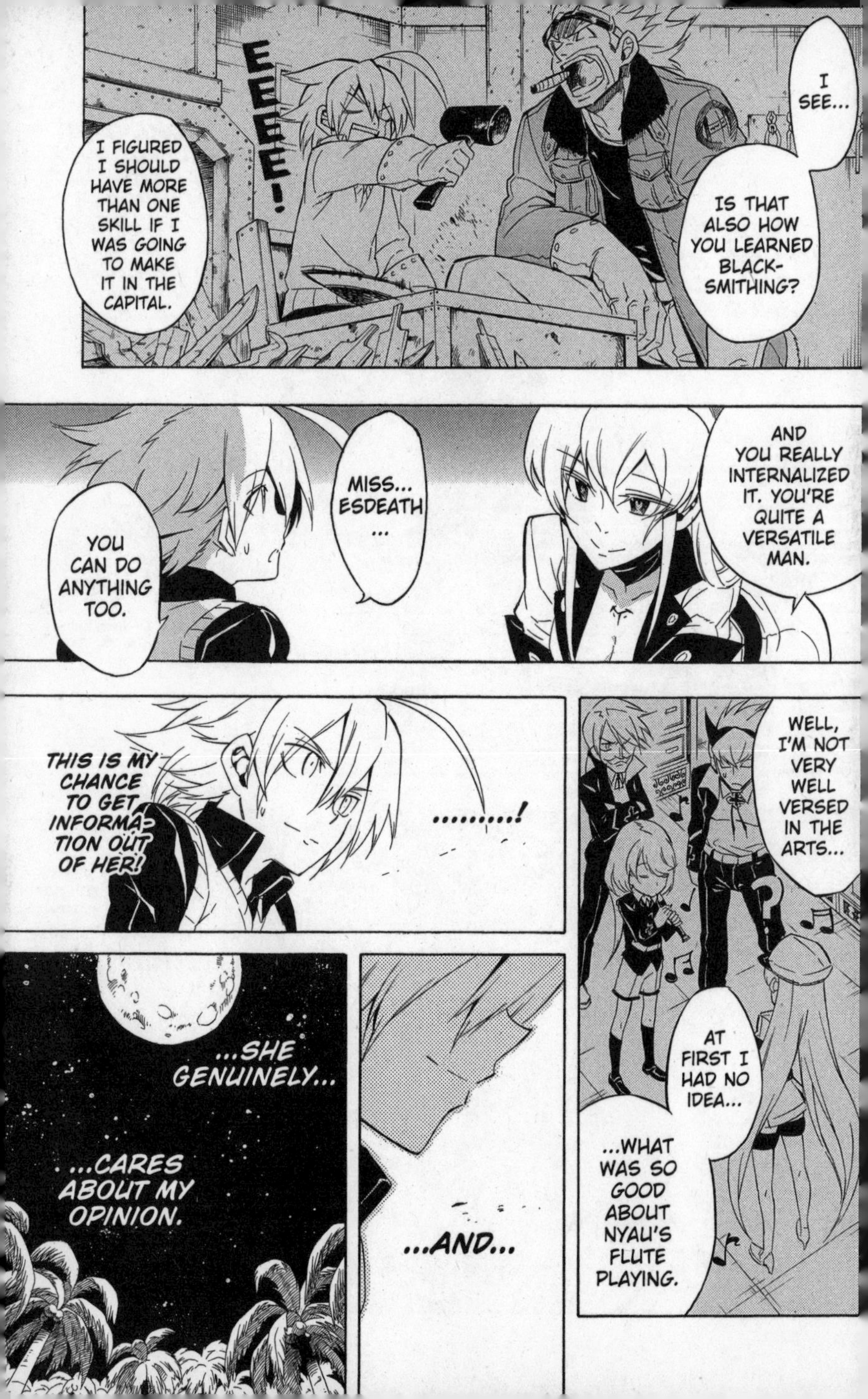
I SEE...
IS THAT ALSO HOW YOU LEARNED BLACK-SMITHING?
EEEE!
I FIGURED I SHOULD HAVE MORE THAN ONE SKILL IF I WAS GOING TO MAKE IT IN THE CAPITAL.
AND YOU REALLY INTERNALIZED IT. YOU'RE QUITE A VERSATILE MAN.
MISS... ESDEATH...
YOU CAN DO ANYTHING TOO.
WELL, I'M NOT VERY WELL VERSED IN THE ARTS...
AT FIRST I HAD NO IDEA...
...WHAT WAS SO GOOD ABOUT NYAU'S FLUTE PLAYING.
.........!
THIS IS MY CHANCE TO GET INFORMATION OUT OF HER!
...AND...
...SHE GENUINELY...
...CARES ABOUT MY OPINION.

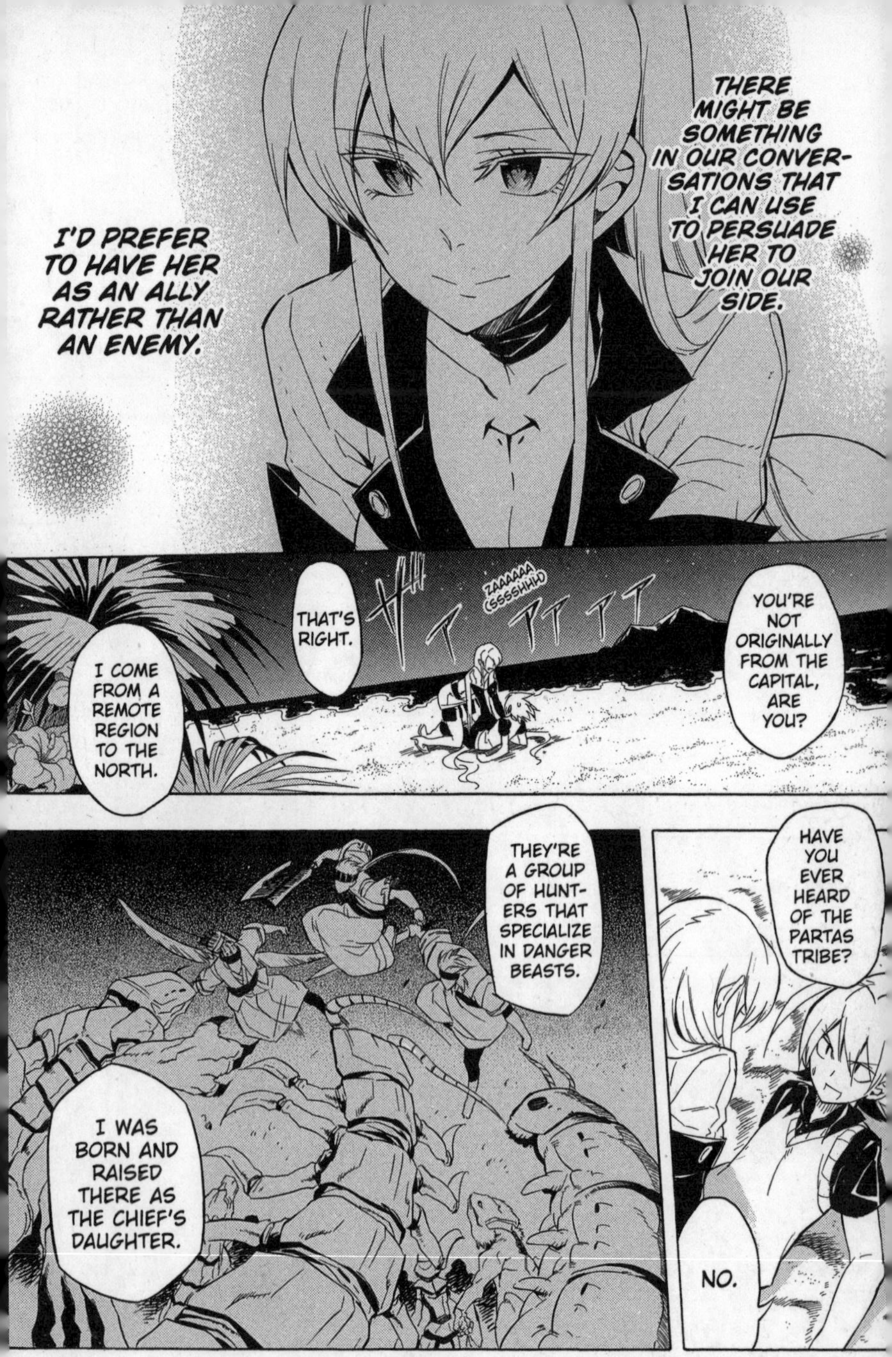
THERE MIGHT BE SOMETHING IN OUR CONVER-SATIONS THAT I CAN USE TO PERSUADE HER TO JOIN OUR SIDE.
I'D PREFER TO HAVE HER AS AN ALLY RATHER THAN AN ENEMY.
YOU'RE NOT ORIGINALLY FROM THE CAPITAL, ARE YOU?
ZAAAAAA (SSSSHHH)
THAT'S RIGHT.
I COME FROM A REMOTE REGION TO THE NORTH.
HAVE YOU EVER HEARD OF THE PARTAS TRIBE?
NO.
THEY'RE A GROUP OF HUNT-ERS THAT SPECIALIZE IN DANGER BEASTS.
I WAS BORN AND RAISED THERE AS THE CHIEF'S DAUGHTER.

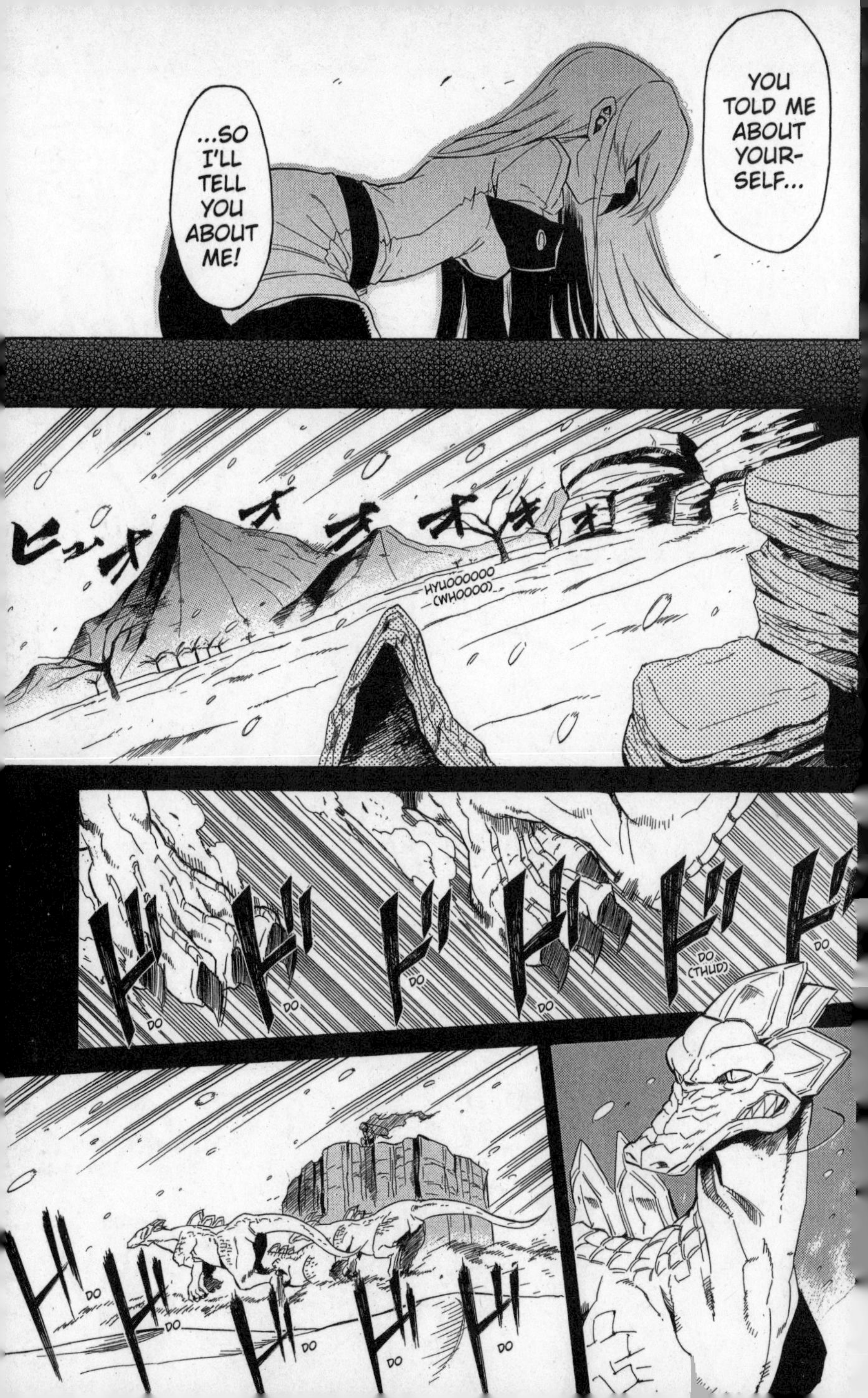
YOU TOLD ME ABOUT YOUR-SELF...
...SO I'LL TELL YOU ABOUT ME!
ヒュオオオオォォ
HYUOOOOOO (WHOOOO)
ドドドドドドド
DO (THUD)
DO
DO
DO
DO
DO
ドドドドドド
DO
DO
DO
DO
DO

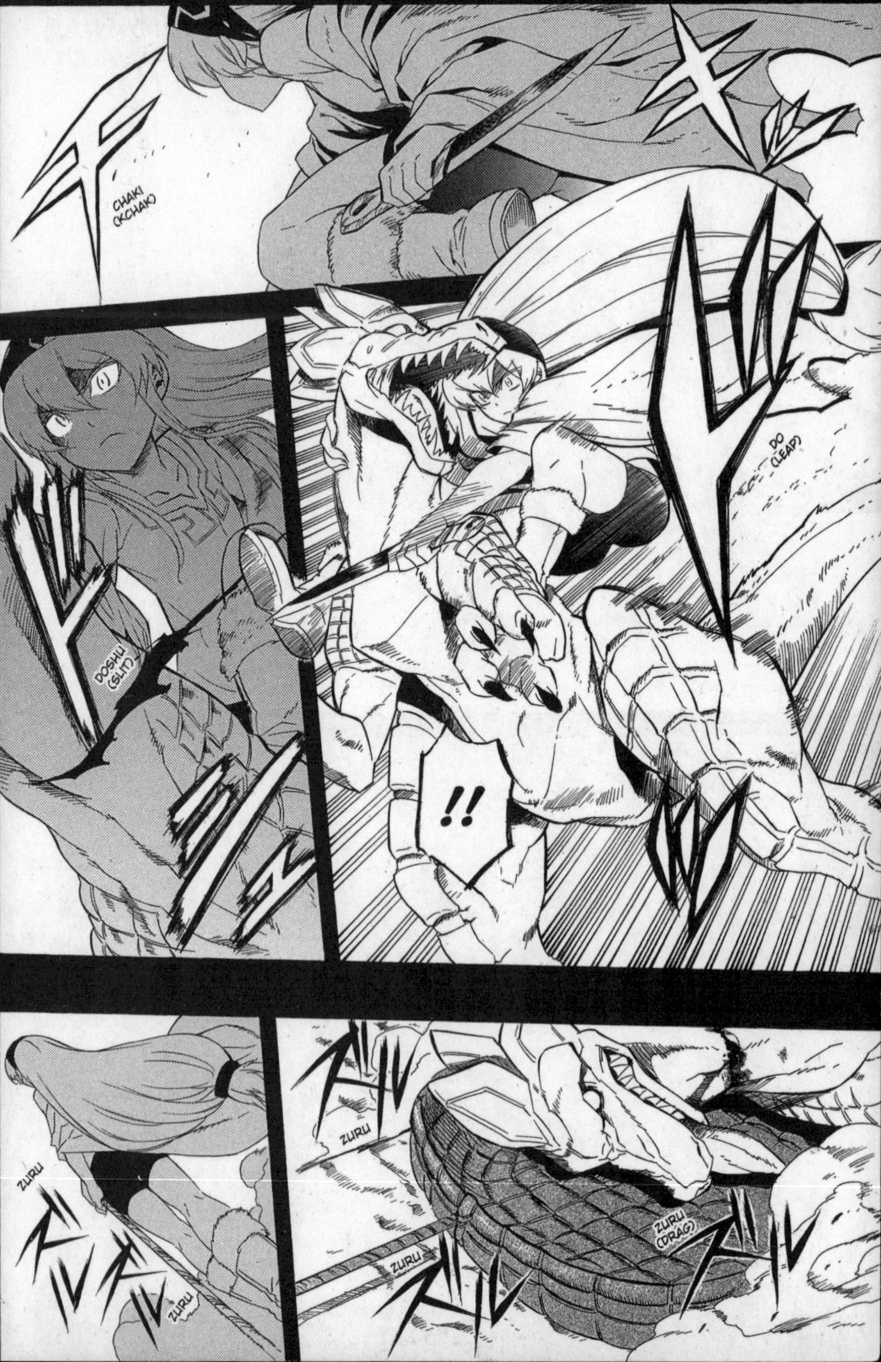
CHAKI (KCHAK)
DO (LEAP)
!!
DOSHU (SLIT)
ZURU
ZURU (DRAG)
ZURU
ZURU
ZURU

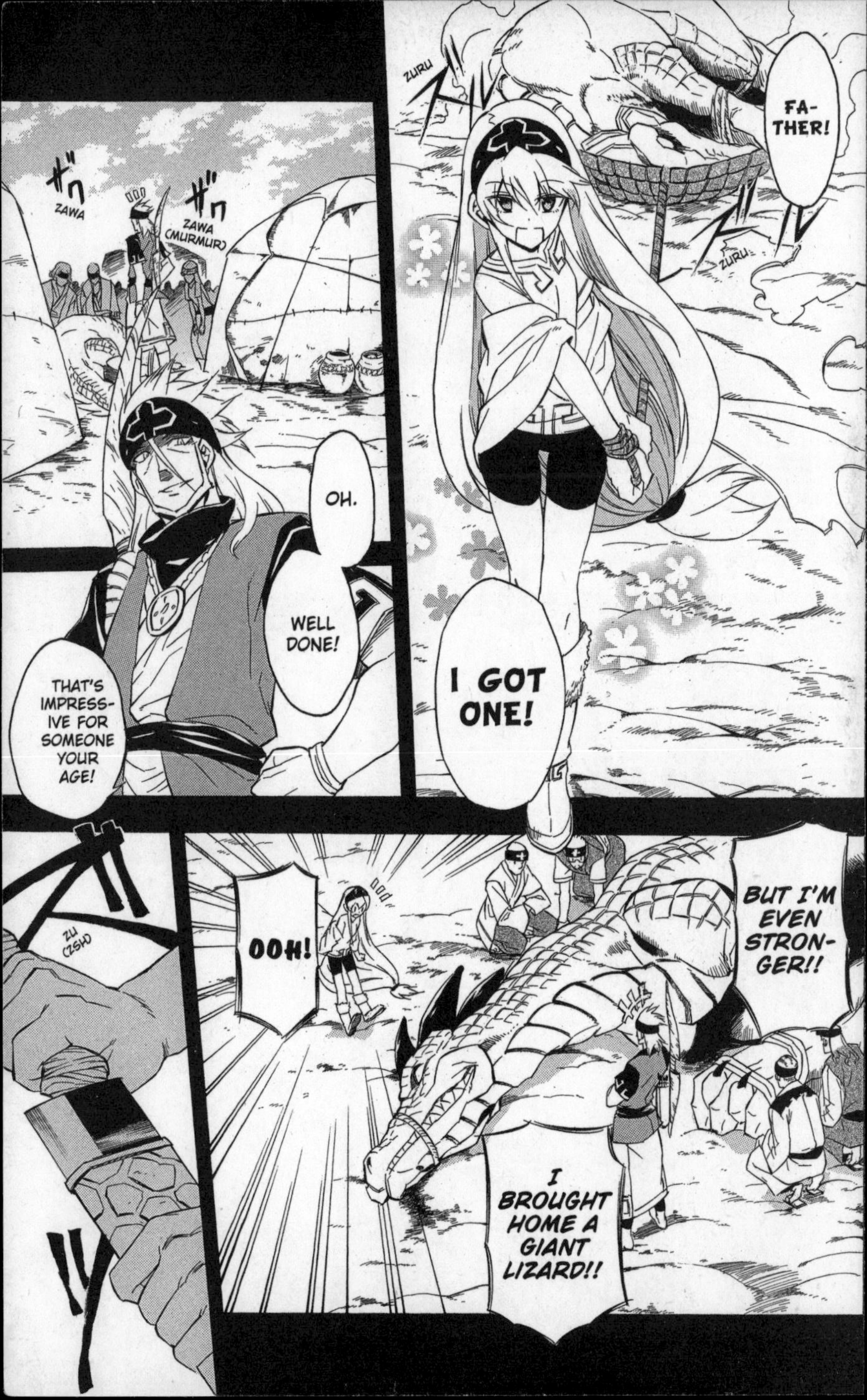
ZURU
FA-
THER!
ZURU
I GOT ONE!
ZAWA
ZAWA (MURMUR)
OH.
WELL DONE!
THAT'S IMPRESS-
IVE FOR SOMEONE YOUR AGE!
BUT I'M EVEN STRON-
GER!!
I BROUGHT HOME A GIANT LIZARD!!
OOH!
ZU (ZSH)

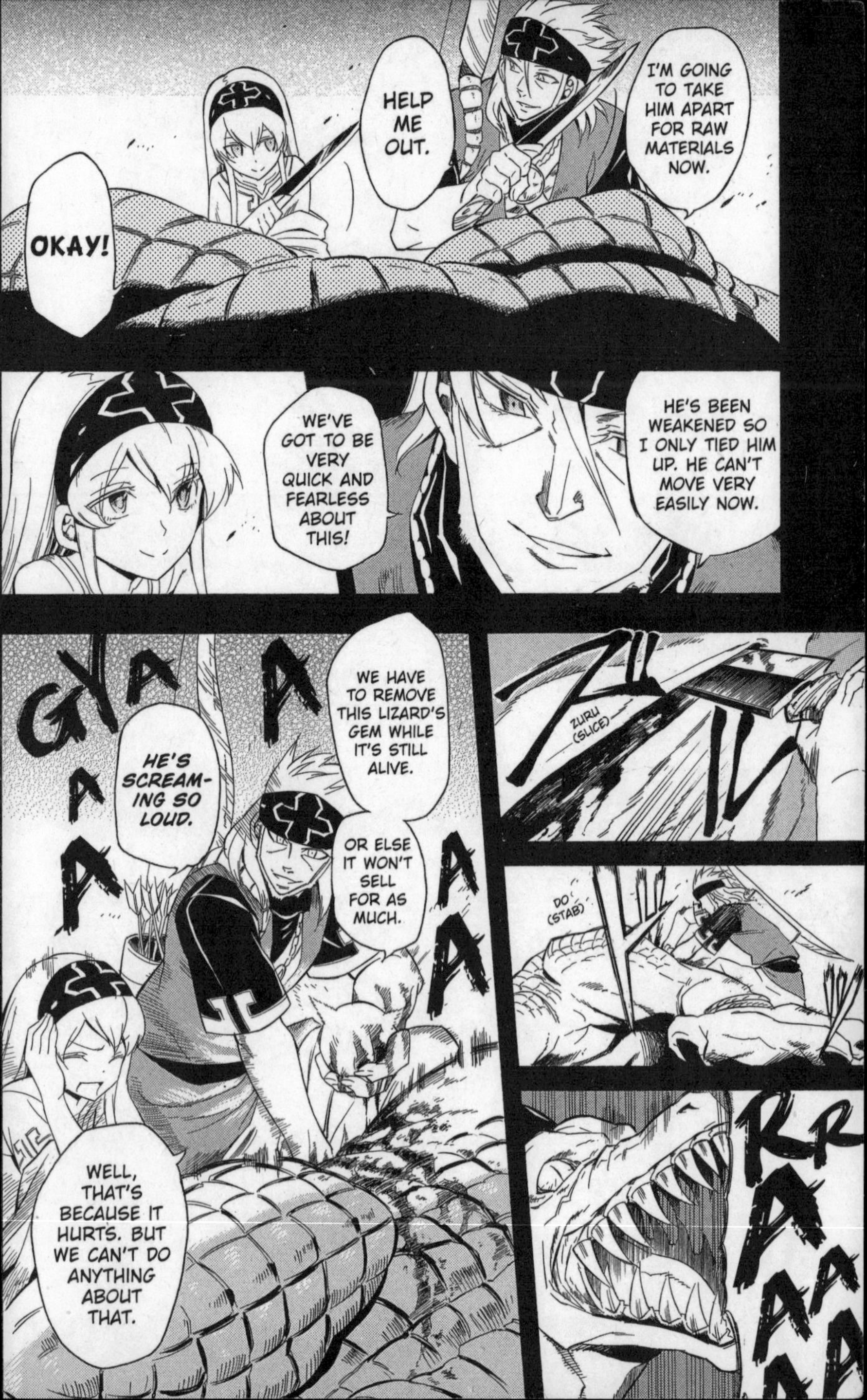
I'M GOING TO TAKE HIM APART FOR RAW MATERIALS NOW.
HELP ME OUT.
OKAY!
HE'S BEEN WEAKENED SO I ONLY TIED HIM UP. HE CAN'T MOVE VERY EASILY NOW.
WE'VE GOT TO BE VERY QUICK AND FEARLESS ABOUT THIS!
ZURU (SLICE)
DO (STAB)
KRRAAAAA
GYAAAAAAA
WE HAVE TO REMOVE THIS LIZARD'S GEM WHILE IT'S STILL ALIVE.
OR ELSE IT WON'T SELL FOR AS MUCH.
HE'S SCREAMING SO LOUD.
WELL, THAT'S BECAUSE IT HURTS. BUT WE CAN'T DO ANYTHING ABOUT THAT.

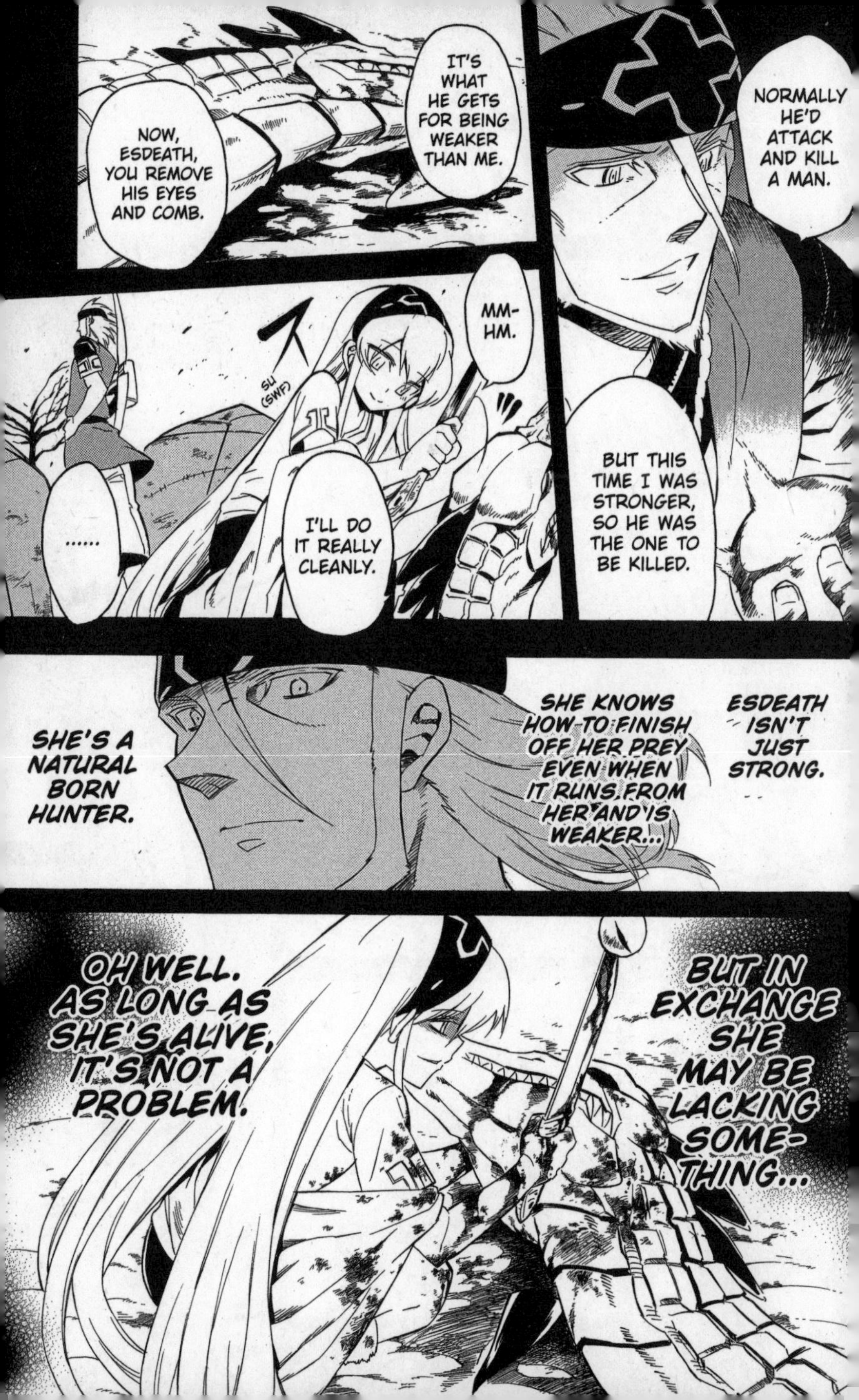
NORMALLY HE'D ATTACK AND KILL A MAN.
BUT THIS TIME I WAS STRONGER, SO HE WAS THE ONE TO BE KILLED.
IT'S WHAT HE GETS FOR BEING WEAKER THAN ME.
NOW, ESDEATH, YOU REMOVE HIS EYES AND COMB.
MM-HM.
SU (SWF)
I'LL DO IT REALLY CLEANLY.
......
ESDEATH ISN'T JUST STRONG.
SHE KNOWS HOW TO FINISH OFF HER PREY EVEN WHEN IT RUNS FROM HER AND IS WEAKER...
SHE'S A NATURAL BORN HUNTER.
BUT IN EXCHANGE SHE MAY BE LACKING SOME-THING...
OH WELL. AS LONG AS SHE'S ALIVE, IT'S NOT A PROBLEM.

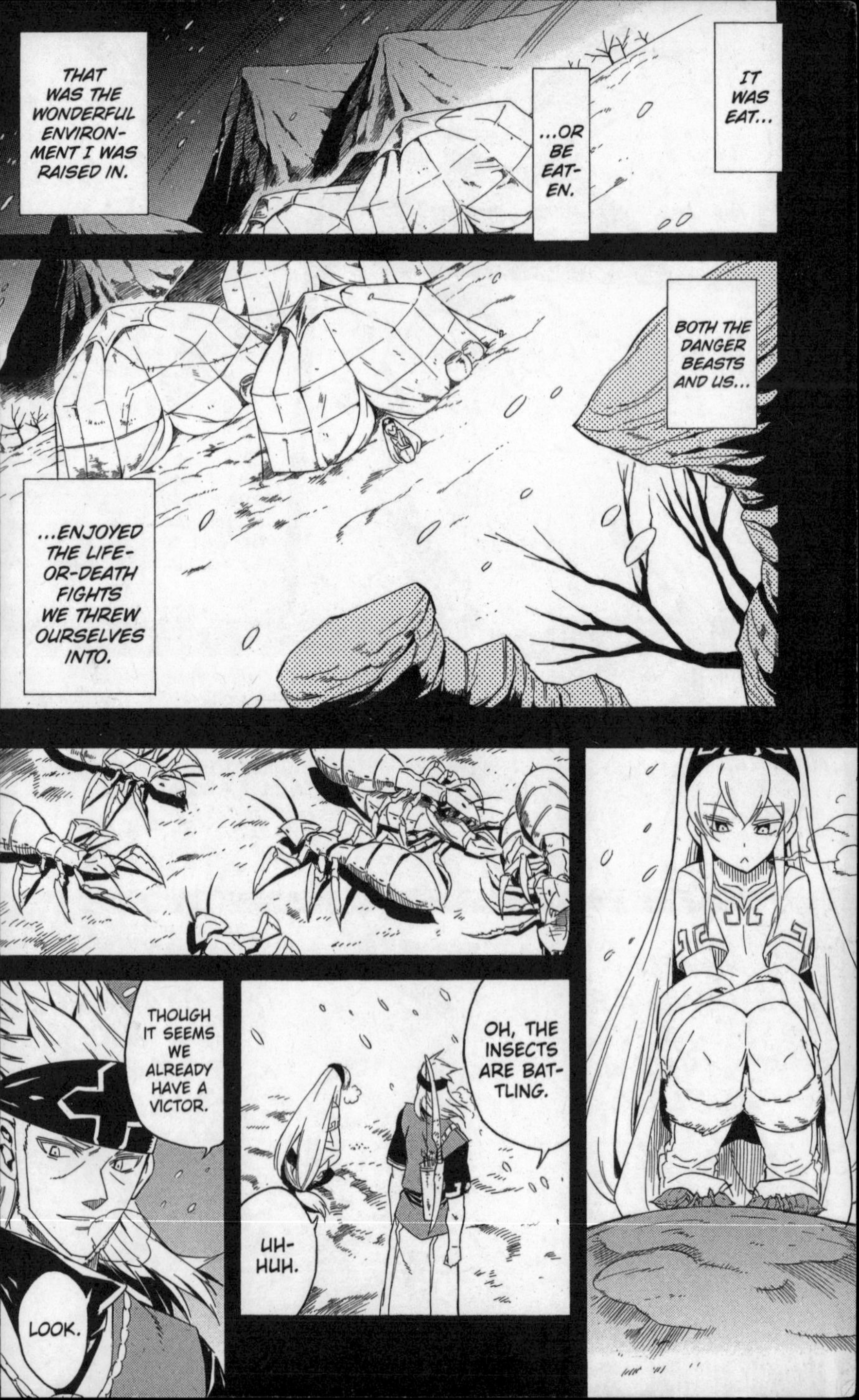
IT WAS EAT...
...OR BE EATEN.
THAT WAS THE WONDERFUL ENVIRONMENT I WAS RAISED IN.
BOTH THE DANGER BEASTS AND US...
...ENJOYED THE LIFE-OR-DEATH FIGHTS WE THREW OURSELVES INTO.
OH, THE INSECTS ARE BATTLING.
UH-HUH.
THOUGH IT SEEMS WE ALREADY HAVE A VICTOR.
LOOK.

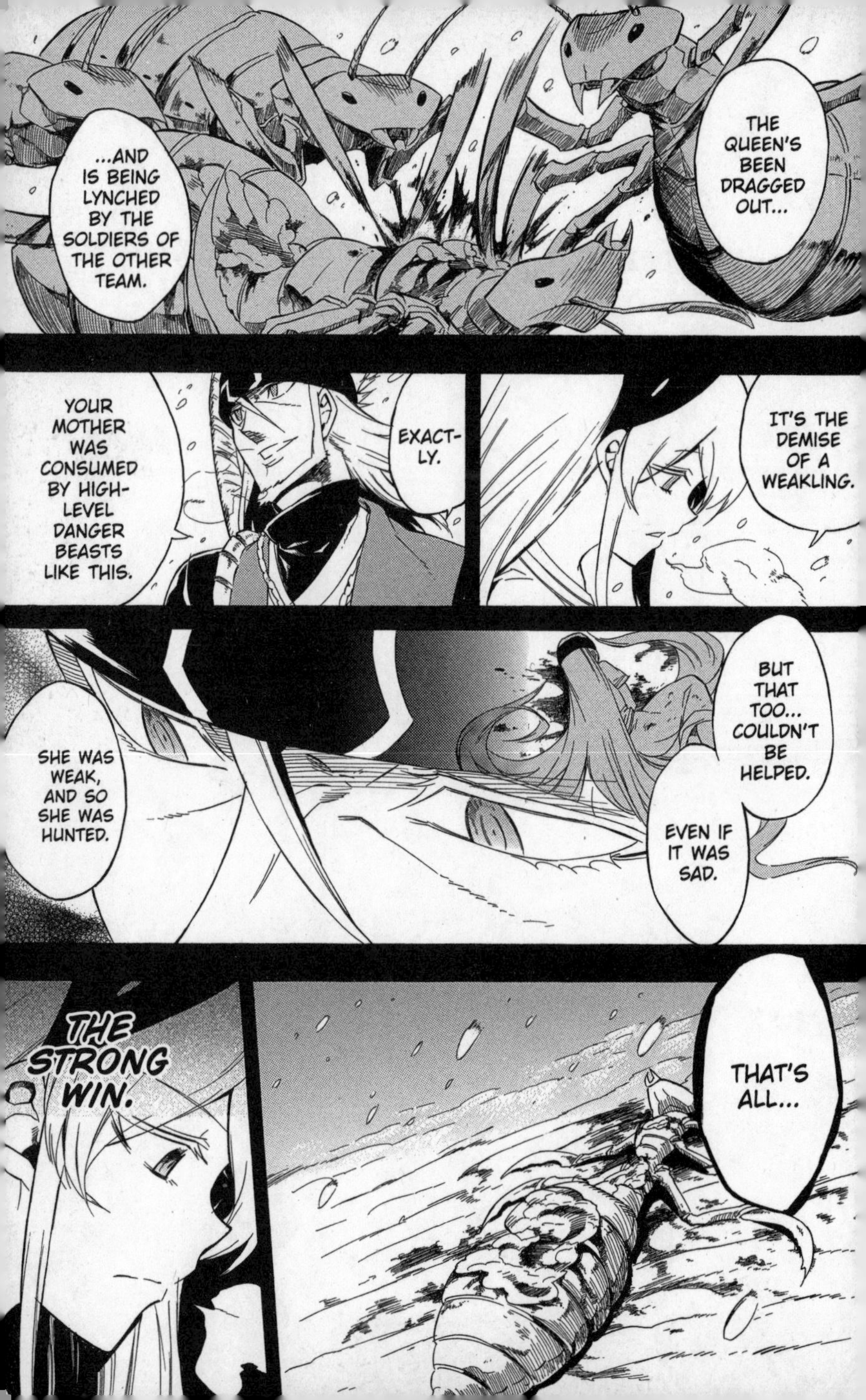
THE QUEEN'S BEEN DRAGGED OUT...
...AND IS BEING LYNCHED BY THE SOLDIERS OF THE OTHER TEAM.
IT'S THE DEMISE OF A WEAKLING.
EXACT-LY.
YOUR MOTHER WAS CONSUMED BY HIGH-LEVEL DANGER BEASTS LIKE THIS.
BUT THAT TOO... COULDN'T BE HELPED.
EVEN IF IT WAS SAD.
SHE WAS WEAK, AND SO SHE WAS HUNTED.
THAT'S ALL...
THE STRONG WIN.

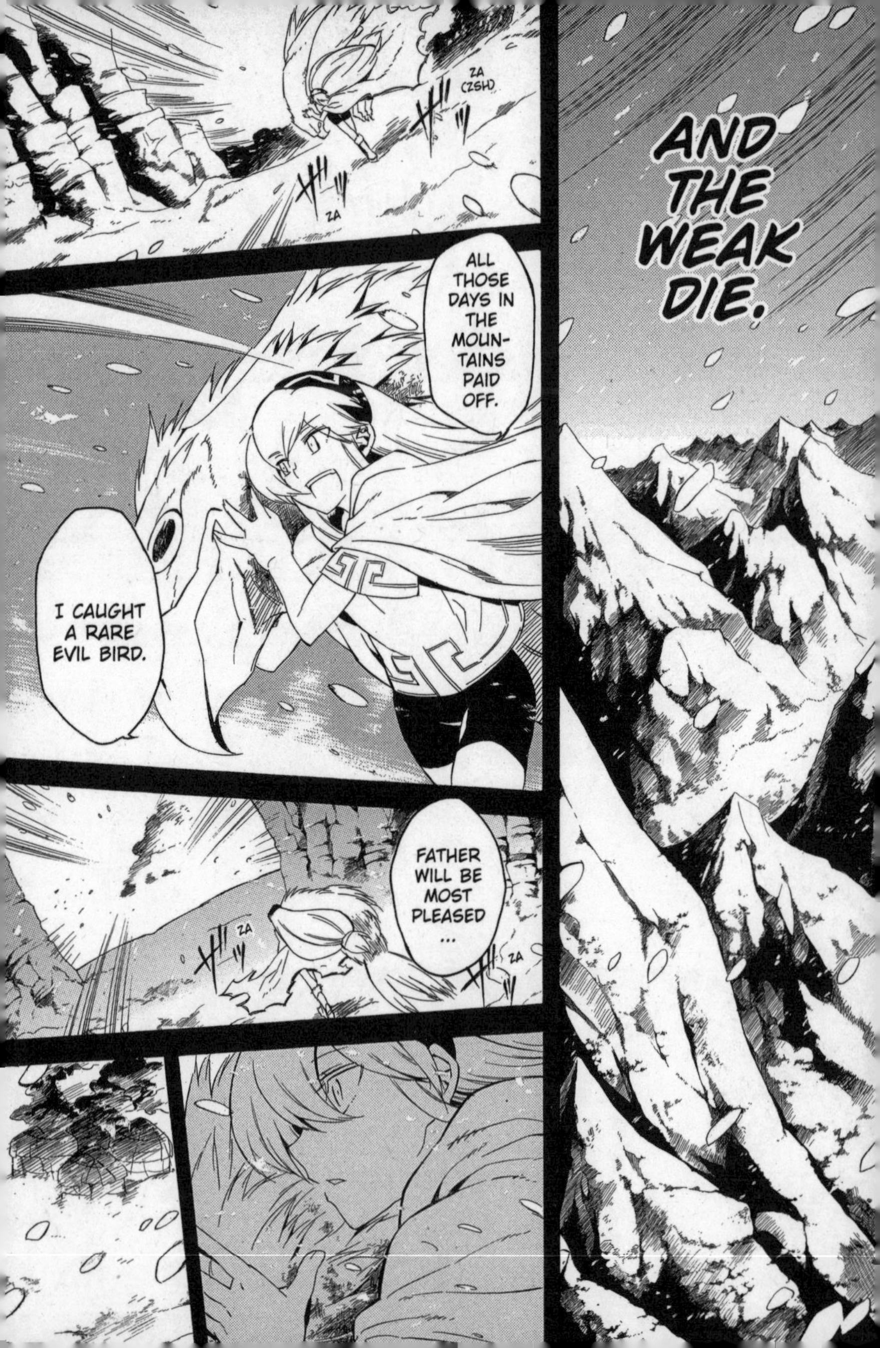
AND THE WEAK DIE.
ZA (ZSH)
ZA
ALL THOSE DAYS IN THE MOUN-TAINS PAID OFF.
I CAUGHT A RARE EVIL BIRD.
FATHER WILL BE MOST PLEASED ...
ZA
ZA

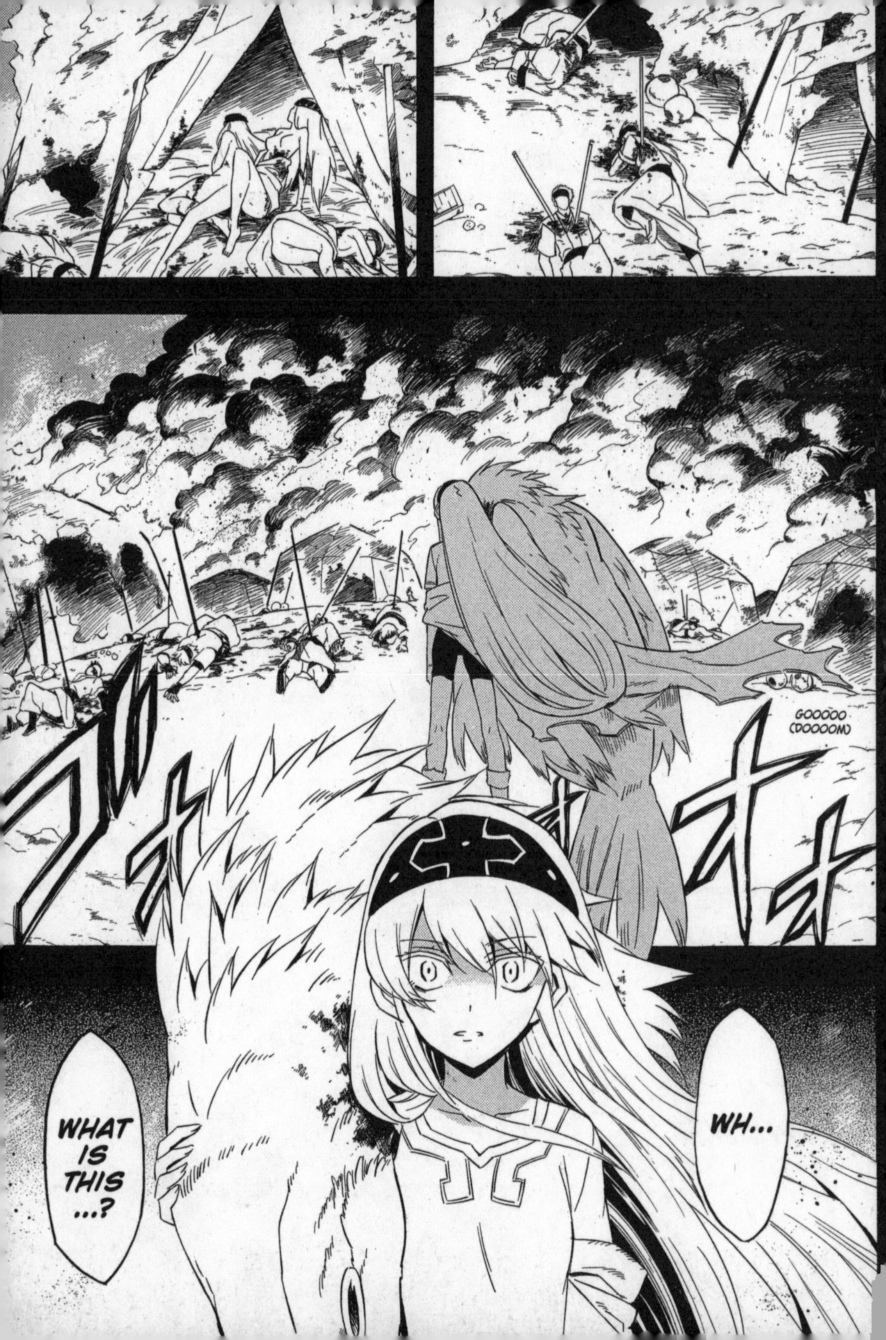

GOOOOO
(DOOOOM)
WH...
WHAT IS THIS ...?

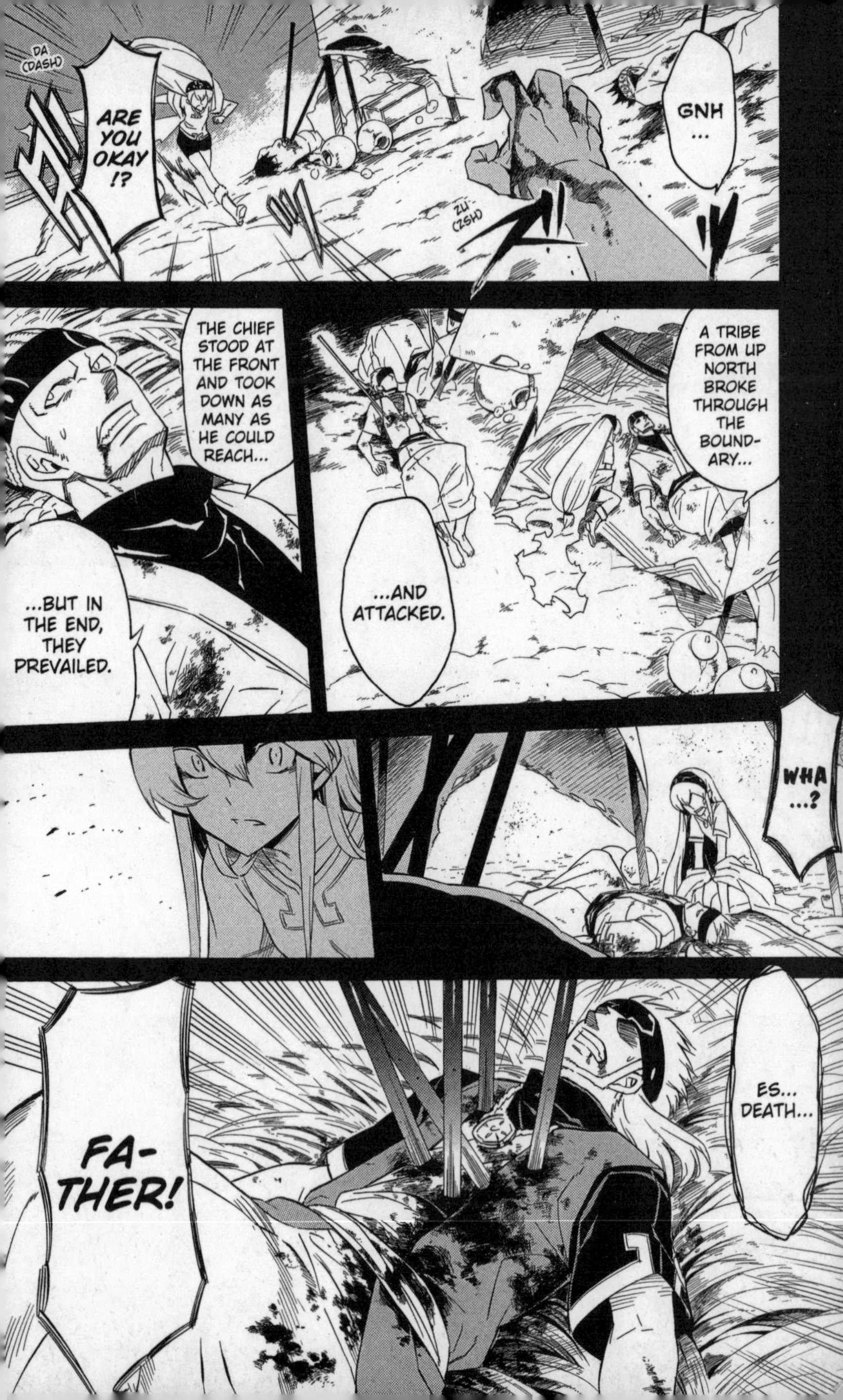
GNH ...
ZU (ZSH)
ARE YOU OKAY !?
DA (DASH)
A TRIBE FROM UP NORTH BROKE THROUGH THE BOUNDARY...
...AND ATTACKED.
THE CHIEF STOOD AT THE FRONT AND TOOK DOWN AS MANY AS HE COULD REACH...
...BUT IN THE END, THEY PREVAILED.
WHA ...?
ES... DEATH...
FA-THER!

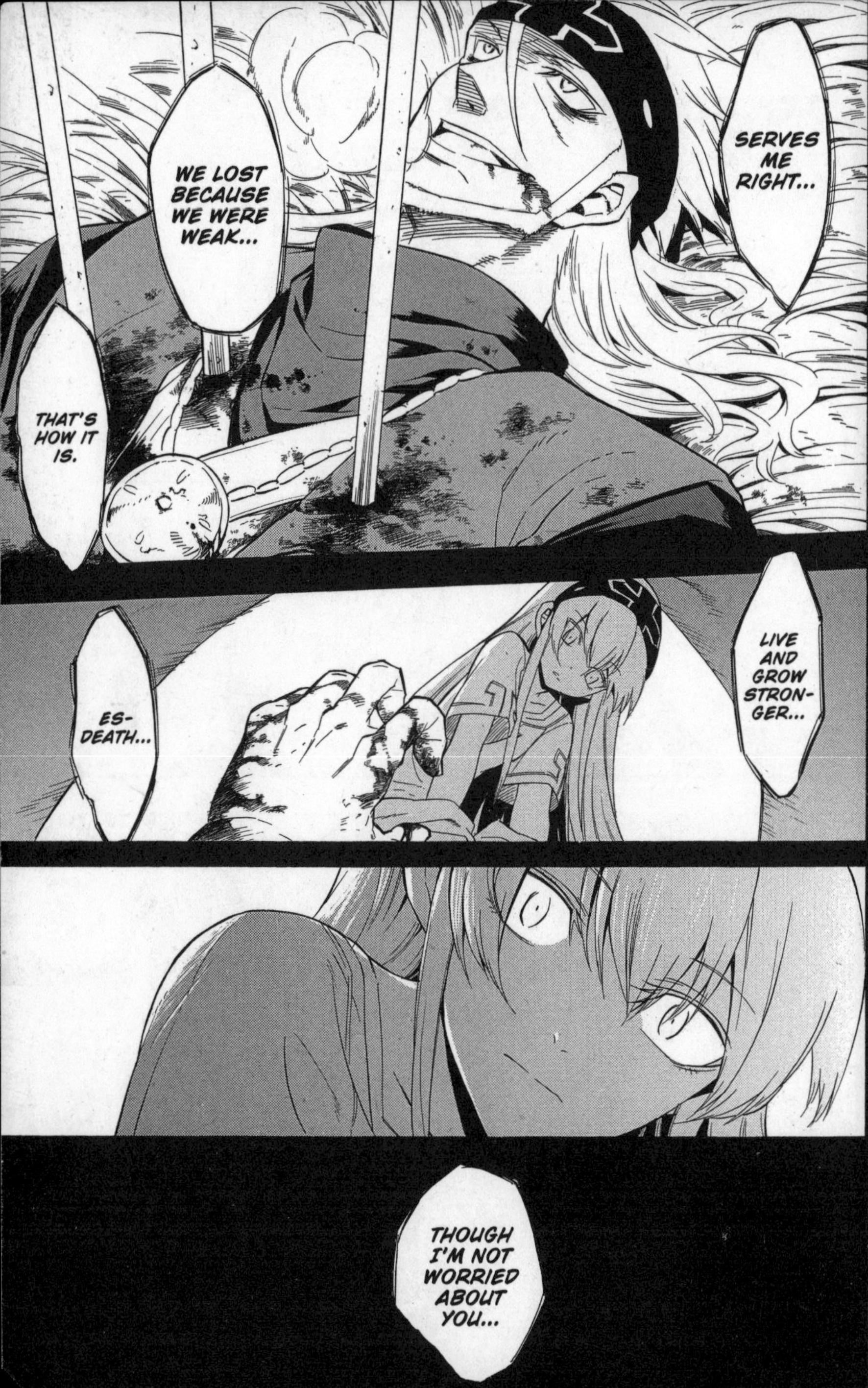
SERVES ME RIGHT...
WE LOST BECAUSE WE WERE WEAK...
THAT'S HOW IT IS.
LIVE AND GROW STRON-GER...
ES-DEATH...
THOUGH I'M NOT WORRIED ABOUT YOU...

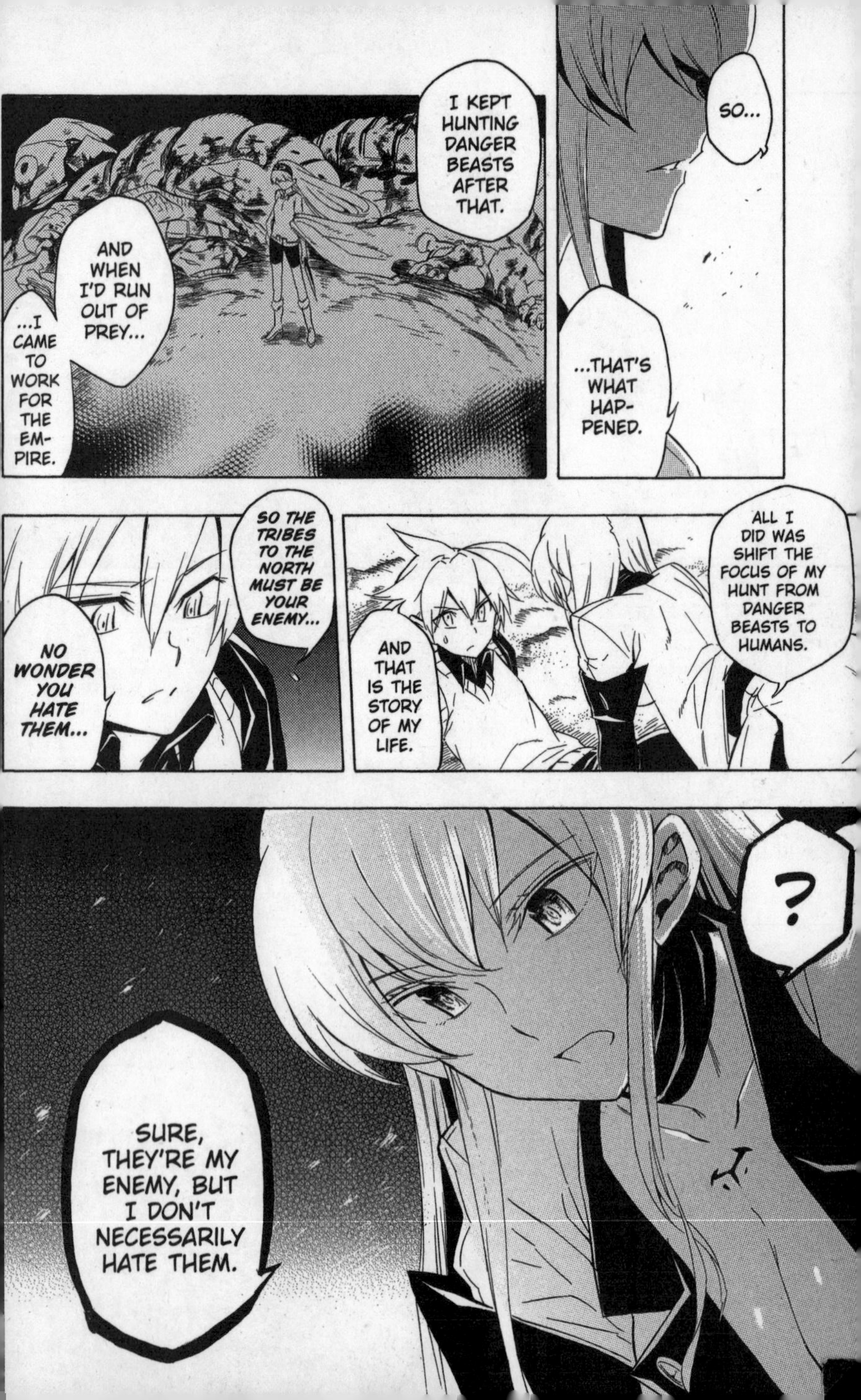
SO...
...THAT'S WHAT HAP-PENED.
I KEPT HUNTING DANGER BEASTS AFTER THAT.
AND WHEN I'D RUN OUT OF PREY...
...I CAME TO WORK FOR THE EM-PIRE.
ALL I DID WAS SHIFT THE FOCUS OF MY HUNT FROM DANGER BEASTS TO HUMANS.
AND THAT IS THE STORY OF MY LIFE.
SO THE TRIBES TO THE NORTH MUST BE YOUR ENEMY...
NO WONDER YOU HATE THEM...
?
SURE, THEY'RE MY ENEMY, BUT I DON'T NECESSARILY HATE THEM.

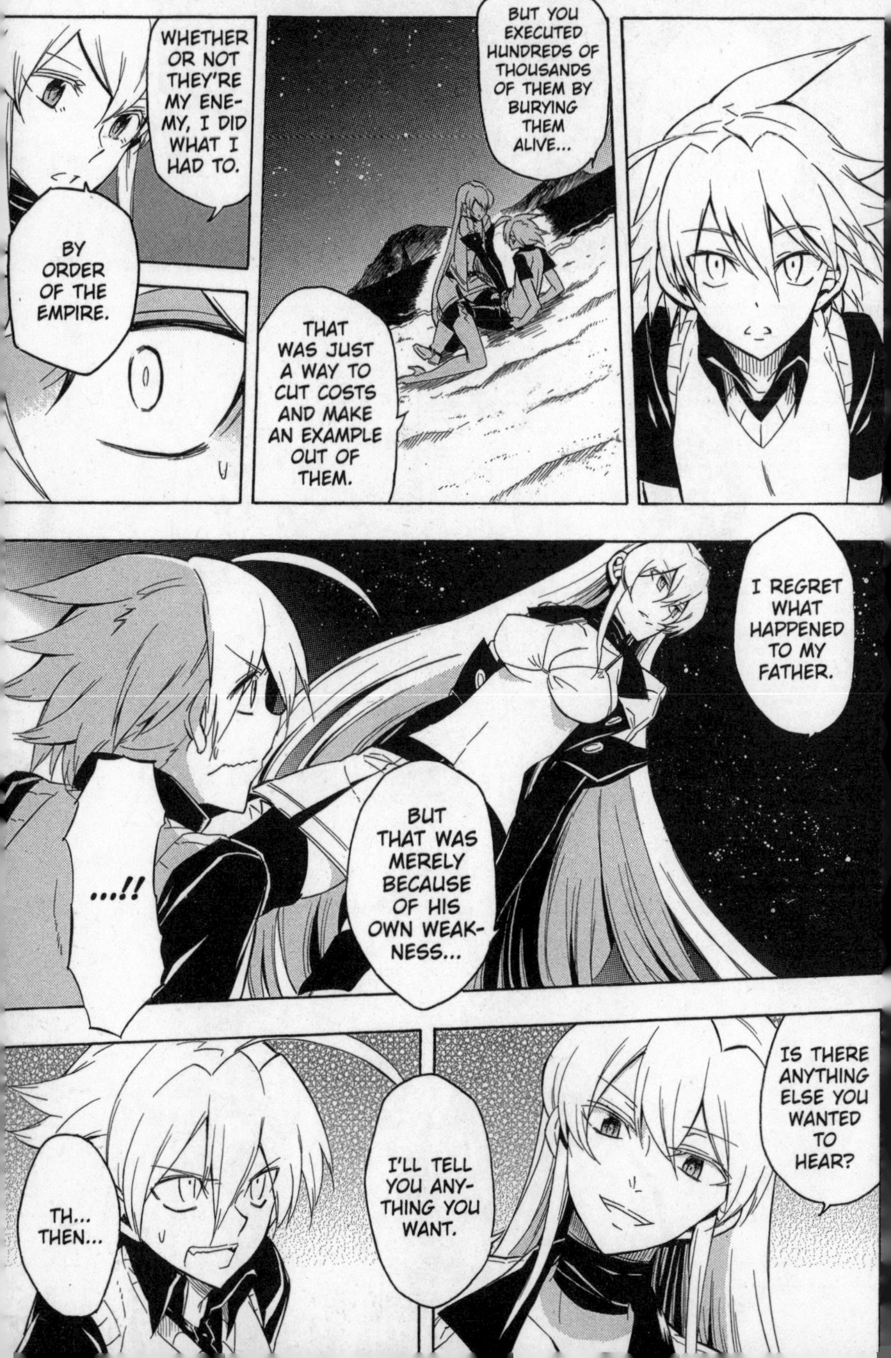

BUT YOU EXECUTED HUNDREDS OF THOUSANDS OF THEM BY BURYING THEM ALIVE...
THAT WAS JUST A WAY TO CUT COSTS AND MAKE AN EXAMPLE OUT OF THEM.
WHETHER OR NOT THEY'RE MY ENEMY, I DID WHAT I HAD TO.
BY ORDER OF THE EMPIRE.
I REGRET WHAT HAPPENED TO MY FATHER.
BUT THAT WAS MERELY BECAUSE OF HIS OWN WEAKNESS...
...!!
IS THERE ANYTHING ELSE YOU WANTED TO HEAR?
I'LL TELL YOU ANYTHING YOU WANT.
TH... THEN...

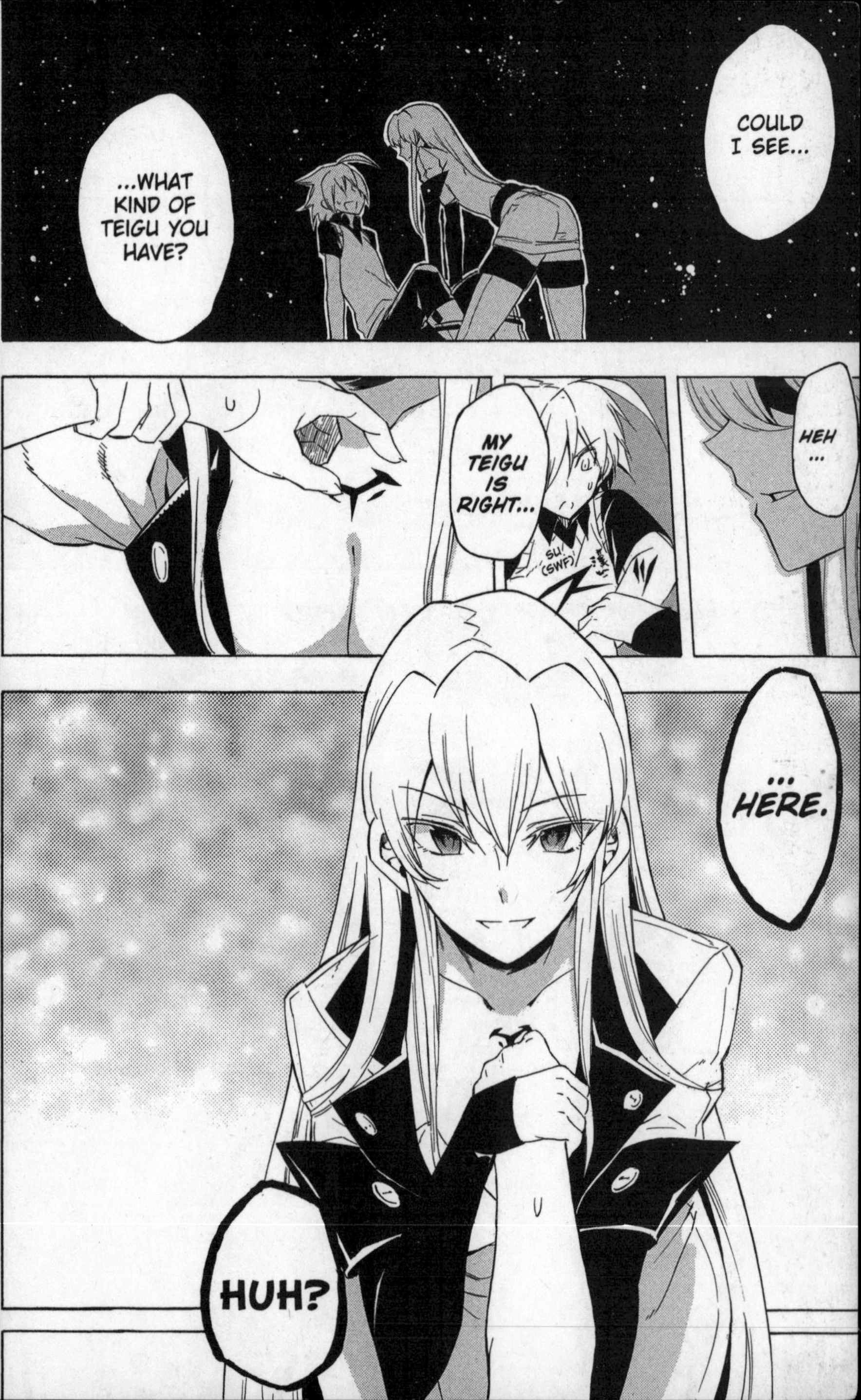
COULD I SEE...
...WHAT KIND OF TEIGU YOU HAVE?
HEH ...
MY TEIGU IS RIGHT...
SU! (SWF)
... HERE.
HUH?

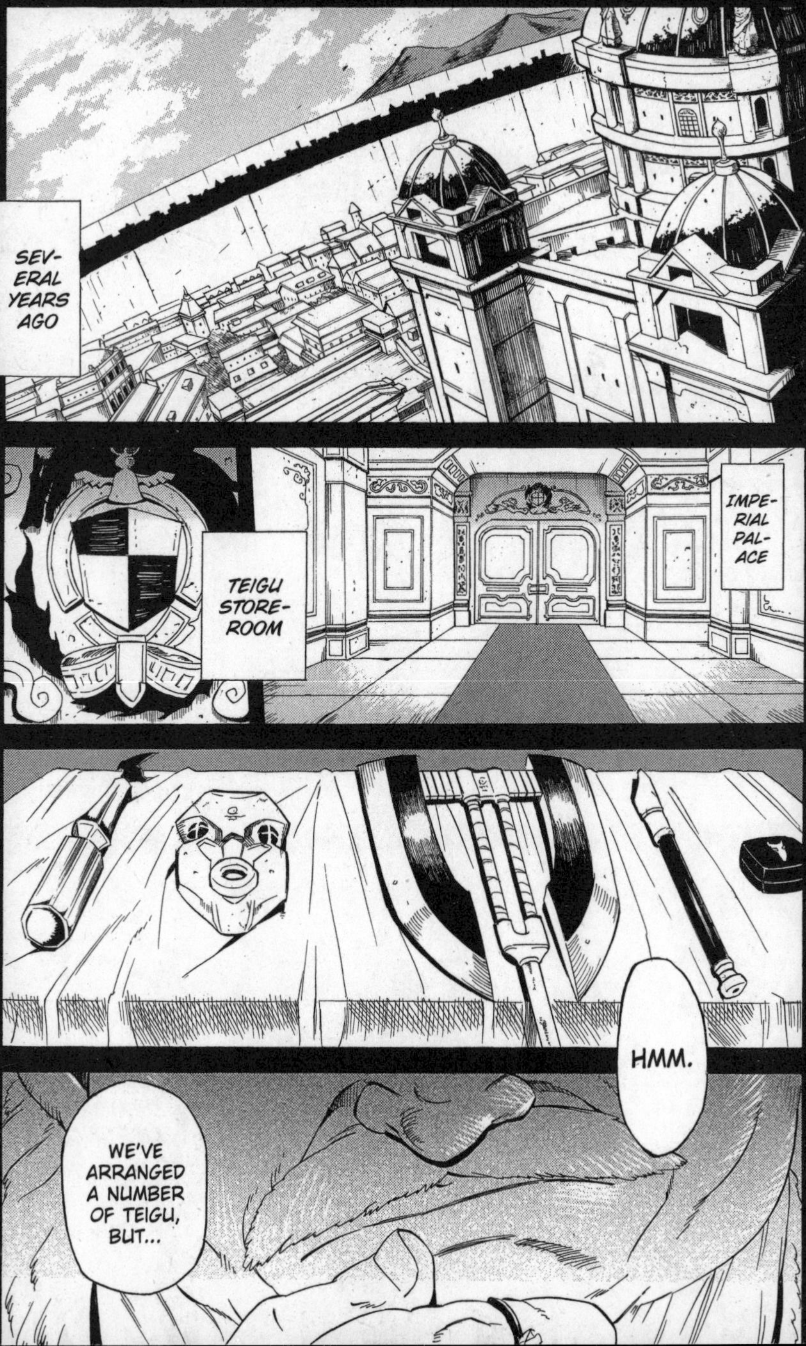
SEV-ERAL YEARS AGO
IMPERIAL PALACE
TEIGU STORE-ROOM
HMM.
WE'VE ARRANGED A NUMBER OF TEIGU, BUT...

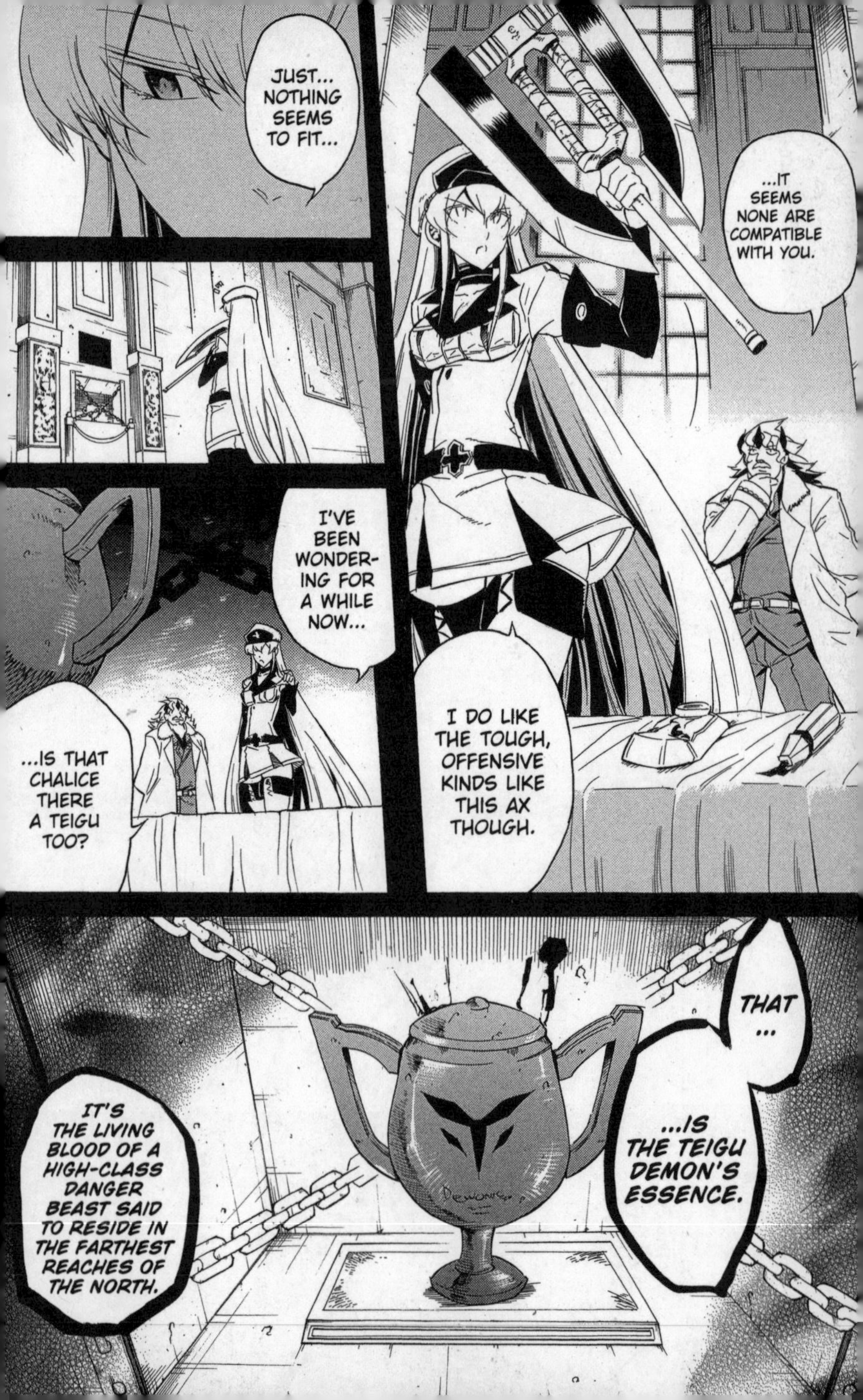
...IT SEEMS NONE ARE COMPATIBLE WITH YOU.
I DO LIKE THE TOUGH, OFFENSIVE KINDS LIKE THIS AX THOUGH.
JUST... NOTHING SEEMS TO FIT...
I'VE BEEN WONDERING FOR A WHILE NOW...
...IS THAT CHALICE THERE A TEIGU TOO?
THAT...
...IS THE TEIGU DEMON'S ESSENCE.
IT'S THE LIVING BLOOD OF A HIGH-CLASS DANGER BEAST SAID TO RESIDE IN THE FARTHEST REACHES OF THE NORTH.

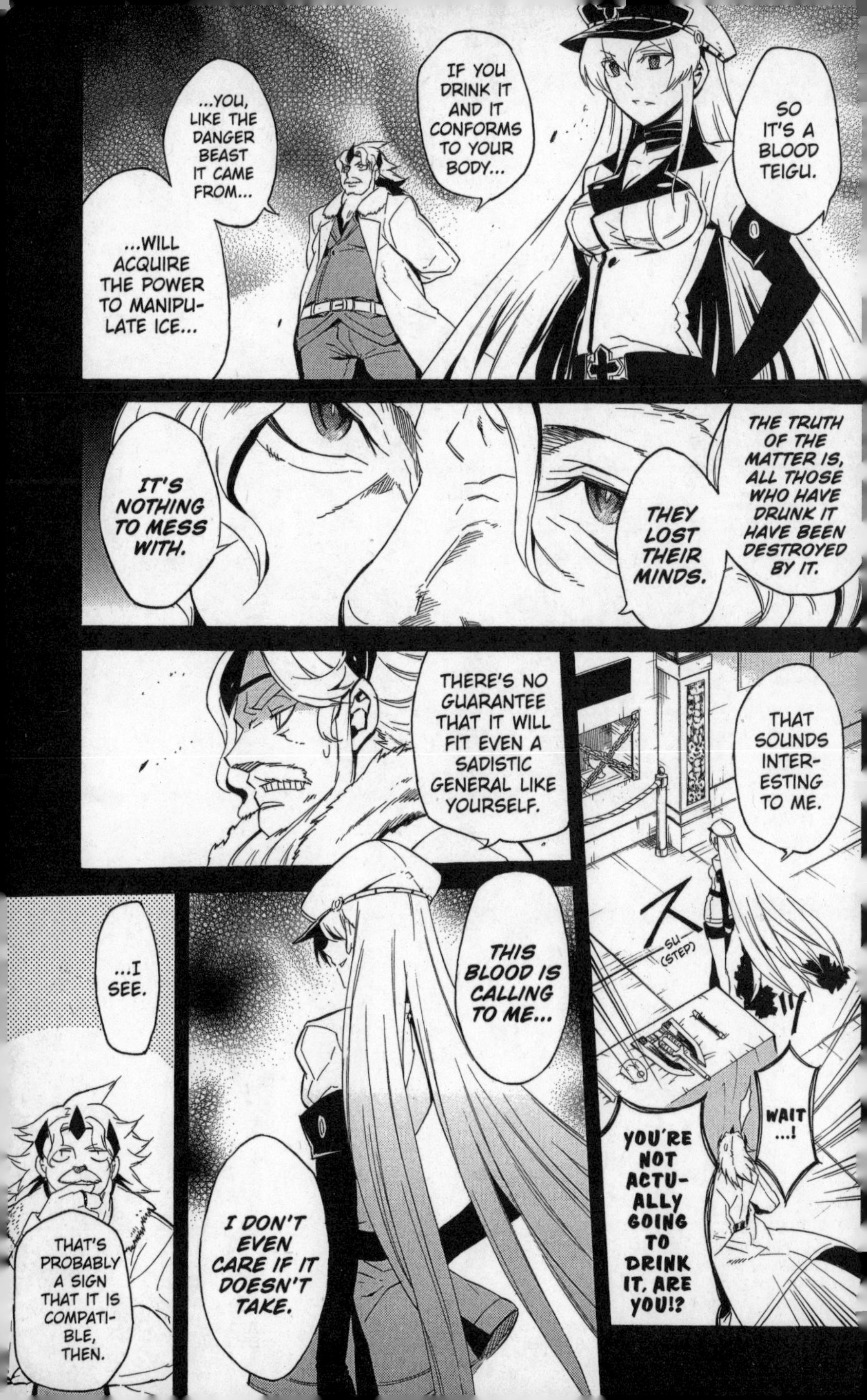
SO IT'S A BLOOD TEIGU.
IF YOU DRINK IT AND IT CONFORMS TO YOUR BODY...
...YOU, LIKE THE DANGER BEAST IT CAME FROM...
...WILL ACQUIRE THE POWER TO MANIPULATE ICE...
THE TRUTH OF THE MATTER IS, ALL THOSE WHO HAVE DRUNK IT HAVE BEEN DESTROYED BY IT.
THEY LOST THEIR MINDS.
IT'S NOTHING TO MESS WITH.
THAT SOUNDS INTERESTING TO ME.
THERE'S NO GUARANTEE THAT IT WILL FIT EVEN A SADISTIC GENERAL LIKE YOURSELF.
SU (STEP)
WAIT ...!
YOU'RE NOT ACTUALLY GOING TO DRINK IT, ARE YOU!?
THIS BLOOD IS CALLING TO ME...
I DON'T EVEN CARE IF IT DOESN'T TAKE.
...I SEE.
THAT'S PROBABLY A SIGN THAT IT IS COMPATIBLE, THEN.

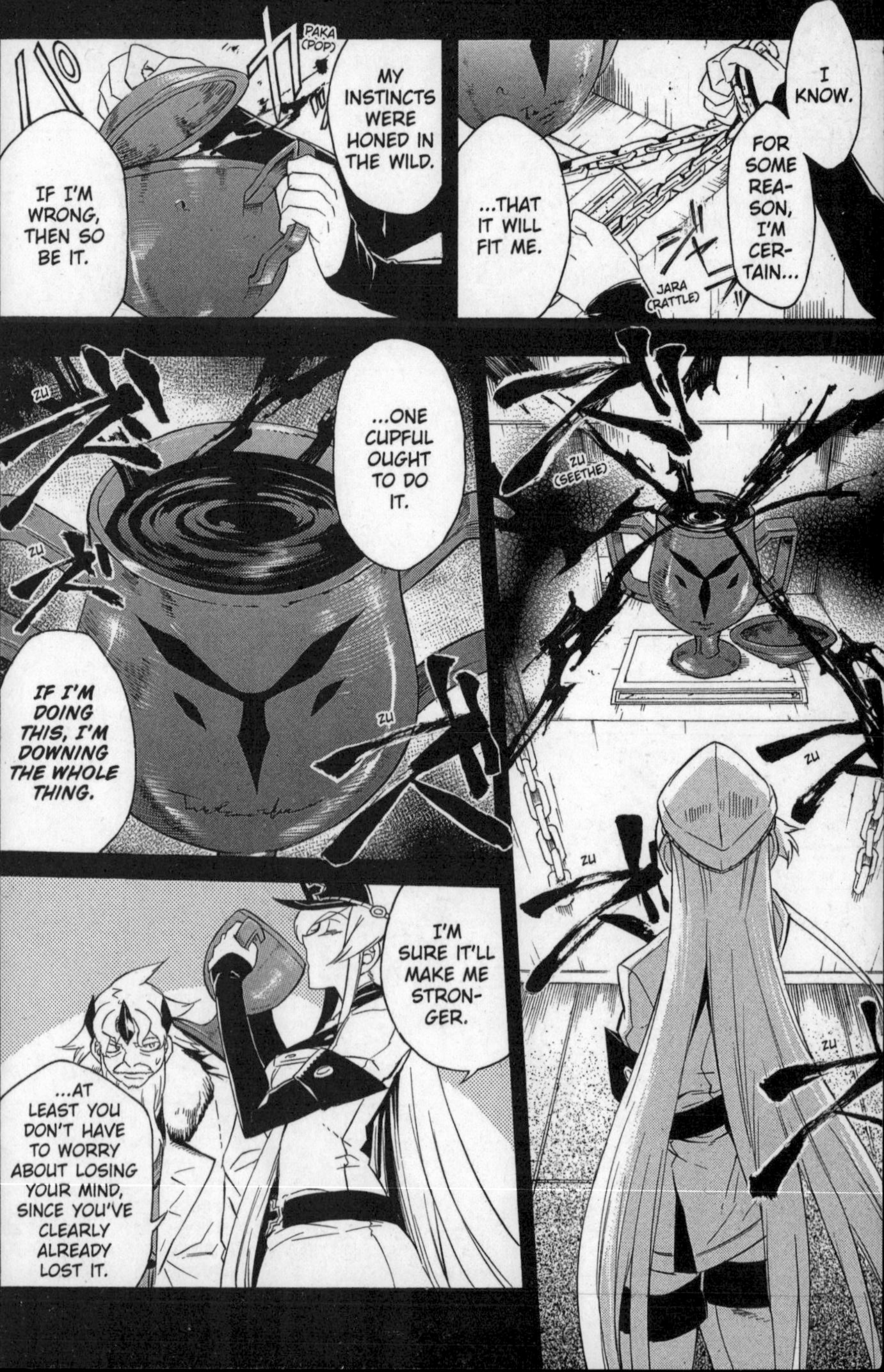
I KNOW.
FOR SOME REASON, I'M CERTAIN...
JARA (RATTLE)
...THAT IT WILL FIT ME.
PAKA (POP)
MY INSTINCTS WERE HONED IN THE WILD.
IF I'M WRONG, THEN SO BE IT.
ZU (SEETHE)
ZU
ZU
...ONE CUPFUL OUGHT TO DO IT.
ZU
ZU
IF I'M DOING THIS, I'M DOWNING THE WHOLE THING.
ZU
ZU
I'M SURE IT'LL MAKE ME STRONGER.
...AT LEAST YOU DON'T HAVE TO WORRY ABOUT LOSING YOUR MIND, SINCE YOU'VE CLEARLY ALREADY LOST IT.

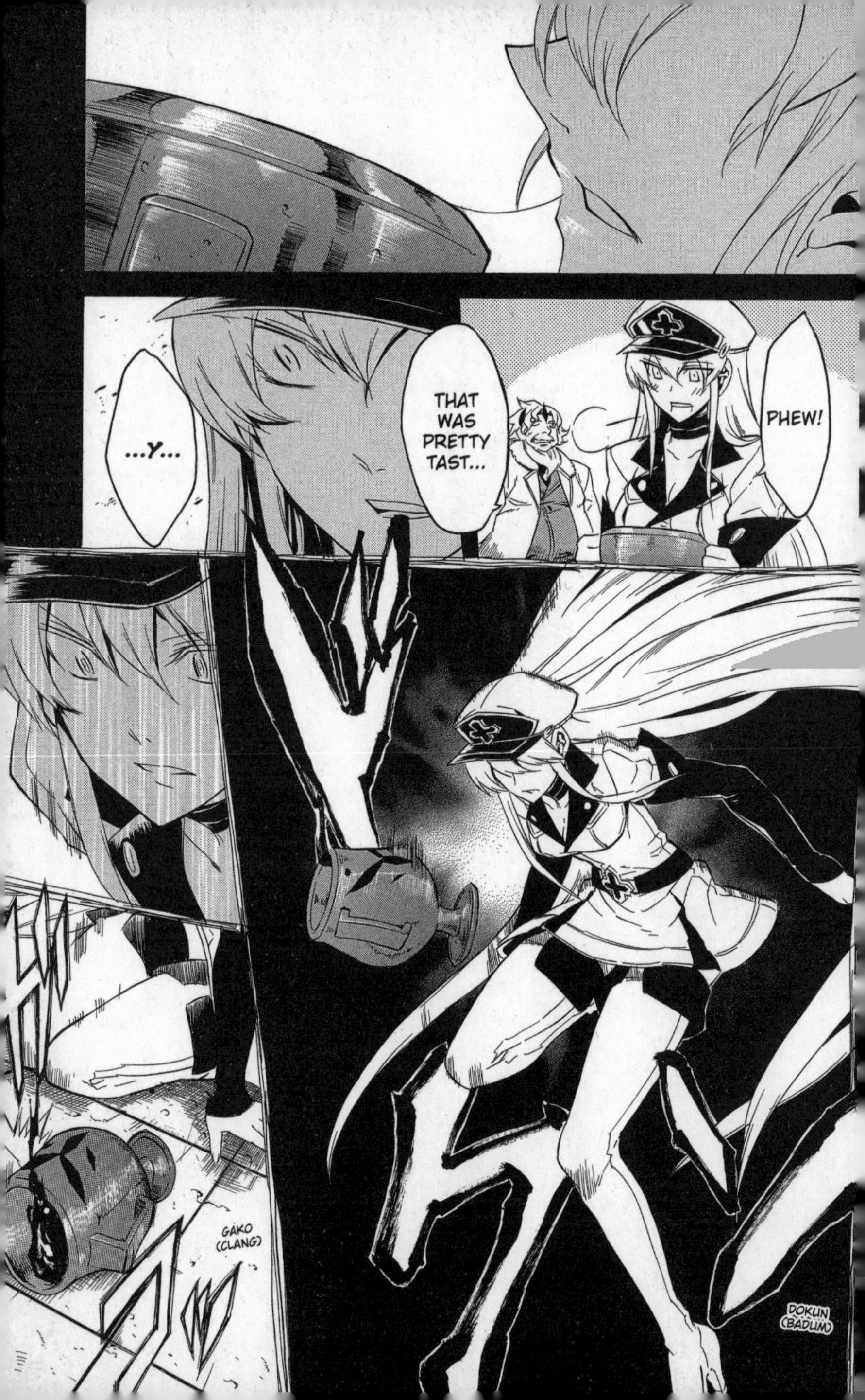
PHEW!
THAT WAS PRETTY TAST...
...Y...
DOKUN (BADUM)
GAKO (CLANG)

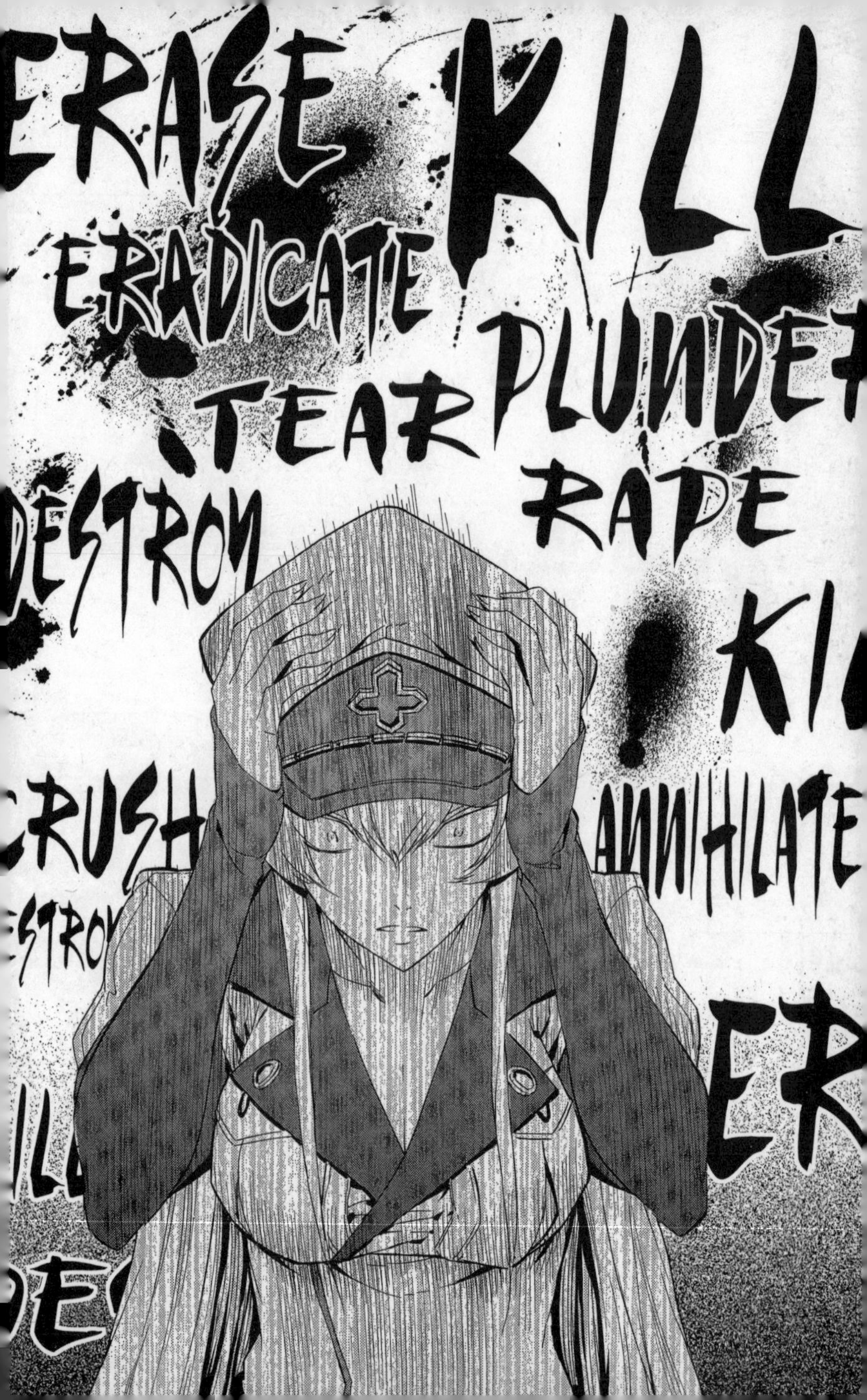
KILL
ERASE
ERADICATE
TEAR
RAPE
DESTROY
ANNIHILATE
CRUSH

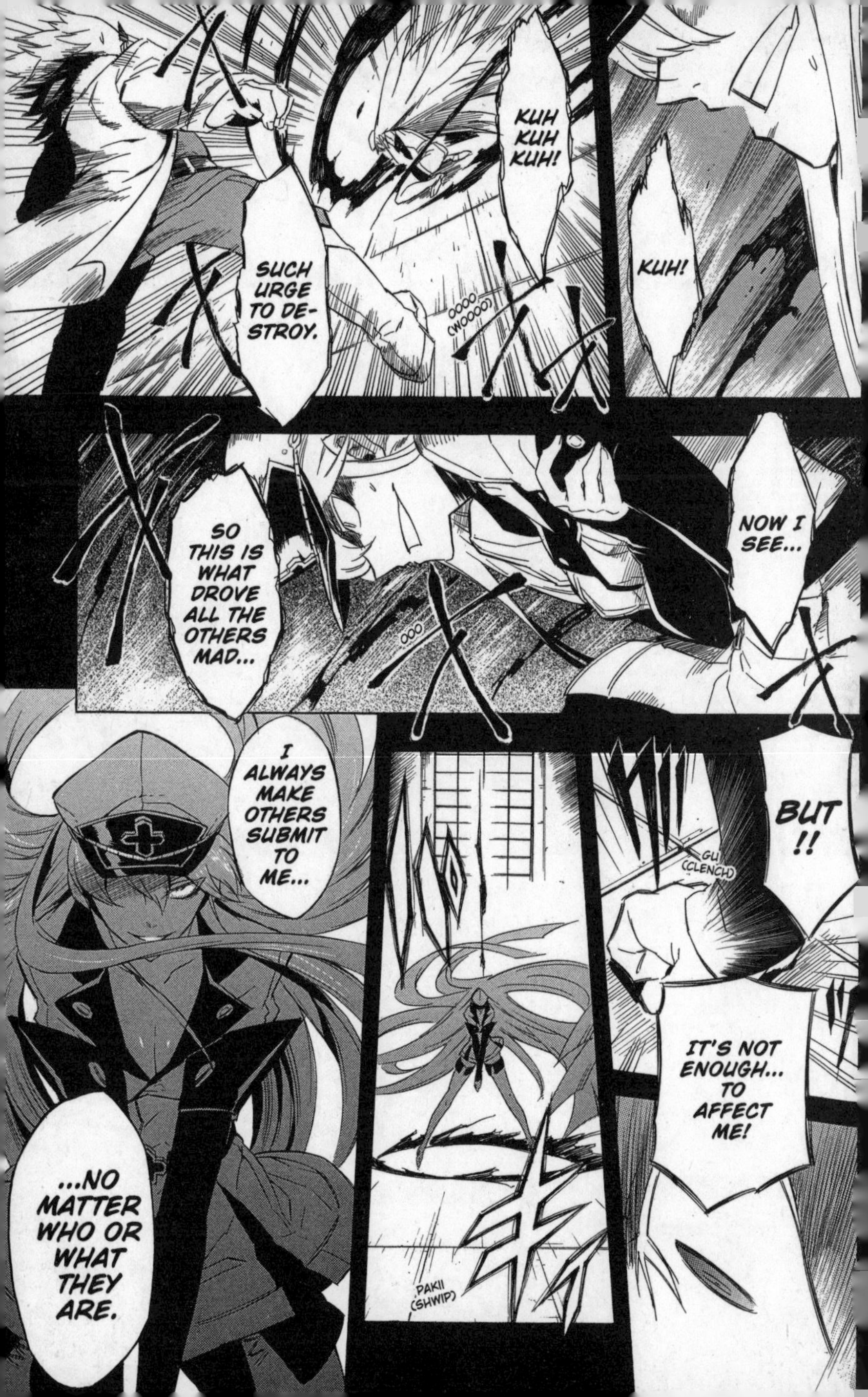
KUH!
KUH KUH KUH!
SUCH URGE TO DE-STROY.
OOOO (WOOOO)
NOW I SEE...
SO THIS IS WHAT DROVE ALL THE OTHERS MAD...
OOO
BUT!!
GU (CLENCH)
IT'S NOT ENOUGH... TO AFFECT ME!
PAKII (SHWIP)
I ALWAYS MAKE OTHERS SUBMIT TO ME...
...NO MATTER WHO OR WHAT THEY ARE.

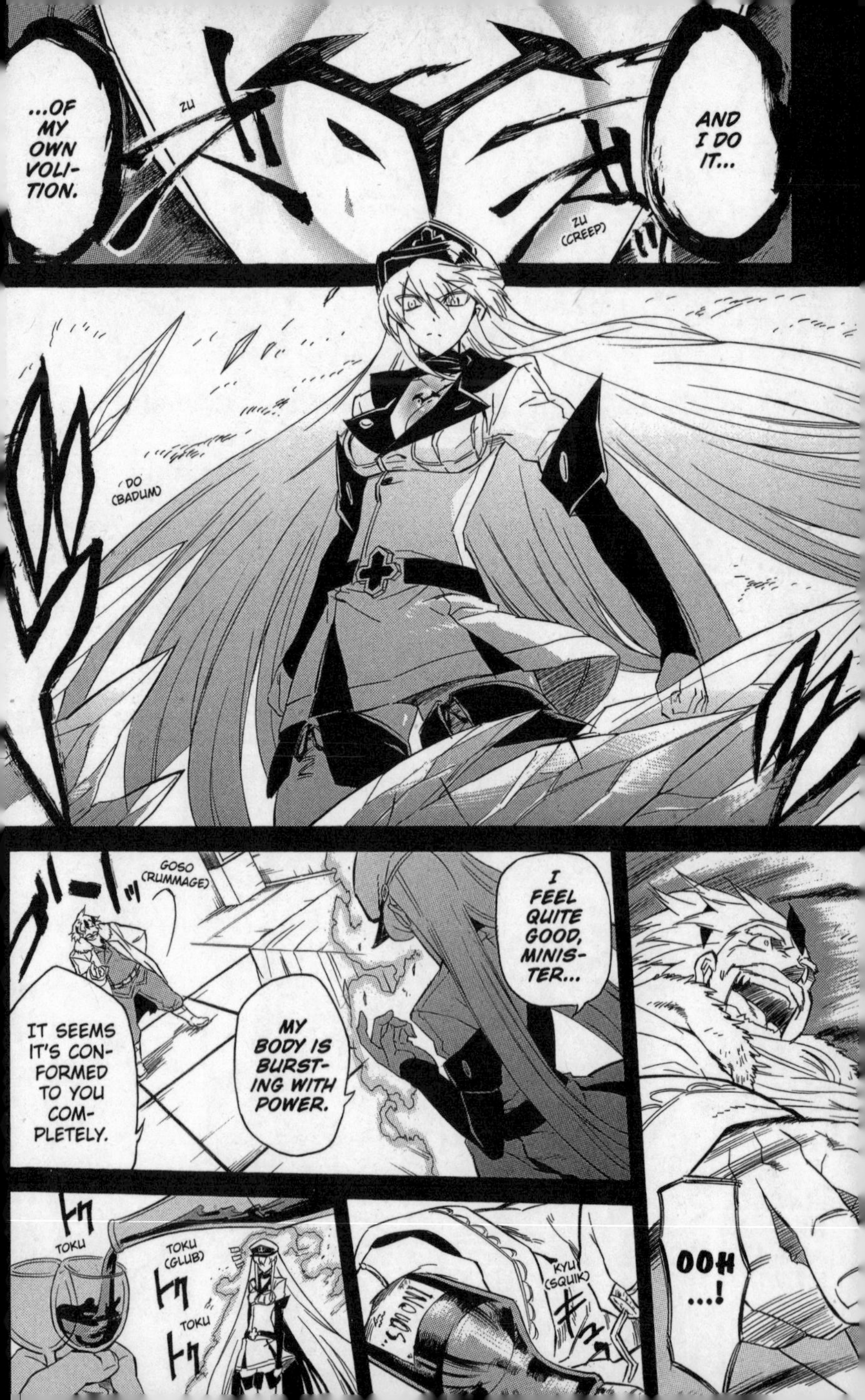
AND I DO IT...
ZU (CREEP)
ZU
...OF MY OWN VOLITION.
DO (BADUM)
I FEEL QUITE GOOD, MINISTER...
MY BODY IS BURSTING WITH POWER.
GOSO (RUMMAGE)
IT SEEMS IT'S CONFORMED TO YOU COMPLETELY.
OOH ...!
KYU (SQUIK)
TOKU (GLUB)
TOKU
TOKU

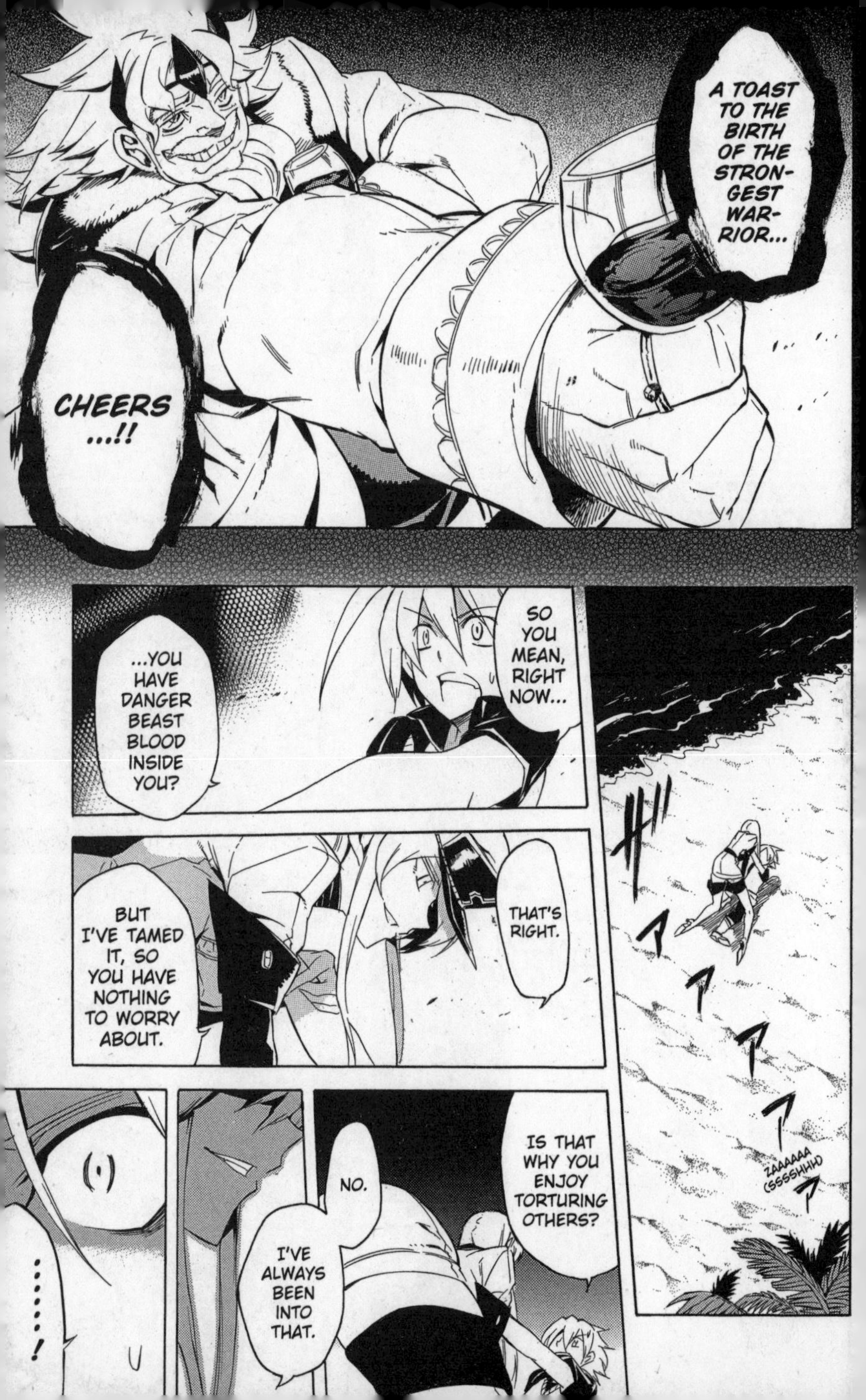
A TOAST TO THE BIRTH OF THE STRONGEST WARRIOR...
CHEERS ...!!
ZAAAAAA (SSSSHHH)
SO YOU MEAN, RIGHT NOW...
...YOU HAVE DANGER BEAST BLOOD INSIDE YOU?
THAT'S RIGHT.
BUT I'VE TAMED IT, SO YOU HAVE NOTHING TO WORRY ABOUT.
IS THAT WHY YOU ENJOY TORTURING OTHERS?
NO.
I'VE ALWAYS BEEN INTO THAT.
......!

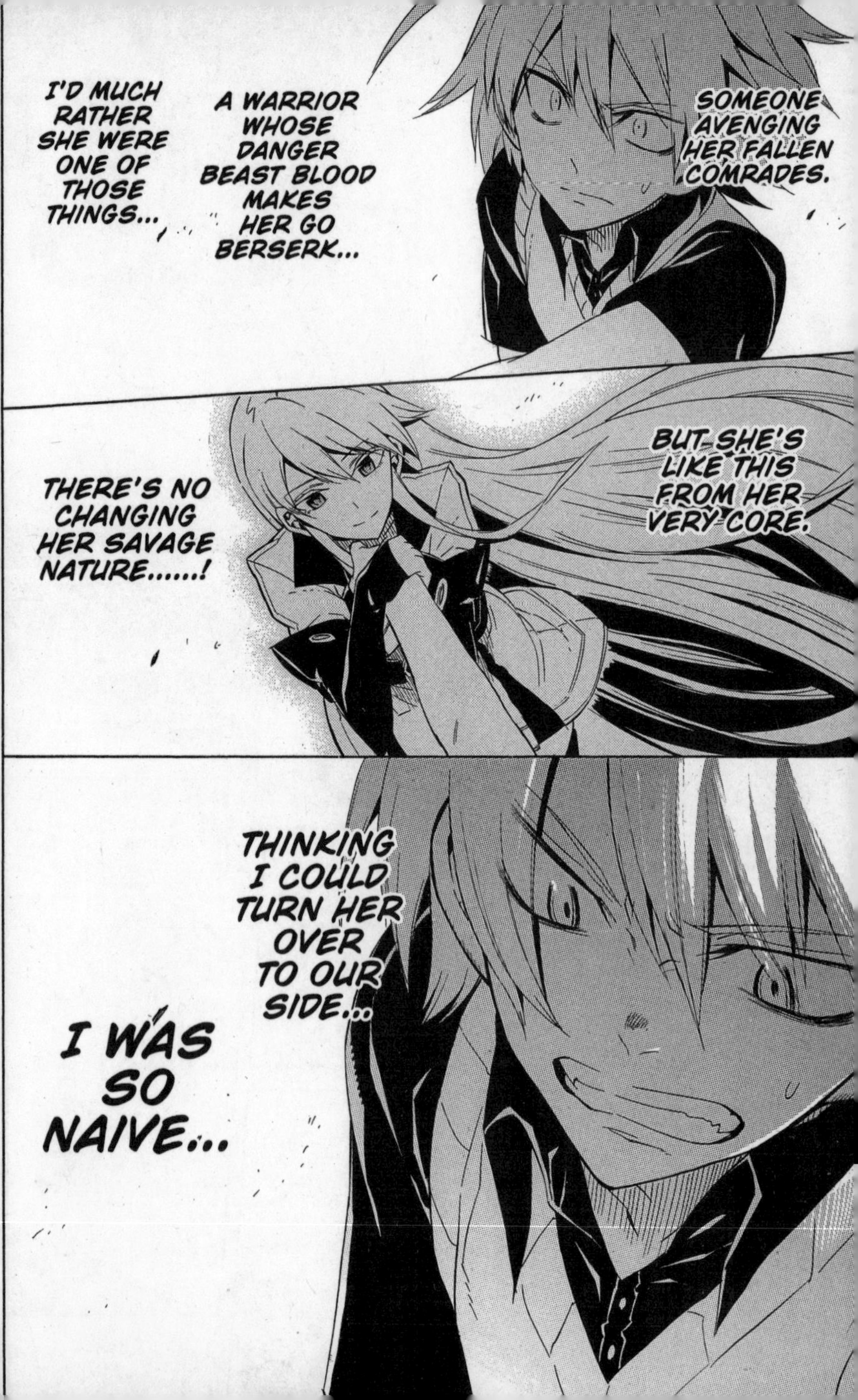
SOMEONE AVENGING HER FALLEN COMRADES.
A WARRIOR WHOSE DANGER BEAST BLOOD MAKES HER GO BERSERK...
I'D MUCH RATHER SHE WERE ONE OF THOSE THINGS...
BUT SHE'S LIKE THIS FROM HER VERY CORE.
THERE'S NO CHANGING HER SAVAGE NATURE......!
THINKING I COULD TURN HER OVER TO OUR SIDE...
I WAS SO NAIVE...

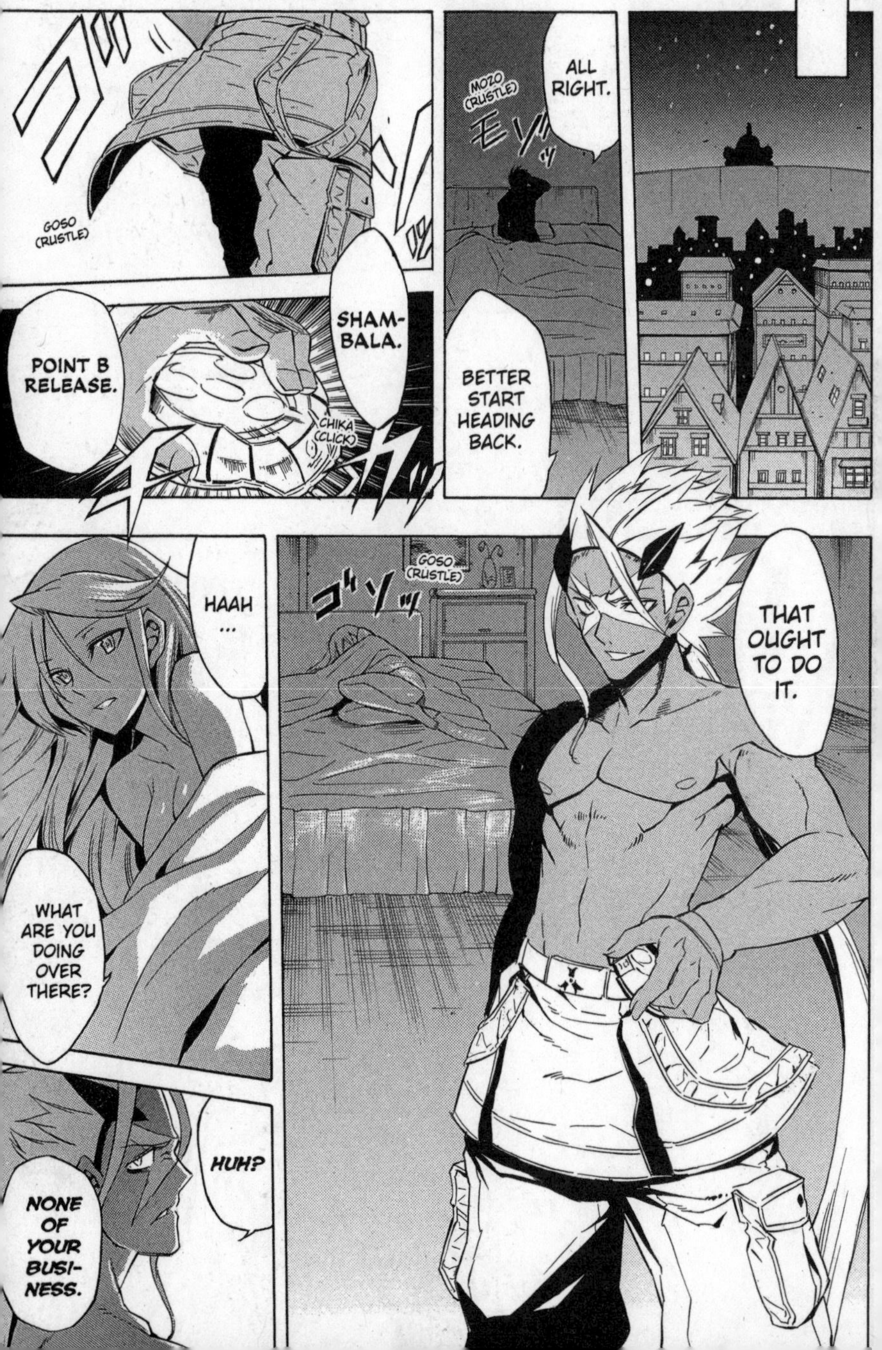
ALL RIGHT.
MOZO (RUSTLE)
BETTER START HEADING BACK.
GOSO (RUSTLE)
SHAMBALA.
POINT B RELEASE.
CHIKA (CLICK)
THAT OUGHT TO DO IT.
GOSO (RUSTLE)
HAAH ...
WHAT ARE YOU DOING OVER THERE?
HUH?
NONE OF YOUR BUSINESS.

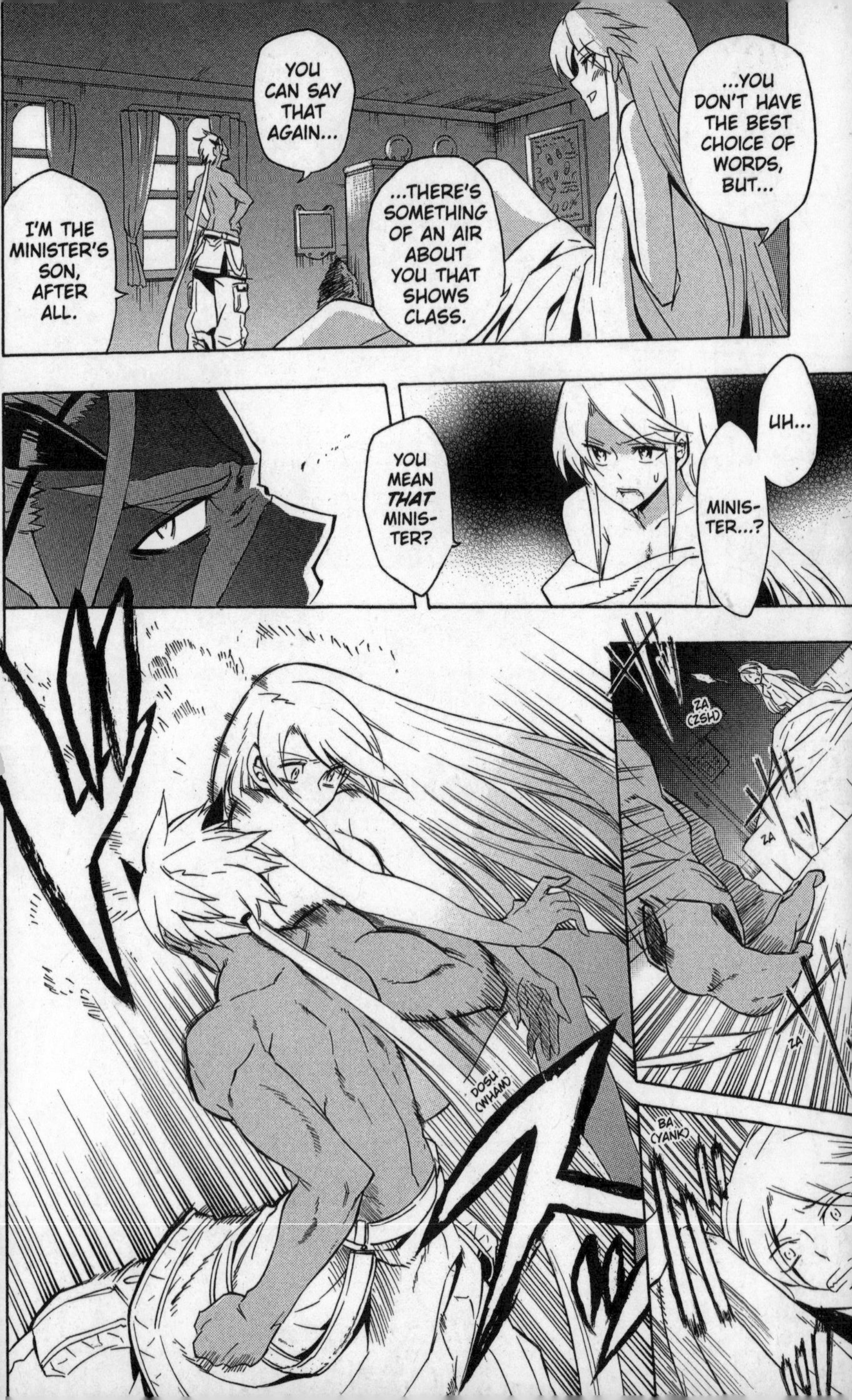
...YOU DON'T HAVE THE BEST CHOICE OF WORDS, BUT...
...THERE'S SOMETHING OF AN AIR ABOUT YOU THAT SHOWS CLASS.
YOU CAN SAY THAT AGAIN...
I'M THE MINISTER'S SON, AFTER ALL.
UH...
MINIS-TER...?
YOU MEAN *THAT* MINIS-TER?
ZA (ZSH)
ZA
ZA
BA (YANK)
DOSU (WHAM)

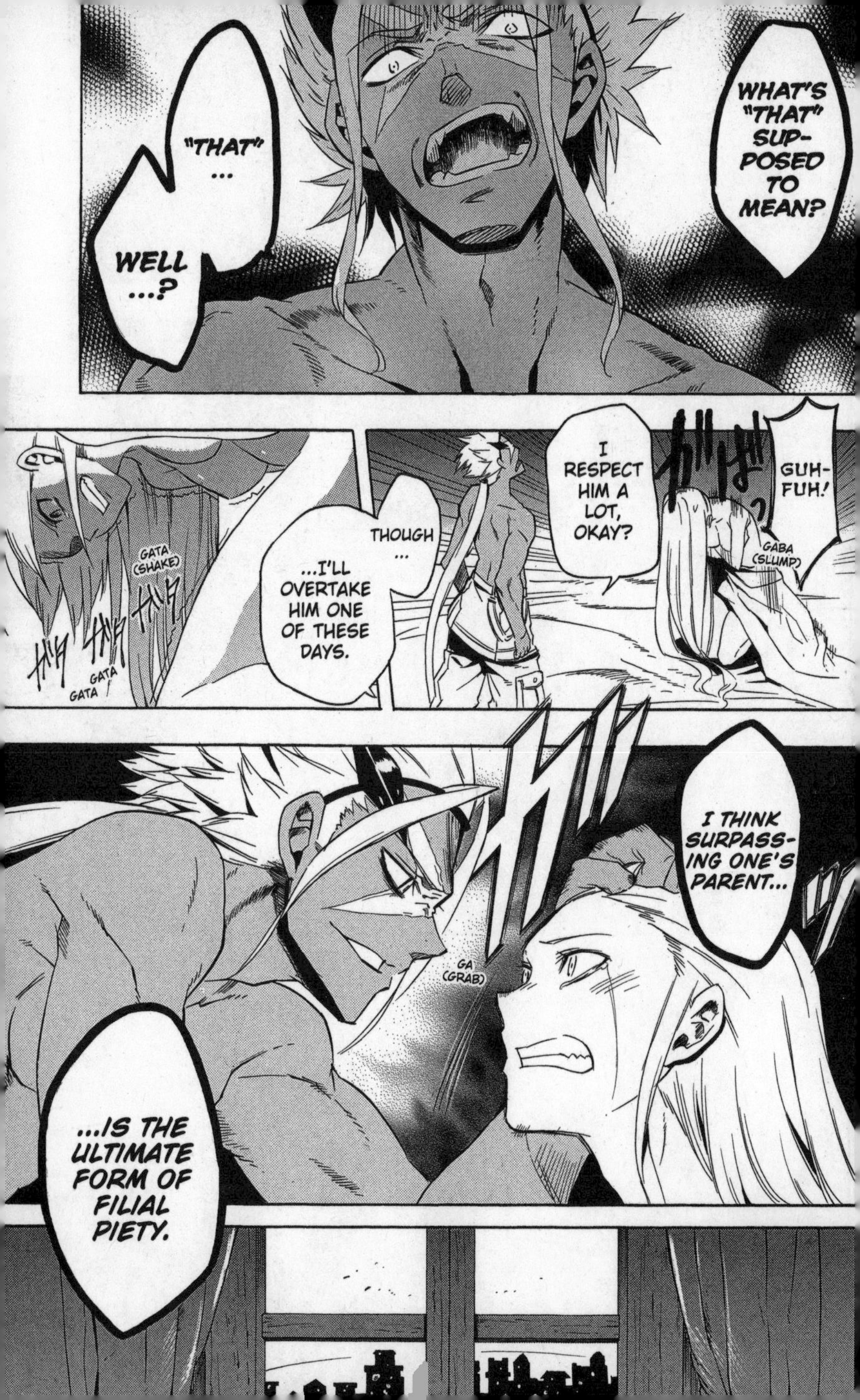
WHAT'S "THAT" SUP-POSED TO MEAN?
"THAT" ...
WELL ...?
GUH-FUH!
GABA (SLUMP)
I RESPECT HIM A LOT, OKAY?
THOUGH ...
...I'LL OVERTAKE HIM ONE OF THESE DAYS.
GATA (SHAKE)
GATA GATA
I THINK SURPASS-ING ONE'S PARENT...
GA (GRAB)
...IS THE ULTIMATE FORM OF FILIAL PIETY.

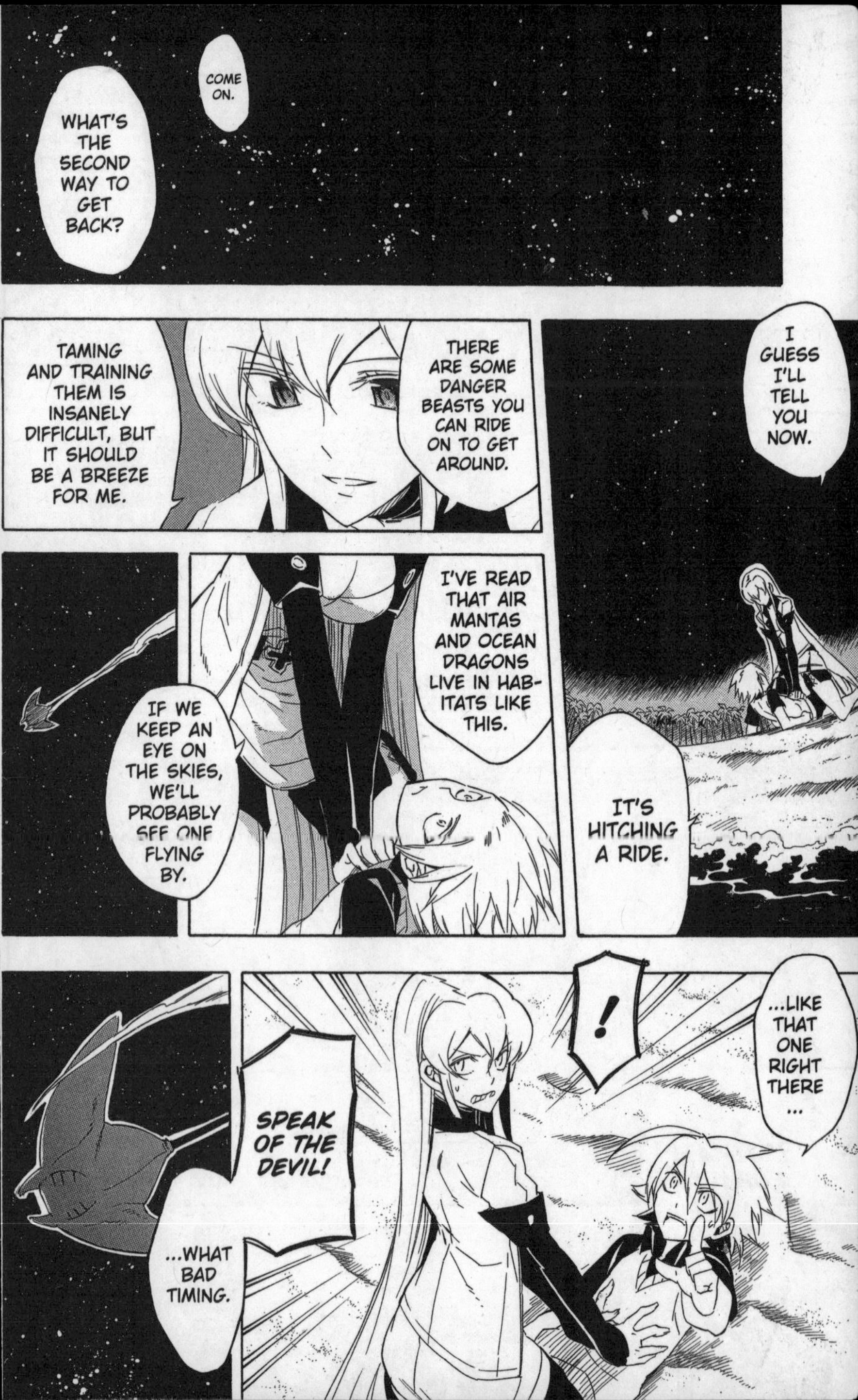
COME ON.
WHAT'S THE SECOND WAY TO GET BACK?
I GUESS I'LL TELL YOU NOW.
IT'S HITCHING A RIDE.
THERE ARE SOME DANGER BEASTS YOU CAN RIDE ON TO GET AROUND.
TAMING AND TRAINING THEM IS INSANELY DIFFICULT, BUT IT SHOULD BE A BREEZE FOR ME.
I'VE READ THAT AIR MANTAS AND OCEAN DRAGONS LIVE IN HAB-ITATS LIKE THIS.
IF WE KEEP AN EYE ON THE SKIES, WE'LL PROBABLY SEE ONE FLYING BY.
...LIKE THAT ONE RIGHT THERE...
!
SPEAK OF THE DEVIL!
...WHAT BAD TIMING.

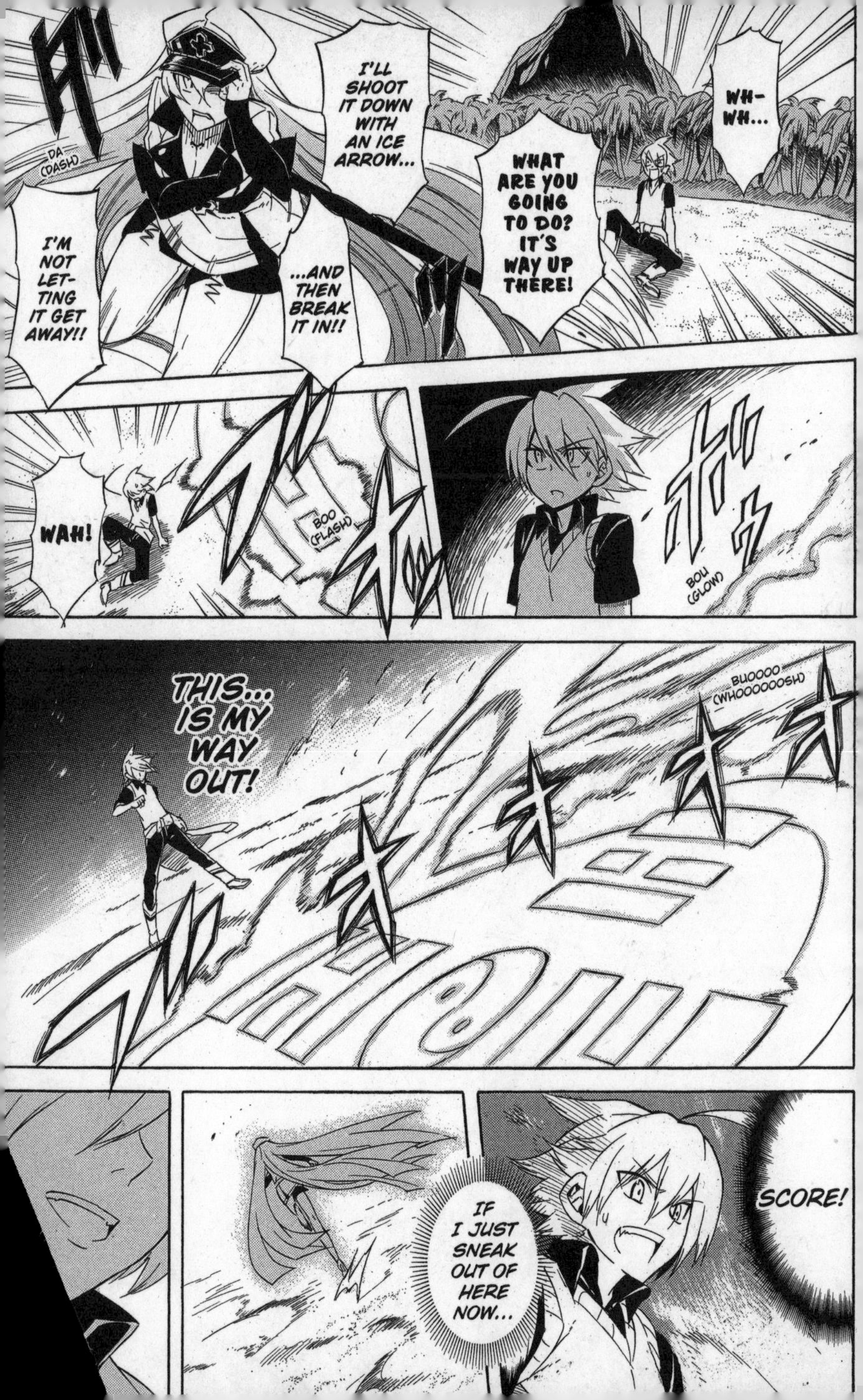
WH-WH...
WHAT ARE YOU GOING TO DO? IT'S WAY UP THERE!
I'LL SHOOT IT DOWN WITH AN ICE ARROW...
...AND THEN BREAK IT IN!!
DA (DASH)
I'M NOT LETTING IT GET AWAY!!
BOU (GLOW)
BOO (FLASH)
WAH!
BUOOOO (WHOOOOOOSH)
THIS... IS MY WAY OUT!
SCORE!
IF I JUST SNEAK OUT OF HERE NOW...

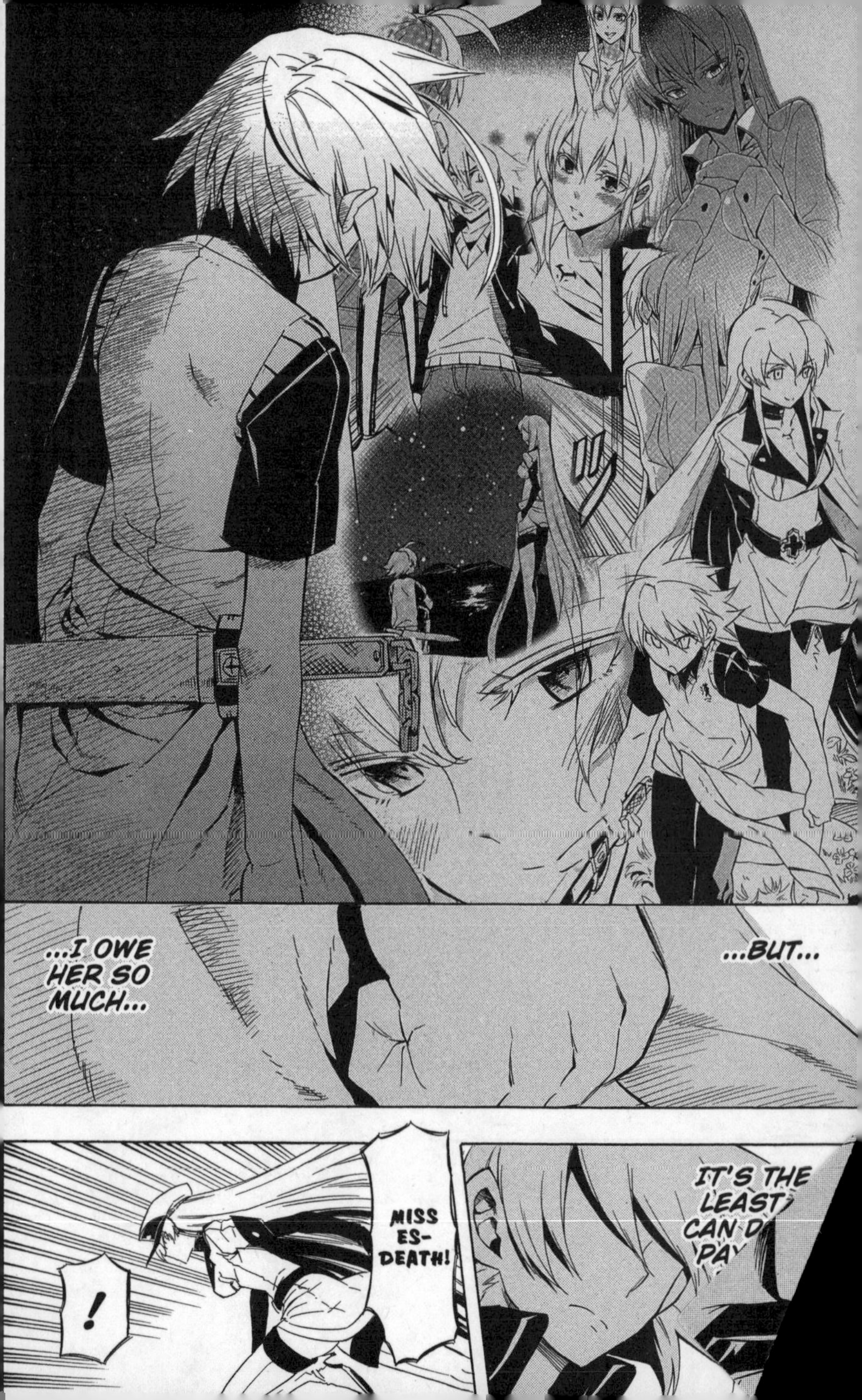
...I OWE HER SO MUCH...
...BUT...
IT'S THE LEAST
MISS ES-DEATH!
!

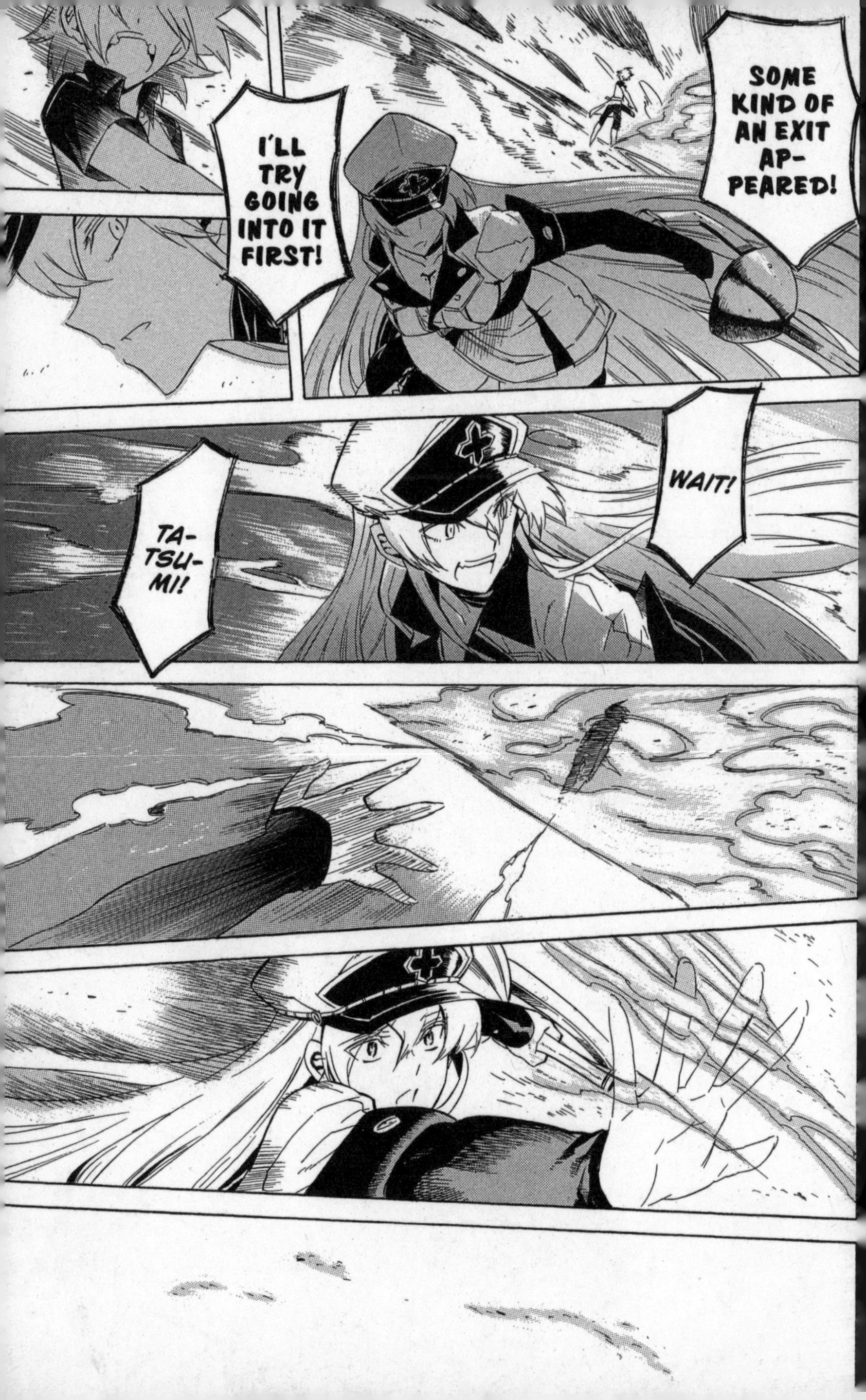
SOME KIND OF AN EXIT AP-PEARED!
I'LL TRY GOING INTO IT FIRST!
WAIT!
TA-TSU-MI!

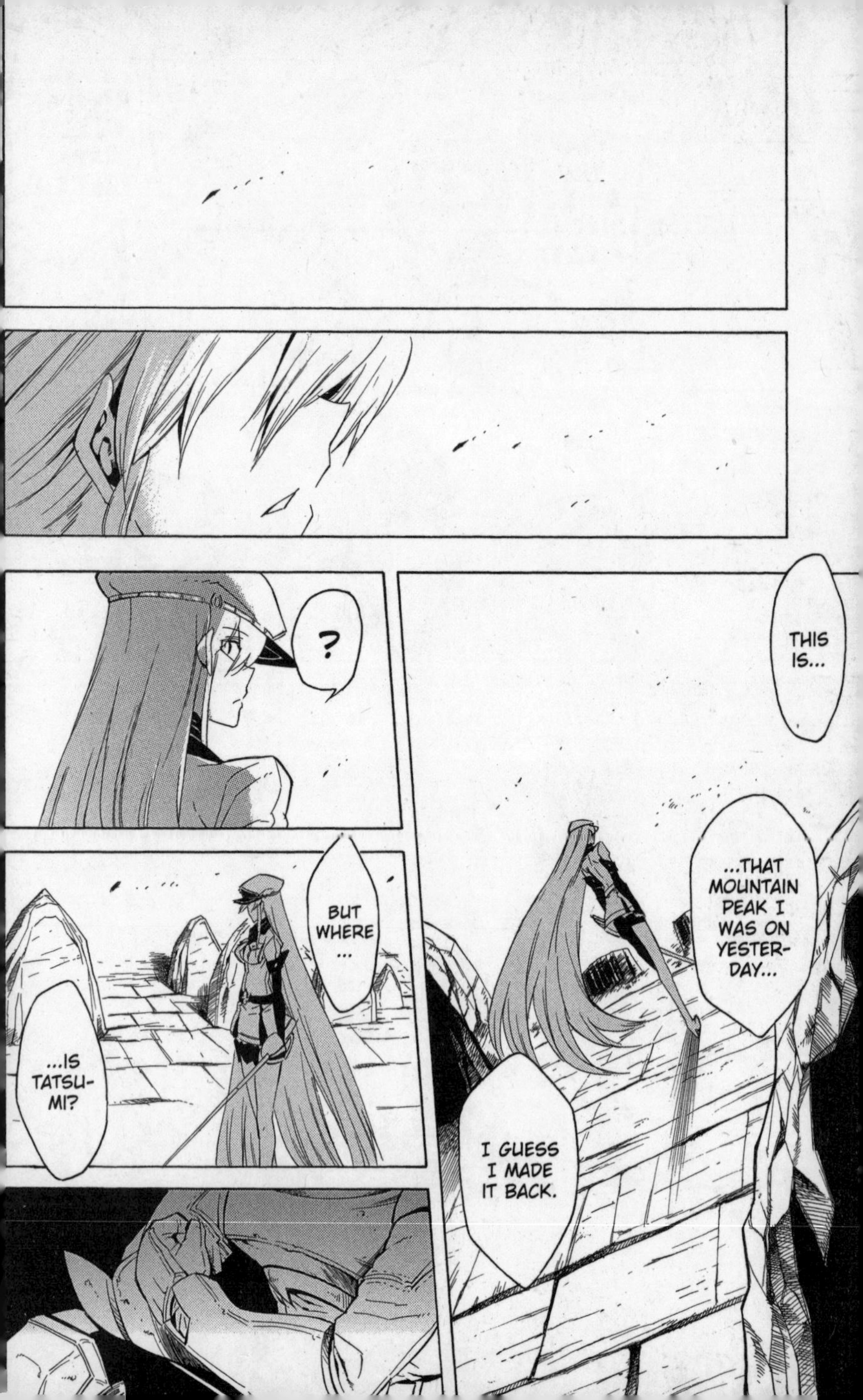
THIS IS...
...THAT MOUNTAIN PEAK I WAS ON YESTER-DAY...
I GUESS I MADE IT BACK.
?
BUT WHERE ...
...IS TATSU-MI?

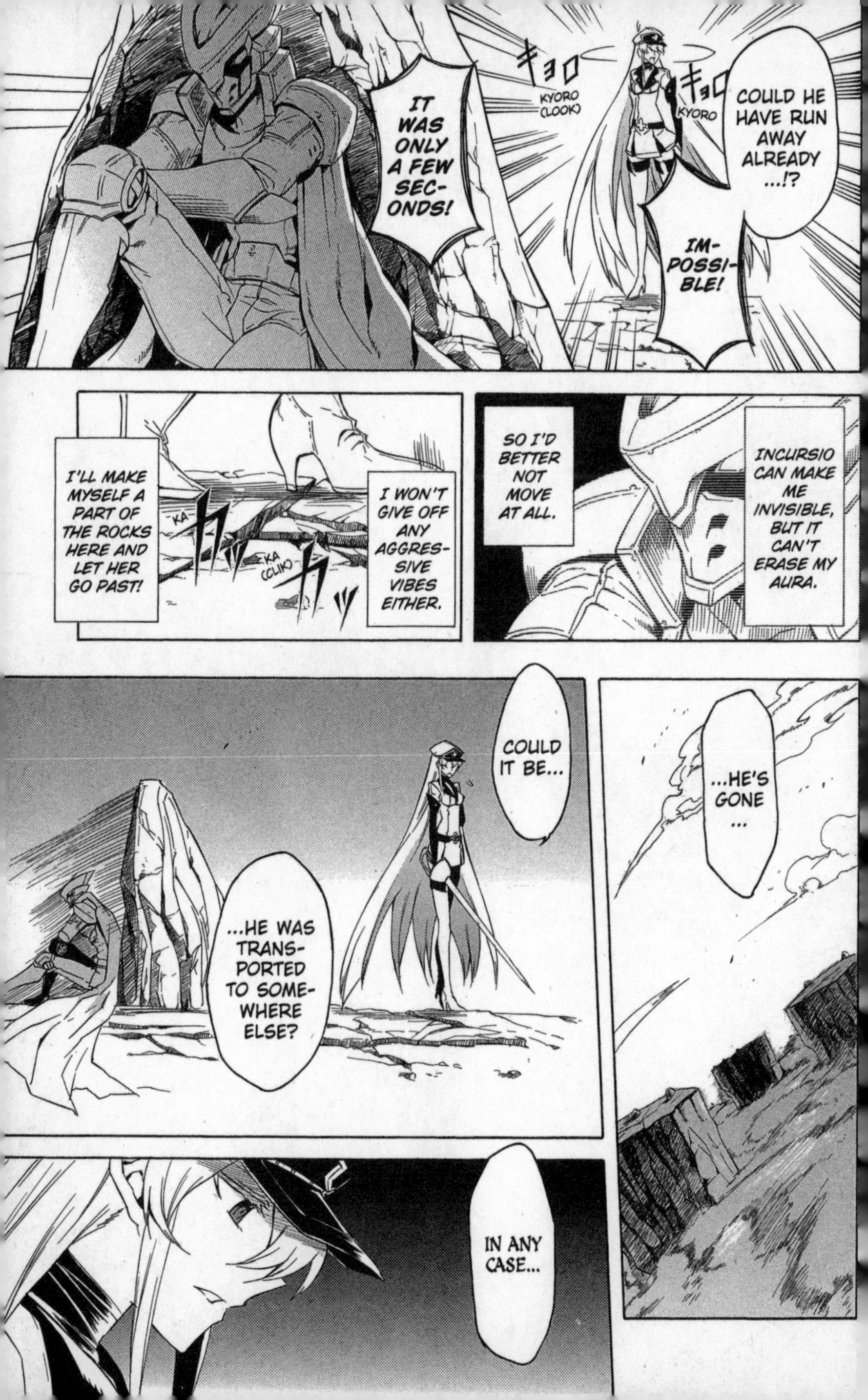
キョロ
KYORO (LOOK)
キョロ
KYORO
COULD HE HAVE RUN AWAY ALREADY ...!?
IMPOSSIBLE!
IT WAS ONLY A FEW SECONDS!
INCURSIO CAN MAKE ME INVISIBLE, BUT IT CAN'T ERASE MY AURA.
SO I'D BETTER NOT MOVE AT ALL.
I WON'T GIVE OFF ANY AGGRESSIVE VIBES EITHER.
I'LL MAKE MYSELF A PART OF THE ROCKS HERE AND LET HER GO PAST!
KA
KA (CLIK)
...HE'S GONE ...
COULD IT BE...
...HE WAS TRANSPORTED TO SOMEWHERE ELSE?
IN ANY CASE...

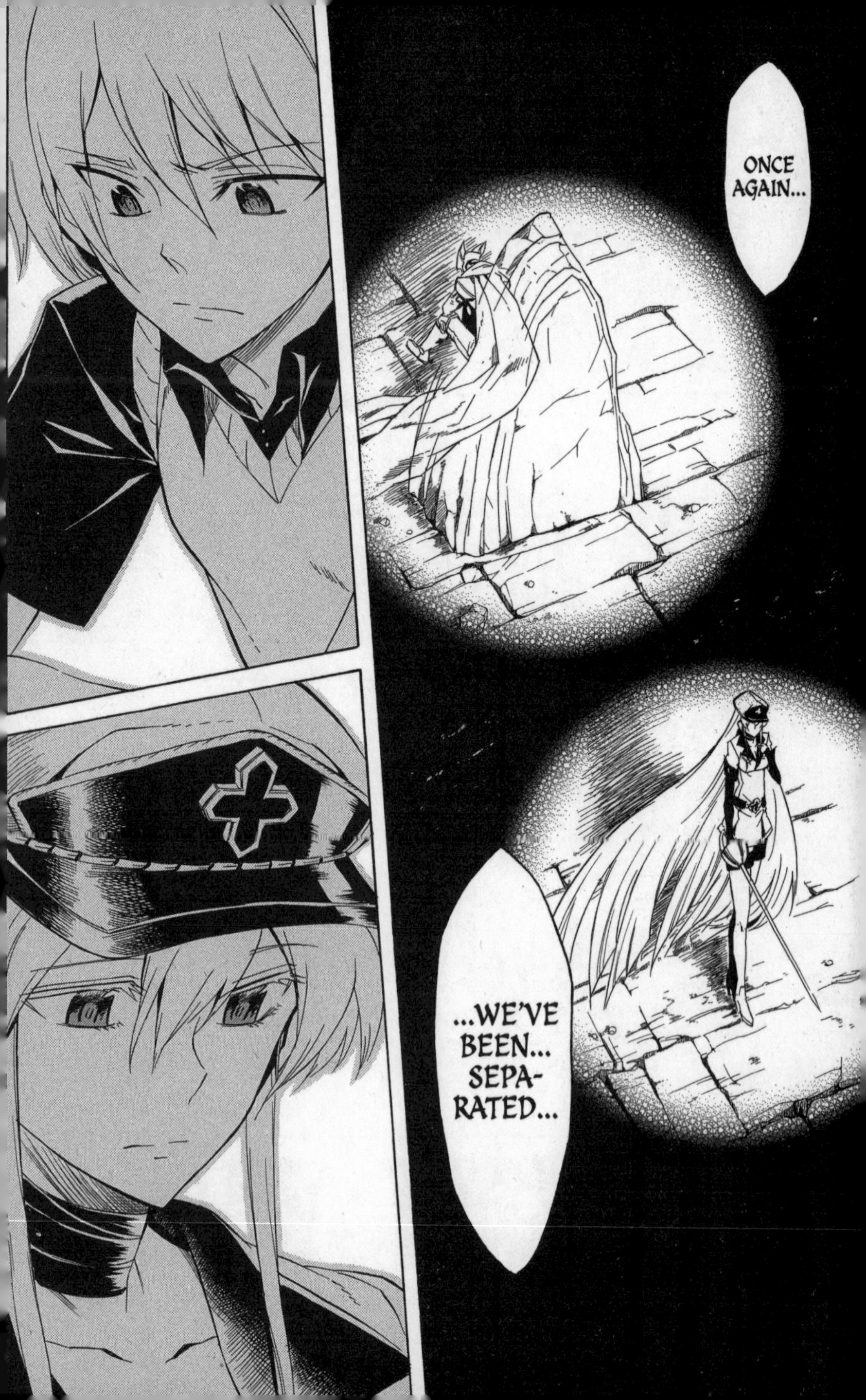
ONCE AGAIN...
...WE'VE BEEN... SEPA-RATED...

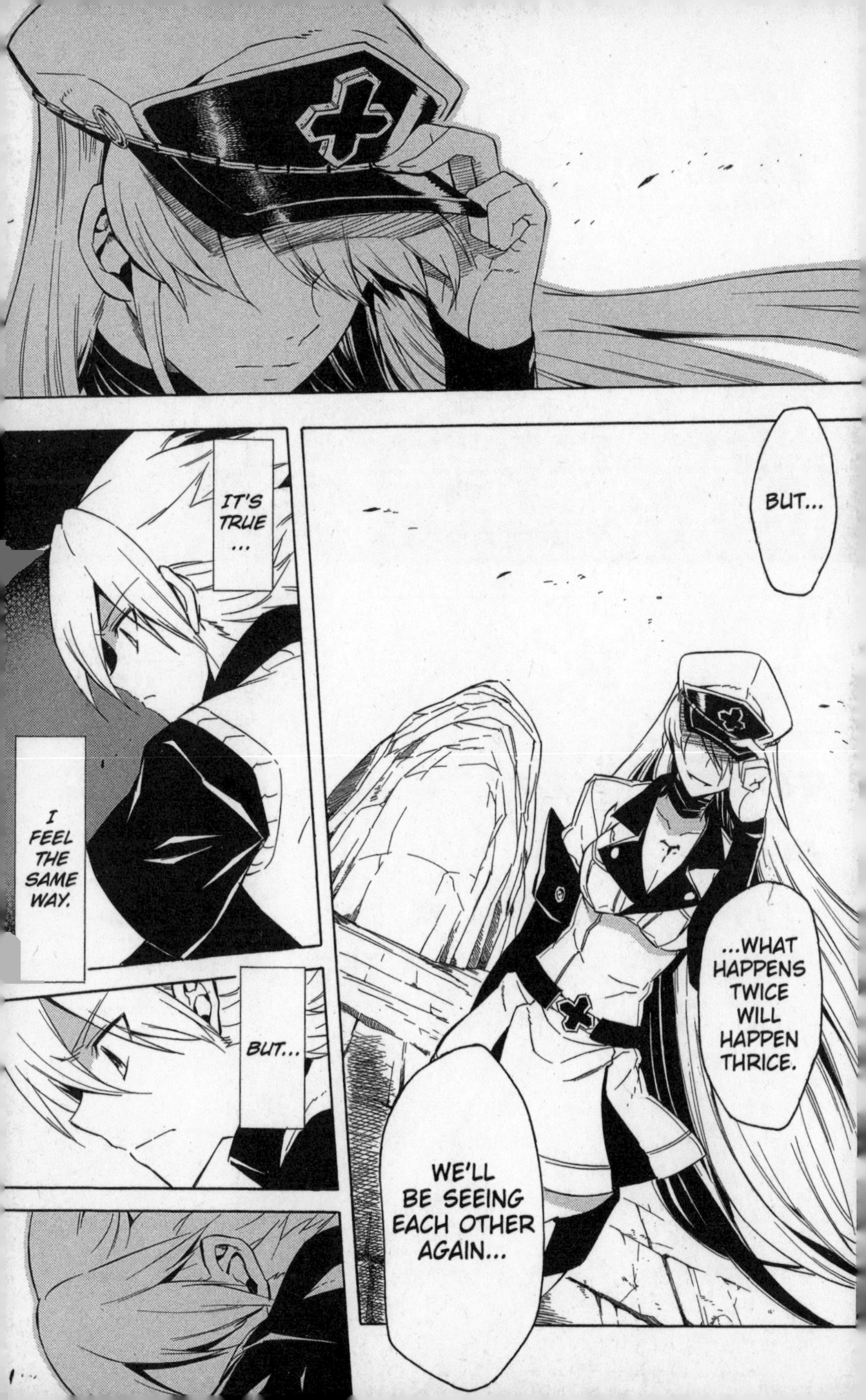
BUT...
...WHAT HAPPENS TWICE WILL HAPPEN THRICE.
WE'LL BE SEEING EACH OTHER AGAIN...
IT'S TRUE...
I FEEL THE SAME WAY.
BUT...

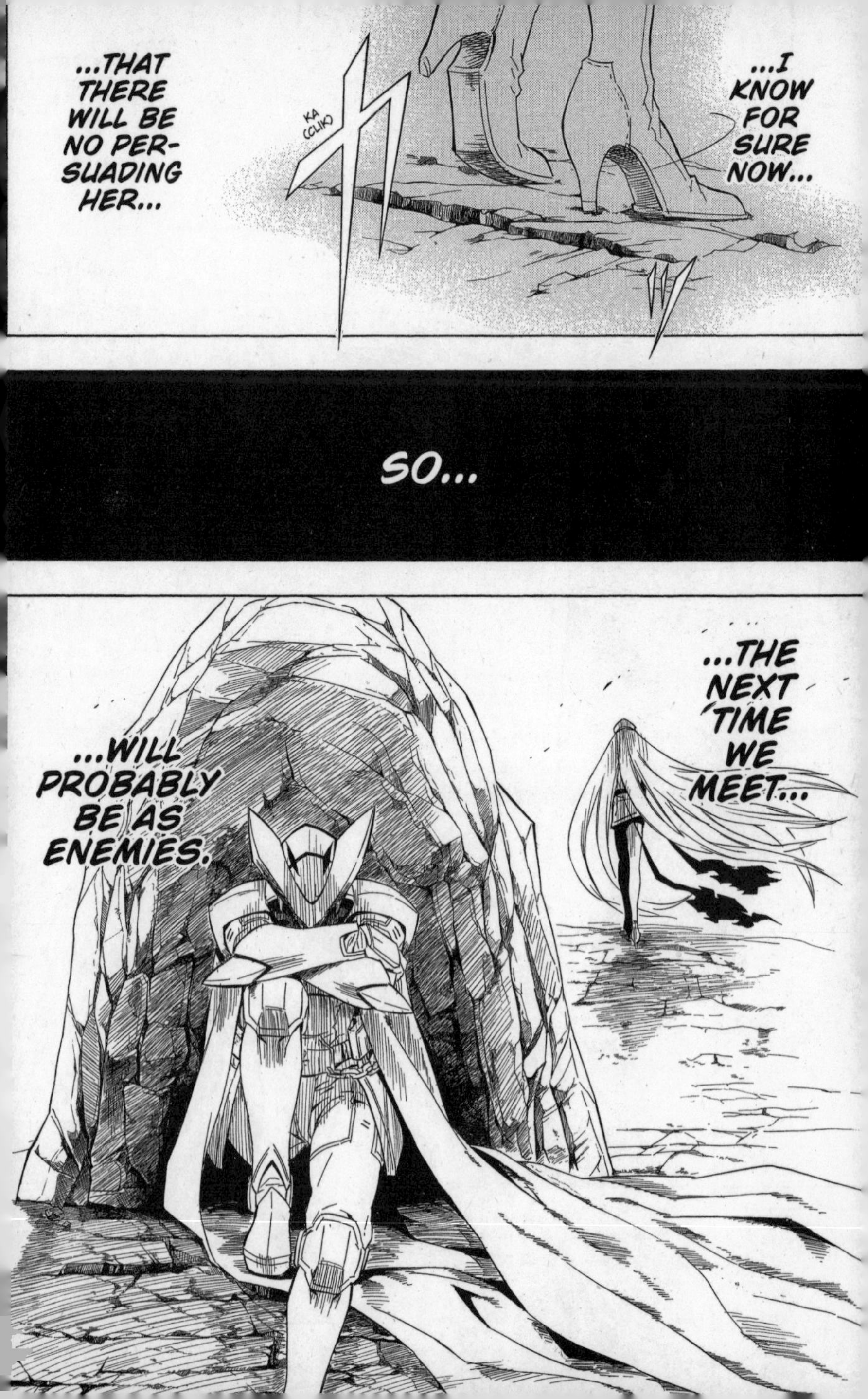
...I KNOW FOR SURE NOW...
KA (CLIK)
...THAT THERE WILL BE NO PERSUADING HER...
SO...
...THE NEXT TIME WE MEET...
...WILL PROBABLY BE AS ENEMIES.

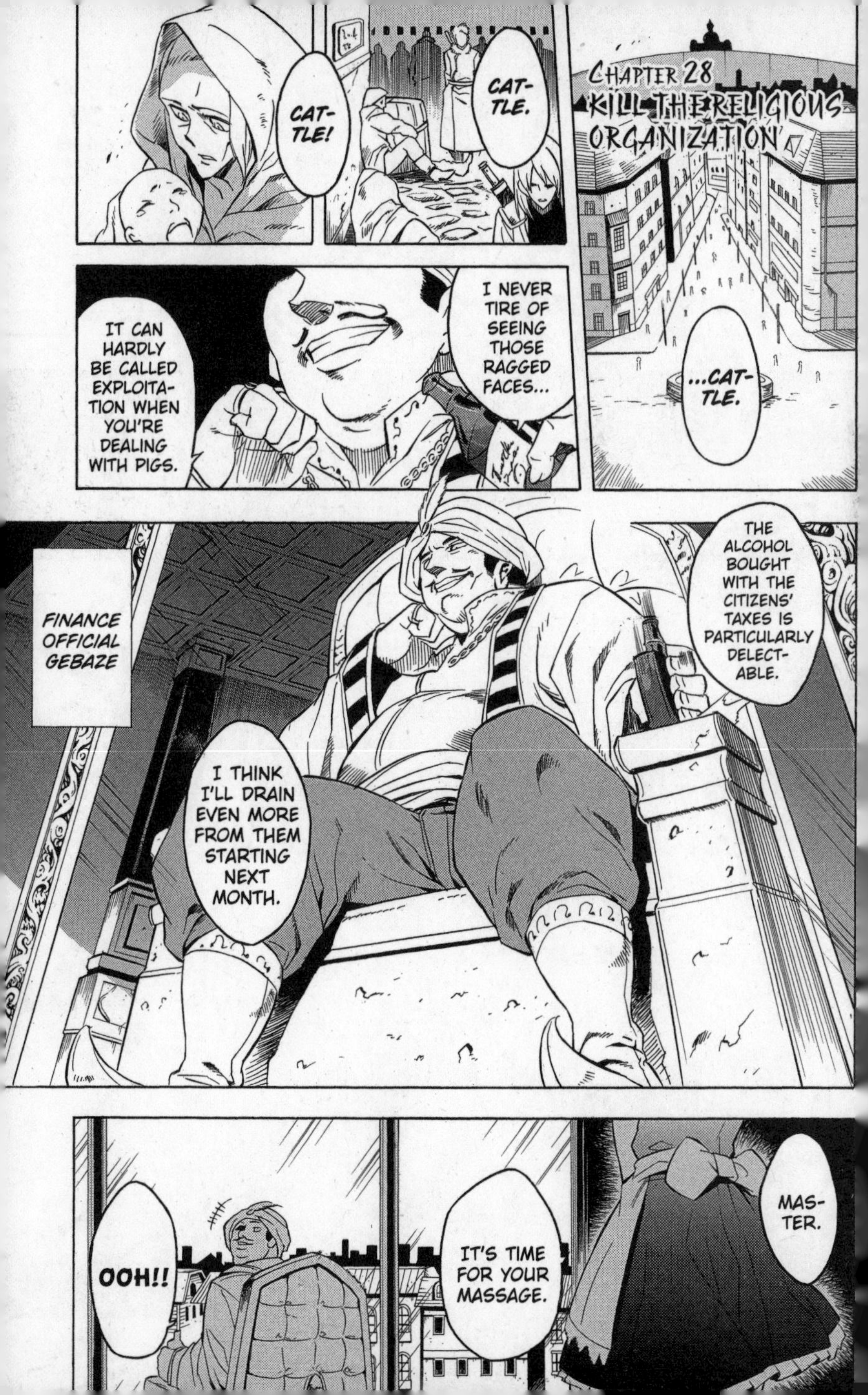
Chapter 28 Kill the Religious Organization
...CAT-TLE.
CAT-TLE.
CAT-TLE!
I NEVER TIRE OF SEEING THOSE RAGGED FACES...
IT CAN HARDLY BE CALLED EXPLOITATION WHEN YOU'RE DEALING WITH PIGS.
THE ALCOHOL BOUGHT WITH THE CITIZENS' TAXES IS PARTICULARLY DELECTABLE.
FINANCE OFFICIAL GEBAZE
I THINK I'LL DRAIN EVEN MORE FROM THEM STARTING NEXT MONTH.
MAS-TER.
IT'S TIME FOR YOUR MASSAGE.
OOH!!

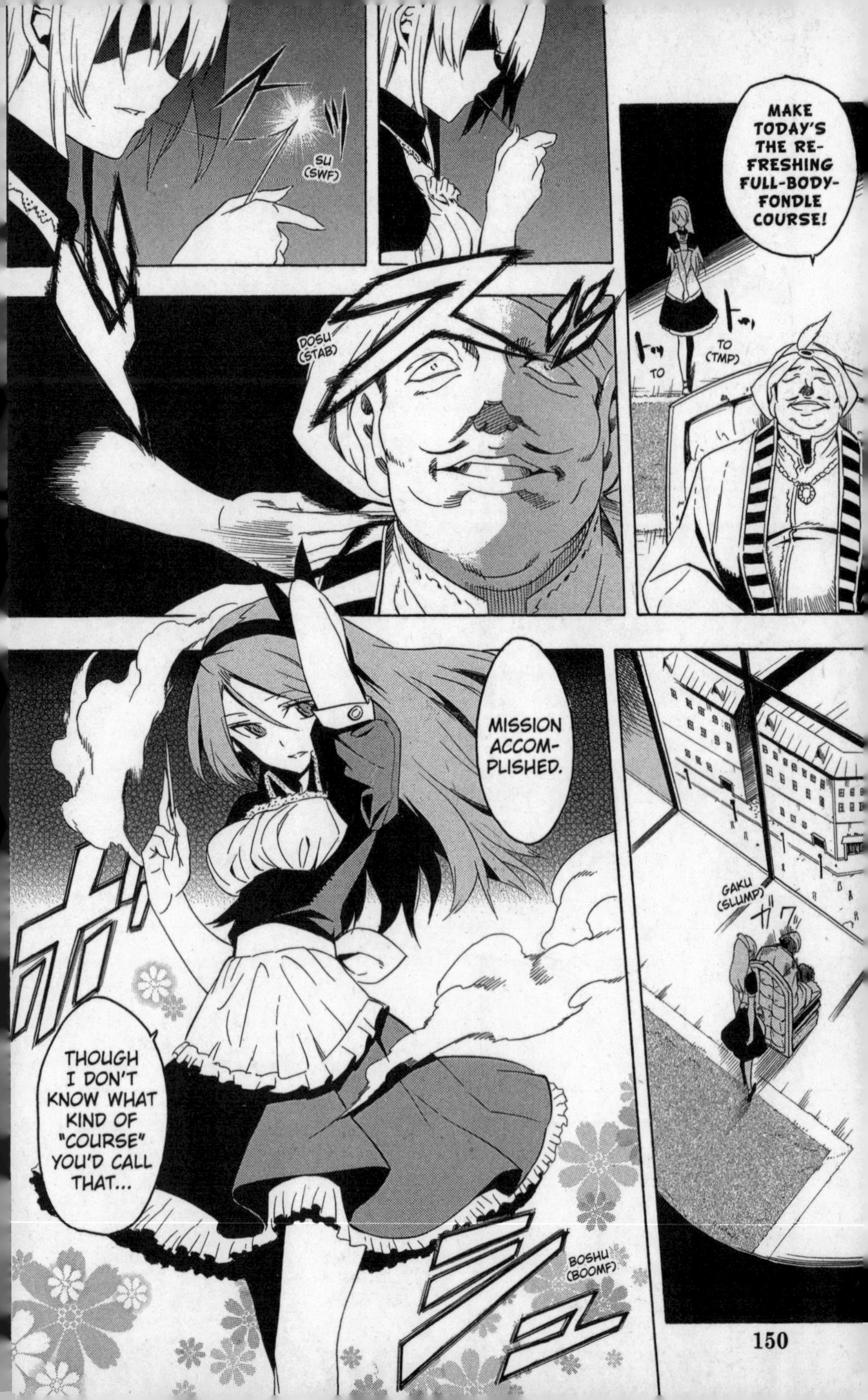

MAKE TODAY'S THE RE-FRESHING FULL-BODY-FONDLE COURSE!
TO (TMP)
TO
SU (SWF)
DOSU (STAB)
GAKU (SLUMP)
MISSION ACCOMPLISHED.
THOUGH I DON'T KNOW WHAT KIND OF "COURSE" YOU'D CALL THAT...
BOSHU (BOOMF)

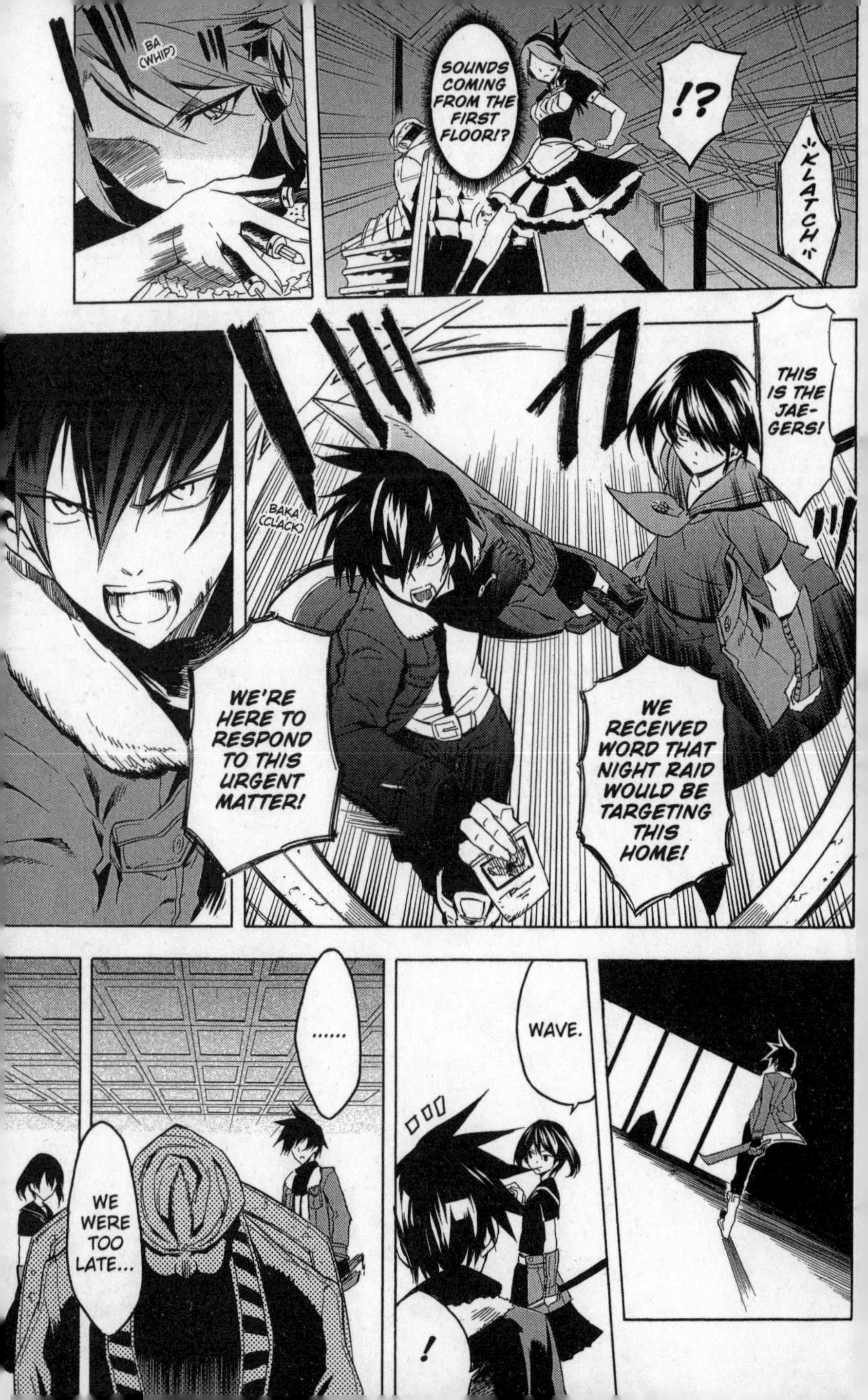
!?
KLATCH
SOUNDS COMING FROM THE FIRST FLOOR!?
BA (WHIP)
THIS IS THE JAEGERS!
WE RECEIVED WORD THAT NIGHT RAID WOULD BE TARGETING THIS HOME!
BAKA (CLACK)
WE'RE HERE TO RESPOND TO THIS URGENT MATTER!
WAVE.
!
......
WE WERE TOO LATE...

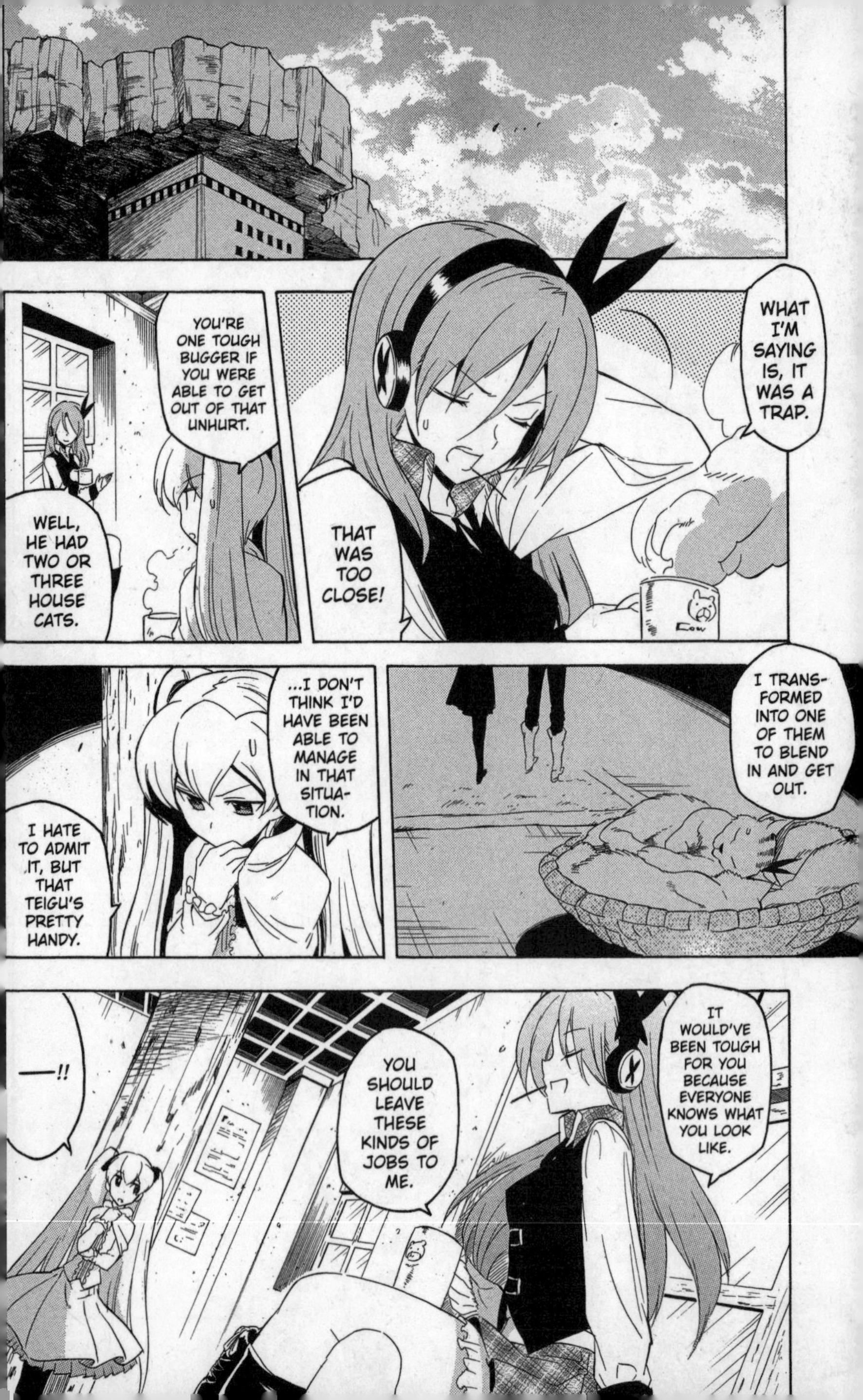
WHAT I'M SAYING IS, IT WAS A TRAP.
THAT WAS TOO CLOSE!
YOU'RE ONE TOUGH BUGGER IF YOU WERE ABLE TO GET OUT OF THAT UNHURT.
WELL, HE HAD TWO OR THREE HOUSE CATS.
I TRANS-FORMED INTO ONE OF THEM TO BLEND IN AND GET OUT.
...I DON'T THINK I'D HAVE BEEN ABLE TO MANAGE IN THAT SITUA-TION.
I HATE TO ADMIT IT, BUT THAT TEIGU'S PRETTY HANDY.
IT WOULD'VE BEEN TOUGH FOR YOU BECAUSE EVERYONE KNOWS WHAT YOU LOOK LIKE.
YOU SHOULD LEAVE THESE KINDS OF JOBS TO ME.
—!!

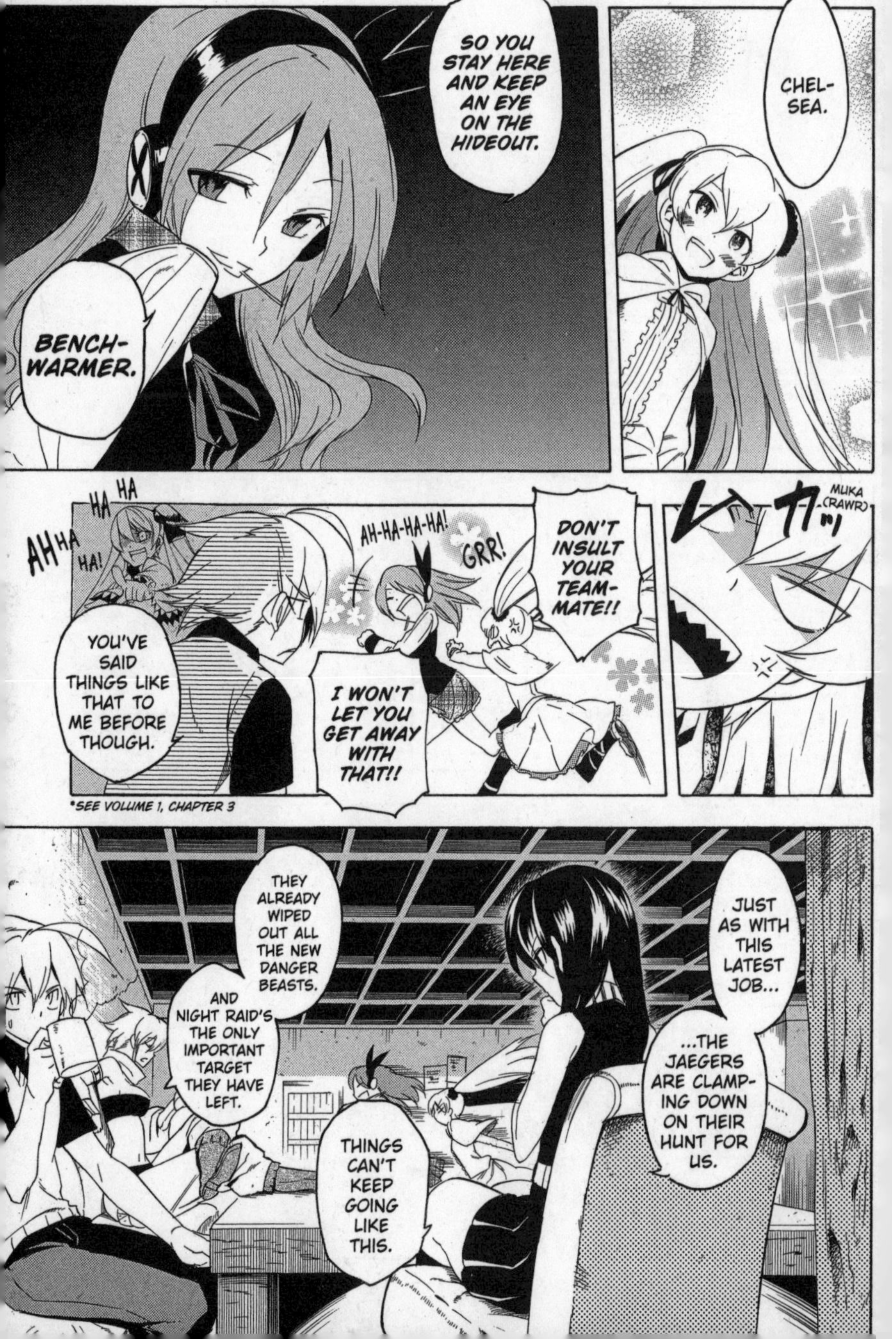
CHEL-SEA.
SO YOU STAY HERE AND KEEP AN EYE ON THE HIDEOUT.
BENCH-WARMER.
MUKA (RAWR)
DON'T INSULT YOUR TEAM-MATE!!
GRR!
AH-HA-HA-HA!
I WON'T LET YOU GET AWAY WITH THAT!!
HA HA
AH HA HA!
YOU'VE SAID THINGS LIKE THAT TO ME BEFORE THOUGH.
*SEE VOLUME 1, CHAPTER 3
JUST AS WITH THIS LATEST JOB...
...THE JAEGERS ARE CLAMP-ING DOWN ON THEIR HUNT FOR US.
THEY ALREADY WIPED OUT ALL THE NEW DANGER BEASTS.
AND NIGHT RAID'S THE ONLY IMPORTANT TARGET THEY HAVE LEFT.
THINGS CAN'T KEEP GOING LIKE THIS.

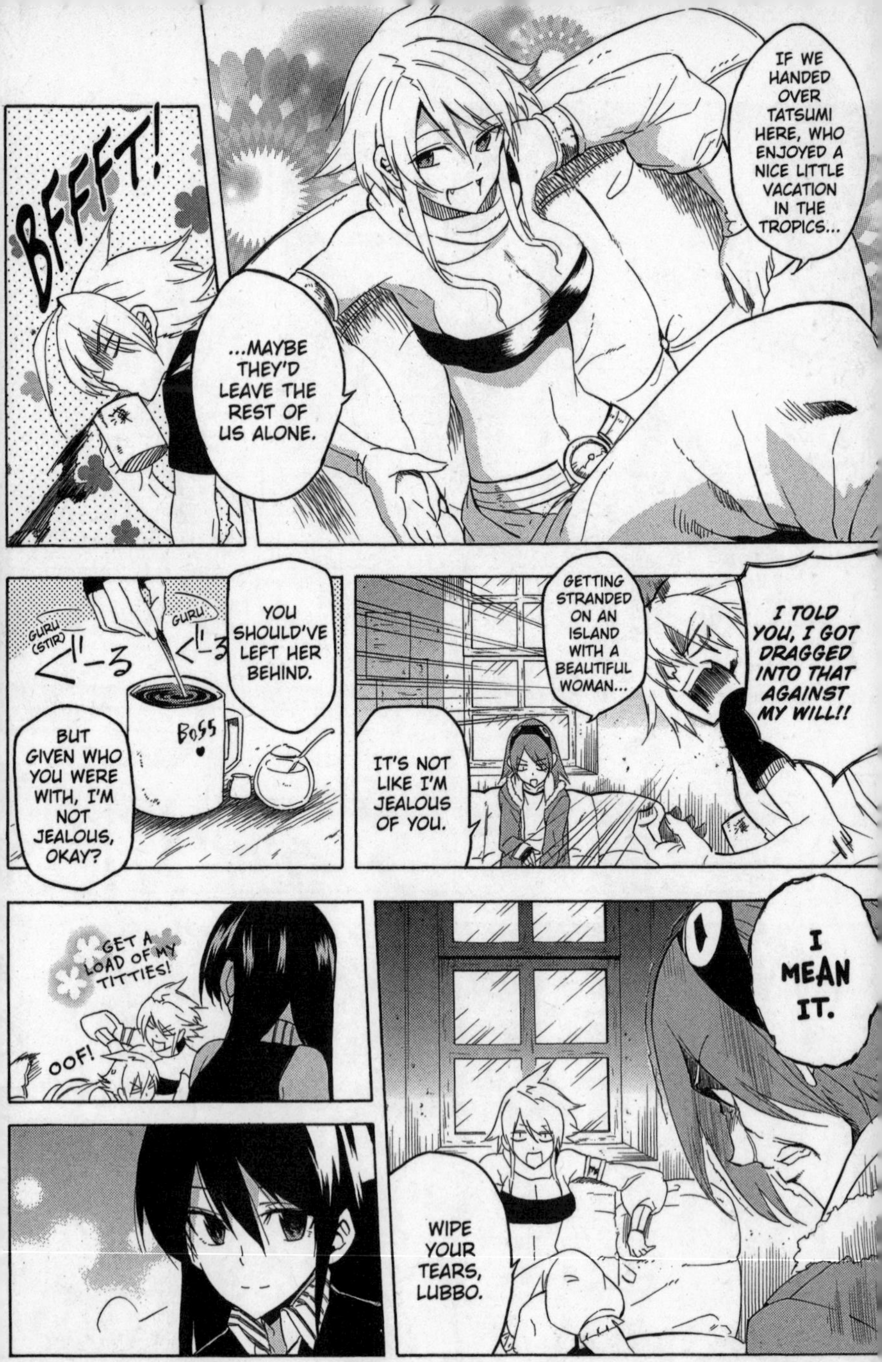

IF WE HANDED OVER TATSUMI HERE, WHO ENJOYED A NICE LITTLE VACATION IN THE TROPICS...
...MAYBE THEY'D LEAVE THE REST OF US ALONE.
BFFFT!
GETTING STRANDED ON AN ISLAND WITH A BEAUTIFUL WOMAN...
I TOLD YOU, I GOT DRAGGED INTO THAT AGAINST MY WILL!!
IT'S NOT LIKE I'M JEALOUS OF YOU.
YOU SHOULD'VE LEFT HER BEHIND.
GURU
ぐーる
GURU (STIR)
ぐーる
BOSS
BUT GIVEN WHO YOU WERE WITH, I'M NOT JEALOUS, OKAY?
I MEAN IT.
WIPE YOUR TEARS, LUBBO.
GET A LOAD OF MY TITTIES!
OOF!

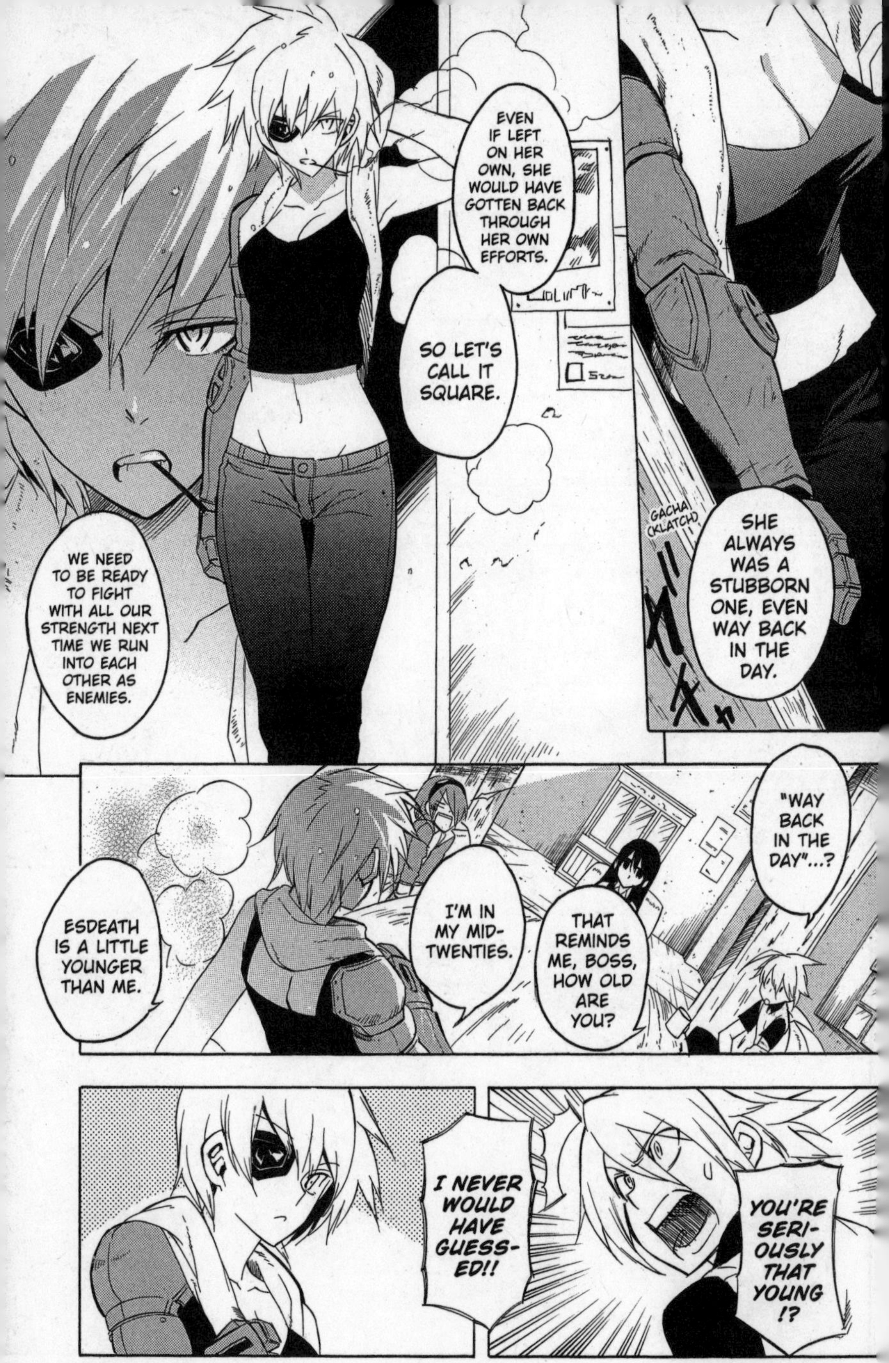

EVEN IF LEFT ON HER OWN, SHE WOULD HAVE GOTTEN BACK THROUGH HER OWN EFFORTS.
SO LET'S CALL IT SQUARE.
WE NEED TO BE READY TO FIGHT WITH ALL OUR STRENGTH NEXT TIME WE RUN INTO EACH OTHER AS ENEMIES.
GACHA (KLATCH)
SHE ALWAYS WAS A STUBBORN ONE, EVEN WAY BACK IN THE DAY.
"WAY BACK IN THE DAY"...?
THAT REMINDS ME, BOSS, HOW OLD ARE YOU?
I'M IN MY MID-TWENTIES.
ESDEATH IS A LITTLE YOUNGER THAN ME.
YOU'RE SERI-OUSLY THAT YOUNG!?
I NEVER WOULD HAVE GUESS-ED!!

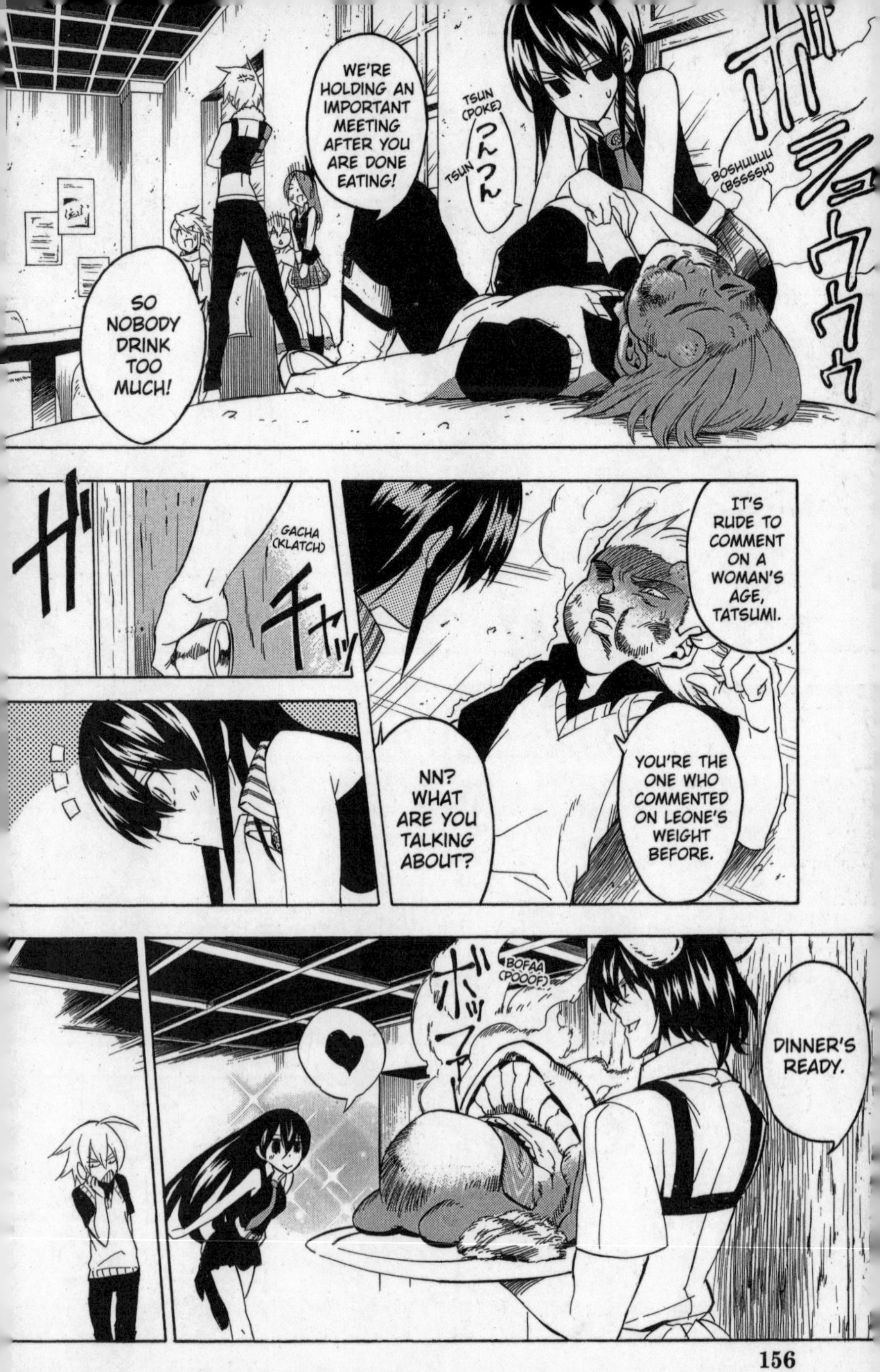
BOSHUUUUU (BSSSSH)
TSUN (POKE) つんつん TSUN
WE'RE HOLDING AN IMPORTANT MEETING AFTER YOU ARE DONE EATING!
SO NOBODY DRINK TOO MUCH!
IT'S RUDE TO COMMENT ON A WOMAN'S AGE, TATSUMI.
GACHA (KLATCH)
YOU'RE THE ONE WHO COMMENTED ON LEONE'S WEIGHT BEFORE.
NN? WHAT ARE YOU TALKING ABOUT?
DINNER'S READY.
BOFAA (POOOF)

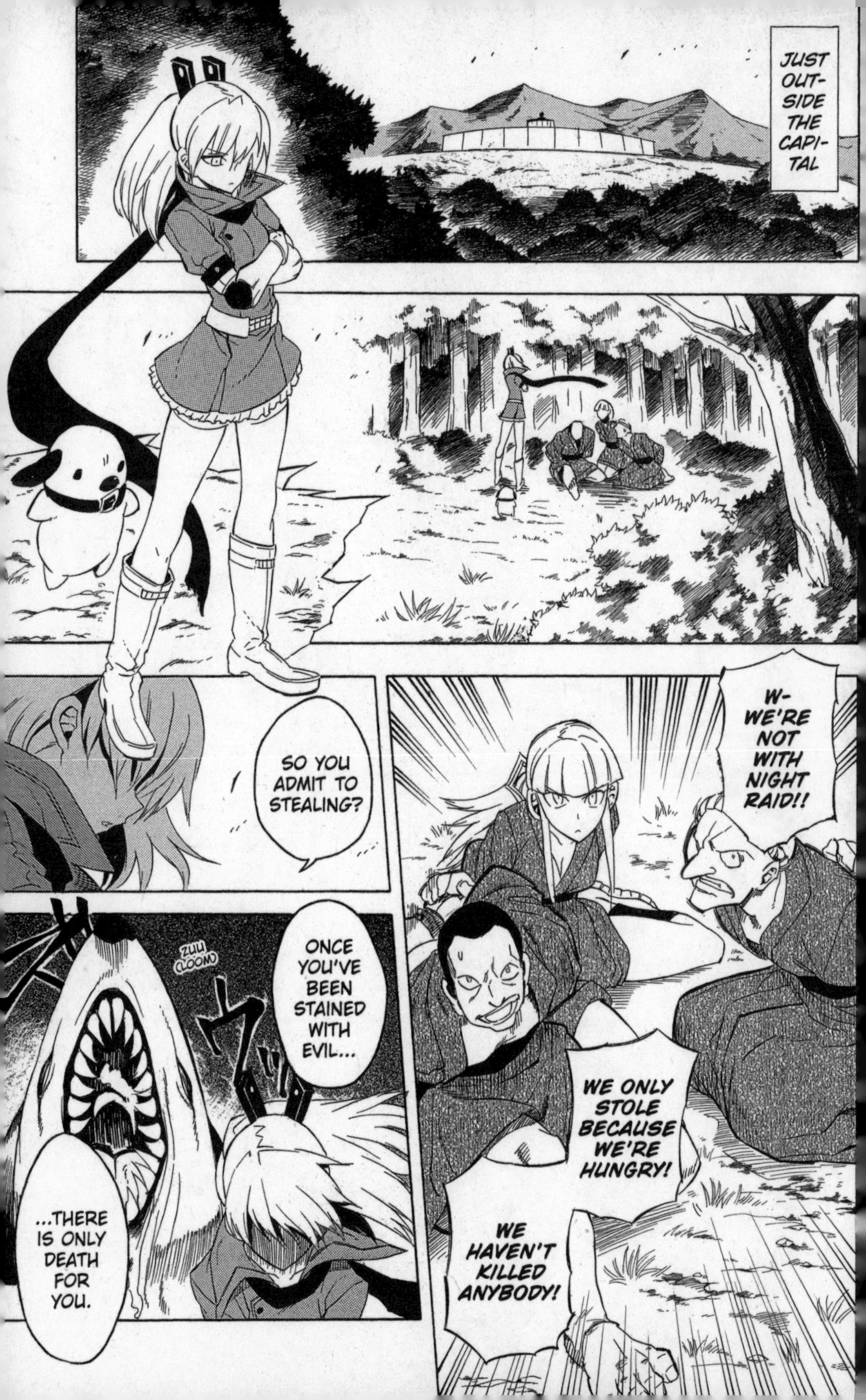
JUST OUTSIDE THE CAPITAL
W-WE'RE NOT WITH NIGHT RAID!!
WE ONLY STOLE BECAUSE WE'RE HUNGRY!
WE HAVEN'T KILLED ANYBODY!
SO YOU ADMIT TO STEALING?
ZUU (LOOM)
ONCE YOU'VE BEEN STAINED WITH EVIL...
...THERE IS ONLY DEATH FOR YOU.

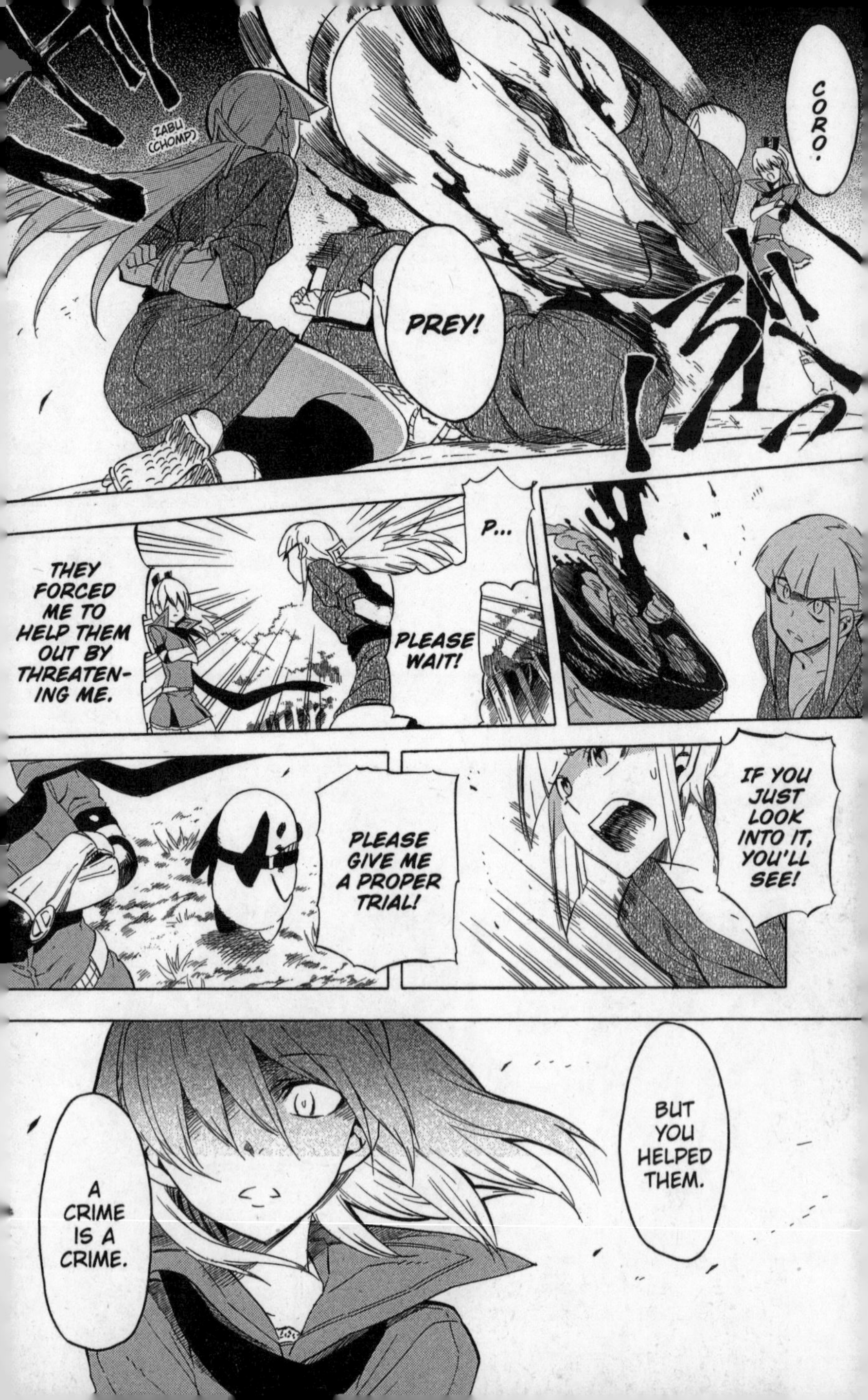
CORO.
ZABU (CHOMP)
PREY!
P...
PLEASE WAIT!
THEY FORCED ME TO HELP THEM OUT BY THREATEN-ING ME.
IF YOU JUST LOOK INTO IT, YOU'LL SEE!
PLEASE GIVE ME A PROPER TRIAL!
BUT YOU HELPED THEM.
A CRIME IS A CRIME.

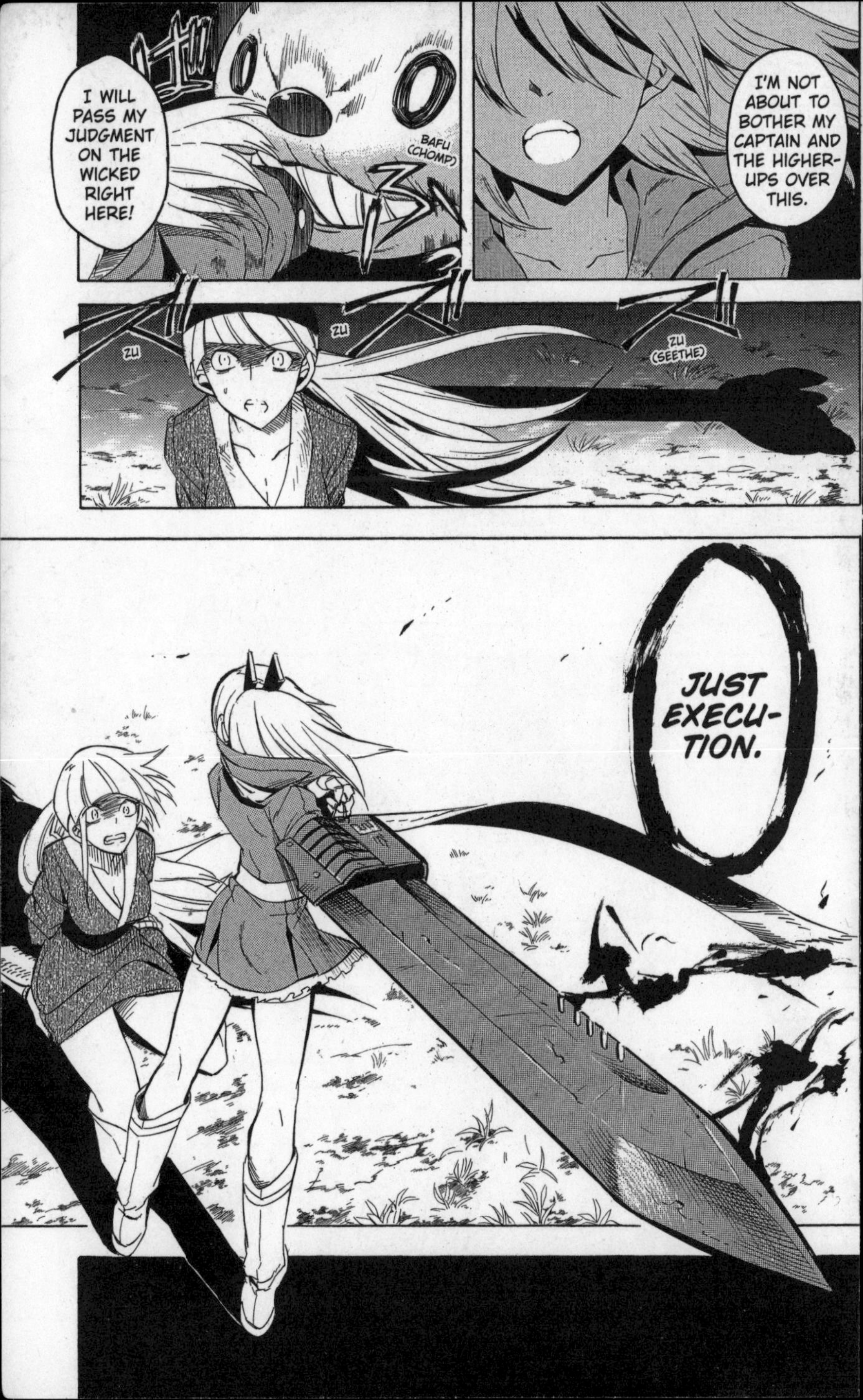

I'M NOT ABOUT TO BOTHER MY CAPTAIN AND THE HIGHER-UPS OVER THIS.
I WILL PASS MY JUDGMENT ON THE WICKED RIGHT HERE!
BAFU (CHOMP)
ZU (SEETHE)
ZU
ZU
JUST EXECU-TION.

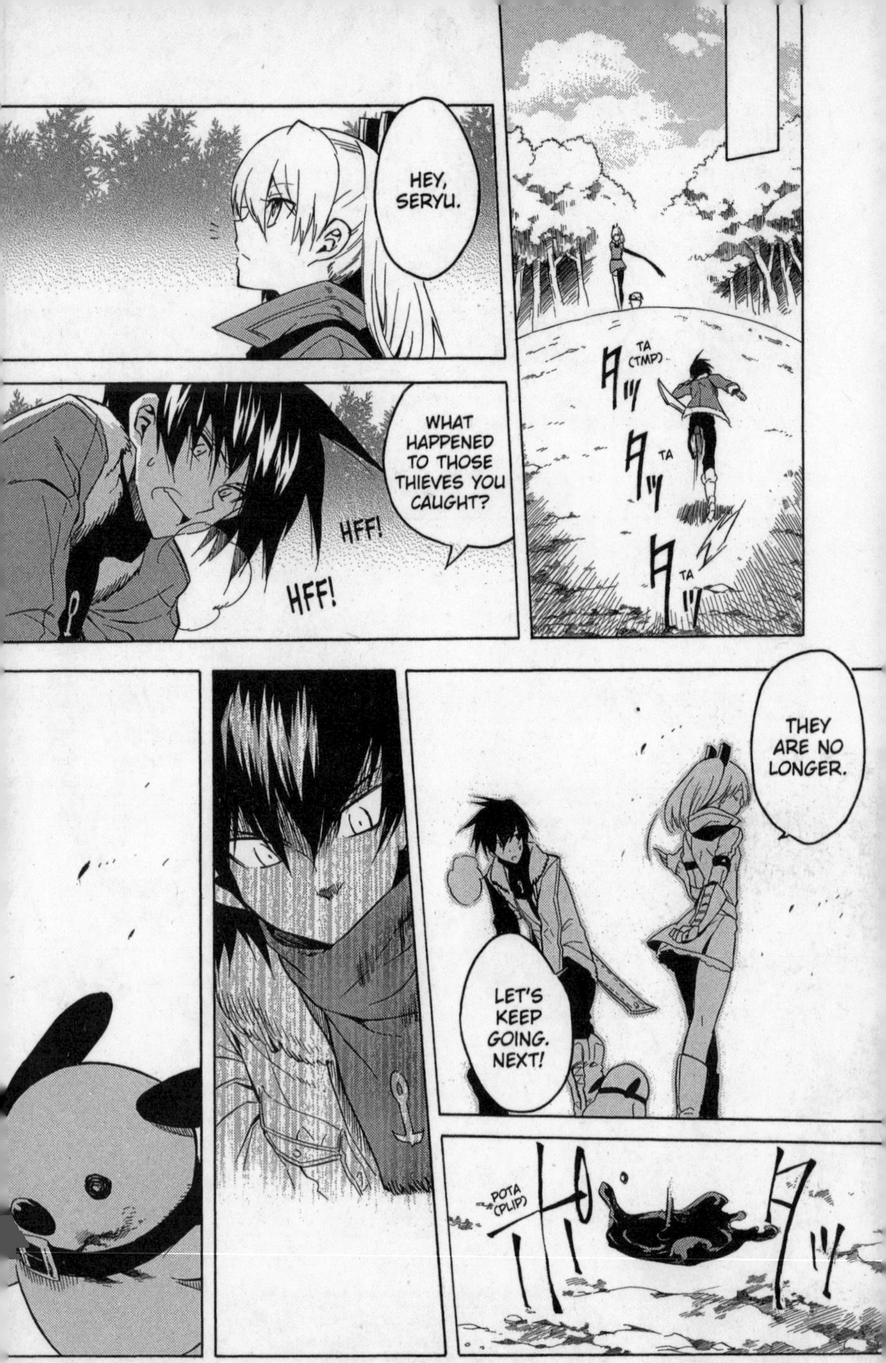
TA (TMP)
TA
TA
HEY, SERYU.
WHAT HAPPENED TO THOSE THIEVES YOU CAUGHT?
HFF!
HFF!
THEY ARE NO LONGER.
LET'S KEEP GOING. NEXT!
POTA (PLIP)

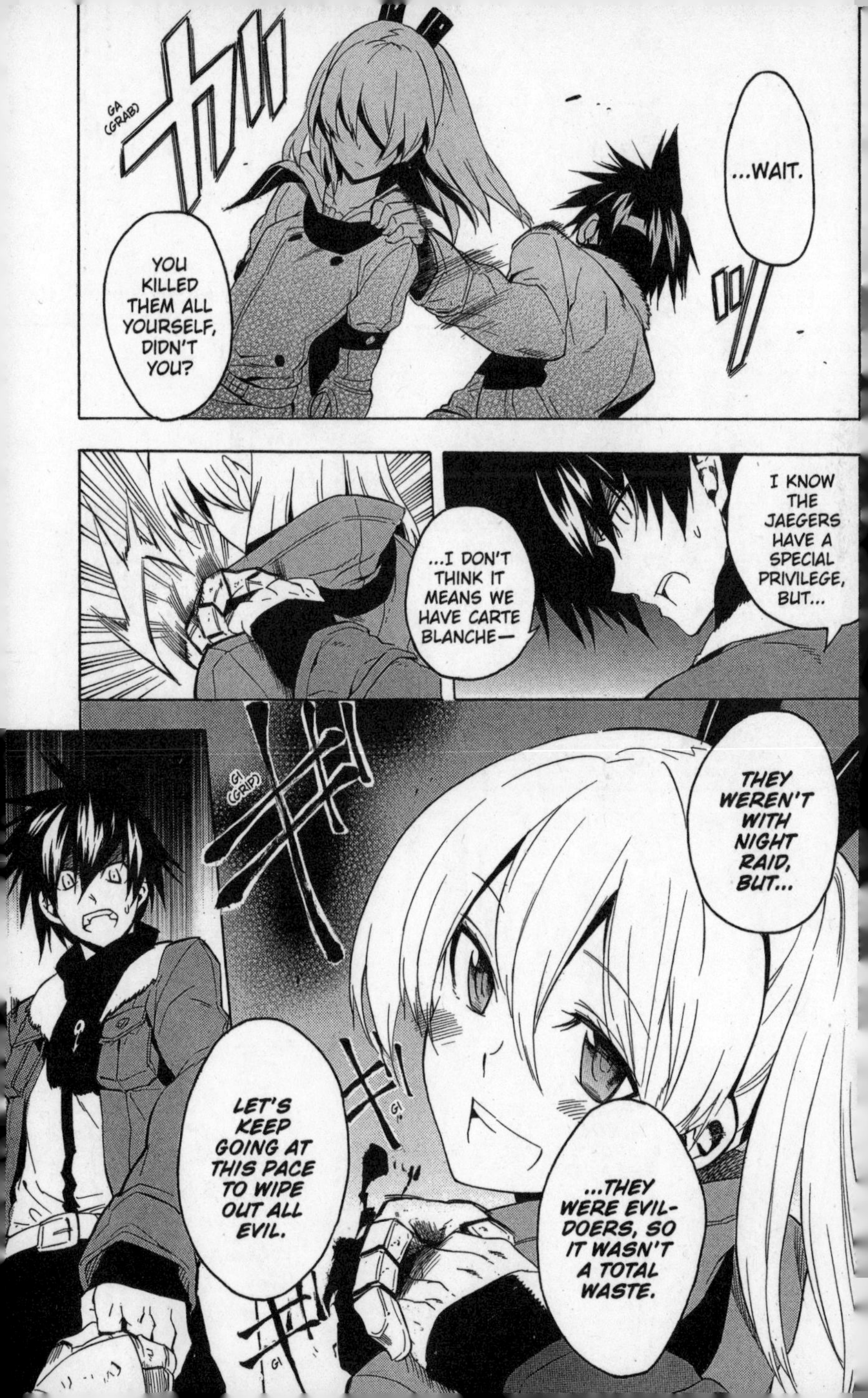
...WAIT.
GA (GRAB)
YOU KILLED THEM ALL YOURSELF, DIDN'T YOU?
I KNOW THE JAEGERS HAVE A SPECIAL PRIVILEGE, BUT...
...I DON'T THINK IT MEANS WE HAVE CARTE BLANCHE—
THEY WEREN'T WITH NIGHT RAID, BUT...
GI (GRIP)
...THEY WERE EVIL-DOERS, SO IT WASN'T A TOTAL WASTE.
LET'S KEEP GOING AT THIS PACE TO WIPE OUT ALL EVIL.
GI
GI

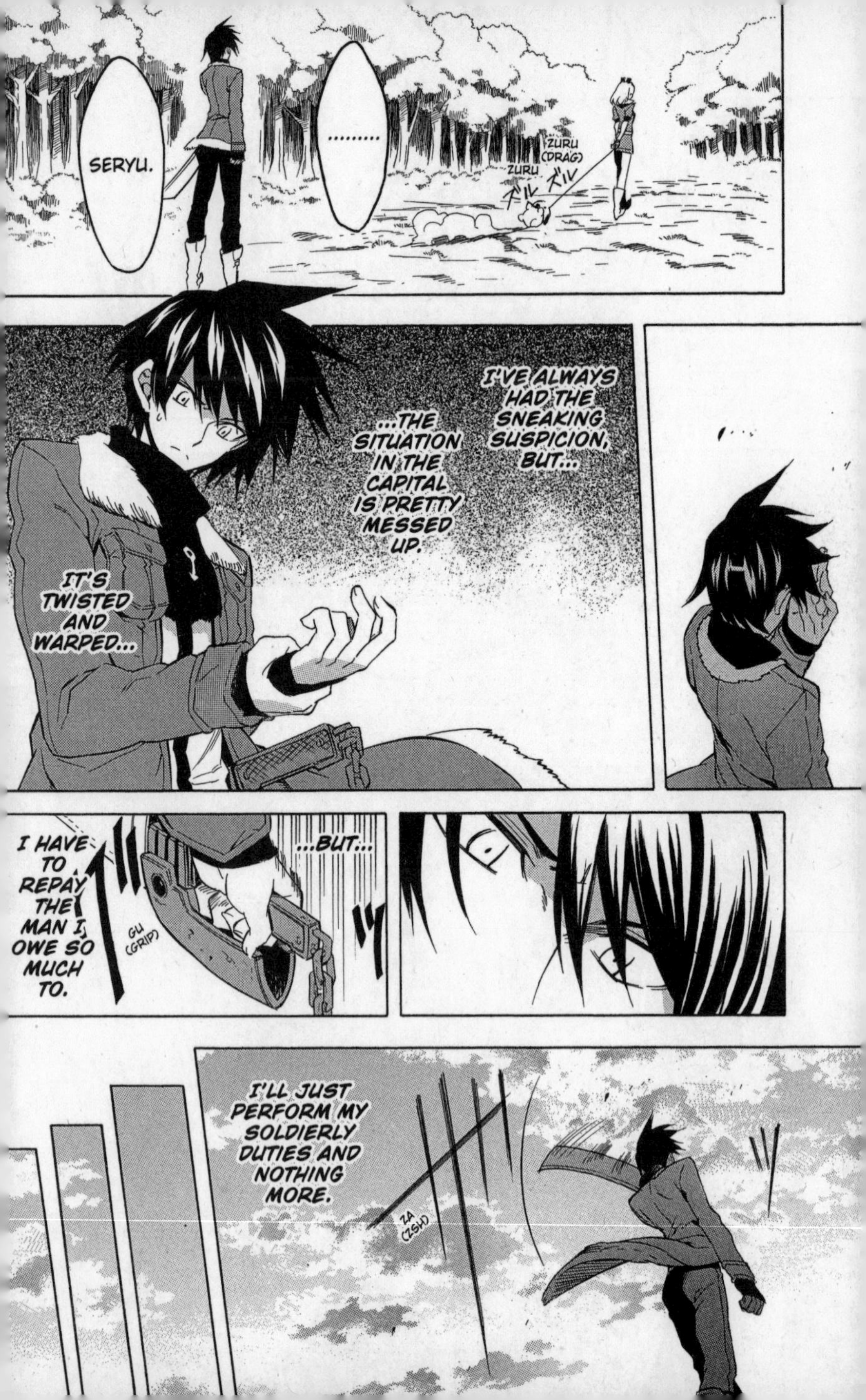
....
SERYU.
ZURU (DRAG)
ZURU
ズル ズル
I'VE ALWAYS HAD THE SNEAKING SUSPICION, BUT...
...THE SITUATION IN THE CAPITAL IS PRETTY MESSED UP.
IT'S TWISTED AND WARPED...
...BUT...
I HAVE TO REPAY THE MAN I OWE SO MUCH TO.
GU (GRIP)
I'LL JUST PERFORM MY SOLDIERLY DUTIES AND NOTHING MORE.
ZA (ZSH)

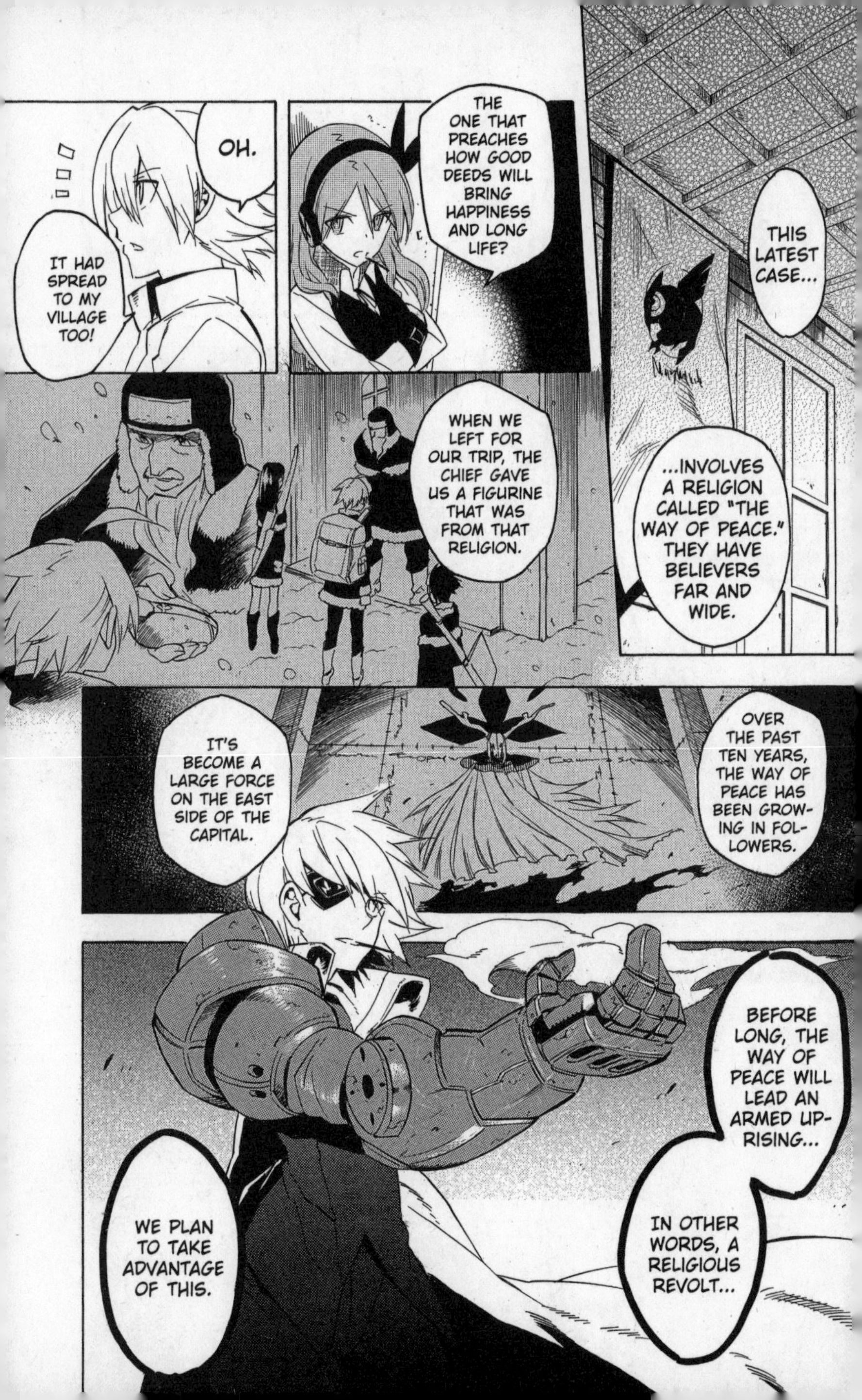
THIS LATEST CASE...
...INVOLVES A RELIGION CALLED "THE WAY OF PEACE." THEY HAVE BELIEVERS FAR AND WIDE.
THE ONE THAT PREACHES HOW GOOD DEEDS WILL BRING HAPPINESS AND LONG LIFE?
OH.
IT HAD SPREAD TO MY VILLAGE TOO!
WHEN WE LEFT FOR OUR TRIP, THE CHIEF GAVE US A FIGURINE THAT WAS FROM THAT RELIGION.
OVER THE PAST TEN YEARS, THE WAY OF PEACE HAS BEEN GROWING IN FOLLOWERS.
IT'S BECOME A LARGE FORCE ON THE EAST SIDE OF THE CAPITAL.
BEFORE LONG, THE WAY OF PEACE WILL LEAD AN ARMED UPRISING...
IN OTHER WORDS, A RELIGIOUS REVOLT...
WE PLAN TO TAKE ADVANTAGE OF THIS.

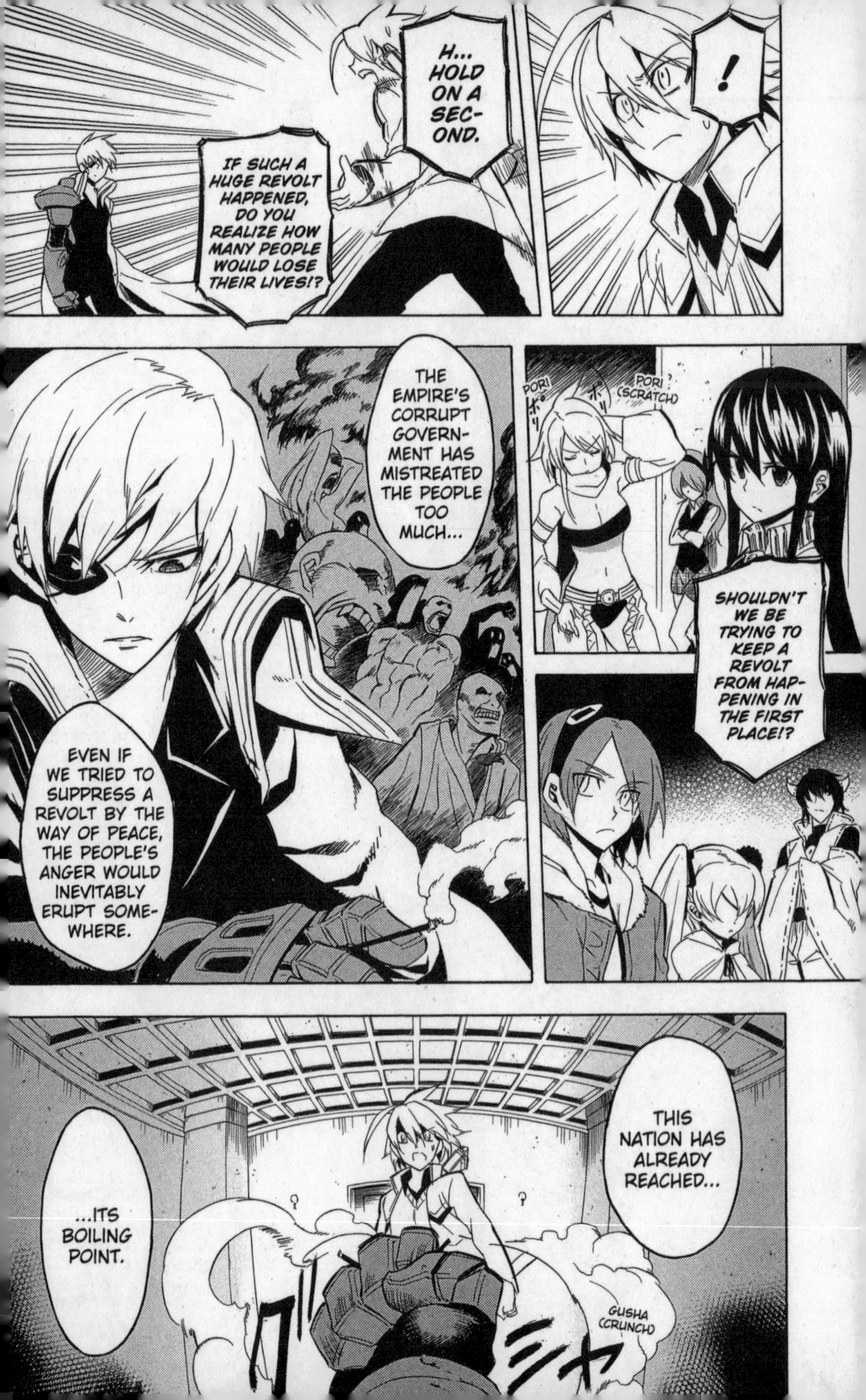
!
H... HOLD ON A SECOND.
IF SUCH A HUGE REVOLT HAPPENED, DO YOU REALIZE HOW MANY PEOPLE WOULD LOSE THEIR LIVES!?
PORI (SCRATCH)
PORI
SHOULDN'T WE BE TRYING TO KEEP A REVOLT FROM HAPPENING IN THE FIRST PLACE!?
THE EMPIRE'S CORRUPT GOVERNMENT HAS MISTREATED THE PEOPLE TOO MUCH...
EVEN IF WE TRIED TO SUPPRESS A REVOLT BY THE WAY OF PEACE, THE PEOPLE'S ANGER WOULD INEVITABLY ERUPT SOMEWHERE.
THIS NATION HAS ALREADY REACHED...
...ITS BOILING POINT.
GUSHA (CRUNCH)

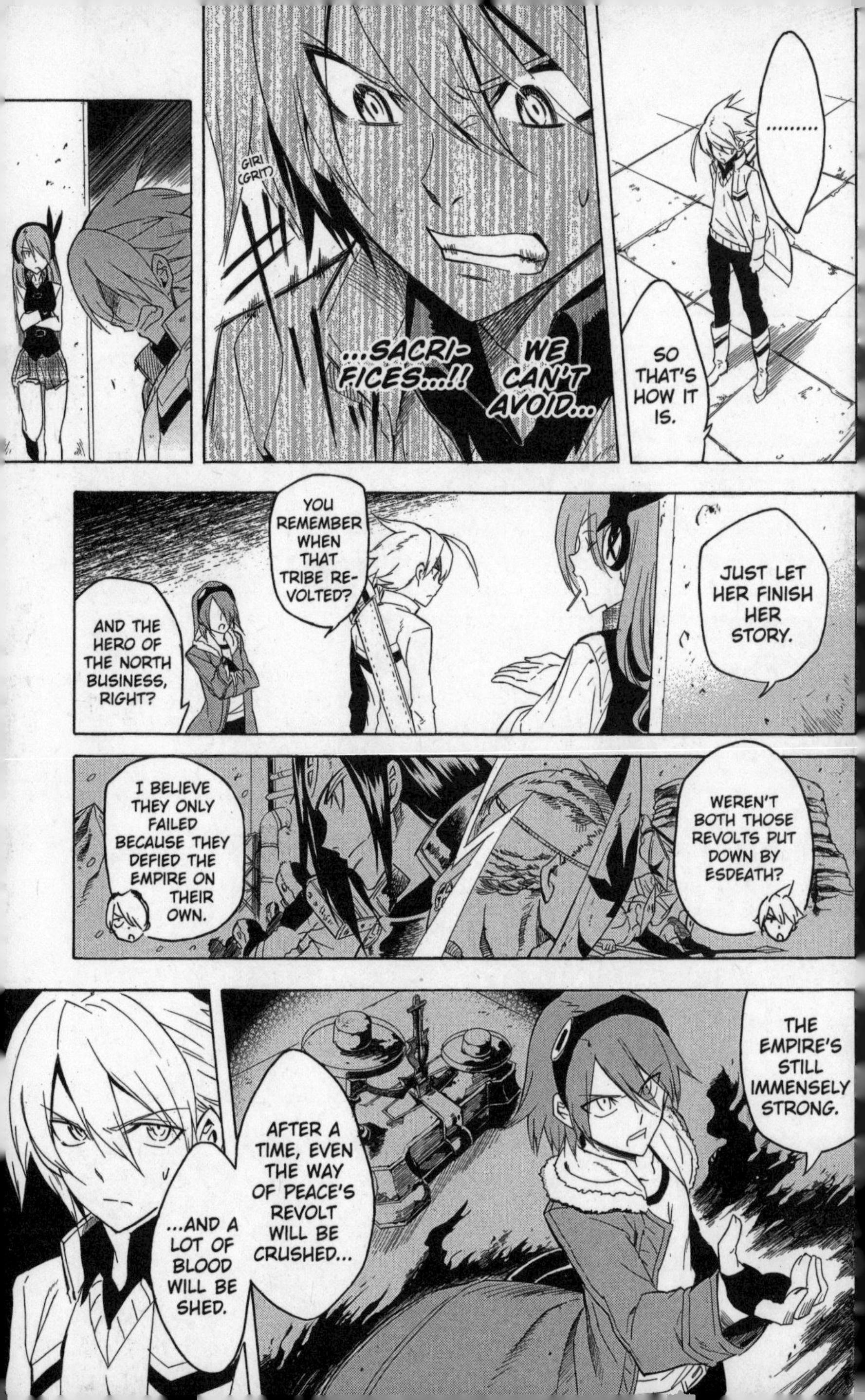
....
SO THAT'S HOW IT IS.
WE CAN'T AVOID...
...SACRIFICES...!!
GIRI (GRIT)
JUST LET HER FINISH HER STORY.
YOU REMEMBER WHEN THAT TRIBE RE-VOLTED?
AND THE HERO OF THE NORTH BUSINESS, RIGHT?
WEREN'T BOTH THOSE REVOLTS PUT DOWN BY ESDEATH?
I BELIEVE THEY ONLY FAILED BECAUSE THEY DEFIED THE EMPIRE ON THEIR OWN.
THE EMPIRE'S STILL IMMENSELY STRONG.
AFTER A TIME, EVEN THE WAY OF PEACE'S REVOLT WILL BE CRUSHED...
...AND A LOT OF BLOOD WILL BE SHED.

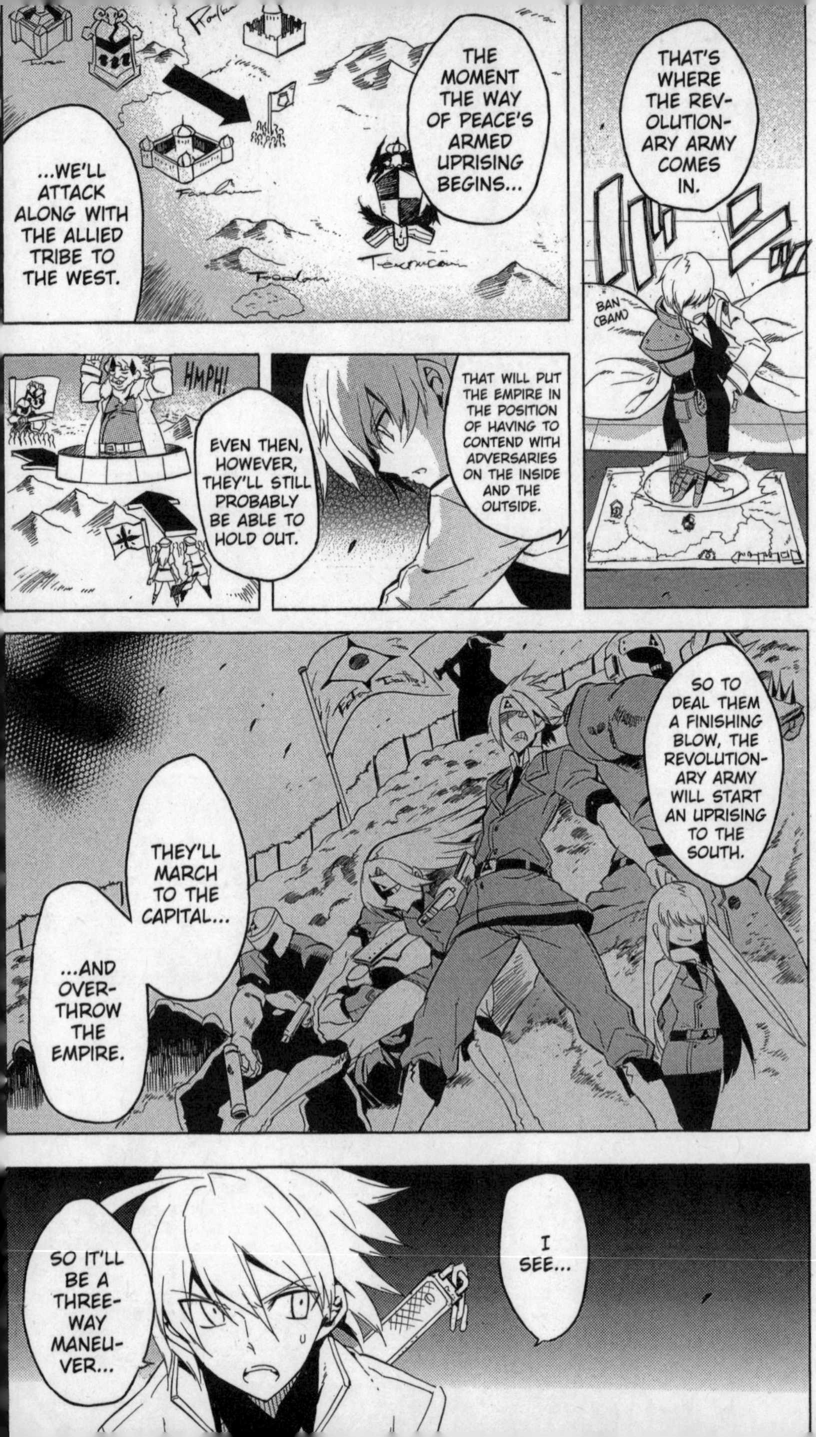
THE MOMENT THE WAY OF PEACE'S ARMED UPRISING BEGINS...
...WE'LL ATTACK ALONG WITH THE ALLIED TRIBE TO THE WEST.
THAT WILL PUT THE EMPIRE IN THE POSITION OF HAVING TO CONTEND WITH ADVERSARIES ON THE INSIDE AND THE OUTSIDE.
HMPH!
EVEN THEN, HOWEVER, THEY'LL STILL PROBABLY BE ABLE TO HOLD OUT.
THAT'S WHERE THE REVOLUTIONARY ARMY COMES IN.
BAN (BAM)
SO TO DEAL THEM A FINISHING BLOW, THE REVOLUTIONARY ARMY WILL START AN UPRISING TO THE SOUTH.
THEY'LL MARCH TO THE CAPITAL...
...AND OVERTHROW THE EMPIRE.
I SEE...
SO IT'LL BE A THREE-WAY MANEUVER...

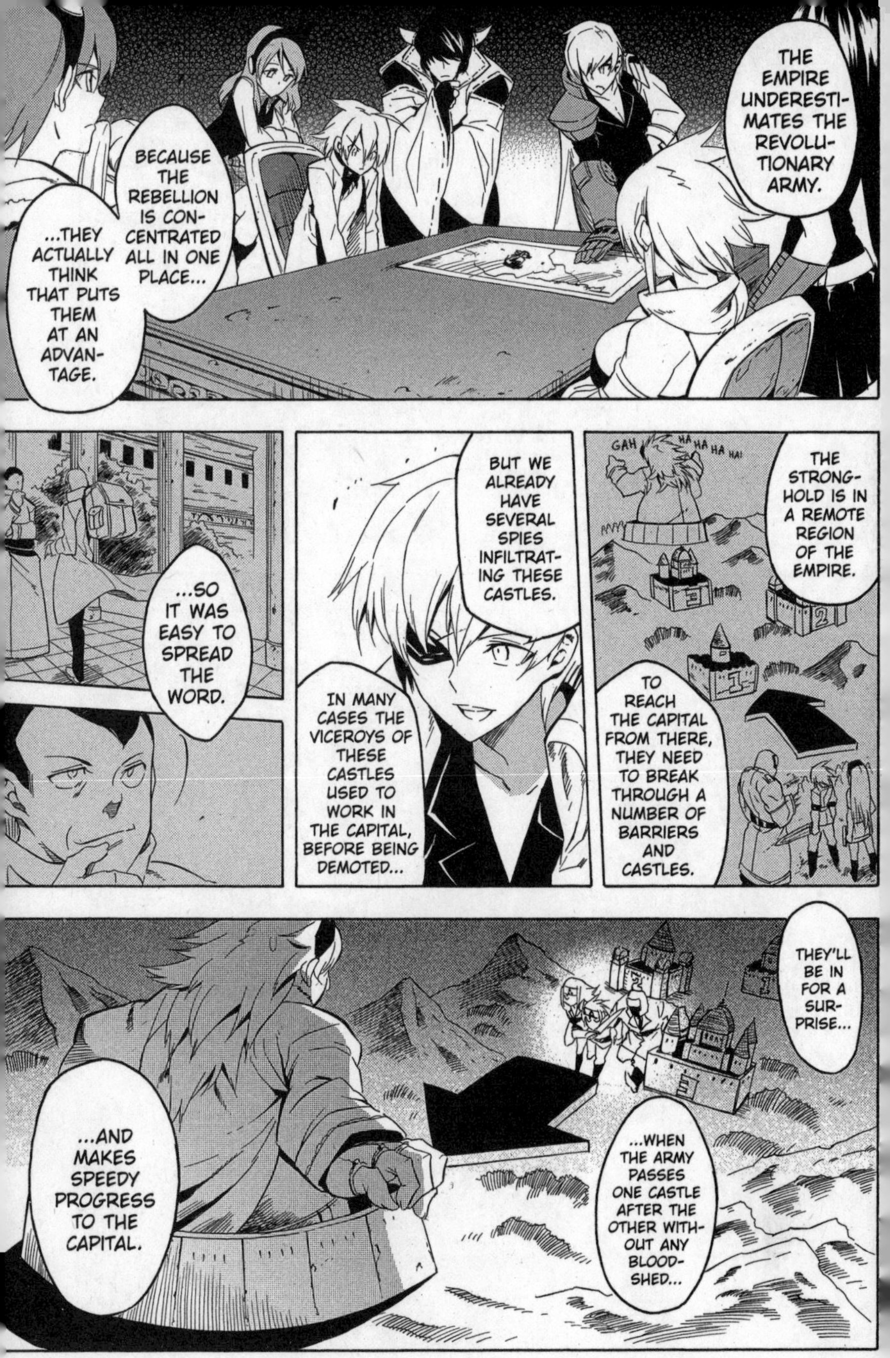
THE EMPIRE UNDERESTIMATES THE REVOLUTIONARY ARMY.
BECAUSE THE REBELLION IS CONCENTRATED ALL IN ONE PLACE...
...THEY ACTUALLY THINK THAT PUTS THEM AT AN ADVANTAGE.
GAH HA HA HA HA HA!
THE STRONGHOLD IS IN A REMOTE REGION OF THE EMPIRE.
TO REACH THE CAPITAL FROM THERE, THEY NEED TO BREAK THROUGH A NUMBER OF BARRIERS AND CASTLES.
BUT WE ALREADY HAVE SEVERAL SPIES INFILTRATING THESE CASTLES.
IN MANY CASES THE VICEROYS OF THESE CASTLES USED TO WORK IN THE CAPITAL, BEFORE BEING DEMOTED...
...SO IT WAS EASY TO SPREAD THE WORD.
THEY'LL BE IN FOR A SURPRISE...
...WHEN THE ARMY PASSES ONE CASTLE AFTER THE OTHER WITHOUT ANY BLOODSHED...
...AND MAKES SPEEDY PROGRESS TO THE CAPITAL.

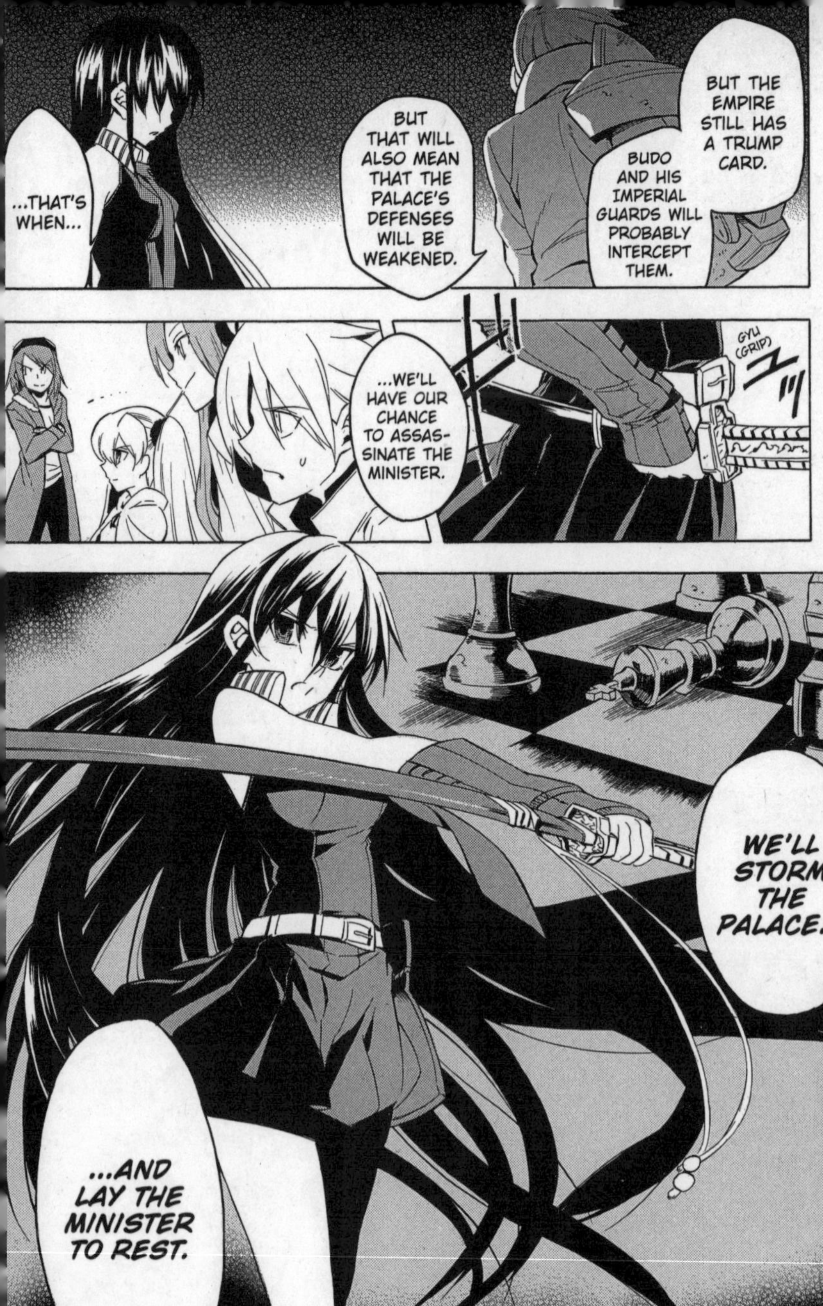
BUT THE EMPIRE STILL HAS A TRUMP CARD.
BUDO AND HIS IMPERIAL GUARDS WILL PROBABLY INTERCEPT THEM.
BUT THAT WILL ALSO MEAN THAT THE PALACE'S DEFENSES WILL BE WEAKENED.
...THAT'S WHEN...
GYU (GRIP)
...WE'LL HAVE OUR CHANCE TO ASSAS-SINATE THE MINISTER.
WE'LL STORM THE PALACE...
...AND LAY THE MINISTER TO REST.

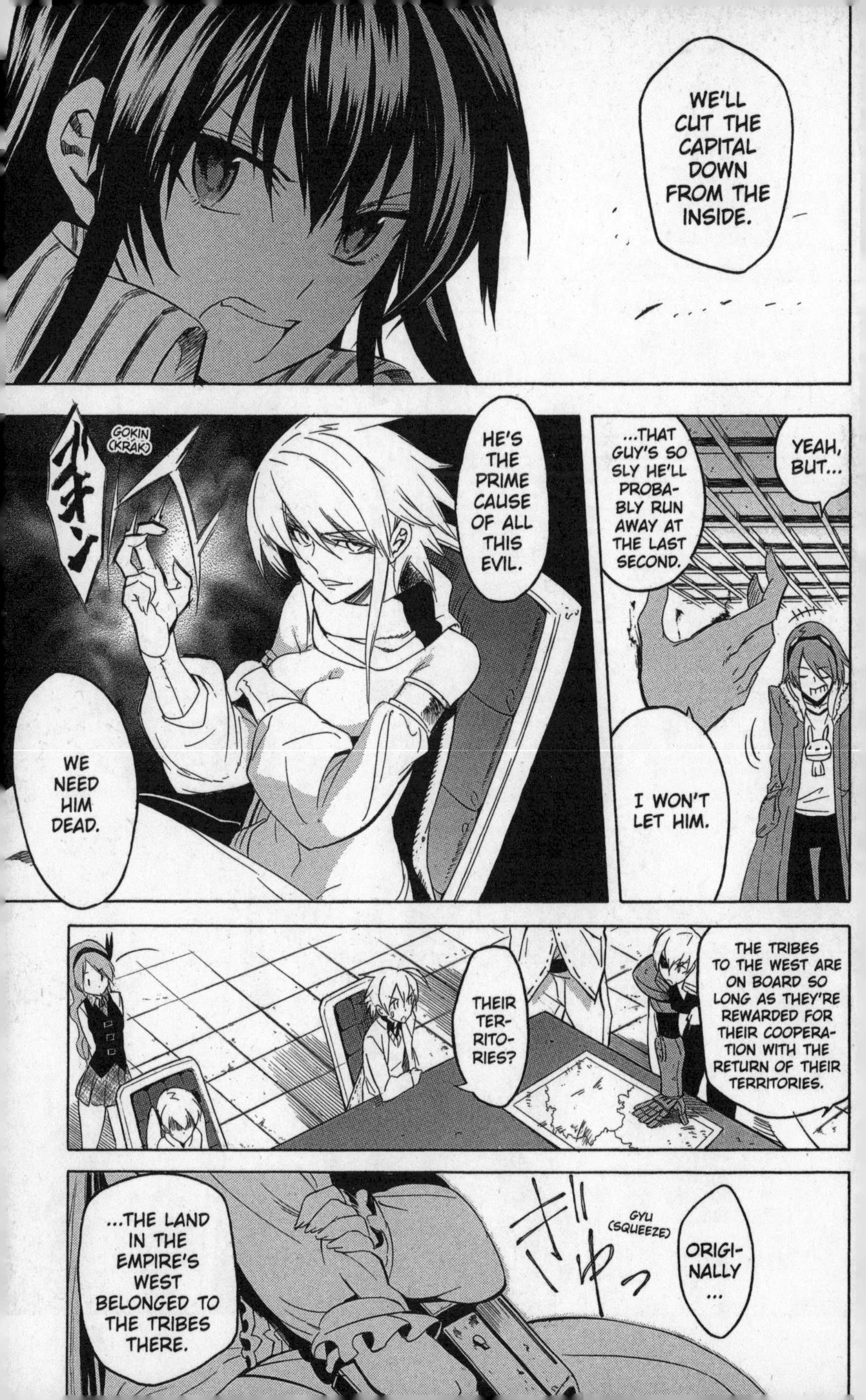
WE'LL CUT THE CAPITAL DOWN FROM THE INSIDE.
YEAH, BUT...
...THAT GUY'S SO SLY HE'LL PROBABLY RUN AWAY AT THE LAST SECOND.
I WON'T LET HIM.
HE'S THE PRIME CAUSE OF ALL THIS EVIL.
GOKIN (KRAK)
WE NEED HIM DEAD.
THE TRIBES TO THE WEST ARE ON BOARD SO LONG AS THEY'RE REWARDED FOR THEIR COOPERATION WITH THE RETURN OF THEIR TERRITORIES.
THEIR TERRITORIES?
ORIGINALLY...
GYU (SQUEEZE)
...THE LAND IN THE EMPIRE'S WEST BELONGED TO THE TRIBES THERE.

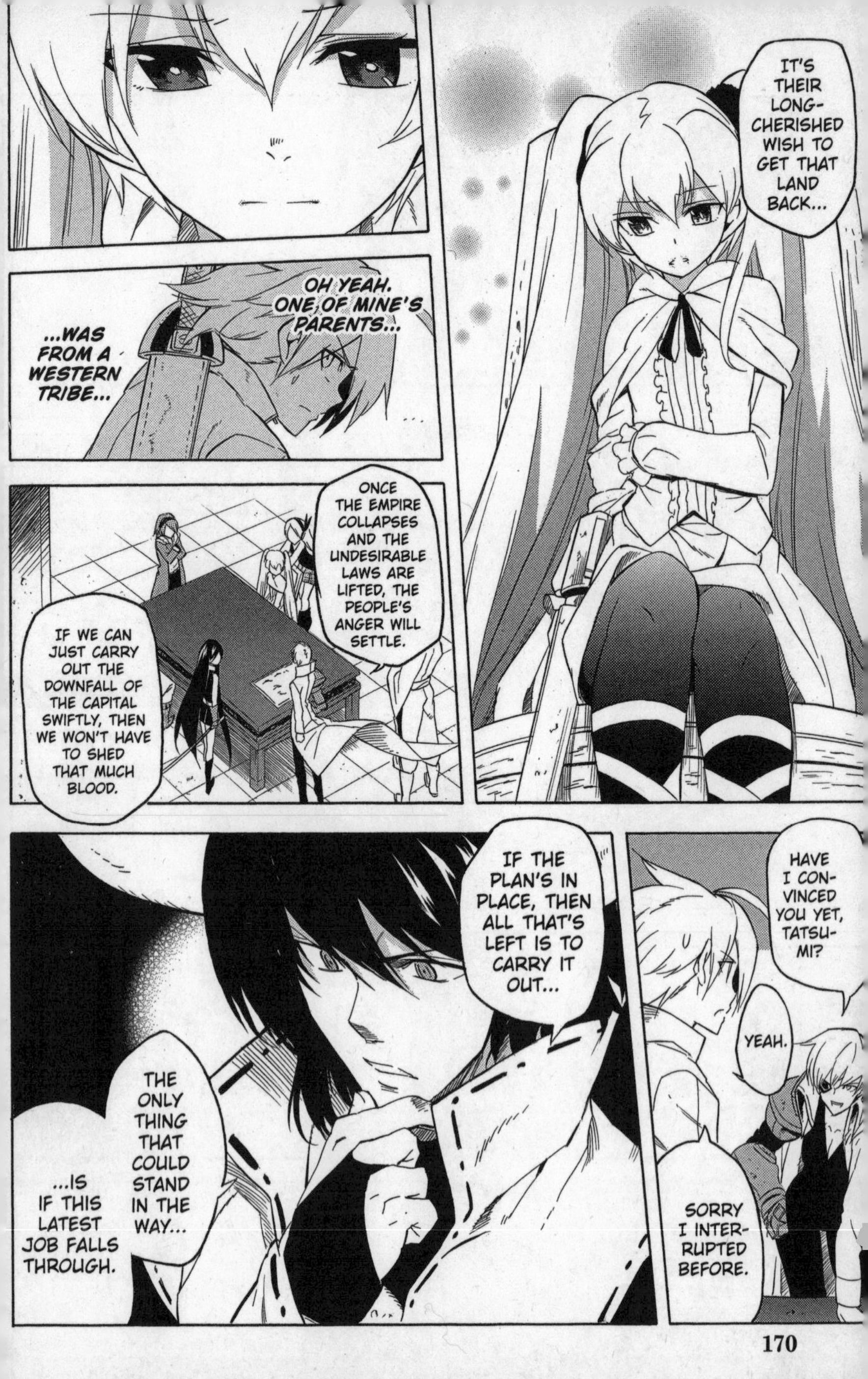
OH YEAH. ONE OF MINE'S PARENTS...
...WAS FROM A WESTERN TRIBE...
IT'S THEIR LONG-CHERISHED WISH TO GET THAT LAND BACK...
ONCE THE EMPIRE COLLAPSES AND THE UNDESIRABLE LAWS ARE LIFTED, THE PEOPLE'S ANGER WILL SETTLE.
IF WE CAN JUST CARRY OUT THE DOWNFALL OF THE CAPITAL SWIFTLY, THEN WE WON'T HAVE TO SHED THAT MUCH BLOOD.
HAVE I CONVINCED YOU YET, TATSUMI?
YEAH.
SORRY I INTERRUPTED BEFORE.
IF THE PLAN'S IN PLACE, THEN ALL THAT'S LEFT IS TO CARRY IT OUT...
THE ONLY THING THAT COULD STAND IN THE WAY...
...IS IF THIS LATEST JOB FALLS THROUGH.

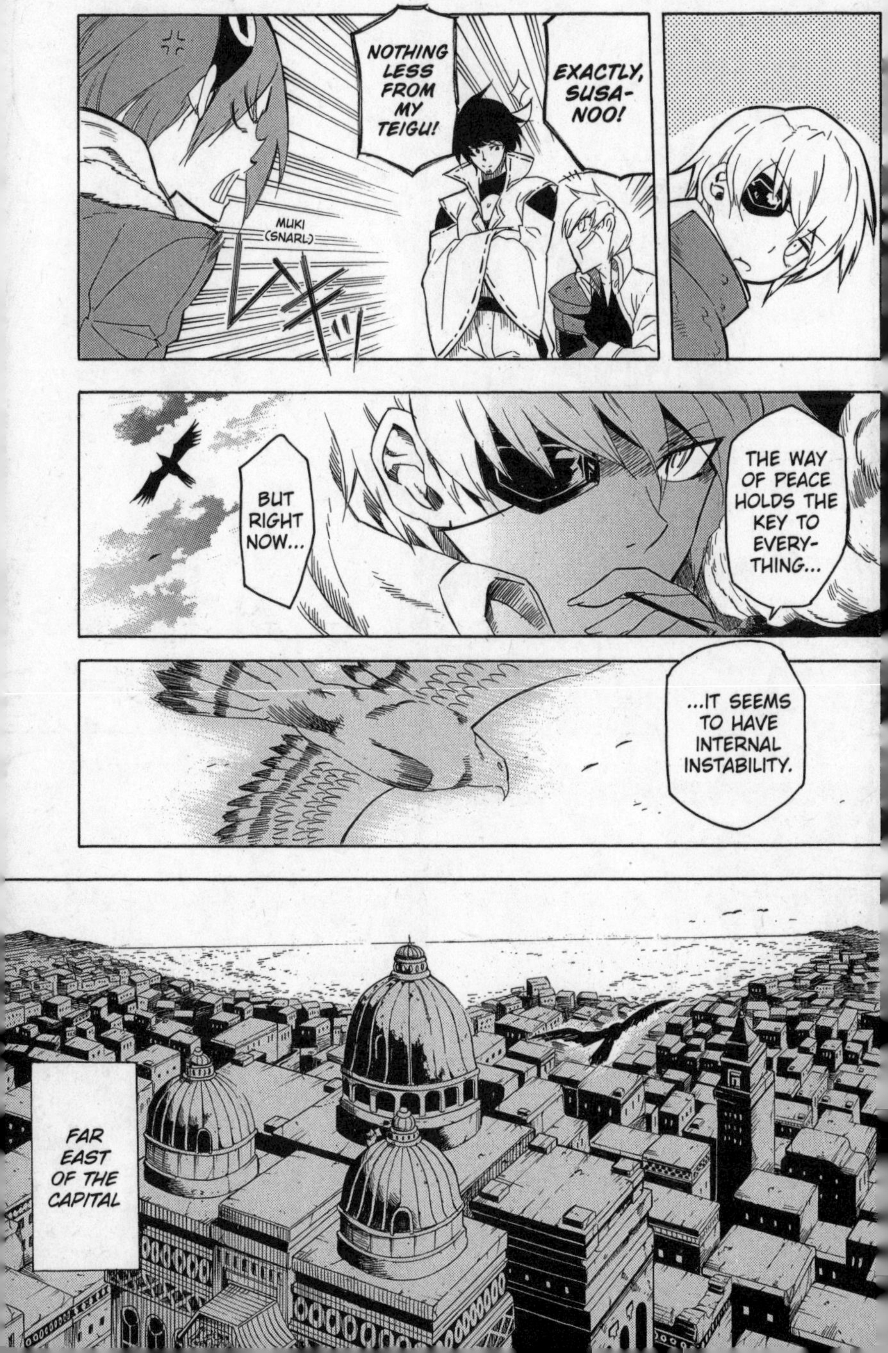
EXACTLY, SUSA-NOO!
NOTHING LESS FROM MY TEIGU!
MUKI (SNARL)
THE WAY OF PEACE HOLDS THE KEY TO EVERY-THING...
BUT RIGHT NOW...
...IT SEEMS TO HAVE INTERNAL INSTABILITY.
FAR EAST OF THE CAPITAL

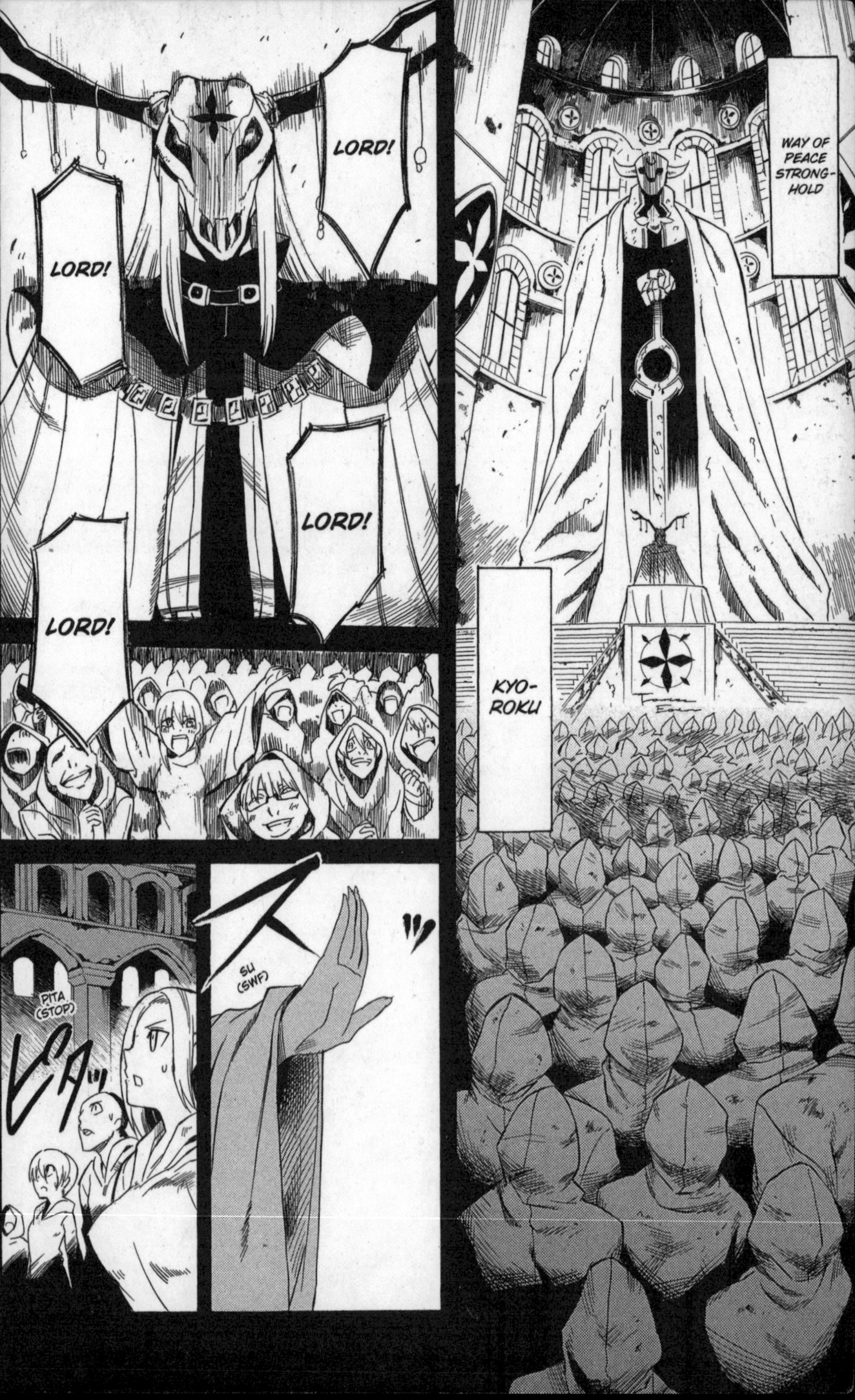
WAY OF PEACE STRONGHOLD
KYO-ROKU
LORD!
LORD!
LORD!
LORD!
SU (SWF)
PITA (STOP)

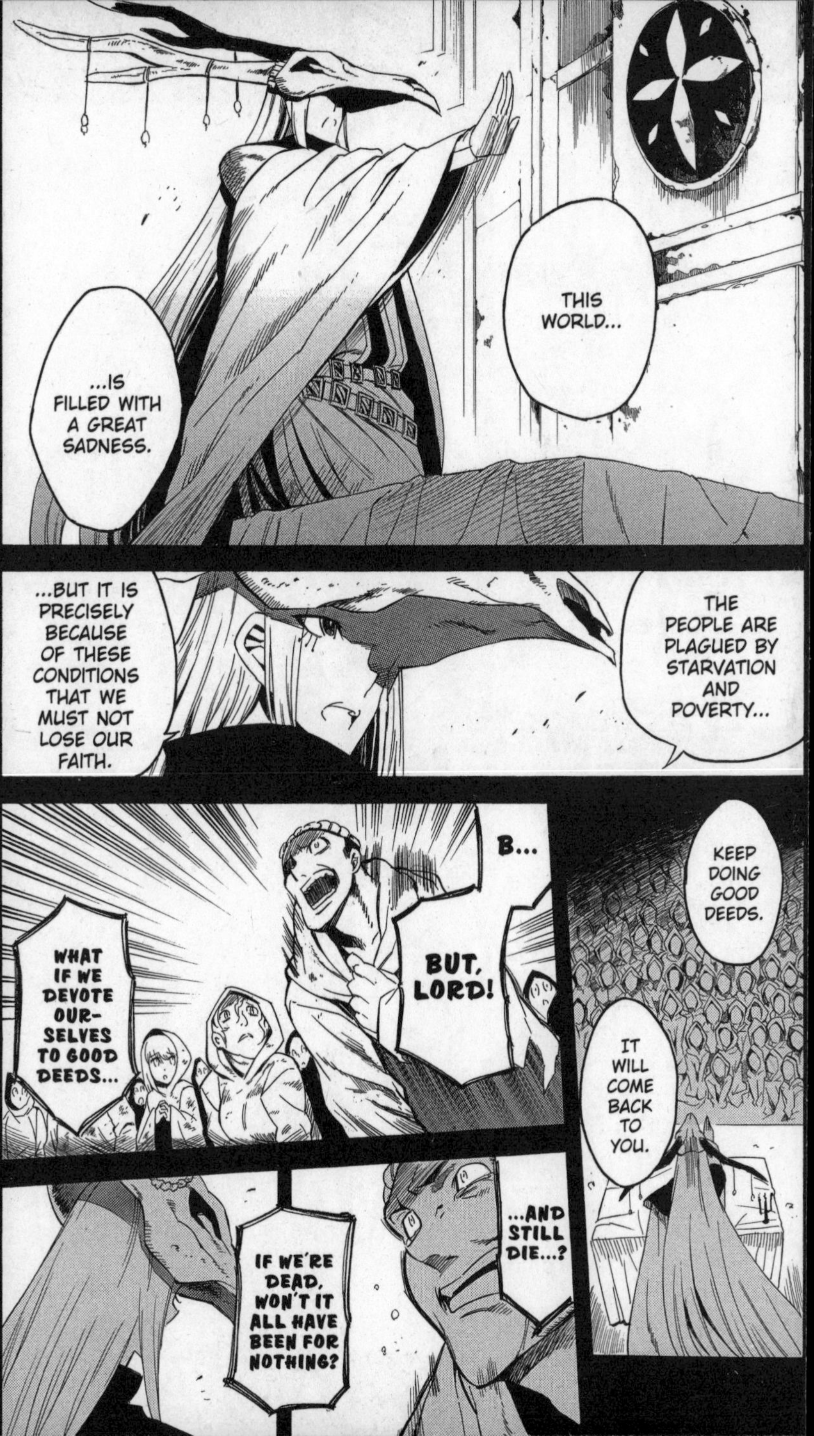

THIS WORLD...
...IS FILLED WITH A GREAT SADNESS.
THE PEOPLE ARE PLAGUED BY STARVATION AND POVERTY...
...BUT IT IS PRECISELY BECAUSE OF THESE CONDITIONS THAT WE MUST NOT LOSE OUR FAITH.
KEEP DOING GOOD DEEDS.
IT WILL COME BACK TO YOU.
B...
BUT, LORD!
WHAT IF WE DEVOTE OURSELVES TO GOOD DEEDS...
...AND STILL DIE...?
IF WE'RE DEAD, WON'T IT ALL HAVE BEEN FOR NOTHING?

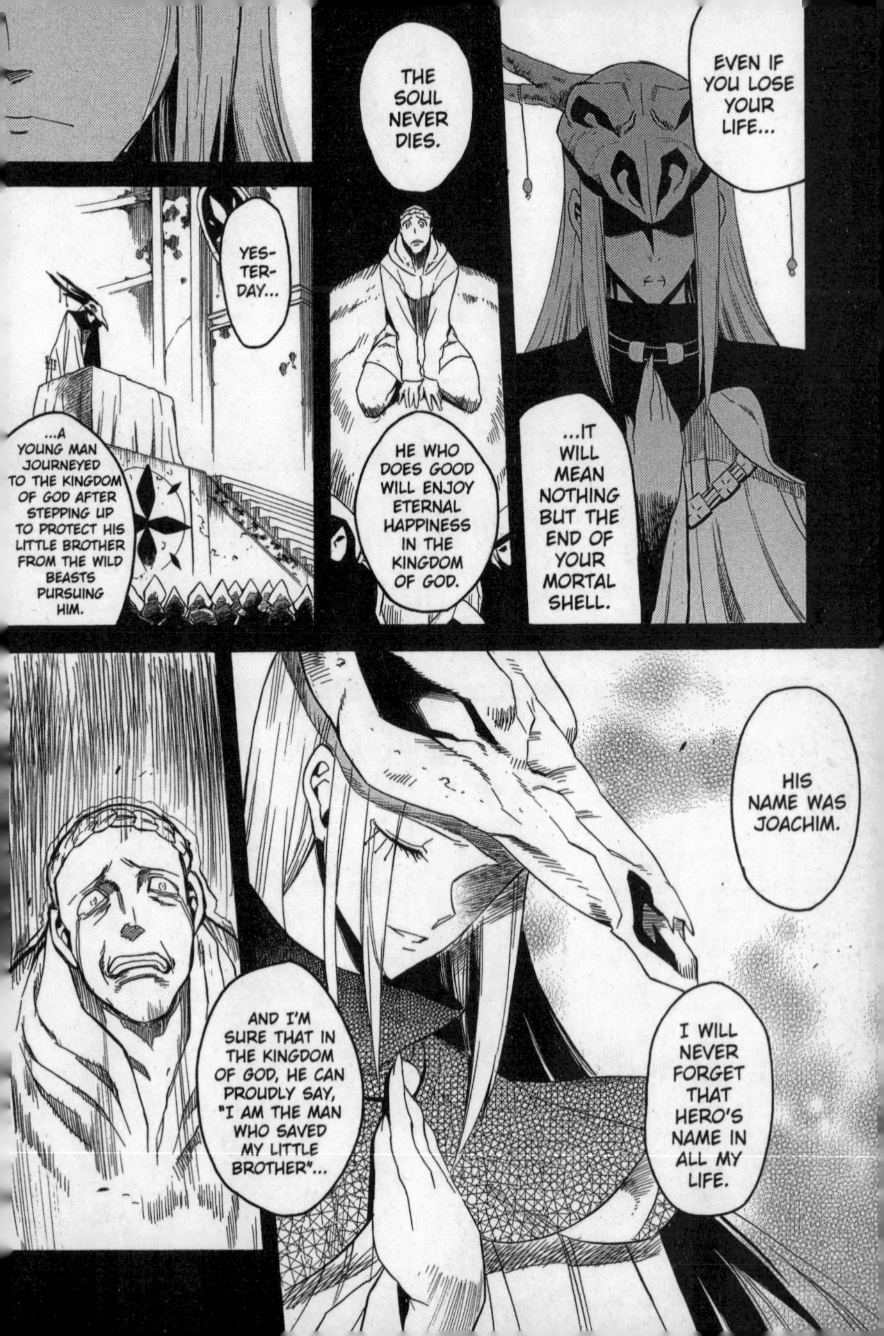
EVEN IF YOU LOSE YOUR LIFE...
THE SOUL NEVER DIES.
...IT WILL MEAN NOTHING BUT THE END OF YOUR MORTAL SHELL.
HE WHO DOES GOOD WILL ENJOY ETERNAL HAPPINESS IN THE KINGDOM OF GOD.
YES-TER-DAY...
...A YOUNG MAN JOURNEYED TO THE KINGDOM OF GOD AFTER STEPPING UP TO PROTECT HIS LITTLE BROTHER FROM THE WILD BEASTS PURSUING HIM.
HIS NAME WAS JOACHIM.
I WILL NEVER FORGET THAT HERO'S NAME IN ALL MY LIFE.
AND I'M SURE THAT IN THE KINGDOM OF GOD, HE CAN PROUDLY SAY, "I AM THE MAN WHO SAVED MY LITTLE BROTHER"...

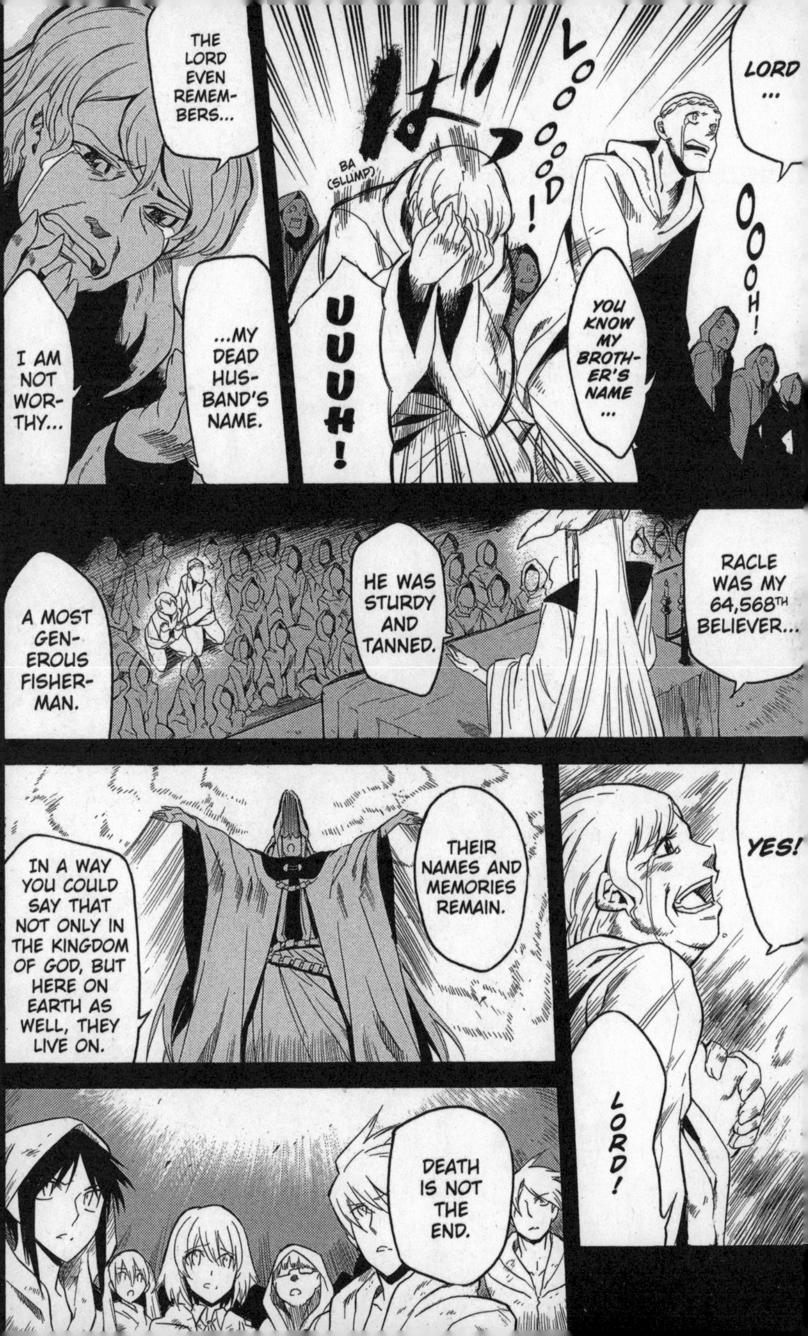

LORD...
OOOOH!
VOOOOOD!
YOU KNOW MY BROTHER'S NAME...
BA (SLUMP)
UUUH!
THE LORD EVEN REMEMBERS...
...MY DEAD HUSBAND'S NAME.
I AM NOT WORTHY...
RACLE WAS MY 64,568TH BELIEVER...
HE WAS STURDY AND TANNED.
A MOST GENEROUS FISHERMAN.
YES!
LORD!
THEIR NAMES AND MEMORIES REMAIN.
IN A WAY YOU COULD SAY THAT NOT ONLY IN THE KINGDOM OF GOD, BUT HERE ON EARTH AS WELL, THEY LIVE ON.
DEATH IS NOT THE END.

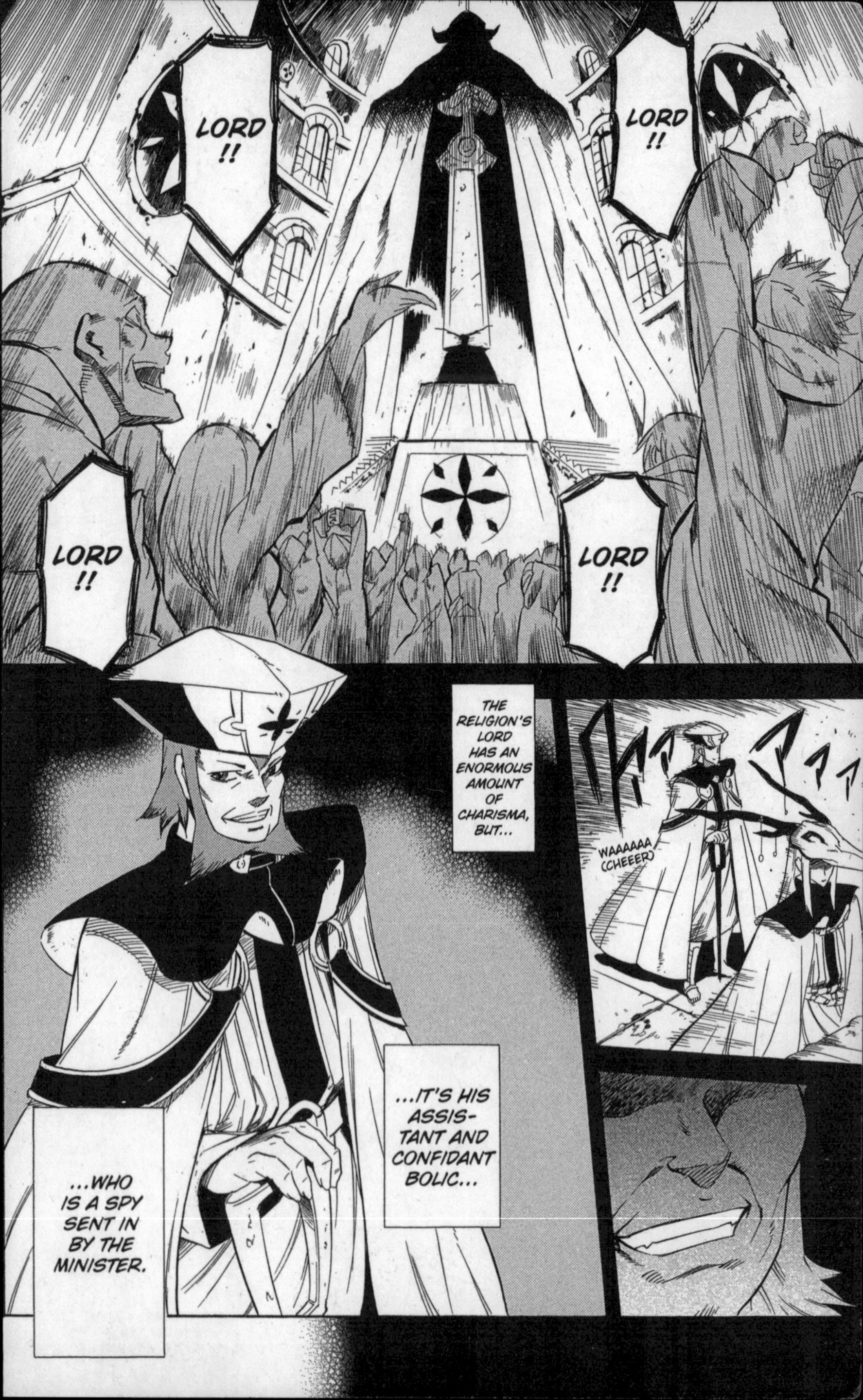
LORD !!
LORD !!
LORD !!
LORD !!
THE RELIGION'S LORD HAS AN ENORMOUS AMOUNT OF CHARISMA, BUT...
WAAAAAA (CHEEER)
...IT'S HIS ASSIS-TANT AND CONFIDANT BOLIC...
...WHO IS A SPY SENT IN BY THE MINISTER.

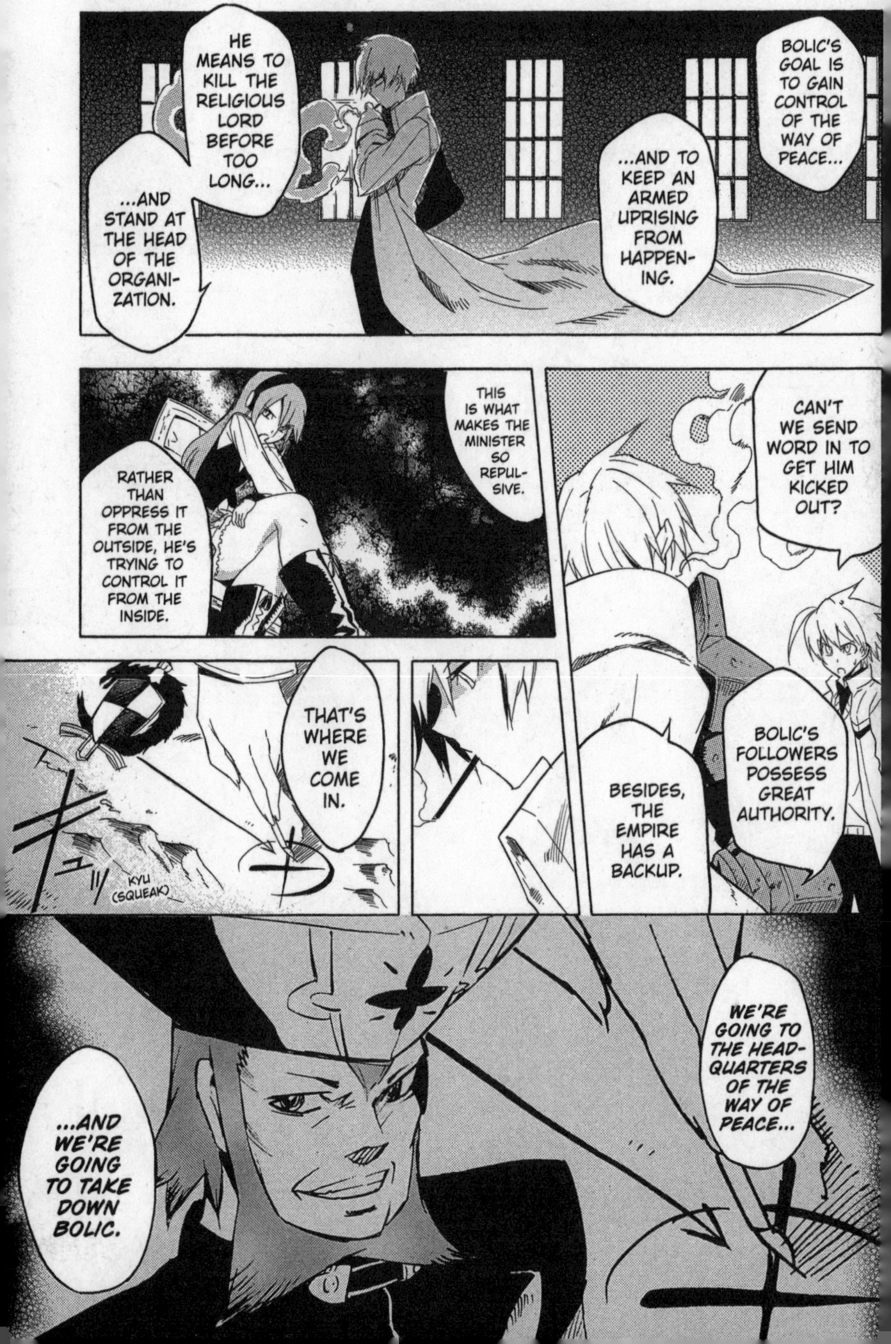
BOLIC'S GOAL IS TO GAIN CONTROL OF THE WAY OF PEACE...
...AND TO KEEP AN ARMED UPRISING FROM HAPPENING.
HE MEANS TO KILL THE RELIGIOUS LORD BEFORE TOO LONG...
...AND STAND AT THE HEAD OF THE ORGANIZATION.
CAN'T WE SEND WORD IN TO GET HIM KICKED OUT?
BOLIC'S FOLLOWERS POSSESS GREAT AUTHORITY.
BESIDES, THE EMPIRE HAS A BACKUP.
THIS IS WHAT MAKES THE MINISTER SO REPULSIVE.
RATHER THAN OPPRESS IT FROM THE OUTSIDE, HE'S TRYING TO CONTROL IT FROM THE INSIDE.
THAT'S WHERE WE COME IN.
KYU (SQUEAK)
WE'RE GOING TO THE HEADQUARTERS OF THE WAY OF PEACE...
...AND WE'RE GOING TO TAKE DOWN BOLIC.

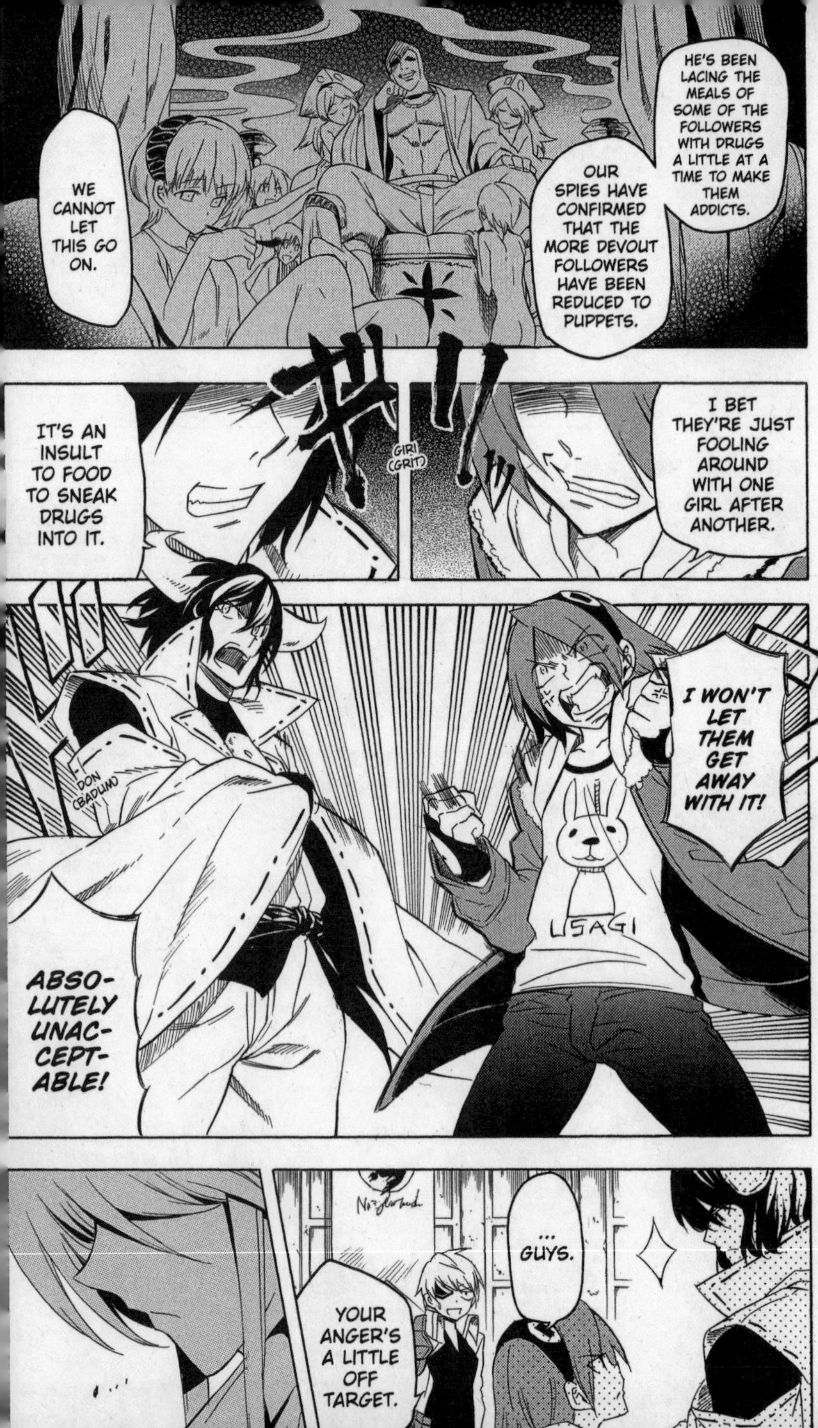
HE'S BEEN LACING THE MEALS OF SOME OF THE FOLLOWERS WITH DRUGS A LITTLE AT A TIME TO MAKE THEM ADDICTS.
OUR SPIES HAVE CONFIRMED THAT THE MORE DEVOUT FOLLOWERS HAVE BEEN REDUCED TO PUPPETS.
WE CANNOT LET THIS GO ON.
I BET THEY'RE JUST FOOLING AROUND WITH ONE GIRL AFTER ANOTHER.
GIRI (GRIT)
IT'S AN INSULT TO FOOD TO SNEAK DRUGS INTO IT.
I WON'T LET THEM GET AWAY WITH IT!
USAGI
DON (BADUM)
ABSO-LUTELY UNAC-CEPT-ABLE!
... GUYS.
YOUR ANGER'S A LITTLE OFF TARGET.
...

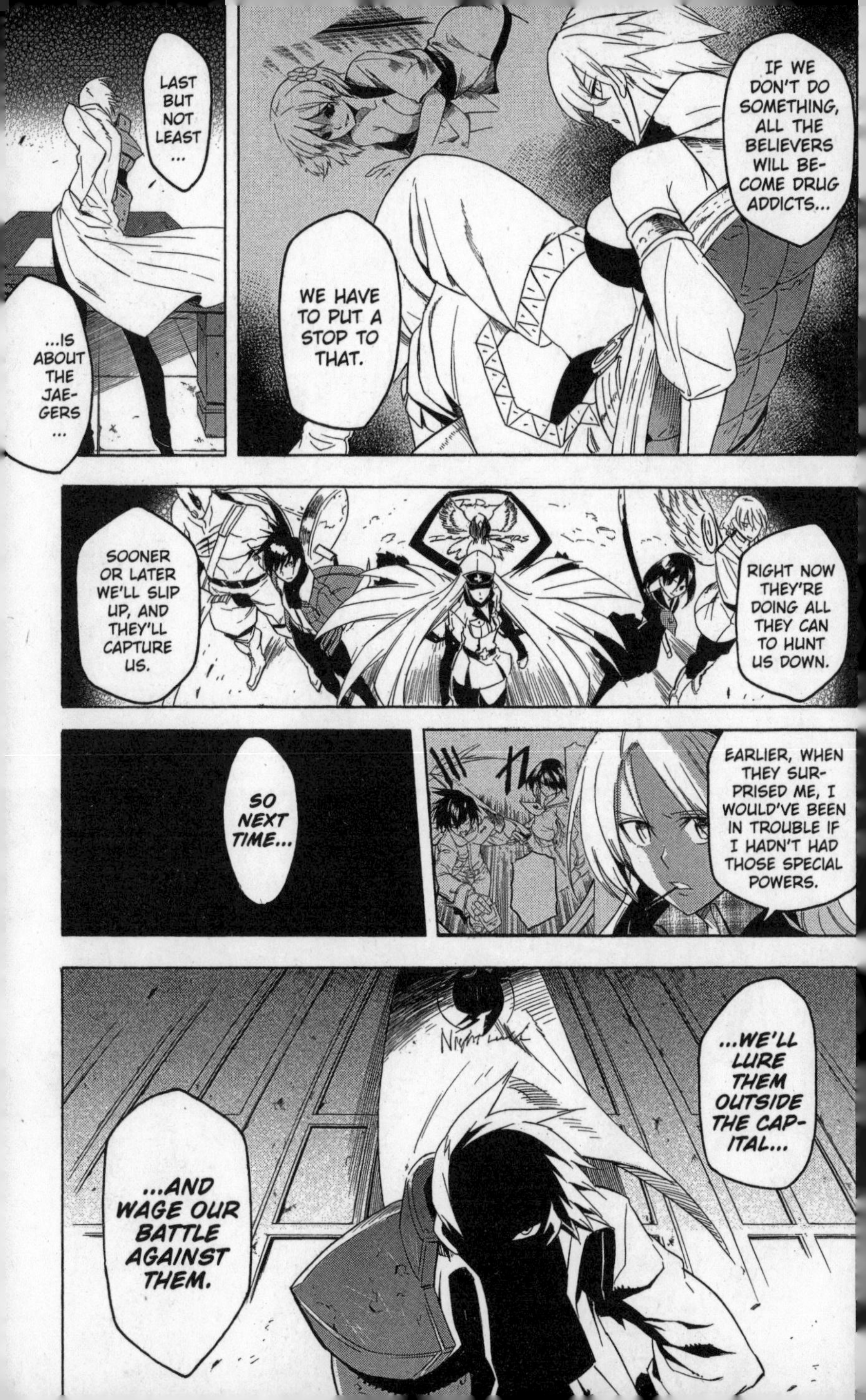
IF WE DON'T DO SOMETHING, ALL THE BELIEVERS WILL BECOME DRUG ADDICTS...
WE HAVE TO PUT A STOP TO THAT.
LAST BUT NOT LEAST...
...IS ABOUT THE JAEGERS...
RIGHT NOW THEY'RE DOING ALL THEY CAN TO HUNT US DOWN.
SOONER OR LATER WE'LL SLIP UP, AND THEY'LL CAPTURE US.
EARLIER, WHEN THEY SURPRISED ME, I WOULD'VE BEEN IN TROUBLE IF I HADN'T HAD THOSE SPECIAL POWERS.
SO NEXT TIME...
...WE'LL LURE THEM OUTSIDE THE CAPITAL...
...AND WAGE OUR BATTLE AGAINST THEM.

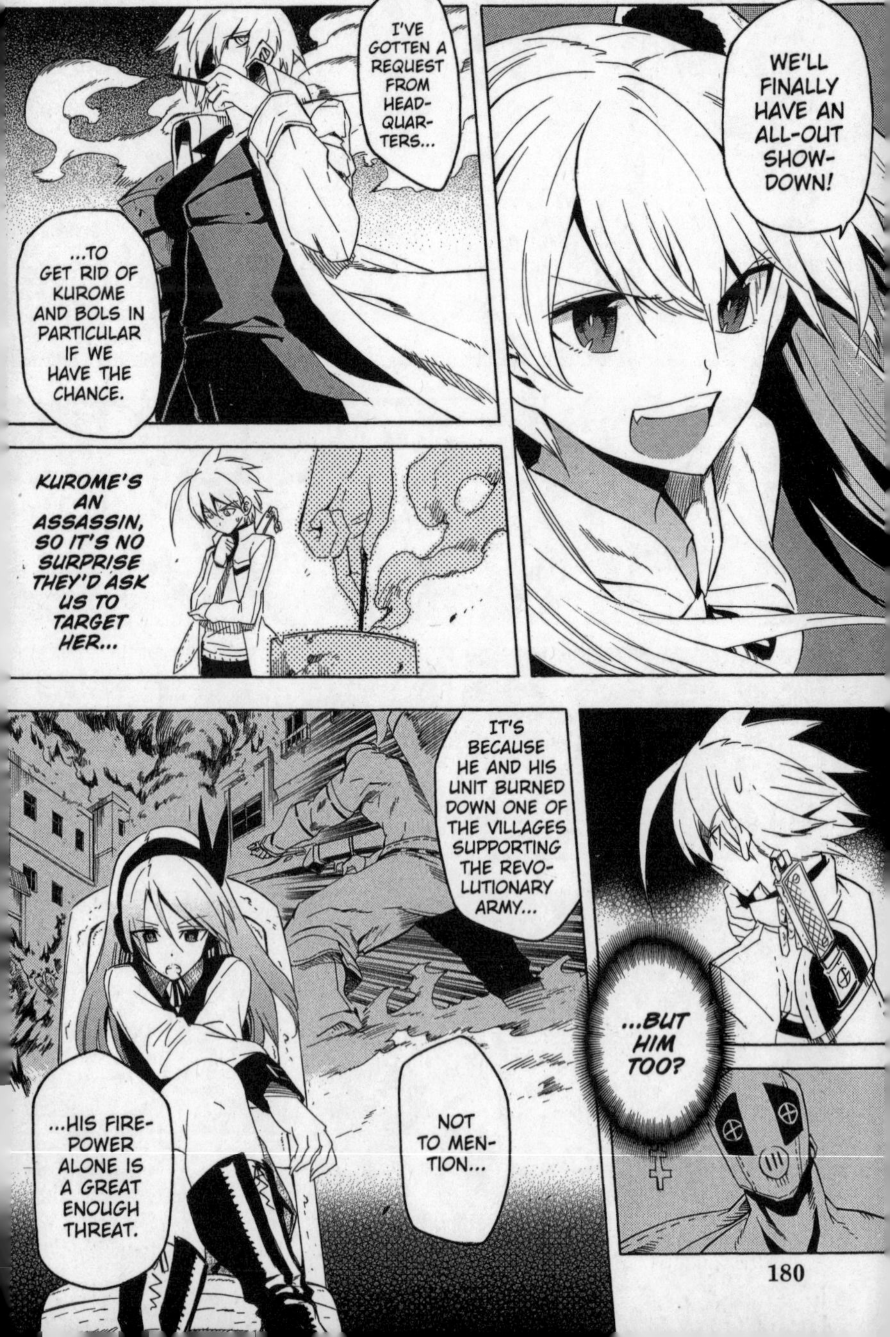
WE'LL FINALLY HAVE AN ALL-OUT SHOW-DOWN!
I'VE GOTTEN A REQUEST FROM HEAD-QUARTERS...
...TO GET RID OF KUROME AND BOLS IN PARTICULAR IF WE HAVE THE CHANCE.
KUROME'S AN ASSASSIN, SO IT'S NO SURPRISE THEY'D ASK US TO TARGET HER...
...BUT HIM TOO?
IT'S BECAUSE HE AND HIS UNIT BURNED DOWN ONE OF THE VILLAGES SUPPORTING THE REVO-LUTIONARY ARMY...
NOT TO MEN-TION...
...HIS FIRE-POWER ALONE IS A GREAT ENOUGH THREAT.

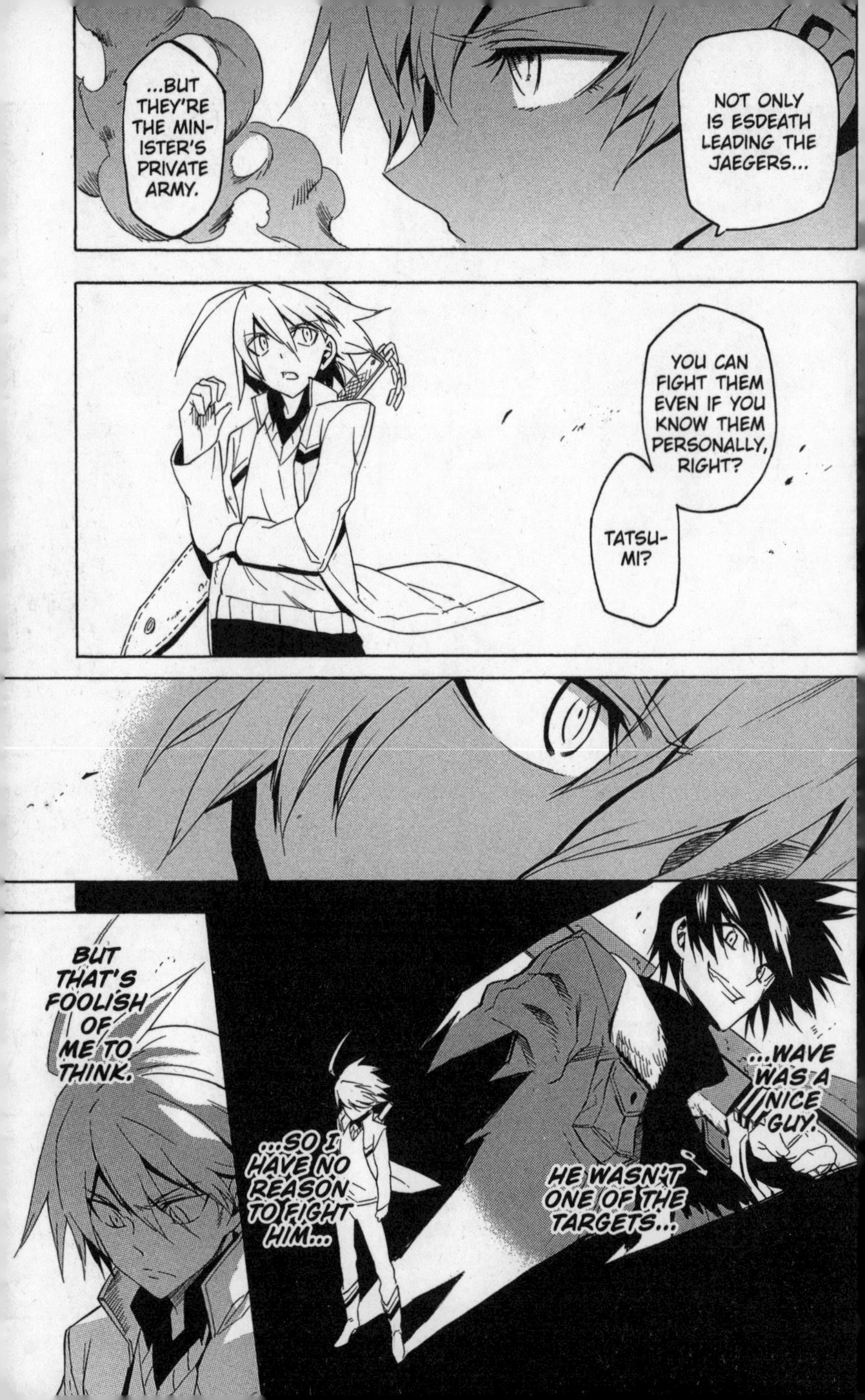
NOT ONLY IS ESDEATH LEADING THE JAEGERS...
...BUT THEY'RE THE MIN-ISTER'S PRIVATE ARMY.
YOU CAN FIGHT THEM EVEN IF YOU KNOW THEM PERSONALLY, RIGHT?
TATSU-MI?
...WAVE WAS A NICE GUY.
HE WASN'T ONE OF THE TARGETS...
...SO I HAVE NO REASON TO FIGHT HIM...
BUT THAT'S FOOLISH OF ME TO THINK.

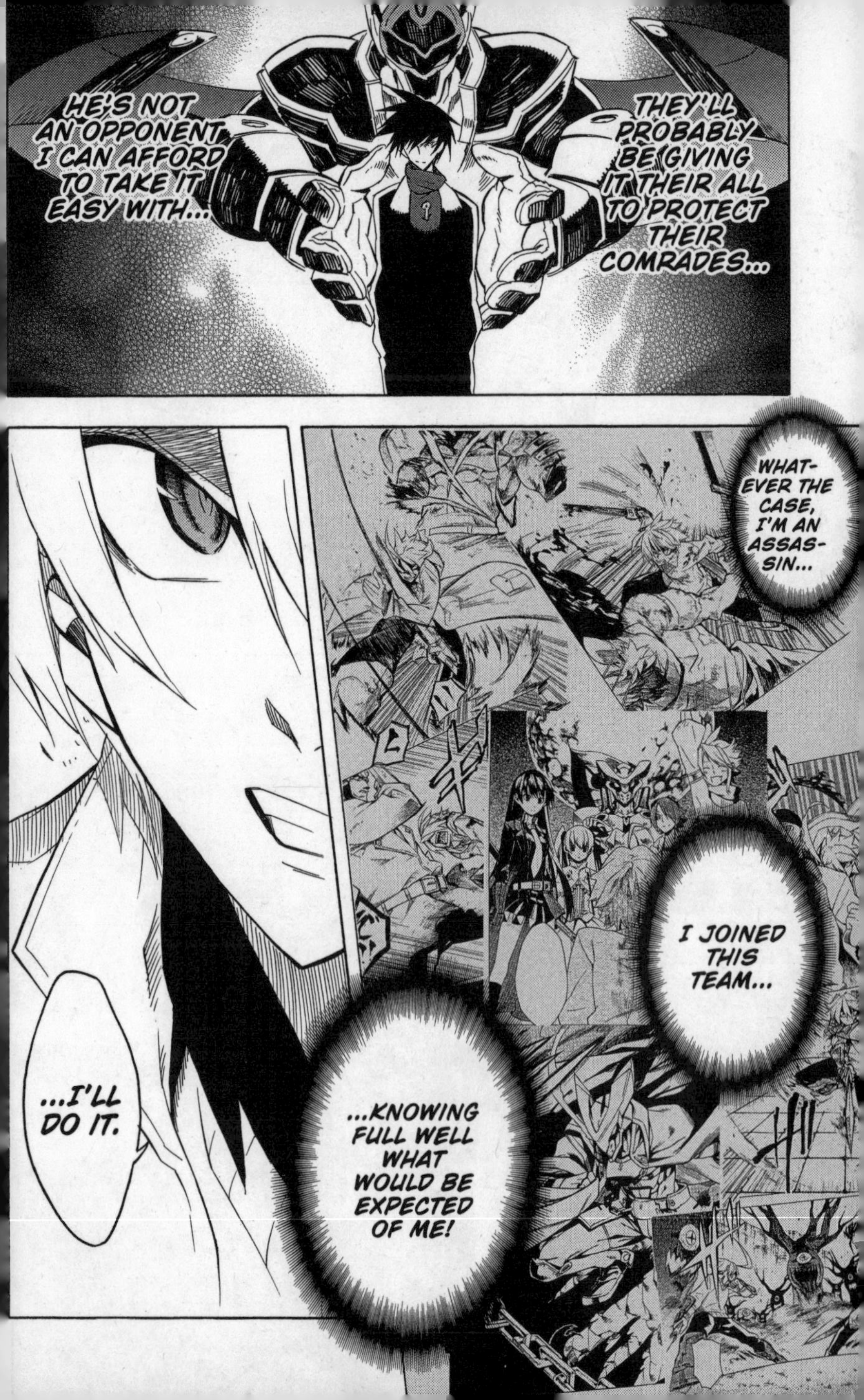
THEY'LL PROBABLY BE GIVING IT THEIR ALL TO PROTECT THEIR COMRADES...
HE'S NOT AN OPPONENT I CAN AFFORD TO TAKE IT EASY WITH...
WHAT-EVER THE CASE, I'M AN ASSAS-SIN...
I JOINED THIS TEAM...
...KNOWING FULL WELL WHAT WOULD BE EXPECTED OF ME!
...I'LL DO IT.

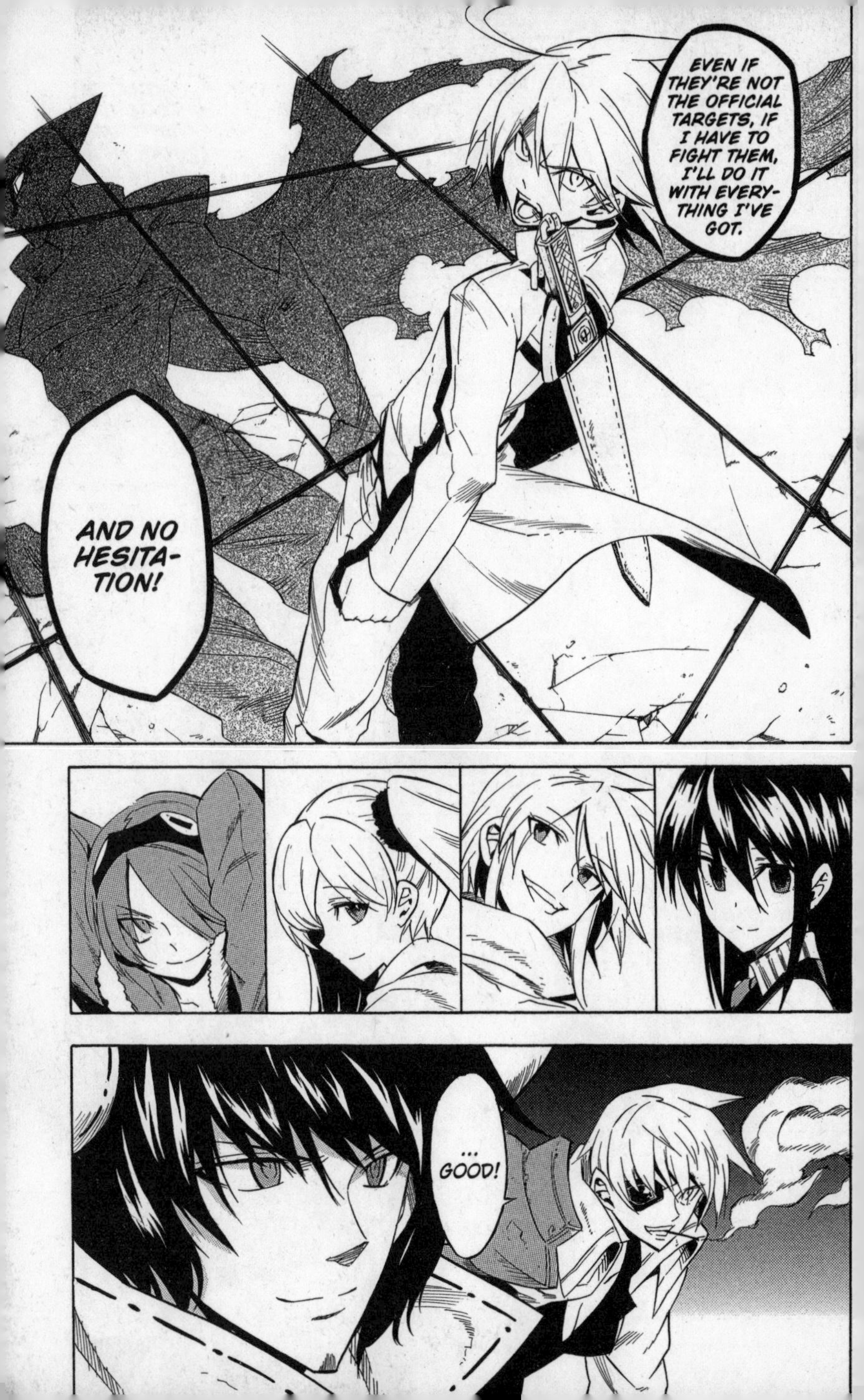
EVEN IF THEY'RE NOT THE OFFICIAL TARGETS, IF I HAVE TO FIGHT THEM, I'LL DO IT WITH EVERYTHING I'VE GOT.
AND NO HESITATION!
...GOOD!

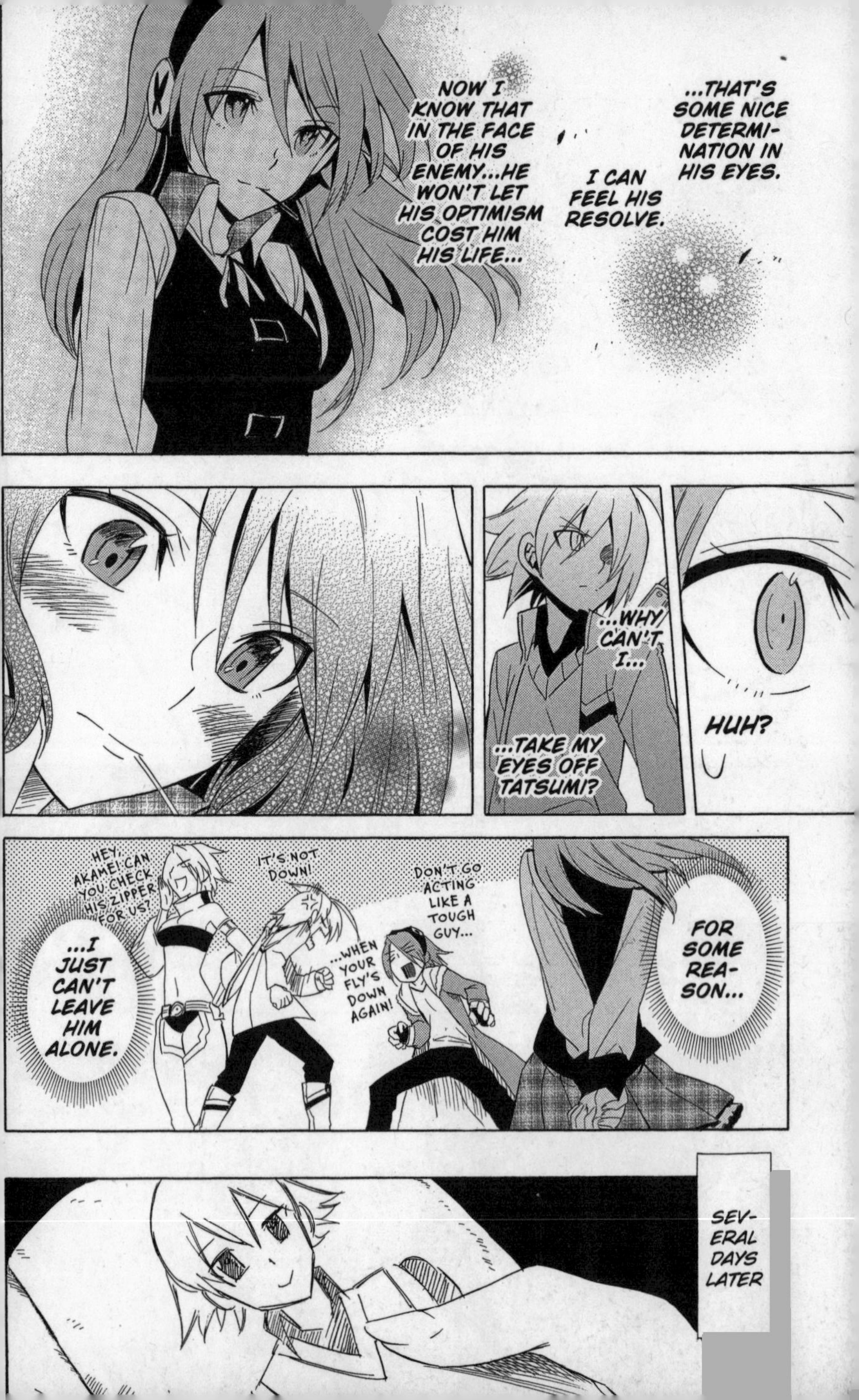
...THAT'S SOME NICE DETERMI-NATION IN HIS EYES.
I CAN FEEL HIS RESOLVE.
NOW I KNOW THAT IN THE FACE OF HIS ENEMY...HE WON'T LET HIS OPTIMISM COST HIM HIS LIFE...
HUH?
...WHY CAN'T I...
...TAKE MY EYES OFF TATSUMI?
FOR SOME REA-SON...
DON'T GO ACTING LIKE A TOUGH GUY...
...WHEN YOUR FLY'S DOWN AGAIN!
IT'S NOT DOWN!
HEY, AKAME! CAN YOU CHECK HIS ZIPPER FOR US?
...I JUST CAN'T LEAVE HIM ALONE.
SEV-ERAL DAYS LATER

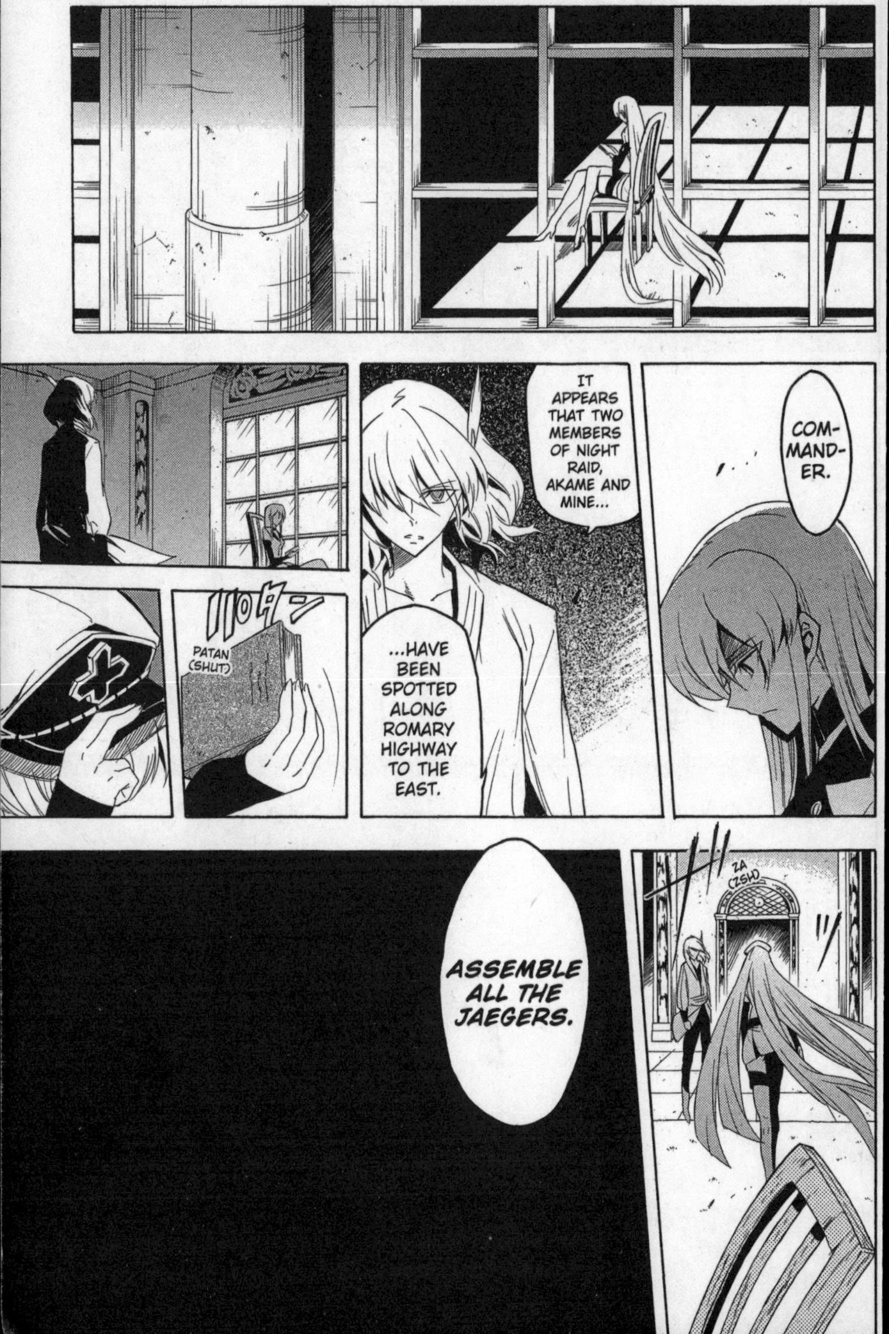
...
COM-MANDER.
IT APPEARS THAT TWO MEMBERS OF NIGHT RAID, AKAME AND MINE...
...HAVE BEEN SPOTTED ALONG ROMARY HIGHWAY TO THE EAST.
PATAN (SHUT)
ZA (ZSH)
ASSEMBLE ALL THE JAEGERS.

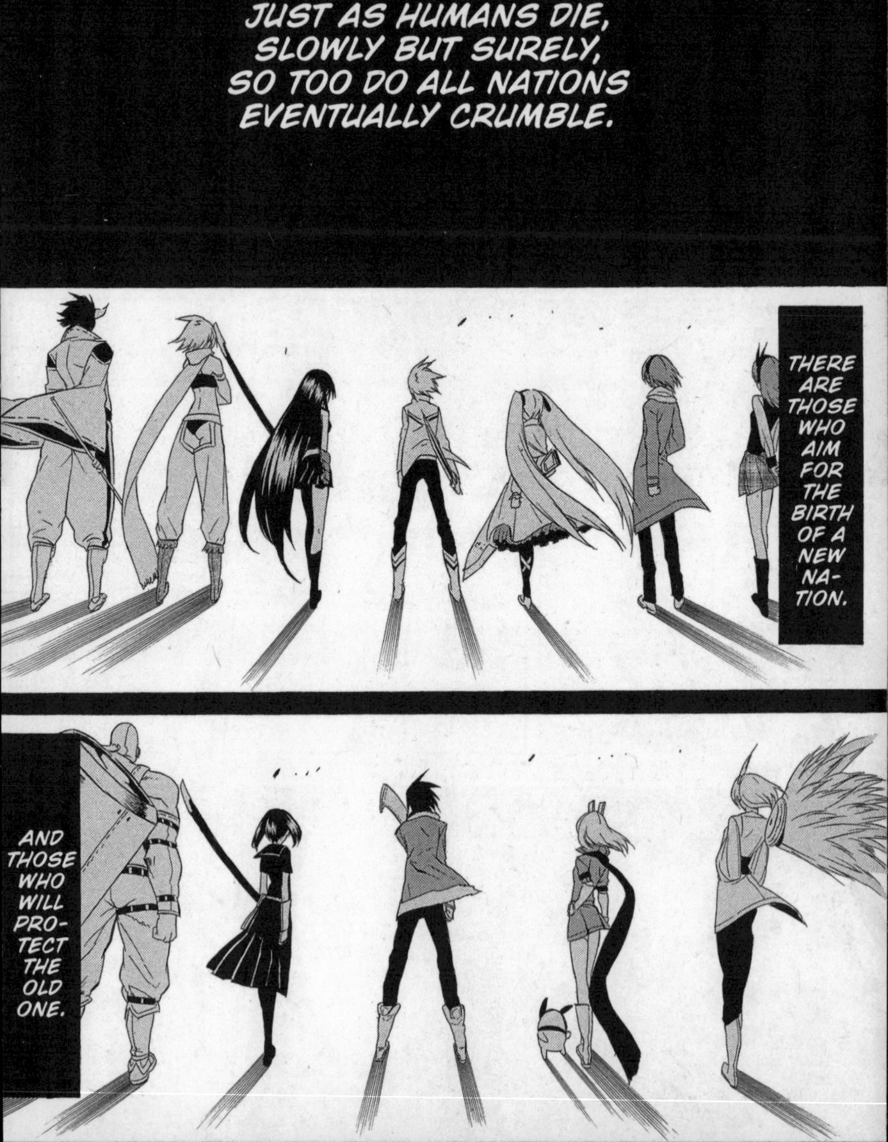
JUST AS HUMANS DIE, SLOWLY BUT SURELY, SO TOO DO ALL NATIONS EVENTUALLY CRUMBLE.
THERE ARE THOSE WHO AIM FOR THE BIRTH OF A NEW NA-TION.
AND THOSE WHO WILL PRO-TECT THE OLD ONE.

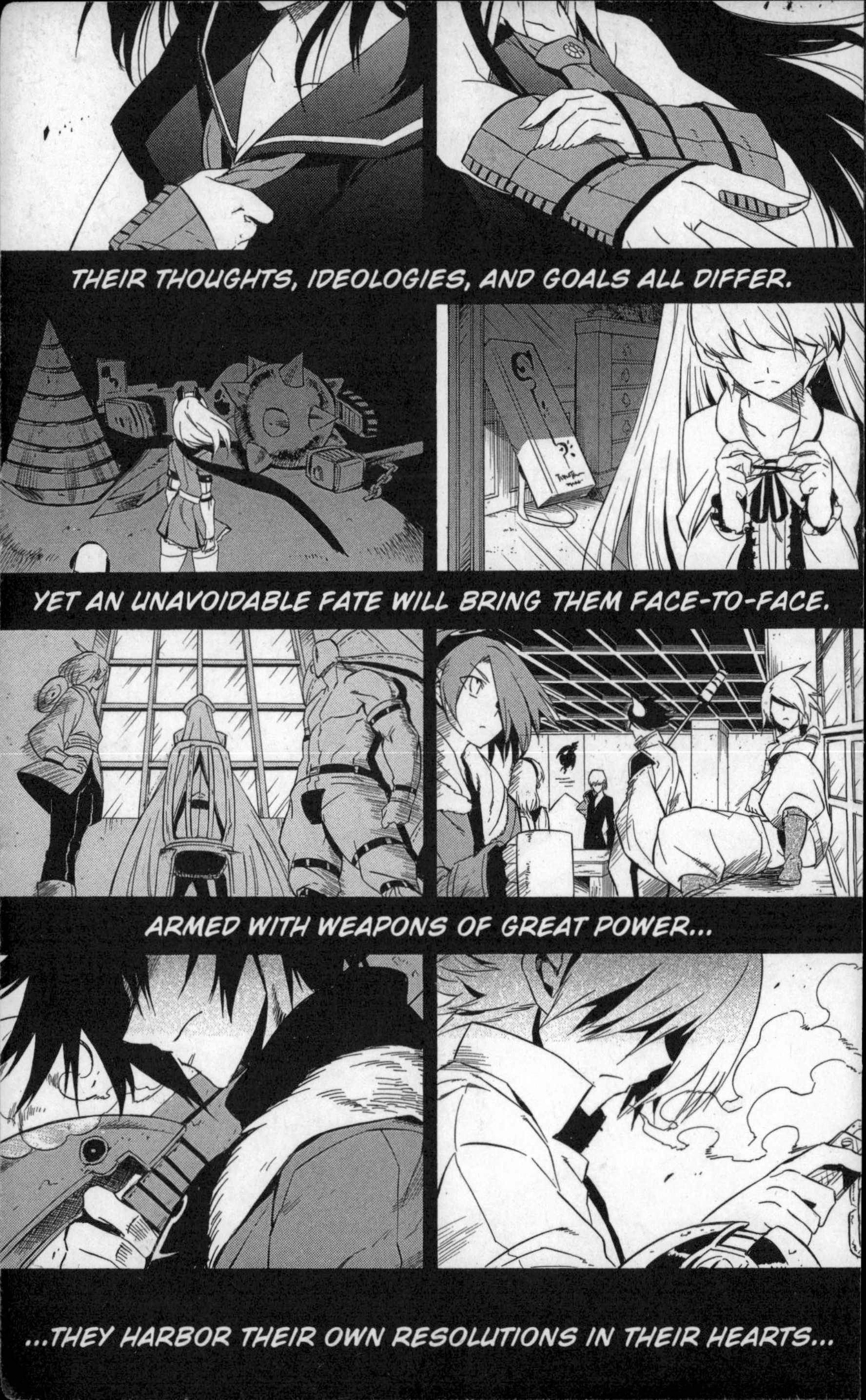
THEIR THOUGHTS, IDEOLOGIES, AND GOALS ALL DIFFER.
YET AN UNAVOIDABLE FATE WILL BRING THEM FACE-TO-FACE.
ARMED WITH WEAPONS OF GREAT POWER...
...THEY HARBOR THEIR OWN RESOLUTIONS IN THEIR HEARTS...

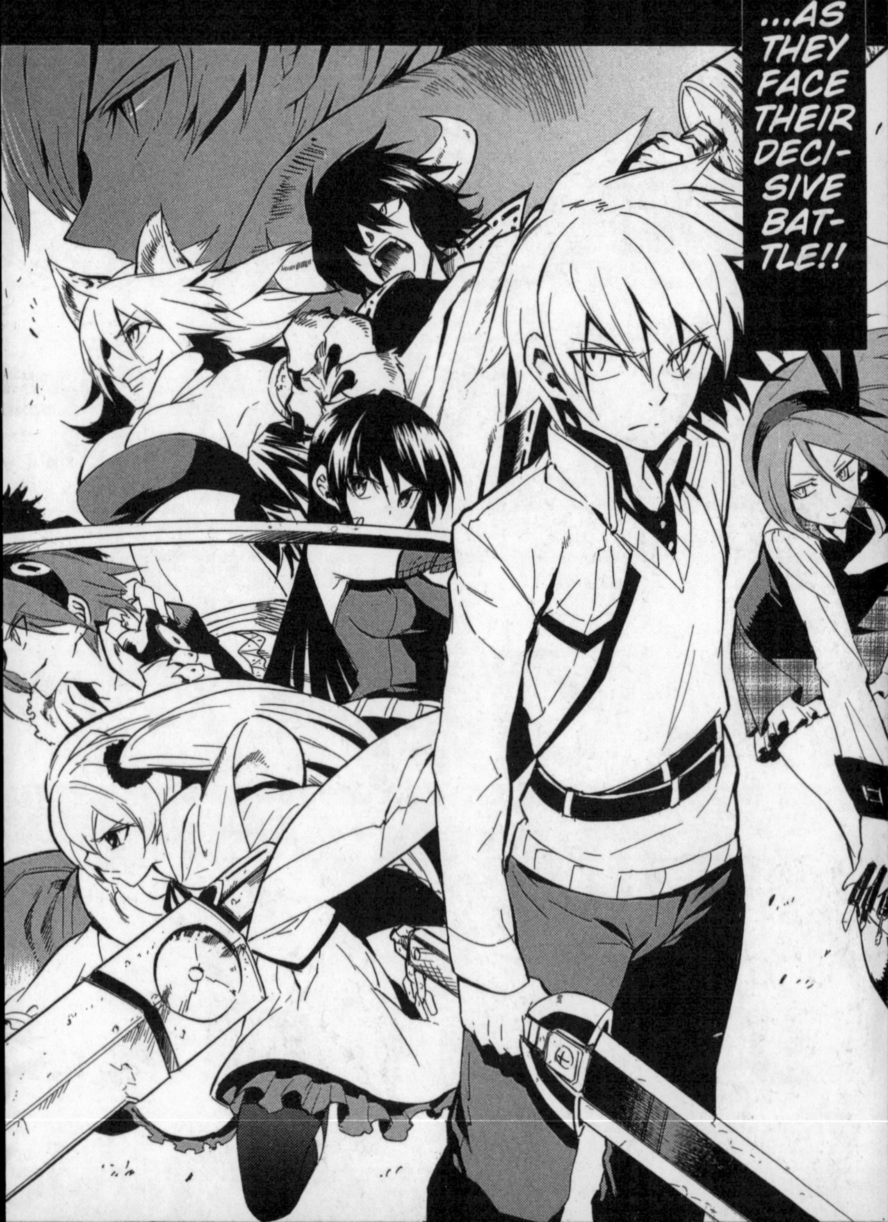
...AS THEY FACE THEIR DECI-SIVE BAT-TLE!!

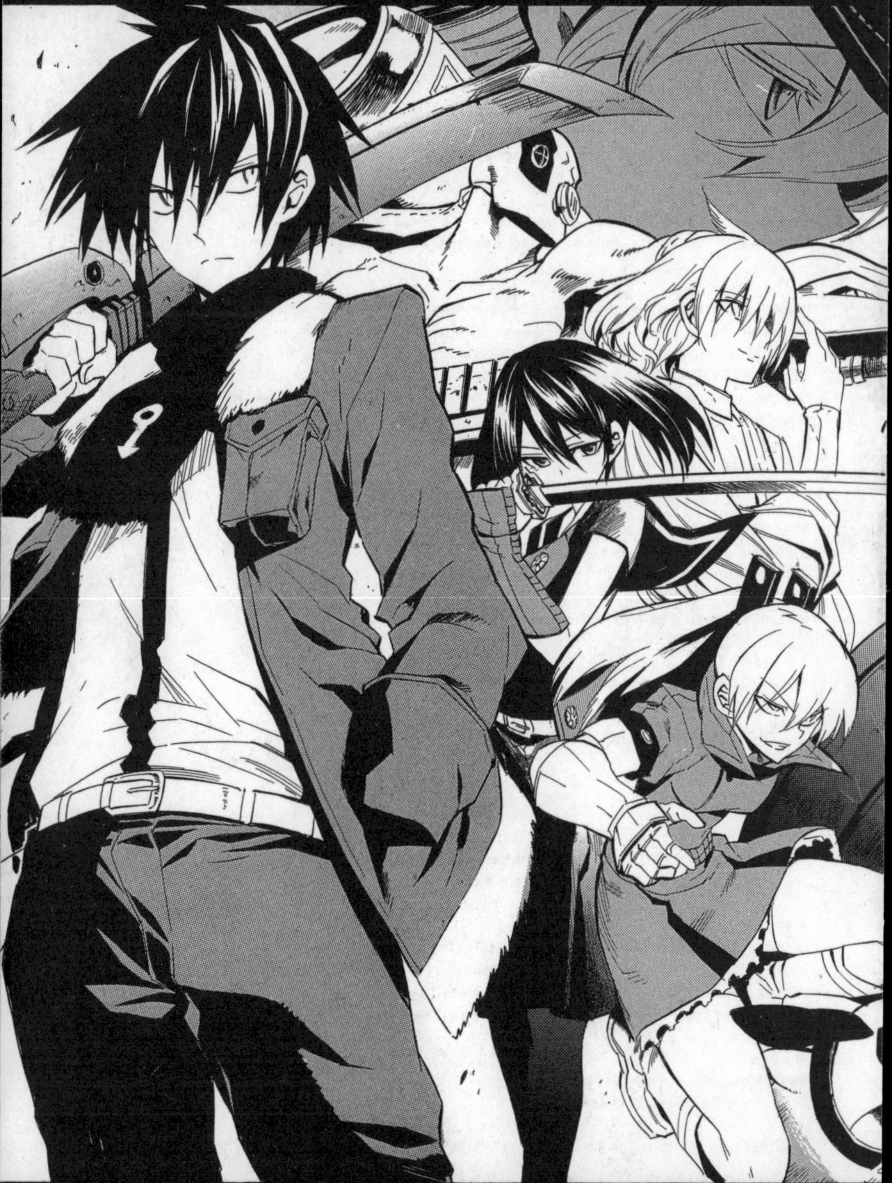

AKAME GA KILL! 6 THE END

TAKAHIRO's
POSTSCRIPT

Thank you very much for picking up Volume 6. This is Takahiro.
I'm going to give you some supplementary explanations
about the characters and elements from the story, so please
read below after you've finished this entire volume.

◆ Seryu's Ten Kings' Judgment
The blade she used in her execution is Number 3 "Sung Dynasty Blade."
As the name "Ten Kings' Judgment" suggests there are ten weapons in total.

◆ The Way of Peace
It developed as a way for the impoverished masses to find solace and will
eventually incite a wide-scale religious revolt...which is like the religious
organization from *Records of the Three Kingdoms* and other such stories. I
already had this arc planned out even before the serialization began, so the
figurine given to Tatsumi in Chapter I was in fact foreshadowing this religion.

◆ Rare Evil Bird
This rare species is so strong that not even Tatsumi would
be able to hunt it alone unless he was using Incursio.

◆ Air Manta
A wild air manta makes an appearance here. I like to give
creatures and characters I've established more than one
appearance in my manga. For example, Kalbi from Chapter
4 might be making another appearance...possibly.

◆ Esdeath (As a Child)
⬆This name was so long that I took to calling her "Loli-death" for
short. I think Tashiro-san has a thing for leggings. It's great.

◆ Partas Tribe
I wanted to give them a strong image, so I took their name from Sparta.

◆ The Minister's Son
This man is still shrouded in mystery, but he will come to
light soon enough. When he punched that woman in the
stomach, it was to show his more brutish side.

◆ New Variety of Danger Beast
Humans who were turned into Danger Beasts through Stylish's experiments.
There are colossal beasts as well, which are the result of the processes
that enabled Stylish to successfully make himself gigantic. Right now they
are linked to the Minister's son and will also be involved in the main story.

◆ Bolic
He rips people off, so he got the name Bolic.
Gebaze got his name from Zeni Geba.

And that's all for now. See you in the next volume.

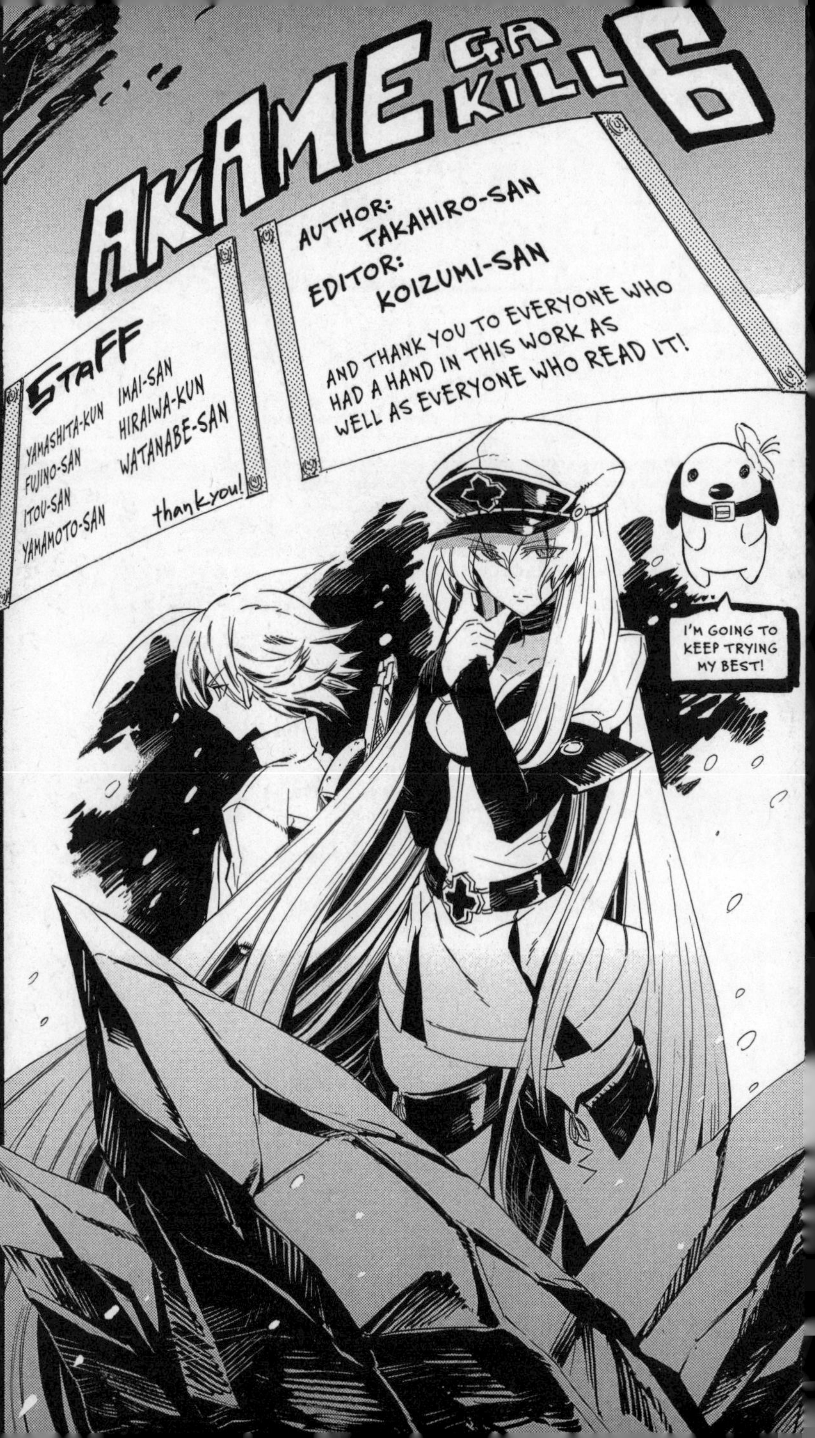
AKAME GA KILL 6
AUTHOR: TAKAHIRO-SAN
EDITOR: KOIZUMI-SAN
AND THANK YOU TO EVERYONE WHO HAD A HAND IN THIS WORK AS WELL AS EVERYONE WHO READ IT!
STAFF
YAMASHITA-KUN
FUJINO-SAN
ITOU-SAN
YAMAMOTO-SAN
IMAI-SAN
HIRAIWA-KUN
WATANABE-SAN
thank you!
I'M GOING TO KEEP TRYING MY BEST!

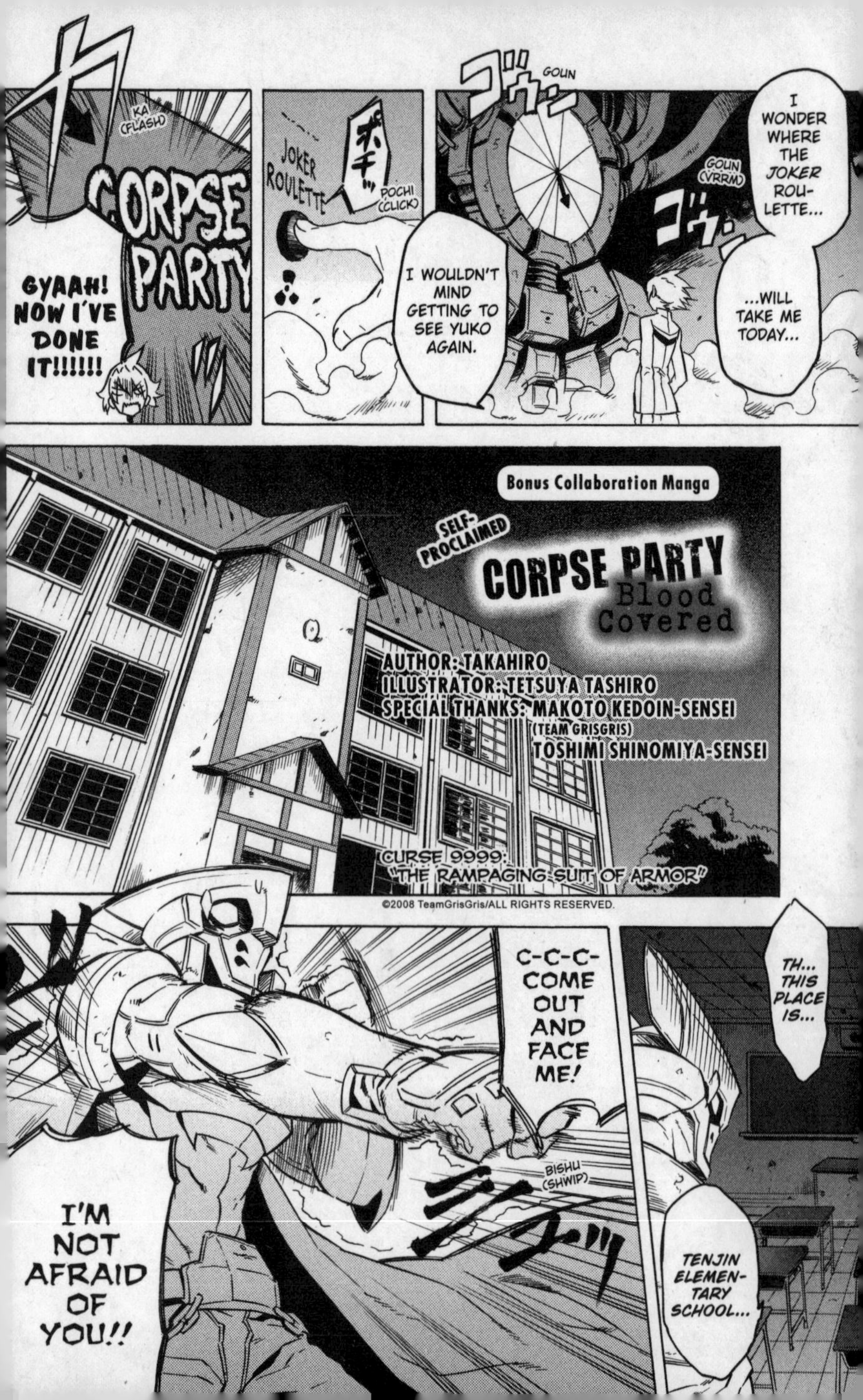
GOUN
I WONDER WHERE THE JOKER ROULETTE...
GOUN (VRRM)
...WILL TAKE ME TODAY...
I WOULDN'T MIND GETTING TO SEE YUKO AGAIN.
JOKER ROULETTE
POCHI (CLICK)
KA (FLASH)
CORPSE PARTY
GYAAH! NOW I'VE DONE IT!!!!!!
Bonus Collaboration Manga
SELF-PROCLAIMED
CORPSE PARTY Blood Covered
AUTHOR: TAKAHIRO
ILLUSTRATOR: TETSUYA TASHIRO
SPECIAL THANKS: MAKOTO KEDOIN-SENSEI (TEAM GRISGRIS)
TOSHIMI SHINOMIYA-SENSEI
CURSE 9999: "THE RAMPAGING SUIT OF ARMOR"
TH... THIS PLACE IS...
TENJIN ELEMENTARY SCHOOL...
C-C-C-COME OUT AND FACE ME!
BISHU (SHWIP)
I'M NOT AFRAID OF YOU!!

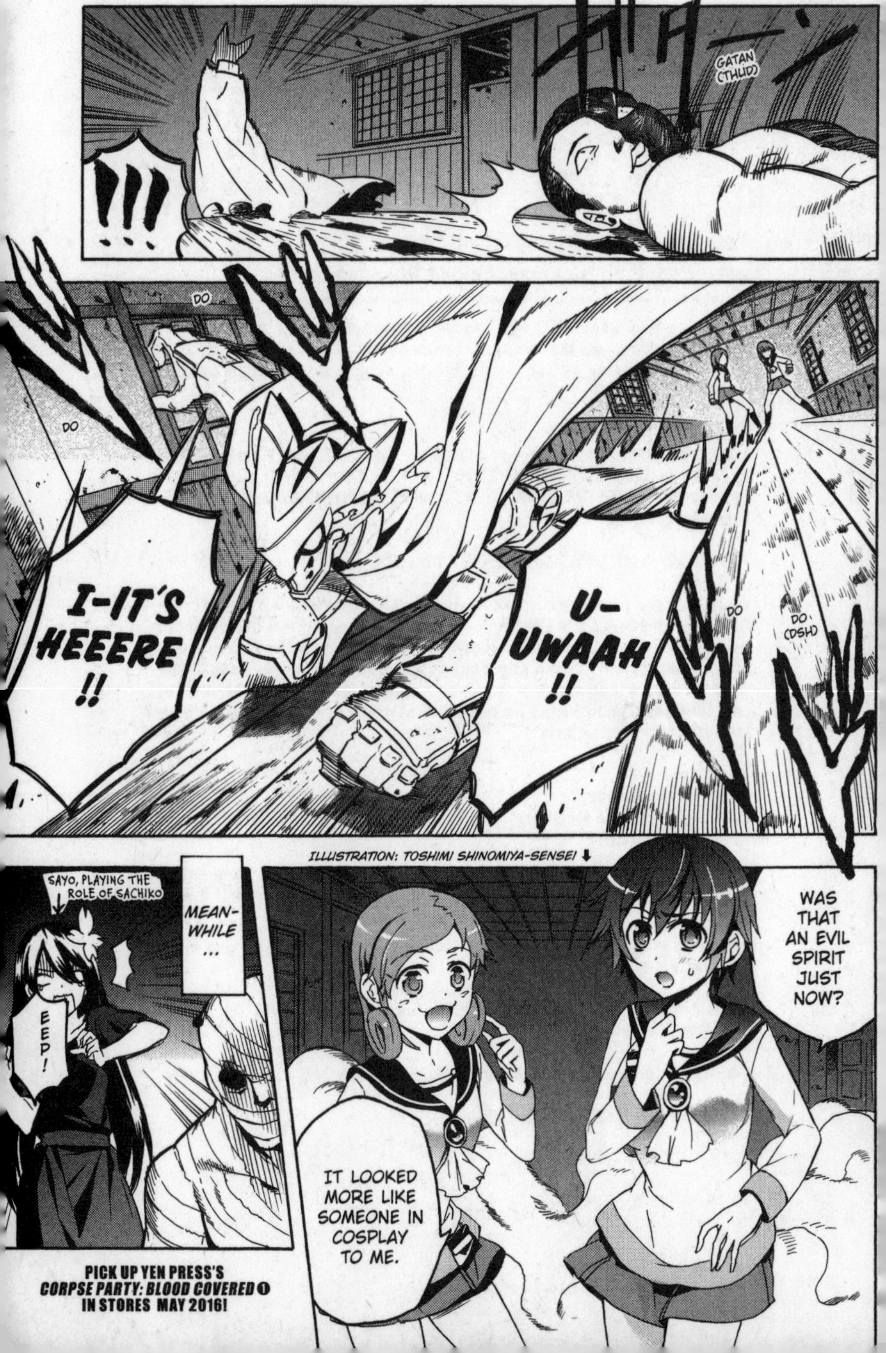
GATAN (THUD)
!!!
DO
DO (DSH)
U-UWAAH!!
I-IT'S HEEERE!!
DO
DO
ILLUSTRATION: TOSHIMI SHINOMIYA-SENSEI
WAS THAT AN EVIL SPIRIT JUST NOW?
IT LOOKED MORE LIKE SOMEONE IN COSPLAY TO ME.
MEAN-WHILE...
SAYO, PLAYING THE ROLE OF SACHIKO
EEP!

AKAME GA KILL! 6

TAKAHIRO
TETSUYA TASHIRO

Translation: Christine Dashiell
Lettering: Erin Hickman, Abigail Blackman

AKAME GA KILL! Vol. 6
© 2012 Takahiro, Tetsuya Tashiro / SQUARE ENIX CO., LTD. First published in Japan in 2012 by SQUARE ENIX CO., LTD. English translation rights arranged with SQUARE ENIX CO., LTD. and Hachette Book Group through Tuttle-Mori Agency, Inc., Tokyo.

Translation © 2016 by SQUARE ENIX CO., LTD.

Yen Press
Hachette Book Group
1290 Avenue of the Americas
New York, NY 10104

www.HachetteBookGroup.com
www.YenPress.com

Yen Press is an imprint of Hachette Book Group, Inc. The Yen Press name and logo are trademarks of Hachette Book Group, Inc.

The publisher is not responsible for websites (or their content) that are not owned by the publisher.

Library of Congress Control Number: 2015960108

First Yen Press Edition: April 2016

ISBN: 978-0-316-34008-3

10 9 8 7 6 5 4 3 2 1

BVG

Printed in the United States of America